The Business of Camp

Ann Sheets
Dave Thoensen

ISBN: 978-1-60679-299-5
Library of Congress Control Number: 2014931285
Cover design: Cheery Sugabo
Book layout: Cheery Sugabo
Front cover image: DWalker44/iStock/Thinkstock (photo),
hynci/iStock/Thinkstock (graphic)
Back cover photo of Dave Thoensen: Lisa Ries, Tamarak Staff

Healthy Learning
P.O. Box 1828
Monterey, CA 93942
www.healthylearning.com

Acknowledgments

No single book will tell you everything you need to know about operating a camp. We have been very lucky throughout our individual careers to have had numerous mentors and colleagues who have shared their knowledge freely, always willing to provide help and guidance about what it takes to be a camp director/owner. Nelson Wieters, Maude Katzenbach, and Jean McMullan were Ann's most influential mentors. Harley Gordon, Bob and Marcy Brower, and Gordie Kaplan were Dave's. All these wonderful people have been our heroes in the camping profession. It is from these professionals that we learned about the business of operating a camp as well as from numerous American Camp Association meetings and conferences, where we've always learned something worthwhile.

In working on this project, we continued to have guidance and help from numerous colleagues to whom we owe tremendous thanks. First, to Grechen Throop and Amy Katzenberger, who guided us throughout the process and provided much needed assistance. Thanks also to the folks from Healthy Learning, who proved their skills as editors with two neophyte authors. Jane Sanborn read all the early drafts and ever so gently suggested revisions and additions. Kim Brosnan read the later drafts and made sure we had our facts right. Many of our colleagues reviewed individual sections and gave valuable input. We are most grateful for their assistance. Thanks also to those colleagues who allowed us to share some of their advice because they really are the pros here. Our families—Jim, Patrick, and Katie Sheets and Lucia, Dianne, and David Thoensen—have been extremely supportive during the process, reading drafts and putting up with piles of books and papers all over our respective dining room tables.

We owe special thanks to Peg Smith, CEO for the American Camp Association, who suggested we combine forces to work on this project and who has provided ongoing encouragement, even promising to buy a copy of the book when completed.

Throughout this book, we have offered some thoughts, suggestions, and recommendations about how camp executives can handle the business aspects of camp operations. As we stated previously, this book alone won't tell you everything about how to run a camp. Great resources exist on programming, risk management, marketing, and camp administration—among other topics—written by some very wise people. We hope camp professionals take advantage of these resources because most of the other authors know a lot more than we do.

Even more importantly, we hope you will pay it forward, sharing your passion and knowledge with those young camp professionals who will someday succeed you—just as Harley, Gordie, Bob and Marcy, Nelson, Maude, and Jean shared important lessons with us. It's a great life, a terrific profession, and we're lucky to be a part of the camp community. Thanks for letting us spend some time with you and share our thoughts.

Ann Sheets, Fort Worth, Texas
Dave Thoensen, Chicago, Illinois

Contents

Introduction

Regardless of tax status, all camps—whether profit or nonprofit, resident or day, general or specialty—are businesses. While the relationships and skills developed in any camp are of utmost importance, the basics of running a small business apply to all camps. Businesses run on systems and they must comply with numerous laws and regulations. With the breadth of most camp operations, it is a challenge to be an expert in everything from accounting to OSHA regulations to youth programming. Not many small businesses include facility management, food service, health care, educational and recreational programming, risk management, transportation, marketing, technology, procurement, large animals, watercraft, high-risk activities, and parent relations—all with a workforce generally made up of 19- to 25-year-olds.

As a camp director or owner, how many times have you heard the question "So, what do you do the rest of the year?" That question shows how little most people know about what it takes to provide or oversee a high-quality, successful camp operation. As a business, every camp requires someone at the helm with business acumen to make the camp successful. This can be the owner, the director, or an organization's executive, but someone must have the ultimate responsibility and judgment to make good business decisions that align with the camp's mission and values.

However, every camp person knows that camp is more than just a business. Camp is a unique business that almost always involves kids, mission-driven people, and a great deal of passion from the owners, directors, and executives who know the value of the camp experience. Just as ignoring the business side of camp can be fatal, so can looking at only the business side. Most camp people give their all to making the entire operation a success. Balance in decision making is the key, maintaining the passion for camp while paying attention to the business of camp.

Advice From a Pro

"It is critical to treat camp like a business or it will absolutely fail, and to know in your head and heart that if you treat camp only as a business it will also fail absolutely: so always make your choices about the business of camp with the greatest care."

— Rodger Popkin, Blue Star Camps (NC)

This book is written for camp owners, directors, and executives of camps of all types and sizes—whether you are new to the camp business or have many years of experience. It is about the business requirements necessary to have a successful camp. Whether you are beginning a new camp, looking for investors, taking over an existing camp, or you simply want to analyze your business operations as you add programs, the information presented in this book is designed to help camp decision makers in their quest to realize the full potential of the camp business—financially and in the marketplace. We definitely don't have all the answers because every camp is different. However, we have provided many questions that should be answered by the individuals in charge of camps. They may serve as a checklist of things you need to consider in your pursuits or simply confirmation of what you're already doing.

We refer to owners, directors, and executives as camp administrators or executives—sometimes as camp officials or professionals—but that's intended to be all inclusive regardless of the exact position you may hold in your camp.

And now, time for the disclaimer. What we are presenting is intended as general advice only, and based on the circumstances of your camp, it may or may not apply. Nothing in this book should be considered as authoritative legal, financial, accounting, or other professional advice. We are presenting the topics because, as camp executives, you need to know what laws affect camp, what types of systems should be developed, and what processes should be analyzed. We also know that camps come in all sizes, shapes, and locations and with many different purposes. We have attempted to be as comprehensive as possible, but not everything you need to know about operating a camp's business and finance will be found here. We recommend you seek the services of qualified professionals if expert assistance is needed in any area.

In addition, when reference is made to a specific commercial product or service by trade name or web address, it does not constitute an endorsement nor do we guarantee the product or service will meet each camp's needs. Specific products, services, or websites are provided as information only and as a starting place where camp administrators can begin a search for options.

Throughout this book are numerous references to websites that will provide more information about the topic addressed. To assist in quick access to some of those sites, QR codes have been inserted that when scanned with a smartphone will take you directly to the referenced websites.

Figure 1-1. Sample QR code

Many fine resources have been written about camp management, risk management, marketing, health care at camp, site management, and hundreds of different programs, among other topics. One book simply cannot cover everything you need to know about the business and financial components of owning, operating, or managing a camp, so we've pointed you in the direction of additional resources—printed and web based—that will help you dig deeper into topics and learn more. Some are camp specific and some are more general and could apply to any business.

We also recommend that one of the best ways to increase your knowledge about the camp profession is to get involved with your state or regional professional association and with the American Camp Association. Through those organizations, you will meet other camp professionals who have been there, done that and who enjoy telling their stories and experiences at camp. We also know that in the camp profession, you will find more cooperation than competition. Sharing is prevalent, as camp people want everyone to be successful so that as a whole, we can serve more children and youth.

In addition, the process of applying for and participating in the accreditation process of the American Camp Association will enable you to grasp the broad range of accepted standards in the field of camp. While it is not required that camps become accredited, it is highly recommended, as accreditation is one of the best measures that a camp owner or director desires to have a high-quality camp operation.

No matter what kind of camp you have, there's no business like the camp business! Welcome to a great experience, but hold onto your hat—whether it be a baseball cap, visor, or Stetson—because you're in for quite a ride.

Best wishes!
Ann Sheets
Dave Thoensen

1

Camp, Business, and Ethics

Alissa Deutsch, Tamarak Staff

The camp profession prides itself on integrity. Most camp operations fall into the category of small businesses regardless of the type of camp and they comply with applicable laws and good business practices. But equally important is doing business and working in an ethical manner at all times. Because ethics is so important, it is presented before anything else about the business of camp.

Ethics

How do you define ethics? Kirk Hanson of Santa Clara University's Markkula Center for Applied Ethics says that ethics is "the study of standards of behavior which promote human welfare and 'the good.'" He further states that ethics is about how people behave, about the standards people hold themselves to, and about how people treat each other—even those they don't know. Equally important is what ethics isn't: It's not just feelings or conscience, it's not just following the law, and it's not the same as religion (Hanson, 2013).

Many camps consider character education as part of their values and program, intentionally working to build character and teaching ethical behavior to their campers. To that end, camp counselors are considered role models for campers, providing examples of how to solve problems, looking at situations from multiple viewpoints before making a decision, and reinforcing good camper behavior.

While character education may be a good camp program, working in an ethical manner is a business principle that all camps should embrace. Camp professionals should model ethical behavior in business practices and in relationships with not only the campers and their parents but also with other camps and the community.

Modeling Ethical Behavior

Concrete ways that ethical behavior can be modeled in camp could include the following:

- Implementation of an enrollment policy for campers that is unswerving in abiding by deadlines and other established requirements
- Consistent and fair treatment of all campers and staff
- Flexibility in the implementation of all policies that take into account not only the business interests of the camp but also the interests of the campers and families served
- Truthfully and realistically representing camp operations in all marketing and promotional materials
- Taking an active role in the community in which your operation resides or which serves your population
- Ethically representing your operation in the community without criticizing or denigrating your competition
- Written human resources policies for staff that are applied without fail in every situation

- Establishment of fee schedules that fully describe what is included and when fees are due
- Fair and responsible application of refund and other policies that are communicated to parents
- Getting all sides of a story before making a decision
- Prompt resolution of complaints
- Written job descriptions and employment agreements that include not only the employee's responsibilities but also what the camp will provide to the employee for training, compensation, supervision, and evaluation
- Accurately reporting enrollment and finances to data collection organizations and entities that charge for their services based on such numbers (such as camper insurance or association membership)

It has been said that what you tolerate, you teach. Whether faced with a deadline for filing a government report or reporting sales tax correctly, camp professionals make a strong statement about integrity by the way in which they do business, never tolerating misstatements–intentional or not–about finances or enrollment nor what you can provide to children and youth who attend your camps.

Moral Abilities to Develop in Your Camp Staff

Camps are just like other organizations–they're made up of individuals. Albert C. Pierce, professor of ethics and national security at the National Defense University in Washington, DC, spoke at Santa Clara University about building and nurturing an ethical culture, noting the following four abilities that organizations should develop in individuals:

- *Moral awareness:* the ability to recognize when a problem has a dimension of right and wrong more than a narrow technical problem
- *Moral reasoning:* the ability to think through a problem, project the consequences, and then decide what to do
- *Moral courage:* the ability to overcome the fear of being ostracized by their peers or getting a poor review of job performance
- *Moral effectiveness:* the ability to persuade someone else to choose the most ethical action (Steen, 2013)

As camp professionals, you have a tremendous opportunity to teach these abilities to your camp employees–many of whom are working for the first time and are poised to learn life lessons at camp. These lessons can be a wonderful gift for the young adults who make up your camp staffs–a development of character and business ethics that will serve them in their future careers.

Camps also have a reputation of working closely with other camps and with professional colleagues, sharing best practices and ideas freely in what some have called "coopertition," cooperating with their competitors based on the belief that what helps one camp helps the entire camping profession. In that spirit, camp professionals generally speak with families and the public about the strengths and characteristics of their own programs, not about what they perceive as weaknesses in other camps. While camp officials may be fiercely recruiting campers and staff who are also being recruited by others, integrity and ethics should always play a significant role, with camp representatives never speaking ill of other camps and their employees or programs.

For more information about business ethics, see *Business Ethics: The Magazine of Corporate Responsibility* (www.business-ethics.com) and the Markkula Center for Applied Ethics at Santa Clara University (www.scu.edu/ethics-center).

You Set the Tone

In any organization, it's the person at the top who sets the tone—whether for ethical behavior, program quality, or customer service. In *How We Do Things Here: Building a Legal, Ethical Workplace Culture*, Stephen M. Paskoff writes about developing a plan for an ethical, legal culture in any industry. He says:

> Executives must live the organization's mission and values through their own words and actions. Their behavior ultimately sets the standard for the company's culture—'how we do things here.' Senior executives must define a clear vision of the organization's commitment to lawful and ethical operations as a cornerstone of the business. ... Words should be simple, clear, and direct. (2002)

Business ethics can be summed up by the following three essential concepts:

- *Respect* for all with whom you work—campers, parents, staff, colleagues, and the community
- *Responsibility* in not just following laws and regulations but also doing what's right
- *Honesty* in all that people say, post, print, imply, and do

Teaching character education at camp is a great idea, but modeling character and values through your business is even better.

2

Camp Philosophy and Culture

Jupiterimages/Creatas/Thinkstock

Camps come in all varieties: for profit, agency, nonprofit, faith based, day, resident, short term, long term, national, local, employee based, volunteer driven, specialty or general, and everything in between. The tax status or any other label or variety of a camp simply doesn't matter when it comes to operations of the camp. Camps are businesses and all must be run as businesses. Period. A very wise person once stated that "if you manage the business, the bucks will take care of themselves." If you take the time to consider the intent of this simple message, it really makes a lot of sense.

Why Camp?

Before making decisions about such things as organizational structure and tax status, owners and directors must answer a simple question: Why camp? Why do you want to offer a camp program? It is crucial to have a well-thought-out purpose because most business decisions should be based on or at least consider the camp's mission, values, and goals.

Organizational Vision, Mission, Values, and Goals

A camp may have a vision, a mission statement, defined values, a program philosophy, and multiple underlying goals—one of which may be to make a profit or to provide a break-even program. No perfect formula exists for a camp mission statement, but every camp needs to know why it is in the business of camp.

Generally speaking, a business needs to answer the following three questions:

- What service do you want to provide?
- To whom do you provide the service?
- How can you be the best at what you do?

The service addressed in this book is camp—in whatever form. Camp professionals need to determine exactly how they want to provide the camp experience as well as to whom. If you are serving children and youth, what ages? What gender? Will you have a day camp or a resident camp? How long will your sessions last? From what geographic area will you draw your campers? And most importantly, what will set you apart from other camps and programs?

You probably have some definite ideas about what you want to do at camp. You may have a location and you may even have campers and have run a camp program before. But how do you describe what you do? Why do you have a camp? Before you invest either your money or someone else's money, think about the big picture:

- What do you want to accomplish by having a camp?
- How will you fund it?
- Where will the campers come from?
- Can you make enough to pay your expenses?
- Can you make a profit?
- Do you want to help children and youth gain skills? If so, what skills?
- Is your goal to provide an experience in the outdoors for your campers?

To begin to answer these and more questions, you must first define the very basis for your interest in having a camp and what you hope to accomplish by writing your vision, mission, values, and goals. While many definitions exist, this book uses the following:

- *Vision* is the preferred future that will exist because of the camp. It's generally very broad. It could be a statement like:

  Camp XYZ's vision is a world where leaders are caring individuals who respect others and our natural world.

- *Mission* is a description of what the business will do to achieve the vision, such as:

  Camp XYZ will prepare future leaders by instilling confidence, a respect for others, and a love of the outdoors.

Eight-Word Mission Statements

Kevin Starr, director of the Mulago Foundation, recommends that mission statements be eight words or fewer. "As investors in impact, we–the Mulago Foundation–don't want to wade through a bunch of verbiage about empowerment, 'capacity-building,' and 'sustainability'–we want to know exactly you're trying to accomplish," Starr says. "We want to cut to the chase, and the tool that works for us is the eight-word mission statement. All we want is this: A verb, a target population, and an outcome that implies something to measure–and we want it in eight words or less. Why eight words? It just seems to work. It's long enough to be specific and short enough to force clarity" (2012).

As an example of the power of brevity, the Trustees of Reservations, the oldest regional land trust in the world with more than 100 special places covering almost 25,000 acres in Massachusetts, has as its mission "To preserve, for public use and enjoyment, properties of exceptional scenic, historic, and ecological value in Massachusetts" (Trustees of Reservations, 2013), although the sign at one of its properties, Crane Beach, says simply: "We save the irreplaceable for everyone, forever" (Howard, 2011).

No magic number exists when writing a mission statement. Some have suggested using a maximum of six or seven words or, like the Mulago Foundation, eight. In the spirit of making mission statements succinct yet meaningful, the previous camp mission statement example could be shortened to: Building future leaders through camp experiences. The following are sample mission statements that are short and to the point:

- Connecting children with nature
- Building character through outdoor activities
- Increasing sports skills of teenagers
- Safe summer fun with friends

Whether you make your mission statement more or fewer than eight words, the important thing is that it *clearly states what the camp intends to accomplish.*

Values

Values are the shared beliefs of the operators of the camp that form the basis for the design of programs and how the camp operates. These could include such statements as:

- At Camp XYZ, we believe that children and youth learn best in informal settings.
- We believe that the camp setting provides one of the best informal settings for lifelong learning.
- We believe that children and youth need adult role models who can interact well with them.
- We believe that informal learning takes place best in small groups of 10 or fewer campers.
- We believe that children and youth will prosper in an outdoor environment.
- We believe that children and youth will grow into healthy adults by developing good habits at camp.
- We believe that diversity is a strength.
- We believe that children and youth learn by taking responsibility for themselves and their living group.

Goals

Goals are generally specific statements that relate to the mission and values but which can be measured over a short period of time, such as:

- Camp XYZ will increase camper attendance.
- Camp XYZ will expand programs offerings.
- Camp XYZ will improve staff training.

Many guides to writing goals and objectives suggest that objectives should give more specificity to goals and should be written by using the SMART method:

- S = Specific
- M = Measureable
- A = Attainable
- R = Responsibility clearly defined
- T = Time bound

Using this method, specific objectives under the aforementioned goals might be:

- Camp XYZ will increase attendance in the youngest boys' cabins by 6, or one cabin, each year over the next three years. (Assigned to Charles)
- Camp XYZ will add two new program activities each year until at least 20 different programs are offered. (Assigned to Mary)
- Camp XYZ will improve staff training by utilizing online courses prior to pre-camp training for all new staff for the next two years. (Assigned to James)

Some will get even more specific by establishing action steps that, for example, label the specific online courses, who the camp wants to take the classes, dates for completion, etc.

Nomads?

Seen on a cartoon: A man on a camel says to a woman, also on a camel, who's carrying two young children, as they're obviously riding in a desert: "Stop asking me if we're almost there. We're nomads, for crying out loud."

Unlike nomads, you must know where you're going. You can't wander from place to place when dealing with a business. Find out where you want to go and then determine how you're going to get there.

The purpose of this section is not to prescribe a camp's vision, mission, values, or philosophy or even to show how to develop these crucial elements. Multiple other resources can provide guidance on how to develop these elements of the camp business plan. How camp administrators go about developing the camp's mission statement, values, and goals is a personal decision, although it can be dictated by affiliation with a larger organization—whether an ownership group or national entity. The point is that everyone needs to know why the business exists, be able to articulate the mission, clearly state your personal values, and measure business decisions against the mission and values.

Some businesses take their mission and values and refer to them throughout their work and marketing. Moz®, a Seattle-based marketing analytics software company, uses the acronym TAGFEE to share its core values. They say: "Our goal is for everything we create and cultivate—our software, content, corporate culture, and relationships—to live up to the tenets of our TAGFEE code. We acknowledge that we are entirely responsible for our own reputation, the level of success we achieve, the brand image we create, and the contributions we make to the marketing industry. They're all a direct reflection of our mission to be as Transparent, Authentic, Generous, Fun, Empathetic, and Exceptional as possible" (Moz, 2013a). By using the acronym TAGFEE, Moz has not only created a symbol of its values that's easy to remember, but also by Moz using it throughout its marketing materials, TAGFEE is known to its customers as well as its employees. Moz also included a refreshing statement in its code to acknowledge that it is responsible for everything the company does.

For this book's purposes, the collective vision, mission, values, and goals will be referred to as "the camp philosophy." The camp philosophy will guide almost every decision that camp executives make regarding camp. For example, using the previous examples, it looks like this camp program and housing will be based on small groups of 10 or fewer campers, that it will have an emphasis on the environment, and that campers will be expected to have group living responsibilities. With these examples, one would not expect to see dorms for 20 campers or a program that emphasized technology or a single focus in its activities.

Whether designing your facilities or implementing new programs, it is essential to ask yourself if your decisions support your values and align with your mission. If they don't, then it's time to rethink the decisions.

Camp Culture

Taken together, the camp philosophy, the campers, the staff, and the program will also shape the camp's culture. The owner or director will also add to the camp's culture, which could be likened to a personality and influenced by everything said, done, and implied at camp.

Jeffrey Leiken and Joseph Riggio, writing in *Camping Magazine*, said:

> There are camps that do the most simple things in the most extraordinary ways—camps that totally commit themselves to fulfilling their "mission." These camps take incredibly precise steps to ensure each aspect of their camp is aligned with this mission and is indeed serving it—from the songs they sing, to the ways they acknowledge kitchen staff, to the way they handle conflicts. It is an incredible experience to be in these camps' cultures. (2002)

They go on to state:

> Within a camp, there are several primary categories or components, which make up culture. Each of these has influence and impact, and changing any one of them impacts the whole. They are signs and symbols, ritual and tradition, stories and metaphors, communication and behavior, and finally, you as a participant in it (the culture you are creating). (Leiken & Riggio, 2002)

Categories Making Up Culture

Signs and symbols include everything from your camp name and logo to your camp T-shirts and how your staff and campers dress as well as the signs at camp on your buildings or providing directions. Are they handmade? Commercially made? Are your signs playful, such as the equestrian center that sports not a sign saying STOP but WHOA or the no parking sign that reads "Don't Even Think About Parking Here."

Ritual and tradition include things like the stories that are told around the campfire, special days at camp, songs sung after a flag raising, or awards presented at closing ceremonies. Some traditions are continued long after the meanings are forgotten. As Leiken and Riggio say, "Sometimes the tradition of traditions is a part of camp culture that limits us, and we don't even realize it" (2002).

Stories and metaphors include not just the legends passed down from year to year but also the more damaging stories accompanied by a few snickers or laughs. Does your camp culture include this type of story or instead the stories about the shy child who overcame her fears at camp and blossomed or the camper whose dream of riding a horse came true?

Communication and behavior may be some of the most obvious indicators of a camp's culture—whether it's an agreement by counselors to deal with issues with campers and fellow counselors in a firm yet caring way or a pattern of practical jokes that just aren't that humorous for the victim.

But the most important part of creating and maintaining the type of culture desired at camp is the behavior and actions of the person in charge—you, the owner, the director, or the executive. How do you deal with your staff? Are you supportive of everyone? Are you friendly and outgoing with the campers, calling each one by name? Are you always on time for meals? Do you approach each day with a positive outlook, greeting the staff and campers with a smile when they arrive at camp or come to the dining hall? Do you participate in all the camp's activities? And most importantly, are you, the camp professional, visible to your staff, campers, and families?

Advice From a Pro

"It's important for the director to be out and about with the campers and staff. There is so much to running a camp that it's easy to fall into the trap of being in the camp office, just taking care of business, because being a camp director is like being in charge of a small, but very active city. However, both staff and campers need to see the director at all meals, observing activities, and being an integral part of the camp program. Even though you may feel the weight of the world, responsible for the safety of all of your campers and staff, they need to see that you are enjoying yourself and that each camper and counselor is important to you."

— Lisa Cook, Camp El Tesoro (TX)

One phrase that sums up how to affect the camp's culture is simple: *Don't just say it—behave it.* If you expect your staff to be neatly dressed, then you need to model that behavior. Do you want counselors to keep their cabins neat? Then, you must keep your cabin and your camp office neat. If your expectation is a friendly, outgoing staff, then as the most influential person in camp, you must be the role model for friendliness, greeting visitors and guests warmly. *You set the tone.*

It is also important to know how you expect disagreements or misunderstandings to be handled. One group of camp professionals agreed that if anything was said during a meeting that offended or hurt, the proper response would be to say "ouch"—a way of letting the group know that the comments were hurtful, which is a far better way of dealing with feelings than not addressing the comment at all. At the end of the day, however, you need to communicate in a tactful and positive manner that everyone understands you have the final call in making decisions. Group discussion is a wonderful concept and having autonomous supervisory staff is too, but at the end of the day, it's your business.

Camp counselors and other staff need training on your expected culture. They need to know how to listen and respond to complaints—whether from parents, campers, or other employees. They need to know where to go when issues come up and they need to know how to follow up. It's important to remember that for many—or sometimes even most—of your employees, camp is the first work experience for them. Providing concrete training on what you expect simply cannot be overlooked.

Everything seems exaggerated at camp—the good and the bad. Where else do you sing to thank the cooks for a particularly good meal? Or award clean cabins? Or treasure a painted rock or a string bracelet? All these things are part of the camp culture.

Stephen Paskoff offered his thoughts on communicating in an age of information overflow, suggesting that you attack the complex with simplicity. In *Simplicity Rules*, he said that the most important messages about culture are:

- "Know our general standards. They're important, not fluff.
- Let us know if you find out about issues or don't know what to do.
- We won't tolerate lying and fabricating information.
- We don't 'shoot' our messengers. We welcome their issues." (2011)

To develop your camp culture, leave nothing to chance. Talk with your staff about your vision, mission, and goals, working with them to identify all the opportunities to create the culture you desire—from program to facilities and from business operations to food service. Decide what the environment should be that will allow you to accomplish your mission. Then, revisit this discussion during camp, checking in to confirm that your philosophy is obvious throughout the camp or if midseason adjustments need to be made. You may want to remember the Moz example and come up with an acronym or a simple way to remember your camp's core values or code.

Vision, mission, values, goals, and culture are not developed just to include in the camp brochure or on the camp website. The camp's philosophy should be evident from the camp's first impression through every single activity, every communication, and every action by camp management and counselors alike.

3

Setting Up a New Business

Daniel Hurst/iStock/Thinkstock

Choosing a Camp Name

Your camp's name is the first impression that most people will have of your program, so make it a good one. Most states will have an online method to search for entity names to see if the name you have chosen is already in use by someone else. Search your state's website for "name reservation" or "starting a business." Do you want your camp name to begin or end with "Camp"? If not, how will you identify your camp as a camp?

If your new venture will be the purchase of an existing program, you need to consider whether to keep the same name of the camp you're purchasing or to change the name to something else. If you are taking over a successful operation, it would be highly advisable to keep the name the same—unless, of course, your mission and goals are entirely different from those of the entity you're purchasing.

Names will last forever, so camp professionals need to spend sufficient time researching the proposed camp name. Do other camps have the same name? Luckily, with online searches, it is now very easy to see if other entities with similar names exist. For example, if you google "Camp Pine Tree," you'll find camps in Maine, Florida, Texas, and Maryland. If you google "Camp Oak Hill," you'll find camps in North Carolina, Minnesota, Tennessee, Connecticut, Mississippi, Florida, Pennsylvania, and Virginia. Even if your camp has beautiful groves of pine trees or oaks on a hill, can you succeed in developing your own identity as a camp (especially a new one) when others share the name?

Numerous stories have been told about manufacturers that had what seemed to be a perfectly good name for a product—only to find out that when they marketed it in other countries, the meaning was detrimental to sales. Camps should consider what their name means in other languages. You never know when your camp may expand to international clientele.

If you are part of a larger organization, find out if naming conventions exist that you must follow. Some national organizations, such as Camp Fire® and the YMCA®, prescribe that the organization name should be the first part of the camp name.

Camp administrators should also take care not to infringe on copyrighted materials or names. Copyright holders have the right and obligation to protect their intellectual property and spend time and money notifying entities that they believe have infringed on their name. Likewise, if you are purchasing an existing camp operation, you want to be certain your purchase agreement includes all intellectual property owned by the former entity, such as patents and trademarks on camp names, logos and marketing slogans, or phrases. Check the U.S. Patent and Trademark Office's Trademark Electronic Search System (TESS) to see if a similar name is trademarked. To do a trademark search, go to tmsearch.uspto.gov. You may want to trademark your camp name. Intellectual property is a complex part of the law, but resources are available at www.stopfakes.gov/learn-about-ip/trademarks/about.

Should you include your own name or an activity in your camp's name, such as "John Jones's Basketball Camp for Boys"? What if you expand to girls or start including soccer? In addition, what will happen if this is a family business but no one in the family wants to—or is able to—carry on the camp business after you retire? Do you want your name attached to the camp if your family is no longer the owner? Some very successful camps named after a founder have been sold to nonfamily members over the years, so that's not out of the question, but if you've built a brand using your family name, will a different owner choose to change it?

Will your camp name appeal to campers and parents? How will it look on the web or as part of a logo? You may want to try out different camp names on a focus group—or even just the neighborhood kids—to get reactions from children. The more your name says about your camp, the less you'll have to communicate about what it is you do. Choose a name that not only appeals to you but also to the campers and families you intend to serve.

Some camp names will be shortened to initials. Try out all the variations on your camp's proposed name. Before you register the name of your camp (necessary in many states), consider all the possibilities for how it could be shortened or misunderstood. Some well-known businesses have creative names with made-up words, but try not to get too cute with things that only you understand or a name that's long or confusing. Give your camp name the T-shirt test and picture how it would look on a camper's T-shirt—or a canoe or however you might envision it being used.

After you've run traps on a proposed name, register it with your state's secretary of state or the appropriate state office. The Small Business Administration's website at www.sba.gov/content/register-with-state-agencies will show where in your state you need to register your name and if it's necessary to register any "doing business as" (DBA) names.

Web Domain Names

Camp executives will also want to check to see if the web domain name associated with your camp name is available. One site that will provide this information is www.networksolutions.com/whois. You may want to purchase the web domain name before you register with the state. Because numerous extensions exist, consider registering multiple extensions of your domain name (for example, .com, .org, .net, .biz, .us, etc.) as well as variations on the name. If you select "Camp What's In a Name," you might register campwhatsinaname.com, camp-whats-in-a-name.net, whatsinanamecamp.org, and so on.

Social media sites are a must. Check Facebook® or other sites and then claim your name as soon as possible. Different sites may require that you have a prescribed number of fans before you can claim a specific name.

Most camp executives want their camp name to be unique. Choosing a camp name will be one of the first major decisions you make about your business. Although name selection seems like a complex process, the camp name will likely be with you for many, many years, so spend the necessary time to select a name that will stand the test of time.

Decide on the Legal Form of Business

The legal structure of your camp will probably be a sole proprietorship, a partnership, a corporation, or a limited liability company. Before deciding which fits your situation, you should consult with an attorney and a tax advisor who can provide professional advice regarding how each is treated under the current tax code and the laws of the state in which you are doing business. Figure 3-1 and the following sections detail general characteristics of these common legal structures.

Sole Proprietorship

When one person operates a business, this structure is very common. In a *sole proprietorship*, income of the business is taxed to the owner personally—usually at a lower rate than for a corporation. The owner receives all the profits of the business and the owner is ultimately responsible for all debts and liabilities. A sole proprietorship is an unincorporated business and taxes are filed with the individual's income tax return.

An advantage of a sole proprietorship is that generally less governmental regulation occurs. A disadvantage is that all liability lies with the individual.

Partnerships

When two or more persons form a business together, it can be formed as a partnership, with each person owning a certain percentage of the business. That percentage would then apply to the division of the profits, but under a general partnership, each partner is responsible for all debts. This structure requires a formal written partnership agreement, outlining who is responsible for which portions of the business; what happens when a partner is incapacitated, dies, or wants to sell his portion of the business; and how major decisions are made.

Limited partnerships can be formed, but these involve different types of partners, including the following:

- *General partners* have more control and can realize unlimited dividends as well as unlimited liability.
- *Limited partners* receive only a percentage of the business profits based on their proportionate share of investment but also have limited liability in a proportionate share.

The IRS requires an information tax return, but the partnership itself does not pay taxes. Instead, the income tax liability passes through to the partners, who report their proportionate share on their own tax returns.

BUSINESS TYPE	ADVANTAGES	DISADVANTAGES
Sole Proprietorship	• Easy to form • Control rests completely with owner, who may mix personal and business assets • Taxes easy to figure	• Personal liability unlimited • Raising money potentially difficult • Doesn't retain value if the owner dies or is incapacitated
General Partnership	• Easy to form • Shared financial commitment • Tax liability passes to partners	• Shared liability among partners • Potential for disagreements • Shared profits • Obtaining loans potentially difficult
Limited Partnership	• Two classes of partners: general and limited • Pass-through taxation • General partners having complete control over business decisions • Limited partners not personally responsible for liability • Flexibility in structure of management	• Unlimited liability for the general partner • Business decisions not available to limited partners
Limited Liability Corporation	• Limited liability • Not as much recordkeeping • Profit sharing • No restrictions on number of members • Flexibility in how management is structured	• Self-employment taxes • Life span can be limited • Little case law for precedents • Specifics depend on how recognized by IRS • Ownership harder to transfer
C Corporation	• Liability limited • Easier to raise money • Taxed at corporate rate • Unlimited number of shareholders • Ownership options for employees, making employment attractive • Easy to transfer ownership through sale of stock	• Taxes doubled • Costly and takes time to form • Requires extensive recordkeeping • Potential for states to impose ongoing fees • Formalities of annual meetings
S Corporation	• Pass-through taxation • Shareholders not personally liable • Unlimited life, extending beyond the death or illness of owner • Can sell shares of stock to raise more capital	• No more than 100 shareholders, who must be individuals, estates, or qualified trusts • Consent to S election by all shareholders • More expensive to form than general partnerships or sole proprietorships
Nonprofit Corporation (if recognized as tax exempt by the IRS)	• No income taxes • Can receive charitable contributions and apply for grants • Liability may be limited; depends on state laws	• Ongoing formalities, such as annual meetings • Takes time to form • Considerable paperwork • Control rests with board, not with founder or camp director

Figure 3-1. Advantages/disadvantages of business types at a glance

Corporations

Corporations are formed when individuals exchange money or property for the capital stock of the corporation. Corporations can be privately held or publicly held. Corporations conduct business, make a profit or a loss, and can return dividends to shareholders as well as pay taxes. Corporations are taxed when they earn profits and shareholders are taxed again when they receive dividends. *S corporations* are a special type of legal structure in which the corporation's profits or losses are passed directly to the shareholders and, therefore, taxed only one time. S corporations have specific tax code requirements, including having no more than 100 shareholders, being a domestic corporation, and having only one class of stock. The standard corporation is known as a *C corporation*, which is taxed as a separate entity. C corporations have no restrictions on ownership.

Limited Liability Companies (LLCs)

These companies limit liability for the owners, as the business is a completely separate entity. *Limited liability companies* (LLCs) are allowed by state statute, with each state setting its own regulations. Owners of LLCs are called members. In some states, an LLC can have only one member. Because of the differences state by state, the IRS will treat LLCs as either sole proprietorships, partnerships, or corporations.

Nonprofit Corporations

Nonprofits are formed at the state level and do not benefit owners or shareholders. Once formed, they can apply for tax-exempt status, which is only available for those organizations formed exclusively for exempt purposes as defined by the IRS in section 501 of the IRS code. Lobbying and political activity are restricted for tax-exempt organizations. Although tax-exempt entities, commonly called "nonprofits," do not pay income taxes, they do have strict reporting requirements, including filing an annual information return (IRS Form 990), as well as additional regulations. Tax-exempt organizations can be organized as a trust, an association, or a corporation, although camps would most likely be organized as corporations. Nonprofit corporations must have a board of directors because they lack owners or shareholders. Choice of the board is critical, as its members will be providing the direction and oversight for the entity.

If you are interested in organizing a camp as a tax-exempt entity, it would be wise to review the IRS guidance found in *Publication 557: Tax-Exempt Status for Your Organization*, which is found online at www.irs.gov/pub/irs-pdf/p557.pdf. If you determine that your camp should be organized as a tax-exempt entity, you will first need to submit your articles of incorporation as a nonprofit organization to your state for approval and then apply to the IRS for recognition of exempt status by submitting IRS Form 1023: *Application for Recognition of Exemption* (Internal Revenue Service, 2013a).

Please note: This information is general in nature and should not be used to guide your decision regarding the legal structure of your camp. Instead, develop questions to pose to your financial advisor and an attorney familiar with small businesses, as the legal structure of your camp will dictate how profits or dividends are distributed to you and any partners or investors, if organized as a for-profit entity.

Governing Documents

If you have any type of business arrangement with another person or a group of people (basically, anything but a sole proprietorship), you'll need some type of governing documents. Names and requirements vary by state, but corporations generally have articles of incorporation and/or bylaws; LLCs have operating agreements; and partnerships have partnership agreements. Check your state law to see what's required.

Even if a formal document isn't required by state law, it's a good business practice to have a written agreement that describes the general operating rules of the business, how disagreements will be settled should they arise, how profits and losses are distributed, what happens to the business if one of the principles dies or wants to sell his part of the business, and under what circumstances the agreement can be amended or terminated. Corporations will usually specify the composition of the board of directors, how members are elected, board terms, corporate officers, and required meetings.

Financial and Accounting

Apply for an Employer Identification Number

If you will have any employees, you'll need to file Form SS-4 with the IRS to receive an Employer Identification Number (EIN). This form and its instructions can be found at www.irs.gov/pub/irs-pdf/fss4.pdf. Camps that operate with only volunteers may also want to apply for an EIN, which is commonly used to identify businesses.

Apply for a Sales Tax Permit

If you are selling any taxable items at your camp, you will most likely need a sales tax permit. Contact your state controller for an application and for more information.

Set Up a Separate Bank Account

Even if you choose a sole proprietorship as your legal structure, a best practice is to set up a separate checking account for your new business so your personal and business expenses will not be comingled. It is advisable that you have an additional signatory on the camp checking account should you ever be incapacitated so camp expenses can continue to be paid. Obviously, this should be someone in which you have a great deal of trust. You may want to discuss this with your attorney and accountant.

Determine Your Tax Year and Accounting Methods

Your tax year can be either a calendar tax year (beginning on January 1 and ending on December 31) or a fiscal tax year (any 12 consecutive months ending on the last day of any month except December). You will also want to determine your accounting method (either cash or accrual) and begin keeping records of all financial transactions for tax purposes.

Permits and Licensure

Obtain Permits

Some states, counties, or local municipalities will require a business permit. Others may require that you get a license to operate a camp. (See Chapter 8 for more.) You will also want to check with your local municipality, township, county, or state agency that's responsible for issuing zoning permits and variances. All property is regulated and zoned at some level and the intricacies of ensuring that you are properly zoned or permitted is critical to ensure that your operation is operating within all legal parameters.

Licensure

Most states have specific rules for the operation of facilities that serve children and require at least some level of government oversight from such agencies as the Department of Children and Family Services (DCFS) and the Department of Public Health or other regulatory agencies. Be prepared! In some cases, these approvals can take up to a year, so you will have to plan accordingly. If your site will have pools or lakes, it will be necessary to obtain the appropriate permits for those water features. If your property water supply will be served by a private well, you may be required to take a well owner operator certification class before you are allowed to open your facility. The same can also be said for any type of food service operation that your facility may have, requiring licensure from a local health department. While the licensing and permit processes can be overwhelming, a good resource to use is a local government office or elected representative. If other camps are in your facility's vicinity, the directors/owners of those operations would also be a good resource in navigating the sometimes confusing maze of government regulations.

Obtain Insurance

Check with your insurance agent to see what type of business insurance you need immediately. Camps will most likely need to obtain additional insurance coverage when you begin operations. Some camps are self-insured, but your agent or broker can provide guidance. If you are renting or leasing property, you will want to obtain a certificate of insurance from the owner to confirm his insurance and to determine whether you have any insurance coverage under his insurance. (Insurance is discussed in detail in Chapter 15.) Also, consider who will handle your workers' compensation insurance coverage. Workers' comp is mandated by every state and it will be necessary to determine who will provide coverage. You can get outside insurance or purchase coverage from a state-managed pool depending on where you can get the best pricing.

Other Decisions

You will have a myriad of other decisions to make, such as the following:

- Will you purchase property?
- Will you lease an existing camp or another site?
- What will your target market be for campers?
- Will you need to consider transportation?
- Will you provide your own food service or contract with a food service management company?
- What programs will you offer?
- How will you advertise?
- Will you seek accreditation by the American Camp Association?

Figure 3-2 provides a checklist to help ensure that you have completed the basic steps necessary to set up your new camp as a business.

Checklist For Setting Up a New Business
❑ Choose a name.
❑ Obtain a web domain.
❑ Decide on your legal form of business.
❑ Apply for a tax identification number.
❑ Apply for a sales tax permit.
❑ Set up a separate bank account.
❑ Determine your tax year and accounting method.
❑ Obtain permits.
❑ Apply for licenses.
❑ Purchase insurance.
❑ Join the American Camp Association.

Figure 3-2. Checklist for setting up a new business

Additional Assistance

Small Business Administration

The Small Business Administration offers excellent resources, training, and financial programs for small business owners. The SBA provides assistance in four primary areas: advocacy, procurement, business development, and financial assistance. In addition, it provides several different loan programs, grants, and other financial assistance. The SBA defines a small business as "one that is independently owned and operated, is organized for profit, and is not dominant in its field. Depending on the industry, size standard eligibility is based on the average number of employees for the preceding twelve months or on sales volume averaged over a three-year period" (Small Business Administration n.d.a). Some small businesses may have up to 1,500 employees and revenues of $21 million, depending on the industry, so camps should qualify for assistance from the SBA.

www.sba.gov

The SBA partners with various other entities (all of which can be accessed via www.sba.gov), including the following:

- Small Business Assistance Centers for anyone running a small business
- Small Business Development Centers, which are 900 sites throughout the United States offering technical assistance in numerous areas
- Women's Business Centers for female entrepreneurs
- Veterans Business Outreach Centers, which provide entrepreneurial development services for armed services veterans
- SCORE (the Service Corps of Retired Executives), which has more than 300 chapters and 13,000-plus volunteer business counselors

Bookstore shelves and Internet sites are filled with resources about starting a business. Read about how to form a business or visit with others who have done so and take advantage of training classes offered by the SBA.

Join a Professional Association

www.ACAcamps.org/membership/join-aca-today

New camp executives should join the American Camp Association (www.ACAcamps.org/membership/join-aca-today) and get to know other camp professionals who can be of considerable help. Networking with your colleagues and taking advantage of the training offered at local and national conferences will be time well spent. Local organizations, such as a chamber of commerce or a Rotary Club®, are also excellent opportunities for new camp owners and directors to network outside of the camping industry.

Family Business Considerations

Many small camp businesses are family owned, a situation that brings a unique set of challenges. Massachusetts Mutual Life Insurance (MassMutual) conducted a survey of more than 500 family business owners and identified the top lessons family business owners wish they had known when they started their business. These lessons included the following:

- Passion and trust among family members and advisors were noted as the most important critical success factors in a family business.
- Boundaries between work and nonwork activities must be set. Even though family businesses have the advantage of control over a work-life balance, family disagreements, stress, and fewer vacations also present challenges.
- Communication is a key not only for business but also for the family, leading to better decision making.

- Define who's in charge and what roles each family member will play.
- Determine how the family will make decisions. Will it be majority rule, negotiation, or some other method?
- Decide at the beginning how the business will be affected should a divorce occur regardless of whether both spouses are involved with the business.
- Look at contingencies as a part of the overall strategic plan of the business. Death or disability happens to people and those families who have acknowledged that are much better prepared to continue the family business.
- Work with your attorneys to develop an exit strategy and have a legal agreement that documents how changes in ownership will be managed.
- Work closely with an accountant and a financial planner to minimize estate tax consequences when the family business ownership is transferred to the next generation. (See Chapter 21 for more on dealing with succession.) (Massachusetts Mutual Insurance, 2010)

These are just the first steps in setting up your camp business, but don't feel discouraged. Remember—camp may have been a simple joy for you as a child or as a counselor or for your children, but camp is still a business—and businesses require a great deal of work to be successful.

4

The Business Plan

mandygodbehear/iStock/Thinkstock

At a recent national conference of the American Camp Association, several new camp owners and directors representing for-profit and nonprofit, day and resident, and private and agency-affiliated camps participated in a panel discussion on challenges they'd faced when starting their programs in the last five years. Diane Tyrrell, writing in *Camping Magazine*, reported that when these new executives were asked for key tips in starting a camp, their first response was to tell those who want to start a camp that they must *remember that camp is a business*—and the second was to *take the time before you do anything else to develop a good, workable business plan* (2010).

Developing a business plan will force you, as the camp owner or director, to take an objective look at your camp in its entirety—free from the emotion you may feel about your camp business. Often, new or prospective camp owners and directors remember all the fun, the relationships, and the excitement of attending camp as a child, overlooking the fact that operating a camp is much, much more. Having a well-thought-out business plan can provide ongoing guidance as the camp is developed as well as provide the foundation for a financial plan that potential lenders or investors can use in evaluating your business.

In his classic book *The Business Planning Guide: Creating a Winning Plan for Success*, David H. Bangs Jr. says that "the importance of planning cannot be overemphasized. By taking an objective look at your business you can identify areas of weakness and strength, pinpoint needs you might otherwise overlook, spot opportunities early, and begin planning how you can best achieve your business goals" (2002).

You will find that although many different ways exist in which to write a business plan, camps may want to include the following parts:

- Cover sheet
- Executive summary
- Introduction
- Program
- Staffing
- Operations, facilities, and equipment
- Marketing
- Financial
- Risk management
- Appendices

You may have reason to add or delete a section or rearrange the order, but remember that this business plan should be thorough and should provide an overall structure for the growth of your new business—which happens to be a camp. A good business plan provides direction for the first three to five years of your venture and should lay out goals in each of the sections and the action steps you will take to accomplish those goals. Keep in mind that this plan is the first impression your camp will make with individuals who may be key to the realization of your dreams, so make certain your plan is professional, well written and with no mistakes or typographical errors, and exhibits the high quality you expect from your business.

Presentation and Graphics

- Throughout your business plan, consider including photos, graphics, and charts to illustrate your goals and the other information you are presenting—but not an excessive number.
- Look at your plan as if it were being presented to you. Is it interesting? Does it keep your attention? Are the illustrations relevant to the topic being presented?
- Consistency in the presentation is important. Select a font that is easy to read and then use the same font throughout your document. Use *italics* and **bold** fonts sparingly. The main text should be in a font no smaller than 10-point or no larger than 12-point depending on the font chosen.
- This is a business document, not a social media post. Don't use emoticons and think twice before using exclamation points.
- Number your pages for easy reference.
- If you can print in color, do so, but don't overwhelm the reader with font color changes. Photos will generally look better in color, as will charts and graphs.
- Bind the document so no one will lose any pages.
- If you are not skilled at developing a professional-looking document, then get someone who is to help you format your business plan. Substance is absolutely the most important, but substantive plans that look unprofessional don't get very far.
- Ask the lender or the potential investor if he prefers a printed copy or an electronic copy of your business plan. If he asks for an electronic copy, do not send a Word or WordPerfect document. Instead, save your document as a PDF file, which will take up much less disk space.
- Take advantage of the spell-check function of your word processing software. Do not have any misspelled words.

Cover Sheet and Executive Summary

Your cover sheet should be simple. At the top of the page, use the words "Confidential Business Plan" and then put your camp name, address, date, and your name. Your business plan will be confidential. You should treat it like any other start-up business. Leave writing the executive summary until last and then limit the summary to one or two pages in length. The executive summary is an overview of your plan and should highlight the most critical components of your camp business plan, including a strong closing summary stating why your camp will be successful.

Introduction

Begin writing with the introduction, explaining what your camp is all about: an overview of the program, the location, and why you're getting into the camp business. Share the mission of your camp and the top three to five goals you have for the first three to five years. You may want to tie your goals to other sections of your business plan. For example, one goal might be a marketing or participation goal, which can be the basis for your marketing plan. Another goal might be accreditation, which could be tied to several different sections of the business plan.

Also, include information about yourself because one of the things you will likely use your business plan for is to obtain financing. Along with selling your idea, you need to sell yourself. Do not be modest, but explain why investors should trust you to use their money wisely. Be honest and don't exaggerate your experience. Instead, provide an objective description of yourself and your other investors (if you have them) or of your organization, whichever is applicable.

Include in the introduction your qualifications to run a camp. What experience do you have in camp management? Have you ever started a business before? Have you ever been in charge of a business or a business unit? Does your organization have a good track record of starting new programs and growing them into successful components of the organization? Explain some of the history of the organization and how this camp fits into its mission.

If you are purchasing an existing camp, review the camp's history and why you're purchasing it. Explain if you will be transferring the license and/ or registration for the camp (if required) or if you will be applying for a new license and any needed business permits and when.

Also included should be the legal structure of your new venture. Is it a sole proprietorship, a partnership, a for-profit corporation, or a nonprofit corporation? If you have partners, list them. If this is a corporation–whether for profit or nonprofit–identify the board of directors. Your partners or board members can give you credibility, so share their names and the roles they will take in your camp. Are they silent partners or will they have an active role? Do you have advisors from the camp community who have experience in starting camps?

You may wish to include in the introduction any information you have about the future of camps and any other information you have access to that will strengthen your proposal and show that camp is a good business. Share the qualities that will make your camp a good business investment. Consider closing the introduction with a recap of the mission and goals of your camp and why you will be successful.

Program

This is your chance to make your readers excited about your camp, to see what makes it special, and to express why it is a good investment. Try to connect with your readers in this section because if you get them hooked on your vision for the camp, the rest of the business plan will be an easier sell.

Be specific about what your program goals are. If you have photos of your campers, this is a great place to use them (with parental permission–and no names). Imagine that your reader is the parent of a potential camper and then sell your program to the reader from that perspective. If you have anecdotes or quotes from campers or parents, include them as appropriate to illustrate what you're doing. Get permission from parents to use their testimonials. They will probably be happy to assist you and could even know some of your potential lenders.

Your competitive advantage will be one of the most important pieces in this section. Without making any comments about your competitors, explain why a camper would want to come to your camp. Do you have programs that others don't? Do you have staff that others don't? If you can't answer those questions in the affirmative, then look deeper and find the unique value that your camp offers. One advantage for new camps may simply be that everything is new—new cabins, new equipment, and new traditions. Is your location outstanding? Is your pricing structure competitive? Do you offer discounts that others don't?

Share whatever research you have about the need for your program, especially any surveys that support your venture. An old marketing axiom says "Find out what they want and then give it to them." If you have not determined a need for your camp, do some research before settling on exactly what your program will offer. If you use general camp research, be sure you attribute it to the author and note that it is general in nature, not specific to your camp.

Explain whether your program is currently in operation or if it is in development. If it's in development, describe where in the process you are and what you're doing to bring your program to fruition. If you listed your short-term (three- to five-year) goals in the beginning of this section, close with what you plan on doing long term and how you anticipate your camp growing and meeting your goals.

Staffing

In the staffing section, provide details about your key staff members, emphasizing their experience and how they can contribute to the success of your new camp. Include photos if possible and past camp experiences, explaining how these are the right people to be on your management team. If you do not yet have staff, describe the type of person you will recruit for key leadership positions and where you will look to find them. Indicate how your key staff will be compensated.

You'll also need an organization chart, showing reporting responsibilities and other staffing relationships. Your organization chart may include the staff you need at present (or during your first summer or program) as well as the staff that will need to be added as you expand and when you project that growth to occur.

If you are seeking accreditation from the American Camp Association, this will be a good opportunity to reference some of the standards related to staffing and explain how your staffing plan will meet or surpass the generally accepted standards in the field. You will want to establish staffing ratios by age and any exceptions to the ratios. In addition, reference your state and/or local regulations for staffing and how your operation will meet those.

Staffing should also include a recruitment plan, indicating where you will find your staff, and a training plan outlining the training provided for your employees, including any certification you will require.

If you will utilize volunteers for any or all positions, provide the same information about your volunteer plan and describe whether the use of volunteers is a short-term or a long-term strategy.

Operations, Facilities, and Equipment

Your operations section will show the details of how your camp will function and is your chance to explain some of the inner workings of your camp, such as registration, maintenance, food service, and any other behind-the-scenes components of your business. It will be helpful to have some type of graphic or diagram showing how these functions support the program. This is also an opportunity to showcase any technology or innovative systems you are using.

Whether you lease or own a facility, this is your opportunity to share the details: location, size, type of living units, program facilities, meeting/dining spaces, natural features, and any other areas at your camp that makes your facility unique or how it aligns with the specific program being offered. If you are seeking funding to purchase or expand your facility, share more details about the features, your master site plan, design considerations, and construction plans.

Similarly, if you have or need equipment to accomplish your goals, describe how you will use it and your plans for maintaining or procuring the equipment. If the equipment plays a key role in your program or operations, explain why and include graphics of the equipment in use, especially if it is unusual.

Marketing

Your marketing strategy can make or break your business plan. No matter how good the program is, you have to have campers and families who will buy the experience at your camp to be successful. Your marketing plan should include at least the following parts:

- *Product:* Exactly what are you selling?
- *People:* A definition of who your customers are, which should include gender, age, interests, geographic location, and any other distinguishing factors. How large is your target market?
- *Pricing strategy:* The tactics you will employ, such as a standard fee, discounts, sliding scale, or different levels of programming.
- *Promotion:* This includes which tools you will use—whether personal visits, advertising, social media, or direct marketing—and which will be the most critical to secure new campers.
- *Competition:* Identification of who your competitors are and what differentiates your camp from theirs. If available, any statistics on your competitor's successes. Are they full?
- *Budget:* How much will you spend on marketing?

- *Repeat business strategy:* You should have specific marketing efforts geared toward existing campers.
- *Key messages:* What will be your key messages in promoting your camp?

Presenting Your Business Plan in a PowerPoint® Slide Show

- If you are asked to make a presentation and can show PowerPoint slides, remember the rule of fives: no more than five lines per slide and no more than five words per line.
- Find out how many people will be in the room for your presentation so you can use an LCD and project the slides if more than two people will be watching your presentation. Confirm ahead of time that it is permissible to use an LCD and that the location has a screen or wall on which to show your presentation. If that is not possible, then make color copies of your slides—one per page—and have enough for everyone in the room.
- Ask how long you have to make your presentation and stay within the allotted time.
- Be prepared to answer questions about everything in your business plan, including your financials. Although your accountant may have had considerable input into the financial section, potential lenders will expect to hear the detailed finances from you, the owner.

Financials

Your potential investors will be most interested in your financial story—what your financial model is, how and when you will reach a breakeven point, and how and when you will meet your financial goals. The following standard financial statements should be included:

- Current and projected income statements for at least two years
- Current and projected balance sheets for at least two years
- Cash flow projection by month for at least two years
- Your personal balance sheet and how you will be compensated
- Similar financial information for your secondary business if you have one (for example, your off-season use of camp and how that will affect your camp business).

In addition, your key financial assumptions should be described:

- The size of your potential customer base
- The rate at which you project to grow over time
- The pricing structure and how it may change over time
- Your fixed and variable costs and how they will change over time
- Research or data on which you base your projections
- Adjustments that must occur should your assumptions change

This is also your opportunity to present your need for start-up money and working capital, explaining how you derive these projected needs. If you have already secured some funding, disclose that as well as any other plans to seek funding. Keep in mind that this business plan is confidential and that your potential investors need reliable information in order to carefully consider your request to invest in you and your camp.

Risk Management

Camp administrators are used to dealing with risks—whether activities that could cause injuries, weather or other natural occurrences, or financial risks due to a low enrollment. Plans to deal with all types of risks should be addressed, noting whether you are retaining risk (and what you're doing to manage the risk retention), reducing risk by specific plans, or transferring risk to others through insurance. The following are some items you may include in your plan:

- Activity risk management plans, with a consideration about listing high risk activities, including an example of your detailed plans as an appendix
- Natural occurrences and how you will respond
- Financial risk identification and plans
- Insurance policies—type and limits of liability
- Risk management analysis conducted in conjunction with your insurance carrier. Most carriers will be willing to do an assessment and provide written suggestions on mitigating the potential risk situations on your property.

Appendices

Any reference material or expanded plans can be attached should the reader desire more information. A business plan will take time, but the investment will be well worth it. The discipline required to develop a thorough plan will allow you to look closely at all the parts, especially your financial roadmap, adjusting as needed and learning the minute details of the business in which you'll put not only a substantial amount of money but also your heart and soul.

Although the Small Business Administration has an online business plan tool that can be accessed at no charge, the website has limited features and not all the sections that relate to a camp are included. By completing the plan yourself in a word processing application, you can edit and have more control over the final product. But the SBA's numerous classes and other online tools may at least assist you in the development of your business plan.

5

Programs

diego_cervo/iStock/Thinkstock

What does your program have to do with the business of camp? Actually, it has everything to do with the business of camp. Your program follows philosophy and business follows your program. Your program is the cornerstone of everything you do in your camp and is what your camp business is built on. Too often, camps try to offer program choices that are not consistent with the philosophical principles and mission upon which they were either founded (in existing camp businesses) or started with (in new camp business ventures).

To clarify, you need to develop and nurture your program and program choices in a way in which you stay true to your camp mission. This is not to say that camp programs should be stagnant or reminiscent of something from decades ago. Wonderful changes have occurred in program options because camper (and camper family) preferences have changed over the years. Twenty years ago, you would have been hard pressed to find a camp of any kind offering program choices consisting of the adventure/challenge programming you see today. At the same time, however, you would be hard pressed to find a camp today that is offering the exact same program choices they offered 20 years ago.

Philosophy and Culture

The first thing a camp should ask of itself in developing a program is what are the core philosophical principles that it as a business entity holds sacred? What is it interested in teaching to its campers as a result of its program? What is the experience it's "selling" in its marketing materials? And perhaps most importantly, what is it that parents and campers are expecting from a camp experience? For example, if you are offering a specialty camp experience in computer technology, it would probably not be in your best interest to focus a program on nature or adventure programming. This is where your program choices as a camp owner, director, or executive become so critical. It determines where your camp will be positioning itself in the marketplace and ultimately how your camp's success or failure will be determined.

After answering the philosophical congruence question with your camp mission, a big question that needs to be addressed is "What will the benefit to the campers be as the result of a program choice?" It is universally accepted that children learn and develop new skills in a wide variety of activities as the result of the camp experience. From learning how to swim in a day camp to learning how to sail or paddle a canoe in an overnight camp, campers are actively engaged and learning as the result of their activities. The same can be said for any of the activities that are found in a camp setting–archery, arts and crafts, music, sports, and adventure challenges are all staples to camps around the world. But as the camp administrator, you and your leadership team must be certain that you are offering program choices that are beneficial to your campers and also represent and align with your camp mission.

Another aspect of a camp program to consider is camp culture. If you are taking over an existing program with decades of history or starting a new operation with a history yet to be written, the decisions you make regarding your camp program will create a history and an expectation in the hearts of your camp families and these will also have an effect on the success of your camp business. Color wars, camp Olympics, and camp carnivals are all program examples of camp culture. The same can be said for rituals recognizing camper achievement or the addition of new program activities as campers age. Program progression is another part of camp culture, with campers advancing from one level to another. In new operations, you have the opportunity to start your own new traditions and you can certainly put your culture stamp on all aspects of the program.

Resources for Camp Programming

Numerous resources for camp programming are available through the American Camp Association bookstore at www.acacamps.org/bookstore. Regional and national conferences sponsored by the association include many sessions on camp programming as well as online training provided through the American Camp Association's Professional Development Center (www.acacamps.org/professional-development-center).

www.ACAcamps.org/bookstore

Expenses

Although costs of programs are not the most important factor, from a business viewpoint, the expenses of programs must be considered. You must know how much a program will cost, including personnel, training, and certification for personnel so they can deliver the program; any equipment that must be purchased; any facilities needed to house the program; expendable supplies; and any recognition items you may provide to campers who complete the program. Additions to programs need to be made in time to include them in marketing materials, especially if the new program will be seen as added value for attending your camp. Ask yourself if your fees must be increased to include the program costs, if the additional costs will be absorbed, or if you will charge extra for participation.

In summary, before adding a new camp program, consider the following questions:

- Is the proposed program aligned with your philosophy?
- What benefit does the program have to the campers?
- Does the program fit within your camp's culture?
- Does the value of the program exceed its expense?

Use Figure 5-1 to help you make decisions about proposed new programming.

Questions to Consider	Potential Programs			
	A	B	C	D
Does the program align with your camp philosophy?				
How will we market the program?				
What's the benefit to campers?				
Does the program align with the camp culture?				
What's the estimated cost?				
What personnel is needed?				
What training is needed?				
What equipment is needed?				
What facilities are needed?				
Will you need any special permits?				

Figure 5-1. Making decisions about potential programs

Program Permissions and Release of Liability

Many camps, especially those with such high-risk activities as horseback riding, adventure/challenge activities, or trip programs, will develop a form for campers and their parents to sign to acknowledge the risk and with the intent to release the camp from any liability should an accident occur. These releases or agreements are often contradictory, including language assuring parents and campers that the camp uses great care in its selection of employees, training the participants, and having the best equipment for use in such activities but then asking them to release the camp from any claims of negligence.

Charles R. Gregg and Catherine Hansen-Stamp, well known in the camping field as attorneys specializing in recreation law, have addressed this topic and have provided the following recommendations to outdoor professionals:

- "Examine your participant agreement to determine if it contains language which might be interpreted as a promise to meet a certain standard of behavior that is inconsistent with your effort to be released from claims of negligence. If there is this type of inconsistency, your release language may be ineffective."
- "Work with experienced legal counsel who is familiar with the law in your jurisdiction, to assess this and other important aspects of your participant agreement." (Gregg & Hansen-Stamp, 2009)

John M. Sadler Jr., a sports insurance specialist and licensed attorney in South Carolina, has noted that a well-drafted waiver or release should include the following items:

- The wording must be clear, simple, and unambiguous.
- The size of the type on the release should be at least 10-point—large enough to be read easily.

- Each camper's parents should sign a waiver/release for their child only, not a form that has "gang signatures," where all participants sign a single document.
- The waiver/release should include the phrase "in consideration of being allowed to participate …" to recognize that all parties receive something of value (consideration), making the release a valid contract.
- In order to show assumption of risk, the release should warn about all possible injuries, including permanent disability or death, and that all risks—known and unknown—are assumed.
- The release should disclaim responsibility for negligence, not gross negligence.
- The release should include the phrase "to the fullest extent permitted by law" when releasing the camp from negligence. (Sadler, 2013)

Participant agreements come in various forms and can be known as a "Release of Liability," a "Waiver of Liability," a "Hold Harmless Agreement," or an "Assumption of Risk." Almost all camps will have some type of release or waiver. The effect can vary substantially based on the circumstances, wording, and state law. Camp executives should heed Gregg and Hansen-Stamp's recommendations and obtain advice from an attorney in the state in which you operate and who has experience in such agreements.

As a camp owner, director, or executive, you know why you're in the camp business—it's not just to make a profit but to provide a positive experience for your campers. Programs and business must go hand in hand, with each priority weighed with the other.

6

Staffing, Human Resources Policies, and Employment Laws

Jupiterimages/Creatas/Thinkstock

While staffing can be one of the most challenging aspects to the business of camp, it is without question the most important function you will have as an owner or director of a camp because these will be the people representing your business to parents. Likewise, the importance of positive interactions between campers and staff cannot be overstated. Most adults who attended camp as children have long forgotten the activities in which they participated, but they remember their counselors because those counselors not only taught activities and tended to the needs of the campers, but they also served as role models. From determining the number and qualifications of staff to hiring, training, and supervising them, the staffing process is critical. Couple this with employment laws and practices and camp executives have considerable responsibilities in the human resources arena.

Staffing Plans

The following are some questions to be answered when developing staffing plans:

- What ratio of staff to campers will you need? Will there be any exceptions during specific times of the day? Does offering a lower camper-to-staff ratio create a marketing advantage?
- What are the qualifications of staff? Age? Skills? Background? What training resources do you have available in house, which allows flexibility in hiring skilled positions?
- How will you recruit staff? Will you depend on local populations, former camper populations, or international staff for your staffing needs?
- What type of screening will you do on prospective staff?
- What will job descriptions include?
- What benefits will you provide to the staff? Time off? Pay?
- What type of supervisory staff will be necessary to ensure line staff is properly mentored and supervised?
- What policies will you develop to guide the staff?
- What training will be necessary for staff? Who'll provide the training? How will you conduct late hire and in-service training?
- How can you ensure that your staff diversity is responsive to and reflective of the diversity of your constituents?
- How will you manage interactions with campers, other staff, and parents?
- What type of evaluation and supervision will you provide?

These important aspects of any staffing plan are addressed by the American Camp Association's standards program and should represent how the camp will put its mission into action.

Numerous models for camp staffing exist. Specific resources that can provide guidance about staffing include *Basic Camp Management: An Introduction to Camp Administration* by Armand and Beverly Ball and *Day Camps From Day One: A Hands-On Guide for Day Camp Administration* by Connie Coutellier. In addition, the American Camp Association's website has articles about staffing previously published in their journal, *Camping Magazine*, available at www.acacamps.org.

Volunteers as Staff

Volunteers will not normally be subject to federal and state laws that apply to employees. However, when using volunteers as staff, they will need a set of human resources policies by which to abide, just as paid employees would. This may be called a "Code of Conduct" or "Volunteer Guidelines," but the same types of regulations should apply to volunteers who are serving in staff roles that apply to employees.

Volunteers as staff work better if the camp director is also a volunteer. The challenge may come when volunteers serving in a staff role are also board members. It's always best to differentiate between their role as a decision maker on the board and their role as a program staff member, which can be done by having well-defined job descriptions for both positions.

Job Descriptions

To employ the right people, you need to know what jobs need to be done. Start with developing a clear job description that includes these parts: title, job classification (is the position exempt from overtime or nonexempt), to whom the person is responsible, the minimum qualifications for the job, any preferred qualifications, the essential functions of the position, and then the key responsibilities.

Qualifications

The minimum qualifications should include education (Does the position require a degree? If so, in what field?), experience (Do you need someone who has supervised others? Someone who has previously worked at a camp?), and any knowledge required (computer skills? youth development skills?) as well as any certification needed by the position.

Preferred qualifications would be such achievements as a degree or a certification that would be ideal but is not a requirement at the present time. These could include training that you can provide to the employee after he's hired. It is also necessary to consider what in-house training opportunities are available that will give you a greater level of flexibility and a larger pool of applicants other than those with specific credentials.

Essential Functions

The Americans with Disabilities Act mandates that it is unlawful to discriminate against persons who are able to fulfill the essential functions of the job—with or without reasonable accommodation. Therefore, it's necessary to identify the essential functions for each position.

No universal or definitive method exists to determine whether a responsibility is an essential function. However, you might judge a responsibility to be an essential function if the position exists to perform this responsibility: if due to the number of employees the task cannot be shared or moved to another job description, if a certain degree of skill or specialization is required to perform the function, or if an inability to perform the function creates a risk to the employee, the organization, or the participants.

The key to writing essential functions statements is identifying the abilities required to fulfill the function rather than disabilities that might disqualify an applicant. Ask yourself which of the following abilities are required to fulfill the responsibilities you have identified as essential:

- Auditory ability
- Visual ability
- Ambulatory ability
- Cognitive ability
- Communication ability
- Physical ability or strength

Key Areas of Responsibility

This section of the job description will identify the broad areas for which the employee will be responsible. For example, if you are hiring a maintenance director, the key areas of responsibility might include vehicles, equipment, buildings, and property. A program director might have as his responsibilities cabin activities, waterfront, equestrian, sports, and all-camp activities. You can devise numerous ways to divide up key areas of responsibility, but grouping responsibilities into just four to six major areas will help define the position.

Interviewing

The single most important part of the employment process will be the interview. Not only will you have the chance to ask questions of the interviewee, but you can also observe how comfortable he is and how well he communicates. The interview is also the first step in staff training because this is your opportunity to share some of the job expectations.

One of the best techniques to use in interviewing job candidates is the behavioral interview, which is a systematic, planned interview based on the job responsibilities and which assumes that the way in which a job candidate used skills in the past is the way in which he will use those same skills in the camp job. Good questions in a behavioral interview will allow the interviewer to recognize the candidates' strengths and weaknesses as well as to see how they measure up to the functions of the job.

Sample Job Description

Camp XYZ
Job Description

Title: Camp Counselor
Classification: Exempt
Responsible to: Unit Director
Minimum Qualifications:

- Completed two years of college
- At least 19 years old
- Experience at a camp as a camper or a counselor
- Experience with programs offered at Camp XYZ

Preferred Qualifications:

- Certification in program areas
- Experience as a camp staff member
- Experience in working with children

Essential Functions:

- Must be able to walk over rough terrain without assistance
- Ability to communicate well with others

Key Area of Responsibility: *Campers and Cabin Management*

- Supervise up to 10 campers in a cabin group.
- Provide for the physical, emotional, and social well-being of campers in a cabin (this may include helping them with basic functions, such as ensuring they brush their hair, take showers, brush their teeth, etc.).
- Be observant of camper interactions and actions, ensuring that camp goals and objectives are being met and that campers' needs are addressed appropriately.
- Ensure that campers get to their activities as scheduled.
- Create a harmonious atmosphere in the cabin.
- Provide informal cabin activities during cabin hour.
- Assist the camp nurse by ensuring that campers with medications get to the health house at scheduled times.

Key Area of Responsibility: *Programs*

- Assist in program areas as assigned.
- Develop program activities for a cabin group as a part of evening unit activities.
- Participate with a cabin in unit and all-camp activities, assuming leadership when required.

Sample Job Description (cont.)

Key Area of Responsibility: *Safety and Standards*

- Be aware of and maintain all applicable camp standards and regulations, including state laws and American Camp Association standards.
- Ensure that all activities for campers are conducted safely and within the established standards.
- Be aware of all activity in camp, reporting anything unusual to camp management.

Key Area of Responsibility: *Cleanliness*

- Ensure that campers perform general cabin cleanup on a daily basis.
- Ensure that campers participate in unit and all-camp cleanup activities.
- Be aware of the general cleanliness of a cabin, a unit, and the camp, taking the initiative to pick up any trash or put away any items left out.

Key Area of Responsibility: *Customer Service*

- Be aware of and respond to needs of campers, their parents, other staff, and camp guests.
- Represent Camp XYZ in a positive manner, upholding the Camp XYZ values at all times.
- Enjoy your time at Camp XYZ so others can tell you're happy to be at camp.
- Share any concerns about campers, their parents, other staff, or camp guests with camp management promptly.

Key Area of Responsibility: *Other*

- Assume other duties as assigned.

Good questions in an interview are open ended. They require more than a "Yes" or "No" answer. Such questions might begin with the following:

- Tell me about a time you …
- What kind of extracurricular activities are you involved in?
- Describe how you …
- Tell me about a time when you have had to make a difficult decision.
- What are your favorite memories about attending camp?
- Do you have a specific counselor you remember from your camp experience?
- Explain how you have …

For example, if you are looking for a team player, you might say "Tell me about a time when you had to put aside something you wanted to do to help the group accomplish its goal." Or if you wanted someone with supervisory experience, you might say "Explain how you managed your subordinates when you were working as a unit director last year."

Additional behavioral interview questions are the following:

- Describe a time when you had a challenge and you met it.
- How do you normally deal with conflict? Give me an example of when you had to deal with conflict.
- Share with me the most creative thing you have ever done.
- Tell me about a time when you have been around children and had to get them motivated to do something.
- Describe a time when you demonstrated good leadership skills.
- What would your teachers say if they were asked to describe you?

Good interview questions will help you discover many qualities about a candidate, but it will be up to you as the camp owner or director to avoid making snap judgments, to remain objective, and to listen very carefully to what the candidate says.

Interviewing Tips

- Applicants may be nervous. Try to put them at ease and offer water, coffee, or a soft drink.
- Keep your mind on the interview. Turn off your cell phone and ask not to be disturbed, allowing sufficient time for the interview.
- Have a common list of questions related to the job that you ask of all applicants, avoiding those that can be answered "Yes" or "No."
- Be prepared, having read the applicant's resume prior to the interview. Ask about any lapses in employment or gaps on their resume as well as any inconsistencies.
- Keep on track. You most likely have a limited amount of time and information that you need to learn about the interviewee, so resist the temptation to wander down an unimportant path.
- Take good notes—but not on the application or the resume.
- Be prepared to discuss not only the job description but also the benefits of working for you at camp. You can always ask that the applicant come in a second time to tour the camp and learn more about the position before either of you makes a decision. You may want to get some of your staff members involved in the interview process, as they will bring a fresh perspective and may see things that you don't.
- Ask about the interviewees' references and how they know them and why they listed them as references. Many times when asked, an interviewee may reveal that the reference is actually a friend or relative. This will also give you an opportunity to ask a more direct question to the reference when conducting your reference check on an interviewee.
- If an interviewee reveals something you feel is potentially alarming during the interview, by all means, focus your line of questions until you're satisfied with the interviewee's response. It is better to have your questions answered completely so you can make the best hiring decision possible.
- Don't be afraid to use obvious questions. Many times, a question such as "Why do you like to work with children?" will reveal surprising answers!

What Not to Ask in an Interview

In general, you should not inquire about any of the follow during an interview: race, color, religion, national origin, age, disability, family status, or genetic information. The Equal Employment Opportunity Commission (EEOC) enforces the laws that make it illegal to discriminate against anyone because of these factors. It is also illegal to retaliate against a person because he has complained of discrimination or has filed a discrimination charge.

www.eeoc.gov/laws/practices

For more details on how to avoid prohibited employment practices and policies, see the EEOC website at www.eeoc.gov/laws/practices.

References and Background Checks

Checking references of potential candidates is essential. Most businesses request three or four references from job applicants—all of whom should be contacted. Using the same principles that were used in developing interview questions, reference questions should be consistent, open ended, and related to the job description. In addition, if you have any questions about college enrollment or degrees, the National Student Clearinghouse provides a fee-based service to verify degrees from and current enrollment at most U.S. higher education institutions. The clearinghouse can be accessed at www.studentclearinghouse.org. Because camp employees work with children, additional care is required, including a check of the National Sex Offender Public Website (www.nsopr.gov) and a criminal background check.

The screening process should include the following elements:

- Verification of any previous employment
- References—at least one personal and one from another employer
- Verification of education, any certifications, and licenses
- Completion of voluntary disclosure form
- Criminal background check
- Motor vehicle report (driving check)
- Drug/alcohol tests
- An interview (preferably in-person, but acceptable through electronic means) (American Camp Association, 2013a)

In its *Accreditation Process Guide* (American Camp Association, 2012), the American Camp Association has a mandatory standard that asks the following:

> Does the camp require annual screening for all camp staff—paid, volunteer, and contracted—with responsibility for or access to campers that includes:
>
> - A voluntary disclosure statement?
> - A check of the National Sex Offender Public Website?

The *Accreditation Process Guide* further states the following:

> All camp staff and volunteers, employed and contracted, full-time, year-round, seasonal, and part time, who could have unsupervised access to children must be included in the screening process. This includes on-site operational personnel as well as staff members working from a central office who come to the camp as a part of their responsibility. 'Contracted' staff working in a typical staff role having contact with campers such as food service, housekeeping, or maintenance personnel, or specialized program leaders, should be screened. Guest program specialists who provide leadership in a limited area and are never with campers in an unsupervised situation would not be subject to screening. (American Camp Association, 2012)

A "Voluntary Disclosure Statement" is a signed statement by the prospective camp employee confirming in writing that he has not been convicted of violent crimes or of crimes against children. Additional information may be included, such as any other criminal behavior, former addresses, and items relevant to the job position. A sample voluntary disclosure statement is found in Appendix E.

Criminal Background Checks

The American Camp Association (2013b) has done extensive work with legislators and the federal government, working toward a uniform criminal background check process that's available in every state. Their work continues on behalf of all camp professionals to expand the Child Protection Act and achieve the following:

- "Create universal access to nationwide background searches, by designating a criminal history review entity or organization to process background checks on prospective employees and volunteers for youth-serving organizations.
- Provide participating organizations with reliable and accurate information as to whether an individual's criminal record bears upon his fitness to work or volunteer with children.
- Create a 'one-stop' system where a local organization could elect to obtain both a state and FBI search in one place.
- Keep the fee for nationwide background checks and criminal history review as low as possible for youth-serving organizations at no more than the actual cost–with a maximum of $25.
- Ensure that individuals that are subject to background checks can request their full criminal histories, challenge their accuracy and completeness, and receive a prompt response from the jurisdiction holding the records."

Background Checks

The American Camp Association (2011) has also provided the following very thorough information about background checks in general (used with permission):

There are several different kinds of criminal background checks available today, each with its strengths and weaknesses. There is no single criminal database in this country that includes every criminal record, so there is no one "perfect" background check.

- Method of Identifying the Individual:
  - ✓ Name-based check: A name-based check uses a person's name and Social Security number to match any possible criminal records.
  - ✓ Fingerprint-based check: A fingerprint-based check uses fingerprints taken from an individual to identify that individual and to match any possible criminal records.
  - ✓ Other biometric-based checks: While the technology is not widely available—there are other ways (besides fingerprints) to determine the identity of an individual in order to match any possible criminal records. These methods will increase in the future and include methods such as retinal scans and DNA extraction.
- Records/Databases that are Checked:
  - ✓ Federal Bureau of Investigation (FBI): The FBI maintains the most complete criminal database in the United States. It contains over 200 million arrest and conviction records concerning over 45 million individuals. All records are fingerprint-based. The database contains all federal crimes plus approximately 70-90% of each state's criminal databases. Low-level misdemeanors, driving citations and DUI's make up the portion of state records that are generally not present in the FBI database.
  - ✓ State Background Checks: These checks include only the crimes committed within that state. These background checks are obtained through a state agency (the agency varies from state to state). Some states allow fingerprint-based checks, some only allow name-based checks, and some offer both types for different fees. Most state checks also include arrests, but a few include only convictions.
  - ✓ County/Local Checks: These checks include only the crimes committed within a local jurisdiction. Background checks of a county or local jurisdiction are obtained through the local police department.
  - ✓ Private Vendor Checks/Databases: There are dozens of private vendors that advertise their ability to conduct criminal background checks. (Visit the ACA Web Site at: www.acacamps.org/buyers-guide to access a list of firms that are Business Affiliates of ACA.) Private background checks are generally name-based. There are two basic methods that these private vendors use for providing background checks:

- ⇨ Some vendors search county record repositories for the county of residence for the past 3 – 5 years (sometimes longer).
- ⇨ Other vendors maintain databases of criminal records, often searchable online. Some of these vendors advertise their background checks as national in scope. But, these databases are actually only really "multi-state." These vendors buy their criminal data from the states. But, many states have strong privacy laws, so they do not sell any criminal data. Other states only sell a portion of their data (for example, parole records–but not the full conviction or arrest files).

✓ Driver's License Check: This would catch any tickets, citations, or convictions related to poor driving, including DUIs.

✓ State Sex Offender Registries: Most states have sex offender registries available online. However, states do not share the same criteria of what constitutes a "sex offender." (Any crimes that would cause an individual to be on a sex offender registry should show up in a state or FBI criminal background check).

✓ U.S. Department of Justice, Dru Sjodin National Sex Offender Public Website: This web site, launched in November 2005, provides the public access to each participating state Sex Offender Web Site (www.nsopw.gov). In most cases, the database includes individuals who have been convicted of sexually violent offenses against adults and children and certain sexual contact and other crimes against victims who are minors.

✓ Child Abuse Registries: A few states will allow organizations that work with children to check an individual against their child abuse registry. These databases often include complaints of abuse that never result in arrest or prosecution and so would not be in a criminal database.

- Special Note on the Records/Databases that are Checked: One of the imperfections with criminal databases is that often an arrest will be recorded, but the courts or police do not update that arrest record with the ultimate result. Without that update, it is not known if the individual was convicted, had the charges dropped, or was found not guilty. These incomplete records are often called "open arrests." Some types of background checks only access convictions. When that happens, the check misses any of those open arrests.

Accessibility of Criminal Background Checks

Currently, each state is the "gatekeeper" for background checks – they decide who can access background check information and for what purpose. Each state sets its own laws on background checks, thus, there is no consistency from state to state on eligibility, process, cost, and turnaround time. In many states, the most thorough types of background checks may not be accessible at all to camps. To find out your state's accessibility, visit: www.acacamps.org/publicpolicy/regulations.

www.nsopw.gov

National Sex Offender Public Website

This website links into one national search site, including sex offender registries from public, state, territorial, and tribal sources, and can be accessed at www.nsopw.gov. The site is very intuitive, with a search box on the landing page. After searching, be sure to click on "print view" so you have a record of the search and the results.

A Final Note About the Screening Process

The objective in a thorough screening process for prospective camp employees is threefold:

- To identify the knowledge, skills, and character of prospective employees who'll be serving as role models for children
- To eliminate known child sexual predators from gaining employment around children
- To verify information provided by job candidates

No screening process is 100 percent foolproof. No guarantee exists that hired candidates will be good camp employees. The following must also be in place after hiring:

- A careful training process
- Ongoing supervision
- Policies and procedures that help protect children

The safety and emotional well-being of the campers in your care is the number one priority of every camp owner, director, and executive. But you also have valid business reasons to make every effort to screen potential employees in the most effective manner possible. The cost for screening—in money and in time—pales in comparison to the harm that could be done to a child, the financial burden that could be placed on a camp owner, and the damage to a camp's reputation should a counselor abuse a child at camp.

Staff Manual/Human Resources Policies

One of the most helpful written guides that camp executives can provide for staff is a manual that includes the camp's human resources policies. The HR policies generally describe the conditions in which employees work and provide guidance to supervisors. A thorough set of human resources policies will do the following three things:

- Ensure you as the employer meet your legal obligations.
- Provide consistent guidance for supervisors that leads to fair treatment of all employees.
- Establish the camp's expectations for employee behavior while on the job.

By carefully describing the camp's expectations and the working conditions, camp administrators can better prepare their workforce for the positions they are filling. This can be extremely helpful in camp situations because the total time worked may be just a few weeks or months. You have an added challenge because the camp work experience may be the first job for many of your employees.

Some of the topics that should be addressed in camp human resources policies are listed in the following sections, with sample policies provided in Appendix B. Please note that policies should always be carefully crafted to meet the needs of the individual camp and not simply copied from a source.

Employment

- Equal employment opportunity policies
- Terms and conditions of employment
- Criminal background investigations and other verifications
- Classification of employees
- Pay dates and methods
- Hours of work
- Personal conduct, including use of tobacco, alcohol, and controlled substances
- Physical examinations, drug screens, and medications
- Sexual and other forms of harassment

Benefits

- Statutory benefits (social security, Medicare®, unemployment, workers' compensation)
- Housing, meals, and laundry (if provided)
- Dress requirements and uniforms
- Training provided by the camp—pre-camp and in service
- Time off and leaves of absence
- Health and accident insurance

Operations

- Safety at camp
- Use of camp owned equipment and vehicles
- Authority to purchase and represent the camp
- Policies on the possession of pets and weapons
- Policies on tips, gratuities, and gifts
- Accident/incident reporting
- Reporting requirements for suspected child abuse
- Supervision ratios used in camp, including exceptions to the ratios
- Use of computers, Internet, telephone, and other electronic equipment (personal and camp owned)
- Social networking
- Cell phone use while driving

Evaluation, Discipline, and Separation

- Evaluation and discipline processes
- Problem resolution procedure
- Administrative leave
- Separation
- Voluntary termination
- Involuntary termination
- Reasons for involuntary termination
- Exit report/interview
- Employment references on former employees

Writing Human Resources Policies

Please note that when writing human resources policies, the choice of words can be extremely important. For example, if you have a policy that prohibits the use of alcohol, a noteworthy difference exists between saying "Any use of alcohol by an employee *will* result in dismissal" and "Any use of alcohol by an employee *may* result in dismissal." The first statement gives you no choice but to terminate the employee, whereas the second statement gives you the option to terminate. Neither is right or wrong. It simply depends on what you want your policy to mean.

You may want to make your policies very specific or very broad. For example, some employers may choose to consolidate their policy on behavior expectations to a concise statement, such as "All employees of Camp XYZ will adhere to the standards of conduct expected by the camp." While simple, this statement leaves much to be interpreted by the counselor, supervisor, and director. What are the standards of conduct? Do you spell those out in detail during training? Do you have a separate document listing your standards of conduct? If so, you may be fine with a concise statement. Otherwise, you may want to be more unambiguous in your policies.

It is also a good policy to clearly enumerate the policies that the camp has regarding a wide variety of topics, ranging from alcohol and tobacco use on the job to dating, sensitive issues, dealing with the media, cell phones, and just about any other potential employee issue that may be foreseeable. Refer to these as "Standards of Business Conduct." It is advisable that the employee understands and accepts the "Standards of Business Conduct" and signs a statement to that effect. Placing it in a manual and asking employees to sign that they have read and understand the rules of conduct may help to reduce any possible disagreements in an employee disciplinary process.

Review of Human Resources Policies by an Attorney

It is strongly recommended that you have an employment attorney review all human resources policies before adoption. While attorneys in a general practice can provide very good advice, when it comes to human resources, having an attorney who specializes in employment law working with you to review your human resources policies is well worth the expense. Your employment attorney can also advise you on benefits and other employment issues.

Sample policies found in Appendix B should not be used verbatim. Each camp has the obligation to develop its own policies that fit its own philosophy and circumstances. Please note that the sample policies aren't intended as either recommendations or as legal advice.

All human resources policies should be developed based on your overall camp philosophy and federal and state law, but a few policies will require more consideration because of evolving technology–in particular, cell phone use, computer and Internet use, and social media. Remember that HR policies are for employees (or volunteers if you have a volunteer camp staff) but not campers. However, it is important to remember the policies you will develop for campers when considering your HR policies for employees.

Cell Phone Use by Staff and Campers

Many camps rely on cell phone communication during the camp season, but some have limits on use by staff and campers. As a camp executive, you will need to develop your own policy. The following are some questions on which to reflect:

- Is your camp in a location that provides easy cell phone reception? If not, the issue may be moot for the present, but you will most likely need to deal with the question at some point in the future.
- Do you depend on cell phone communication within camp? For example, does your canoeing or sailing instructor have a cell phone at your waterfront to use in case of an emergency?
- Do you want to be able to get in touch with any staff member at any time via cell phone?
- Do you want to require that counselors have cell phones for emergency use?
- If you allow staff to have their phones with them at all times, do you regulate when they may use them for either calls or texting?
- Do you allow campers to bring cell phones? Unfortunately, it is not unusual for parents to send two phones with their children: one to "burn" (i.e., be confiscated) and one to hide and use to call home.
- If you collect all cell phones, how do you identify them and where will you keep them?
- Do you have a place for staff to store or charge their cell phones?
- Do you have a policy on the use of cell phone cameras and sharing photos of children? (See the section on the Children's Online Privacy Protection Act of 1998 [COPPA].)
- Does your camp ban the use of cellular phones with the exception of extreme emergencies to notify camp or call 911?

While cell phone use has no right or wrong answer, each camp must determine what works best for them. Regardless of your stance, it will be important that you have a written policy so employees know what to expect and that the use of cell phones, including texting, is addressed from the beginning.

Computer Use, the Internet, and Social Media

Most camp staff members have grown up using computers, the Internet, and social media. Although the unlimited use of technology and social media may be the norm for camp employees during the school year, many camps have strict rules and regulations about their use during camp. Your policies should be broad enough to encompass the dynamic nature of technology and social media yet specific enough to provide guidance to your staff on what they can and cannot do—during work time and while they're on break. You may want to include in your policy detailed guidance on blogging or posting online, prohibited content, use of system resources, downloading of music and other content, and limits on computer usage.

Photos, Campers' Privacy, and the Children's Online Privacy Protection Act of 1998 (COPPA)

While the Children's Online Privacy Protection Act (COPPA) basically applies to personal information, including photographs, uploaded by children under age 13, camp executives have an obligation regarding the privacy of their campers. Collecting campers' personal information is addressed in Chapter 10, but other issues related to digital and cell phone cameras, posting of photos on social media sites, and employees must be discussed. A policy prohibiting camp staff from posting photos of any campers online is generally considered the best practice. Staff should be cautioned that no photos or videos of campers should ever be uploaded to a counselor's social media site. Only the camp should upload camper photos and videos and then only to a COPPA-compliant site. The camp's privacy policy should be explained thoroughly to camp staff and monitored for compliance.

Social Interaction With Campers and Parents

Another topic that should be explored in greater detail is that of social interaction with campers and parents. Whether or not you encourage or permit camp social relationships between camp staff and camper families, you should make your policy known to the camp staff. As a word of caution, camp families may feel that a former camp counselor is still representing the camp, even during the year when he has no formal employment agreement with you. Because of that, some camps request that former camp staff members don't develop personal relationships outside of camp with either campers or their parents. Camps may sponsor reunions or other types of social events during the off-season, encouraging former counselors and other staff to participate with the campers and their parents. For other camps, the benefits of such off-season interaction outweigh the concerns.

Staff Manuals—Other Contents

Your staff manual may also include camp procedures—everything from how you check in campers on opening day to how you communicate with parents.

The camp staff organization chart and risk management plans should be a part of the staff manual. American Camp Association standards or state and/or local regulations can require that certain documents, rules, or charts be provided to camp staff. Including such items in the staff manual ensures that all employees have easy access to them.

Most staff manuals also include written guidance for the camp staff on such topics as behavior management of campers, general camp rules and regulations, program-specific rules, and program how-to information as well as the camp history, songs, and games. Some camps will have a staff manual that is printed and bound in such a way as to add other resources to it, whereas other camps provide an electronic copy. Either way, your staff manual can be a beneficial resource for your staff.

Employment and Tax Law

The business of camp requires a great deal of attention to employment and tax law. Regardless of the camp's tax status as for profit or nonprofit, camp personnel must understand and adhere to numerous laws and regulations. The information presented in this book should not be construed as legal or tax advice. Each camp should have an attorney and a financial advisor to provide professional advice on employment and tax law.

Contractors vs. Employees

Persons who are physicians, tradesmen, and attorneys who offer their services to the public are generally not employees but instead are independent contractors. In general, the rule for independent contractors is that if the person for whom the services are performed has only the right to control or direct the result of the work and not the means or methods of accomplishing the result, then those persons performing the work are considered independent contractors. Employers do not pay social security, Medicare, or unemployment taxes on independent contractors.

Camp executives should be wary of classifying camp staff as independent contractors. Specific situations exist in which any person can be considered an independent contractor. Most camp staff members do not qualify as such. The IRS offers guidance in helping to determine if a person should be classified as an independent contractor (in *Publication 15 [Circular E]: Employer's Tax Guide*). It lists the following three categories that must be considered when looking at the relationship between the worker and the business:

- *Behavioral control:* "whether the business has a right to direct and control what work is accomplished and how the work is done, through instructions, training, or other means"
- *Financial control:* whether the business has a right to direct or control the financial and business aspects of the worker's job, such as "the extent of the worker's investment in tools used in performing services and the extent to which the worker makes his or her services available to the relevant market"

- *The relationship of the parties:* whether a written contract is used, whether the business provides benefits to the worker, and "the extent to which services performed by the worker are a key aspect of the regular business of the company" (Internal Revenue Service, 2013b)

It is highly likely that most—if not all—camp staff should be considered employees and therefore the business should pay its portion of social security (FICA) and Medicare taxes as well as deducting the employee's portion and the appropriate income taxes.

Exceptions to the "worker as employee" status might occur in certain contracted services. For example, if a camp contracts with a public pool that others may use, the lifeguards would most likely not be considered camp employees. Similarly, if the camp contracts with a riding facility to provide not only horses but also equine program instruction, the riding instructors would probably not be employees, provided that such instruction is available to members of the public.

However, the question becomes muddled if a contract requires horses to be provided and housed at the camp, along with instructors who are living at the camp and working solely to provide equine instruction for campers. When situations occur that may indicate an employer/employee relationship, it is best to seek advice from a legal or tax professional in determining the proper classification for such a worker.

Camp executives should be aware that when individuals are properly classified as independent contractors, the camp has an obligation to provide an IRS Form 1099 (Miscellaneous Income) to the contractor if he is paid $600 or more during a calendar year. All contractors should be asked to complete an IRS Form W-9 at the time of engagement so the camp has the contractor's social security number or employer identification number, which is required on Form 1099.

Employer Tax Responsibilities

In general, employers should calculate the employer's and the employee's amount due for social security and Medicare as well as the employee's income tax, as these amounts will need to be deposited with the federal government each payday. The IRS provides specific guidance on how to make these calculations and deductions in its *Publication 15 (Circular E): Employer's Tax Guide* and *Publication 15-A: Employer's Supplemental Tax Guide.* You should refer to these guides and ensure that the appropriate deductions are being taken from employee's paychecks.

Employers must make deposits of the amounts withheld from employees' pay in addition to the amounts due by the employer for social security, Medicare, and unemployment taxes (Federal Unemployment Tax [FUTA]) on a regular basis by electronic funds transfer. This is known as the federal deposit. Most financial institutions have programs by which employers can process their payroll electronically and make federal deposits if the camp has chosen a financial software program that doesn't provide for federal deposits. Another option is to consider contracting with a payroll processing firm, which can make the federal deposits in addition to processing the payroll.

A word about 501c(3) organizations: While nonprofit organizations themselves are exempt from federal income tax, they must still withhold federal income tax from their employees' pay. An organization exempt under section 501c(3) of the IRS Code is also exempt from the Federal Unemployment Tax (FUTA). If your camp is a tax-exempt entity under section 501c(3) and you outsource your payroll, confirm that the payroll service fully understands your exemption from FUTA, as this exemption can't be waived (Internal Revenue Service, 2013c).

www.irs.gov

State Requirements and Payday Laws

State or local taxes might also need to be withheld from employees' pay. If you are using a financial institution to pay employees electronically and submit your federal deposit, they should be able to provide information on state or local taxes. If not, consult with your tax advisor or accountant to ensure you are making all the proper deductions and deposits.

Most states have a payday law that specifies how often employees must be paid and the maximum time after working that the employer has to issue payment to the employee. The U.S. Department of Labor's Wage and Hour Division has published information about each of the state payday requirements, which is found in Appendix C (U.S. Department of Labor, 2012a).

IRS Checklist

In its *Publication 15 (Circular E): Employer's Tax Guide*, the IRS includes the following checklist items for employer responsibilities:

For New Employees

- Verify work eligibility (use INS Form I-9).
- Record employees' names and social security numbers exactly as noted on their social security cards.
- Obtain Form W-4 from employees.

Each Payday

- Withhold federal income tax based on the employee's W-4.
- Withhold the employee's share of social security (FICA) and Medicare.
- Deposit withheld income taxes.
- Deposit the employee's and the employer's share of social security and Medicare.

Quarterly

- Deposit the FUTA (federal unemployment) tax.
- File Form 941.

Annually

- Ask employees for a new W-4.
- Provide employees with Form W-2, listing their wages for the previous year (due to them by January 31).
- File all W-2s and Form W-3 with the Social Security Administration (due by the end of February).
- Furnish independent contractors with Form 1099 (by January 31).
- File Form 940. (Internal Revenue Service, 2013b)

Exempt vs. Nonexempt

You will often see employees classified as either "exempt" or "nonexempt." Exempt employees are exempt from the minimum wage and overtime provisions of the Fair Labor Standards Act (FLSA). Nonexempt employees must be paid according to the FLSA, which specifies minimum wages and that for any hours over 40 worked in a workweek, employees must be paid at an overtime rate of 1.5 times their regular rate. Therefore, if a nonexempt employee makes $10 per hour and works 45 hours in a workweek, then his pay would be calculated as 40 hours x $10/hour plus 5 hours x $15/hour, or $400 + $75–a total of $475.

Employees may be classified as exempt from the minimum wage and overtime provisions of the FLSA if they fall into one of the following categories:

- Executive
- Administrative
- Professional
- Outside sales
- Computer

These exemptions are described in the Department of Labor Fact Sheet #17A (which can be accessed at www.dol.gov/whd/regs/compliance/fairpay/fs17a_overview.pdf.):

> **Executive Exemption**
>
> To qualify for the executive employee exemption, all of the following tests must be met:
>
> - The employee must be compensated on a salary basis (as defined in the regulations) at a rate not less than $455 per week;
> - The employee's primary duty must be managing the enterprise, or managing a customarily recognized department or subdivision of the enterprise;

- The employee must customarily and regularly direct the work of at least two or more other full-time employees or their equivalent; and
- The employee must have the authority to hire or fire other employees, or the employee's suggestions and recommendations as to the hiring, firing, advancement, promotion or any other change of status of other employees must be given particular weight.

Administrative Exemptions

To qualify for the administrative employee exemption, all of the following tests must be met:

- The employee must be compensated on a salary or fee basis (as defined in the regulations) at a rate not less than $455 per week;
- The employee's primary duty must be the performance of office or non-manual work directly related to the management or general business operations of the employer or the employer's customers; and
- The employee's primary duty includes the exercise of discretion and independent judgment with respect to matters of significance.

Professional Exemption

To qualify for the *learned professional* employee exemption, all of the following tests must be met:

- The employee must be compensated on a salary or fee basis (as defined in the regulations) at a rate not less than $455 per week;
- The employee's primary duty must be the performance of work requiring advanced knowledge, defined as work which is predominantly intellectual in character and which includes work requiring the consistent exercise of discretion and judgment;
- The advanced knowledge must be in a field of science or learning; and
- The advanced knowledge must be customarily acquired by a prolonged course of specialized intellectual instruction.

To qualify for the *creative professional* employee exemption, all of the following tests must be met:

- The employee must be compensated on a salary or fee basis (as defined in the regulations) at a rate not less than $455 per week;

- The employee's primary duty must be the performance of work requiring invention, imagination, originality or talent in a recognized field of artistic or creative endeavor.

Computer Employee Exemption

To qualify for the computer employee exemption, the following tests must be met:

- The employee must be compensated either on a salary or fee basis (as defined in the regulations) at a rate not less than $455 per week or, if compensated on an hourly basis, at a rate not less than $27.63 an hour;
- The employee must be employed as a computer systems analyst, computer programmer, software engineer or other similarly skilled worker in the computer field performing the duties described below;
- The employee's primary duty must consist of:
  - ✓ The application of systems analysis techniques and procedures, including consulting with users, to determine hardware, software or system functional specifications;
  - ✓ The design, development, documentation, analysis, creation, testing or modification of computer systems or programs, including prototypes, based on and related to user or system design specifications;
  - ✓ The design, documentation, testing, creation or modification of computer programs related to machine operating systems; or
  - ✓ A combination of the aforementioned duties, the performance of which requires the same level of skills.

Outside Sales Exemption

To qualify for the outside sales employee exemption, all of the following tests must be met:

- The employee's primary duty must be making sales (as defined in the FLSA), or obtaining orders or contracts for services or for the use of facilities for which a consideration will be paid by the client or customer; and
- The employee must be customarily and regularly engaged away from the employer's place or places of business. (U.S. Department of Labor, 2008a)

Minimum Wage Requirements/Exemption for Seasonal Amusement or Recreational Establishments

www.dol.gov/whd

As employers, camp administrators are responsible for knowing which employment laws apply to their employees. The U.S. Department of Labor's Wage and Hour Division offers excellent online resources at www.dol.gov/whd. The Fair Labor Standards Act requires that most employees in the United States be paid at least the federal minimum wage and time and one-half for all hours worked over 40 hours in a workweek, but many camps will be exempt from paying minimum wage under Section 13(a)(3): Exemption for Seasonal Amusement or Recreational Establishments Under the Fair Labor Standards Act (FLSA). However, an employer must comply with the most stringent of state or federal provisions and some states may not recognize or permit this exemption. Therefore, camps should review state and local laws thoroughly before applying this exemption.

Section 13(a)(3) provides an exemption from the minimum wage and overtime provisions of the FLSA for:

> any employee employed by an establishment which is an amusement or recreational establishment, if (A) it does not operate for more than seven months in any calendar year, or (B) during the preceding calendar year, its average receipts for any six months of such year were not more than 33-1/3 per centum of its average receipts for the other six months of such year. (U.S. Department of Labor, 2008b)

The Wage and Hour Division's Fact Sheet #18 (which can be accessed at www.dol.gov/whd/regs/compliance/whdfs18.pdf) provides a test for exemption:

- An "amusement or recreational establishment" will be exempt under Section 13(a)(3) of the Act if it meets either Test (A) or Test (B) as explained in the following paragraphs.

  A. "Does not operate for more than seven months in any calendar year." Whether an amusement or recreational establishment "operates" during a particular month is a question of fact, and depends on whether it operates as an amusement or recreational establishment. If an establishment engages only in such activities as maintenance operations or ordering supplies during the "off season" it is not considered to be operating for purposes of the exemption.

  B. 33-1/3 % Test. Because the language of the statute refers to receipts for any six months (not necessarily consecutive months), the monthly average based on total receipts for the six individual months in which the receipts were smallest should be tested against the monthly average for six individual months when the receipts were largest to determine whether this test is met. To illustrate:

- An amusement or recreational establishment operated for nine months in the preceding calendar year. The establishment was closed during December, January and February. The total receipts for May, June, July, August, September and October (the six months in which the receipts were largest) totaled $260,000, a monthly average of $43,333; the total receipts for the other six months totaled $75,000, a monthly average of $12,500. Because the average receipts of the latter six months were not more than 33-1/3% of the average receipts for the other six months of the year, the Section 13(a)(3) exemption: would apply. (U.S. Department of Labor, 2008b)

Thus, a camp operating only in the summer months will most likely be exempt from paying minimum wage, provided that state laws are not more stringent. This is especially important for resident camps, where the camp staff is in residence and works more than eight hour days. However, because the more stringent of either state or federal laws apply, it's imperative that camps have a thorough understanding of their state and local laws. For example, in the state of Washington, the minimum wage is $9.32 per hour (as of January 1, 2014) and covers all employees ages 16 or older unless they are specifically exempt.

Minimum Wage: Federal vs. State Laws

Camps that are not exempt based on the Seasonal or Amusement Recreational Establishment section noted earlier need to have a thorough understanding of minimum wage laws—federal and state. Nineteen states have minimum wages that are higher that the federal minimum wage and the most stringent of the laws will apply, which means that the higher of the two minimum wages is required. See Appendix D for minimum wages by state. Note that in most states, changes to minimum wages are usually made effective January 1, so it's advised that camps check with their state employment office for the most current information on state minimum wages or search the Department of Labor's Wage and Hour Division website (www.dol.gov/whd) for "state minimum wages."

Exemptions for Nonprofits and Faith-Based Camps

Nonprofits and faith-based camps are *not* exempt from either minimum wage provisions or paying overtime based simply on their status as a nonprofit organization or faith-based institution. However, camps sponsored by these organizations may be exempt from minimum wage and overtime if they meet the definition of a seasonal amusement or recreational establishment as noted earlier.

Exemption for Seasonal Amusement or Recreational Establishments

Many camps will be exempt from paying minimum wage to their employees under Section 13(a)(3): Exemption for Seasonal Amusement or Recreational Establishments Under the Fair Labor Standards Act. If the camp does not operate for more than seven months in any calendar year or during the preceding calendar year or its average receipts for any six months of such year were not more than 33.3 percent of its average receipts for the other six months of the year, then the camp will be exempt from paying employees minimum wage—unless a state law is more stringent.

The American Camp Association's website offers an excellent list by state of regulations applying to camps (www.acacamps.org/print/29754). The site notes that in the state of Washington, for example, exemptions include:

> employees who sleep or reside at the place of employment or spend a substantial part of their work time on call and not actually working; employees of charitable institutions charged with child care responsibilities engaged primarily in development of character or citizenship or promoting health or physical fitness or providing or sponsoring recreational opportunities or facilities for young people or members of the armed forces; volunteers or nonemployees for an educational, charitable, or nonprofit organization, or a state or local government body or agency; bona fide executives, administrators, or professionals; full-time state and local volunteer services. (American Camp Association, 2013b)

Camp officials should consult the American Camp Association website (as noted in the previous paragraph) for general information about their state's laws and regulations related to employment law. Links are available to the specific agency in each state that handles camp regulations.

www.ACAcamps.org/publicpolicy/regulations

Age Requirements

The Fair Labor Standards Act also addresses age requirements for employees. Generally, persons must be at least 14 years old to be employed and those under age 16 may only work a limited number of hours. In general, children of any age may work for businesses owned entirely by their parents, although restrictions apply to youth working in hazardous jobs. Hazardous jobs that could be found in camps and which youth under 18 may not fill include processing occupations (such as filleting fish, dressing poultry, laundering, or developing photographs), work related to any boiler equipment or power-driven machinery (including lawn mowers, weed eaters, edgers, food slicers, food processors, and food mixers), washing windows, anything requiring the use of a ladder, baking or cooking, work in freezers, or construction (U.S. Department of Labor, 2013a). Additional positions defined as hazardous jobs are listed at www.dol.gov/whd/regs/compliance/childlabor101_text.htm.

As with other employment laws, many states have laws regulating child labor. Whichever laws are most protective of employees will apply—whether state or federal. Camp officials should also consult American Camp Association standards to assist in determining the age requirements for certain positions. Many positions of responsibility or those programs deemed high risk may require the employee to be at least 21 years old.

Family and Medical Leave Act (FMLA)

The Family and Medical Leave Act (FMLA) was enacted to provide a means for employees to balance their work and family responsibilities by taking unpaid leave for certain reasons. The FMLA applies to "any employer in the private sector who engages in commerce, or in any industry or activity affecting commerce, and who has 50 or more employees each working day during at least 20 calendar weeks in the current or preceding year" (U.S. Department of Labor, 2012b). While the FMLA may not apply to camps operating only on a seasonal basis, those employers who have year-round employees may want to consider the spirit of the law when deciding which benefits to provide for employees, even if it's not mandatory that they provide the unpaid leave addressed by the FMLA.

Employee Polygraph Protection Act of 1988 (EPPA)

The Employee Polygraph Protection Act of 1988 (EPPA) applies to most private employers and prohibits the use of lie detector tests for pre-employment screening or during the course of employment. Although no reporting requirements exist for the EPPA, it's necessary for employers to post information about the act and employee rights (U.S. Department of Labor, 2008c).

Personal Responsibility and Work Opportunity Reconciliation Act of 1996 (PRWORA)

The Personal Responsibility and Work Opportunity Reconciliation Act of 1996 (PRWORA) was signed into law in 1996 and requires all states to implement a new hire reporting program, which ultimately strengthens the Child Support Enforcement Program administered by the Department of Health and Human Services. The New Hire Report must include the name, address, and social security number of all newly hired employees and must be filed within 20 days of the date of hire. States then match new hire information with child support records to locate parents, enforce an order, or establish an order for child support. Employers should contact their state for more information on the reporting of new hires (Office of Child Support Enforcement, 1996).

Immigration Reform and Control Act of 1986 (IRCA)

All employers must comply with the Immigration Reform and Control Act (IRCA) by hiring only persons who may legally work in the United States and employers are required to verify the identity and employment eligibility of anyone to be hired through completion of a Form I-9. Employers must keep all Form I-9s on file for at least three years or one year after employment ends, whichever is longer.

Camp job applicants should be aware that they must provide certain documents on their first day of work for pay. Employers must physically examine the documents provided to determine if they reasonably appear to be genuine. Employees must present either one document that establishes identify and employment authorization (such as a passport) or a document that establishes identity (such as a driver's license or a school ID card with a photograph) and a document that establishes employment authorization (such as a social security card or an original or certified copy of a birth certificate issued by a state or local authority bearing an official seal). Employers cannot specify which documents will be accepted, but the complete list is found on the current Form I-9, which may be found at www.uscis.gov/files/form/i-9.pdf. Camp directors should notify their employees that it's necessary to bring these documents with them on their first day of work at camp as a condition of employment. Some employees new to the workforce may not have easy access to these documents and will have to get them from their parents, so informing them early of this requirement may save time and problems later (U.S. Citizenship and Immigration Services, 2013).

Uniformed Services Employment and Reemployment Rights Act (USERRA)

The Uniformed Services Employment and Reemployment Rights Act (USERRA) covers virtually all employers in the United States and prohibits discrimination against any person on the basis of past service, current obligations, or the intent to serve–whether voluntarily or involuntarily in the uniformed services, which are defined as the Army, Navy, Marines, Air Force, Coast Guard, and Public Health Service commissioned corps as well as their corresponding reserve units. Under the USERRA, an employer must re-employ service members returning from a period of service in the uniformed services and who meet certain criteria related to such things as the length of time absent from the job and the advance notice given to the employer prior to leaving for service in the uniformed services. The USERRA is administered by the Veterans' Employment and Training Service (VETS) (U.S. Department of Labor, n.d.a).

Health Information Portability and Accountability Act (HIPAA)

The Health Information Portability and Accountability Act (HIPAA)—originally passed by Congress in 1996—may or may not apply to your camp. In a recent article in *Campline*, attorneys Charles R. Gregg and Catherine Hansen-Stamp concluded that the HIPAA most likely doesn't apply to most camps. However, they caution that it's always best for camps to seek advice from their own attorneys and the Department of Health and Human Services website, especially with regard to updates as a result of the 2009 Health Information Technology for Economic and Clinical Health Act (HITECH), which expanded HIPAA regulations (Hansen-Stamp & Gregg, 2013).

Patient Protection and Affordable Care Act (PPACA)

Healthcare reform was addressed through the enactment of the Patient Protection and Affordable Care Act (PPACA) in 2010. However, the law hasn't yet been fully implemented, with some implementation still being delayed as of late 2013. The initial law included the provision for tax credits for small businesses, which could be a positive for camps. The Department of Labor, the Department of Health and Human Services, and the IRS have web pages dedicated to interpreting the Affordable Care Act. It is recommended that camp executives check with these or other reliable sources for guidance on how this act will affect camps (Internal Revenue Service, 2013d).

Fair Credit Reporting Act (FCRA)

The Fair Credit Reporting Act (FRCA) requires that employers using any consumer reports (including employment background checks, credit reports, and criminal records) to make employment decisions must comply with the FCRA. As an employer, you must tell the applicant that you may use information from consumer reports (typically a criminal background check) in making a decision about his employment. This information must be conveyed to the applicant in a stand-alone format (not as part of an application) and you must get written permission to obtain the information. Generally, if you use companies that specialize in this type of report, they will provide you with forms that meet the requirements of the FCRA as well as the monograph "A Summary of Your Rights Under the Fair Credit Reporting Act," which you must provide to employees before taking any adverse employment action, such as releasing them or denying them a promotion. Additional information about your responsibilities under the FCRA can be found at business.ftc.gov/documents/bus08-using-consumer-reports-what-employers-need-know (Federal Trade Commission, 2012).

Americans with Disabilities Act (ADA)

www.ada.gov

The Americans with Disabilities Act (ADA) prohibits discrimination against qualified individuals with disabilities in public and private sector employment, requiring covered employers to make reasonable accommodations for known physical and mental limitations of qualified applicants and employees, as long as such accommodations do not impose an undue hardship on employers. This applies to all employers of 15 or more employees. For more information, see the ADA website at www.ada.gov. ADA requirements regarding sites and facilities are addressed in Chapter 9 (U.S. Department of Justice, 2011a).

Occupational Health and Safety (OSHA)

Occupational Health and Safety (OSHA) regulations will apply to all camps. In particular, the OSHA regulations regarding exposure to blood-borne pathogens, personal protective equipment, and hazard communication (maintenance and communication of material safety data sheets) are some of the most common related to camp operations, in addition to requirements mandating that work-related injuries and illnesses be logged on OSHA Form 300. Some American Camp Association standards may refer to OSHA regulations, so camp officials should be aware of potential changes in the law. A recommended place to start is OSHA's Small Business Handbook (found at www.osha.gov/Publications/smallbusiness/small-business.pdf) and the Department of Labor's "Employment Law Guide on Occupational Health and Safety" (found at www.dol.gov/compliance/guide/osha.htm). More information about OSHA as it relates to health and safety is found in Chapter 16 (Occupational Safety and Health Administration, 1989).

Required Posters

All employers are required to post certain notices to employees, including the following:

- Employee Rights Under the Fair Labor Standards Act (FLSA/Minimum Wage)
- Job Safety and Health: It's the Law (Occupational Safety and Health Act/OSHA)
- Employee Rights and Responsibilities Under the Family and Medical Leave Act (FMLA)
- Equal Employment Opportunity Is the Law (EEO)
- Employee Rights for Workers With Disabilities Paid at Special Minimum Wages
- Employee Polygraph Protection Act Notice (EPPA)
- Your Rights Under USERRA (Veterans) (U.S. Department of Labor, n.d.b)

To determine which posters are required for your camp, check www.dol.gov/compliance/topics/posters.htm. Note that no exemption exists for nonprofits regarding posting requirements. All the required posters can be downloaded at no cost from the Department of Labor website. Individual states may require additional notifications, so check with your state employment agency.

As a camp executive, you are an employer. As such, one of your most important jobs will be to manage your staff, ensure fair treatment, and abide by all applicable employment and tax laws. It may appear that you can't possibly manage all the laws and regulations, but you will find that many resources are available to you, including professionals who understand the complexity of employment and tax issues.

7

Recognizing Child Abuse and Reporting Requirements

Louis-Paul St-Onge/iStock/Thinkstock

It is essential that all camp administrators understand their legal responsibilities to recognize and report suspected child abuse and provide training to their employees about the responsibilities of all camp personnel. In addition to the serious harm to children, any failure to report child abuse could have an adverse effect on a camp. Thus, the issue is a business one that must always be addressed. Without a doubt, the safety and well-being of children in the care of camps is the first priority. But camp executives need to know how to recognize signs of potential abuse, take appropriate action, and acknowledge that lack of attention to potential child abuse could cause irreparable harm to the reputation of a camp as a safe, fun place for children in addition to the potential for legal action against the camp or individual should there be a failure to report suspected abuse.

Federal Child Abuse Prevention and Treatment Act (CAPTA)

www.childwelfare.gov

Although laws will differ from state to state, the Federal Child Abuse Prevention and Treatment Act (CAPTA) and the CAPTA Reauthorization Act of 2010 is the basis for most state laws, according to the U.S. Department of Health and Human Services' Administration on Children, Youth and Families (ACYF). The ACYF has established a Child Welfare Information Gateway, which provides detailed information to help protect children and strengthen families and is available at www.childwelfare.gov.

Employees as Possible Abusers

Camp executives have the responsibility to be aware of employees who might abuse children. As professionals caring for children, camp executives take precautions with thorough background checks during the employment process, ample training for camp staff, and careful supervision of all who have contact with children. Policies and procedures, training, and supervision should always include an awareness by all staff of any unusual behavior of other staff that could be indicative of a child abuser. Any concerns should be reported and investigated immediately by camp management and appropriate local authorities.

What Is Child Abuse and Neglect?

The information that follows is from the Child Welfare Information Gateway (2013) factsheet *What Is Child Abuse and Neglect? Recognizing the Signs and Symptoms* and is used with permission. Additional information is available online at www.childwelfare.gov.

What Is Child Abuse and Neglect? Recognizing the Signs and Symptoms

The first step in helping abused or neglected children is learning to recognize the signs of child abuse and neglect. The presence of a single sign does not mean that child maltreatment is occurring in a family, but a closer look at the situation may be warranted when these signs appear repeatedly or in combination. This factsheet is intended to help you better understand the legal definition of child abuse and neglect, learn about the different types of abuse and neglect, and recognize the signs and symptoms of abuse and neglect. Resources about the impact of trauma on well-being also are included in this factsheet. [Note: This information is not reprinted in this book and can be found at www.childwelfare.gov/pubs/factsheets/whatiscan.pdf].

How Is Child Abuse and Neglect Defined in Federal Law?

Federal legislation lays the groundwork for state laws on child maltreatment by identifying a minimum set of acts or behaviors that define child abuse and neglect. The Federal Child Abuse Prevention and Treatment Act (CAPTA), (42 U.S.C.A. §5106g), as amended and reauthorized by the CAPTA Reauthorization Act of 2010, defines child abuse and neglect as, at minimum:

> *"Any recent act or failure to act on the part of a parent or caretaker which results in death, serious physical or emotional harm, sexual abuse or exploitation; or an act or failure to act which presents an imminent risk of serious harm."*

Most federal and state child protection laws primarily refer to cases of harm to a child caused by parents or other caregivers; they generally do not include harm caused by other people, such as acquaintances or strangers. Some state laws also include a child's witnessing of domestic violence as a form of abuse or neglect.

What Are the Major Types of Child Abuse and Neglect?

Within the minimum standards set by CAPTA, each state is responsible for providing its own definitions of child abuse and neglect. Most states recognize the four major types of maltreatment: physical abuse, neglect, sexual abuse, and emotional abuse. Signs and symptoms for each type of maltreatment are listed below. Additionally, many states identify abandonment and parental substance abuse as abuse or neglect. While these types of maltreatment may be found separately, they often occur in combination. For state-specific laws pertaining to child abuse and neglect, see Child Welfare Information Gateway's State Statutes Search page:

www.childwelfare.gov/systemwide/laws_policies/state

What Is Child Abuse and Neglect? (cont.)

Information Gateway's Definitions of Child Abuse and Neglect provides civil definitions that determine the grounds for intervention by state child protective agencies: www.childwelfare.gov/systemwide/laws_policies/statutes/define.pdf

Physical abuse is nonaccidental physical injury (ranging from minor bruises to severe fractures or death) as a result of punching, beating, kicking, biting, shaking, throwing, stabbing, choking, hitting (with a hand, stick, strap, or other object), burning, or otherwise harming a child, that is inflicted by a parent, caregiver, or other person who has responsibility for the child.[1] Such injury is considered abuse regardless of whether the caregiver intended to hurt the child. Physical discipline, such as spanking or paddling, is not considered abuse as long as it is reasonable and causes no bodily injury to the child.

Neglect is the failure of a parent, guardian, or other caregiver to provide for a child's basic needs. Neglect may be:

- Physical (e.g., failure to provide necessary food or shelter, or lack of appropriate supervision)
- Medical (e.g., failure to provide necessary medical or mental health treatment)[2]
- Educational (e.g., failure to educate a child or attend to special education needs)
- Emotional (e.g., inattention to a child's emotional needs, failure to provide psychological care, or permitting the child to use alcohol or other drugs)

Sometimes cultural values, the standards of care in the community, and poverty may contribute to maltreatment, indicating the family is in need of information or assistance. When a family fails to use information and resources, and the child's health or safety is at risk, then child welfare intervention may be required. In addition, many states provide an exception to the definition of neglect for parents who choose not to seek medical care for their children due to religious beliefs.[3]

1. Nonaccidental injury that is inflicted by someone other than a parent, guardian, relative, or other caregiver (i.e., a stranger), is considered a criminal act that is not addressed by child protective services.
2. *Withholding of medically indicated treatment* is a specific form of medical neglect that is defined by CAPTA as "the failure to respond to the infant's life-threatening conditions by providing treatment (including appropriate nutrition, hydration, and medication) which, in the treating physician's or physicians' reasonable medical judgment, will be most likely to be effective in ameliorating or correcting all such conditions..." CAPTA does note a few exceptions, including infants who are "chronically and irreversibly comatose"; situations when providing treatment would not save the infant's life but merely prolong dying; or when "the provision of such treatment would be virtually futile in terms of the survival of the infant and the treatment itself under such circumstances would be inhumane."
3. The CAPTA amendments of 1996 (42 U.S.C.A. § 5106i) added new provisions specifying that nothing in the act be construed as establishing a federal requirement that a parent or legal guardian provide any medical service or treatment that is against the religious beliefs of the parent or legal guardian.

What Is Child Abuse and Neglect? (cont.)

Sexual abuse includes activities by a parent or caregiver such as fondling a child's genitals, penetration, incest, rape, sodomy, indecent exposure, and exploitation through prostitution or the production of pornographic materials.

Sexual abuse is defined by CAPTA as "the employment, use, persuasion, inducement, enticement, or coercion of any child to engage in, or assist any other person to engage in, any sexually explicit conduct or simulation of such conduct for the purpose of producing a visual depiction of such conduct; or the rape, and in cases of caretaker or inter-familial relationships, statutory rape, molestation, prostitution, or other form of sexual exploitation of children, or incest with children."

Emotional abuse (or psychological abuse) is a pattern of behavior that impairs a child's emotional development or sense of self-worth. This may include constant criticism, threats, or rejection, as well as withholding love, support, or guidance. Emotional abuse is often difficult to prove, and therefore, child protective services may not be able to intervene without evidence of harm or mental injury to the child. Emotional abuse is almost always present when other types of maltreatment are identified.

Abandonment is now defined in many states as a form of neglect. In general, a child is considered to be abandoned when the parent's identity or whereabouts are unknown, the child has been left alone in circumstances where the child suffers serious harm, or the parent has failed to maintain contact with the child or provide reasonable support for a specified period of time. Some states have enacted laws—often called safe haven laws—that provide safe places for parents to relinquish newborn infants. Child Welfare Information Gateway produced a publication as part of its State Statute series that summarizes such state laws. Infant Safe Haven Laws is available on the Information Gateway website: www.childwelfare.gov/systemwide/laws_policies/statutes/safehaven.cfm.

Substance abuse is an element of the definition of child abuse or neglect in many states. Circumstances that are considered abuse or neglect in some states include the following:

- Prenatal exposure of a child to harm due to the mother's use of an illegal drug or other substance
- Manufacture of methamphetamine in the presence of a child
- Selling, distributing, or giving illegal drugs or alcohol to a child
- Use of a controlled substance by a caregiver that impairs the caregiver's ability to adequately care for the child

For more information about this issue, see Child Welfare Information Gateway's *Parental Drug Use as Child Abuse* at www.childwelfare.gov/pubs/factsheets/parentalsubabuse.cfm.

What Is Child Abuse and Neglect? (cont.)

Recognizing Signs of Abuse and Neglect

In addition to working to prevent a child from experiencing abuse or neglect, it is important to recognize high-risk situations and the signs and symptoms of maltreatment. If you do suspect a child is being harmed, reporting your suspicions may protect him or her and get help for the family. Any concerned person can report suspicions of child abuse or neglect. Reporting your concerns is not making an accusation; rather, it is a request for an investigation and assessment to determine if help is needed.

Some people (typically certain types of professionals, such as teachers or physicians) are required by state law to make a report of child maltreatment under specific circumstances—these are called mandatory reporters. Some states require all adults to report suspicions of child abuse or neglect. Child Welfare Information Gateway's publication Mandatory Reporters of Child Abuse and Neglect discusses the laws that designate groups of professionals as mandatory reporters: www.childwelfare.gov/systemwide/laws_policies/statutes/manda.pdf.

For information about where and how to file a report, contact your local child protective services agency or police department.

Childhelp National Child Abuse Hotline (800.4.A.CHILD) and its website offer crisis intervention, information, resources, and referrals to support services and provide assistance in 170 languages: www. childhelp.org/pages/hotline-home.

For information on what happens when suspected abuse or neglect is reported, read Information Gateway's *How the Child Welfare System Works*: www.childwelfare.gov/pubs/factsheets/cpswork.cfm.

Some children may directly disclose that they have experienced abuse or neglect. The factsheet *How to Handle Child Abuse Disclosures*, produced by the "Childhelp Speak Up Be Safe" child abuse prevention campaign, offers tips. The factsheet defines direct and indirect disclosure, as well as tips for supporting the child: www.speakupbesafe.org/parents/disclosures-for-parents.pdf.

The following signs may signal the presence of child abuse or neglect.

The Child:

- Shows sudden changes in behavior or school performance
- Has not received help for physical or medical problems brought to the parents' attention
- Has learning problems (or difficulty concentrating) that cannot be attributed to specific physical or psychological causes
- Is always watchful, as though preparing for something bad to happen
- Lacks adult supervision

What Is Child Abuse and Neglect? (cont.)

- Is overly compliant, passive, or withdrawn
- Comes to school or other activities early, stays late, and does not want to go home
- Is reluctant to be around a particular person
- Discloses maltreatment

The Parent:

- Denies the existence of—or blames the child for—the child's problems in school or at home
- Asks teachers or other caregivers to use harsh physical discipline if the child misbehaves
- Sees the child as entirely bad, worthless, or burdensome
- Demands a level of physical or academic performance the child cannot achieve
- Looks primarily to the child for care, attention, and satisfaction of the parent's emotional needs
- Shows little concern for the child

The Parent and Child:

- Rarely touch or look at each other
- Consider their relationship entirely negative
- State that they do not like each other

The previous list may not be *all* the signs of abuse or neglect. It is important to pay attention to other behaviors that may seem unusual or concerning. In addition to these signs and symptoms, Child Welfare Information Gateway provides information on the risk factors and perpetrators of child abuse and neglect fatalities: www.childwelfare.gov/can/risk_perpetrators.cfm

Signs of Physical Abuse

Consider the possibility of physical abuse when the *child:*

- Has unexplained burns, bites, bruises, broken bones, or black eyes
- Has fading bruises or other marks noticeable after an absence from school
- Seems frightened of the parents and protests or cries when it is time to go home
- Shrinks at the approach of adults
- Reports injury by a parent or another adult caregiver
- Abuses animals or pets

Consider the possibility of physical abuse when the *parent or other adult caregiver:*

- Offers conflicting, unconvincing, or no explanation for the child's injury, or provides an explanation that is not consistent with the injury

What Is Child Abuse and Neglect? (cont.)

- Describes the child as "evil" or in some other very negative way
- Uses harsh physical discipline with the child
- Has a history of abuse as a child
- Has a history of abusing animals or pets

Signs of Neglect

Consider the possibility of neglect when the *child:*

- Is frequently absent from school
- Begs or steals food or money
- Lacks needed medical or dental care, immunizations, or glasses
- Is consistently dirty and has severe body odor
- Lacks sufficient clothing for the weather
- Abuses alcohol or other drugs
- States that there is no one at home to provide care

Consider the possibility of neglect when the *parent or other adult caregiver:*

- Appears to be indifferent to the child
- Seems apathetic or depressed
- Behaves irrationally or in a bizarre manner
- Is abusing alcohol or other drugs

Signs of Sexual Abuse

Consider the possibility of sexual abuse when the *child:*

- Has difficulty walking or sitting
- Suddenly refuses to change for gym or to participate in physical activities
- Reports nightmares or bedwetting
- Experiences a sudden change in appetite
- Demonstrates bizarre, sophisticated, or unusual sexual knowledge or behavior
- Becomes pregnant or contracts a venereal disease, particularly if under age 14
- Runs away
- Reports sexual abuse by a parent or another adult caregiver
- Attaches very quickly to strangers or new adults in their environment

Consider the possibility of sexual abuse when the *parent or other adult caregiver:*

- Is unduly protective of the child or severely limits the child's contact with other children, especially of the opposite sex
- Is secretive and isolated
- Is jealous or controlling with family members

What Is Child Abuse and Neglect? (cont.)

Signs of Emotional Maltreatment

Consider the possibility of emotional maltreatment when the *child:*

- Shows extremes in behavior, such as overly compliant or demanding behavior, extreme passivity, or aggression
- Is either inappropriately adult (parenting other children, for example) or inappropriately infantile (frequently rocking or head-banging, for example)
- Is delayed in physical or emotional development
- Has attempted suicide
- Reports a lack of attachment to the parent

Consider the possibility of emotional maltreatment when the *parent or other adult caregiver:*

- Constantly blames, belittles, or berates the child
- Is unconcerned about the child and refuses to consider offers of help for the child's problems
- Overtly rejects the child

Child Abuse Reporting Requirements

All states have identified those persons who by their profession or relationship with children *must* report suspected child abuse. In most states, mandatory reporters include the following:

- Child care providers
- Pediatricians and other healthcare workers
- Law enforcement officers
- Mental health professionals
- Clergy
- School personnel
- Social workers

Although the laws will differ in each state, in general, camp counselors and administrators have a mandatory responsibility to report suspected child abuse to state or local authorities—without coaching from their supervisors or the camp management—because they could be classified as "child care providers." In California, Louisiana, Maine, Nevada, New York, Ohio, Oregon, Vermont, Virginia, and West Virginia, camp personnel are specifically mandated to report suspected child abuse. In Arizona, Hawaii, Illinois, Massachusetts, Missouri, Texas, and Washington, camp counselors appear to be mandated to report suspected child abuse based on the wording in the state statutes. *Note also that states frequently change their laws, so it is imperative that the most current information be available.* Checking with your local Child Protective Services office or with the

Child Welfare Information Gateway at www.childwelfare.gov is recommended (Child Welfare Information Gateway, 2012). In addition, some states license camps as they would child care facilities, so mandatory reporting for camp personnel would be the same as for child care personnel. Check with your state for confirmation. The information included in this section is the most recent at the time of publication, but you should confirm your local and state laws.

In another 18 states, *all persons* who have reasonable cause to suspect that a child has been harmed *must* report. Most of the other state statutes indicate that any individuals who have reasonable cause to suspect that a child has been harmed *may* report. See Appendix H for a list by state of mandatory reporters and implied mandatory reporters related to camp personnel.

Standards for Making a Report

Most state statutes are worded so any persons described as a mandatory reporter must make a report whenever he suspects or has reason to believe that a child has been abused or when the reporter observes a child being harmed. Those reporters who are not mandated to make a report follow the same standards when choosing to report suspected abuse (Child Welfare Information Gateway, 2012).

How to Report and Confidentiality

Most states have toll-free telephone numbers. (See Appendix I for telephone numbers and website addresses for the state agencies charged with accepting reports of abuse.) In addition, the confidentiality of reporters is generally assured through the process. All states provide immunity from civil liability and criminal penalty for mandated reporters who report in good faith, which means that if a camp counselor or administrator suspects that a child is the victim of child abuse, he won't be subject to negative legal consequences by making a report (Karageorge & Kendall, 2008).

The U.S. Department of Health and Human Services' Administration on Children, Youth and Families says:

> Responding to child abuse and neglect involves protecting children from harm and supporting families to reduce the risk of future harm to children. Reports from professionals and concerned citizens are received by child protective services (CPS) staff alerting them to concerns about a child's welfare. CPS staff may initiate an investigation to determine if a child has been or is at risk of being harmed. Staff may also assess the child's and family's needs or engage in other interventions to support the family's efforts to provide a safe, nurturing environment for their children. CPS professionals may work with law enforcement, courts, other professionals, and community members to protect children and support families. (Child Welfare Information Gateway, 2013)

Camp Counselors Reporting Requirements for Suspected Child Abuse

In the following states, camp counselors are specifically named among those mandated to report suspected child abuse:

- California
- Louisiana
- Maine
- Nevada
- New York
- Ohio
- Oregon
- Vermont
- Virginia
- West Virginia

Based on wording in individual state laws, it appears that camp counselors, although they are not mentioned by name, are mandated to report suspected child abuse in the following states:

- Arizona
- Hawaii
- Illinois
- Massachusetts
- Missouri
- Texas
- Washington

In addition, some states license camps as they would child care facilities, so camp personnel may be included when child care professionals have a mandatory reporting responsibility. Check with your state to confirm.

All persons who suspect or have reason to believe that a child has been harmed must report in the following states:

- Delaware
- Florida
- Idaho
- Indiana
- Kentucky
- Maryland
- Mississippi
- Nebraska
- New Hampshire
- New Jersey
- New Mexico
- North Dakota
- Oklahoma
- Rhode Island
- Tennessee
- Utah
- Wyoming

Note: This information was correct at the time of publication, but laws are changed frequently. Check with local or state officials to confirm the requirements in your state.

Camp personnel need to be aware of the state laws where the camp is located and consider not only their legal responsibility to report suspected child abuse—either the director or the nurse, counselor, or another employee to whom the camper made an outcry for help—but also their ethical responsibility. Not reporting suspected abuse could ultimately cause further harm to a child as well as lead to potential criminal charges against anyone who had reason to believe abuse had occurred and cause irreparable damage to the reputation of a camp.

American Camp Association Hotline

The American Camp Association offers a hotline to its members, providing assistance in the event of suspected child abuse or other challenging situations. Members receive the toll-free number when they join the association.

Additional Assistance

Childhelp® is a national organization that provides crisis assistance and other counseling and referral services. The Childhelp National Child Abuse Hotline is staffed 24 hours a day, 7 days a week, with professional crisis counselors who have access to a database of 55,000 emergency, social service, and support resources. All calls are anonymous. Contact them at 1-800-4ACHILD (1-800-422-4453).

8

Other Laws and Regulations Affecting Camps

Stock Foundry_Design Pics/Valueline/Thinkstock

No federal laws or regulations specifically deal with the operations of camps, but camps must still comply with numerous federal regulations. In addition, almost every state requires that camps be licensed and most have camp-specific laws and regulations for camp operations as well as regulations for typical camp activities.

The American Camp Association has a summary of state licensing requirements for camps: www.acacamps.org/print/29754. This listing includes the state governing body responsible for camps; license requirements and general camp license information; criminal background check requirement; whether the state allows FBI background checks; driving license checks; state sex offender registry; minimum wage information, coverage, and exemptions; overtime and exemptions; meal/rest period requirements; and more (American Camp Association, 2013c). The American Camp Association updates this listing on a regular basis. See Appendix F for a listing of states and the state agencies responsible for camp regulations.

The following sections discuss some of the laws that will affect most camps. Please note that nothing contained in this chapter or book should be construed as legal advice. Note also that laws and regulations may be updated at any time. Camps should check with authorities regarding applicability of the laws and regulations listed in this book and to get the most current revision if any. This list is not intended to be a comprehensive list.

Employment Laws

See Chapter 6 for more information about staffing, human resources policies, and employment laws.

The Americans with Disabilities Act

The Americans with Disabilities Act (ADA) is in three parts:

- Title I, which deals with employment issues (discussed in Chapter 6)
- Title II, which addresses state and local government requirements
- Title III, the public accommodations section, which will be especially important to any camp executives who are building facilities

Most architects will have an ADA review prior to construction to ensure that the design complies with the ADA. An inspection after construction is required, as virtually every business that serves the public—regardless of the size of the business or age of buildings—must comply with the requirements of the ADA for public accommodations.

Of particular note are the relatively new regulations developed in response to the ADA's requirements to make pools more accessible to persons with disabilities. Implementation of the latest revisions was delayed from the original date, but you should be aware of the new requirements and check with pool designers and contractors before building new pools as well as look at modifications that may be necessary to existing pools.

The Department of Justice has a publication titled *ADA Update: A Primer for Small Business*, available at www.ada.gov/regs2010/smallbusiness/smallbusprimer2010.htm, that includes information that describes what small businesses should do to make reasonable accommodations to provide their goods and services to the more than 50 million Americans with some type of disability (U.S. Department of Justice, 2011b).

Although the U.S. Department of Justice is charged with implementing the Americans with Disabilities Act, numerous federal agencies have ADA-related responsibilities, including the Equal Employment Opportunity Commission, the Department of Transportation, the Federal Communications Commission, the Department of Labor, the Department of Human Services, the Department of the Interior, the Department of Education, and others. Additional information can be accessed at the ADA portal at www.ada.gov (U.S. Department of Justice, 2011b).

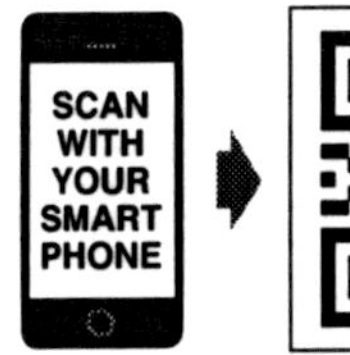

www.ada.gov

Pool & Spa Safety Act

The Pool & Spa Safety Act, also known as the Virginia Graeme Baker Act, is a federal law designed to prevent drain entrapments, and requires that public pools be equipped with compliant drain covers. Camp pools are considered public pools and must comply with new construction and existing pools. Details are at www.poolsafely.gov (U.S. Consumer Product Safety Commission, 2012). In addition, this website also addresses basic pool safety measures, including supervision, fencing, and the need to teach swimming to children.

States and localities are charged with enforcement of the Virginia Graeme Baker Act as well as their own regulations. The National Swimming Pool Foundation has links to all state and county regulations related to swimming pools as well as additional resources, including the Pool & Spa Safety Act and the Americans with Disabilities Act (www.nspf.org/en/Resources) (National Swimming Pool Foundation, 2013).

Boating, Canoeing, and Sailing

Camps using federal or state waterways for boating, canoeing, and sailing should be conscious of the numerous regulations regarding watercraft. The U.S. Coast Guard Boating Safety Resource Center is an excellent source for these regulations. Its website is www.uscgboating.org (U.S. Coast Guard Boating Safety Resource Center, 2013).

In addition, the United States Power Squadrons is a "non profit, educational organization dedicated to making boating safer and more enjoyable by teaching classes in seamanship, navigation and related subjects." They also have information about state boating laws at www.americasboatingcourse.com/lawsbystate.cfm (United States Power Squadrons, 2010).

Bicycle Safety Laws

As of mid-2013, no federal laws in the United States required bicycle helmets. The Bicycle Helmet Safety Institute's website lists the 22 states that have state laws as well as the more than 200 municipalities with local ordinances. Its web address is www.helmets.org/mandator.htm (Bicycle Helmet Safety Institute, 2013).

Challenge Courses

No laws regulating challenge courses existed as of mid-2013, but the Association for Challenge Course Technology has developed standards that have been recognized in most courts. Camp administrators can learn more information about this organization at www.acct.affiniscape.com (Association for Challenge Course Technology, 2012).

Children's Online Privacy Protection Act (COPPA)

The Children's Online Privacy Protection Act (COPPA) was enacted by Congress in 1998 and amended in 2012 with the primary goal of ensuring that parents have control over the information collected online from their young children. The Federal Trade Commission is responsible for issuing and enforcing regulations concerning children's online privacy, including what website operators and online services must do to protect children online. Camp executives should be aware of COPPA when determining if the camp will collect children's personal information online. For more information, see www.business.ftc.gov/privacy-and-security/childrens-privacy (Federal Trade Commission, 2013).

Copyright Laws—Movies and Music

As a camp owner or director, do you plan on having dive-in movies at the pool? Or how about showing a movie on a rainy day? Have you noticed the large warning at the beginning of movies on DVDs, prohibiting the presentation of movies to public groups? You should, because the Federal Copyright Act (Public Law 94-553: Title 17 of the U.S. Code) (www.copyright.gov/title17/circ92.pdf) limits the use of such DVDs (and older tapes) to personal home use (U.S. Copyright Office, 2011). Any presentation in a camp setting is considered a public performance and, therefore, a public performance license is required to show movies or DVDs at camp. Camps can purchase a license to legally show movies at camp from the Motion Picture Licensing Corporation (MPLC), an independent copyright licensing agency authorized by movie studios to issue the Umbrella License®. American Camp Association members pay a discounted rate to purchase this license. Contact the American Camp Association national office at 765-342-8456 or the MPLC at 800-462-8855 or visit www.mplc.org for more information (American Camp Association, 2013d).

Similarly, a license is also required for music used or sung on the camp premises. The American Society of Composers, Authors and Publishers (ASCAP) and the American Camp Association have an agreement that permits accredited camps to use ASCAP licensed music without paying any licensing fees, as the American Camp Association pays a nominal fee per camp per year for all ASCAP licensed music. (Note that not all music is licensed through ASCAP. Some is licensed through BMI or other licensing agencies.) Limitations exist as to how ASCAP licensed music is used by camps. You can obtain additional information from the American Camp Association at 765-342-8456 or the ASCAP at 212-621-6272 (American Camp Association, 2013e).

Equine Activity Liability Acts

Traditionally, the liability that camp professionals faced for any harm caused to people by horses was governed by common law. The Michigan State University College of Law, through its Animal Legal and Historical Center (ALHC), notes that:

> In an effort to encourage equestrian activities, 44 states have enacted the Equine Activity Liability Act (EALA), which limits the liability equine professionals face for the injury or death of an equestrian participant—with certain exceptions. EALA terms vary by state, but in most states, the EALA makes equine professionals not liable for the death or injury of an equestrian participant if such death or injury resulted from a risk inherent to equine activities. (Hodges, 2010)

As of mid-2013, all but four states (California, Maryland, Nevada, and New York) have some type of equine liability laws—most of which apply to horseback riding activities. The ALHC maintains and annually updates a listing of these state laws at animallaw.info/articles/armpequineliability.htm (Animal Legal and Historical Center, 2013). See Appendix G for the equine laws current as of publication. Note that:

> the equine professional is only protected if a participant suffers injury or death due to an inherent risk involved with interacting with horses. EALA does not shield an equine professional from liability if the injury or death was caused by a non-inherent risk or caused by the equine professional's own negligence. (Hodges, 2010)

For more information about equine liability, see the topic paper provided by the ALHC at animallaw.info/topics/tabbed%20topic%20page/spusequineliability.htm

Many of the equine liability laws require that warning signs be posted to alert participants of the inherent risk in participating in such activities. One source of warning signs is www.statelinetack.com/item/equine-liability-signs.

Transportation Laws

See Chapter 17 for more information about transportation laws.

Child Care Tax Credit for Parents With Children Attending Day Camps

According to the IRS, the Child and Dependent Care Credit can be claimed for the expense of day camps but not for overnight camps. The credit can be as much as 35 percent of the qualifying expenses (Internal Revenue Service, 2012). More information is available from the IRS in its *Publication 503: Child and Dependent Care Expenses* (www.irs.gov/pub/irs-pdf/p503.pdf). Directors and owners of day camps will want to make the parents of their campers aware of this child care tax credit and provide documentation for tax purposes.

Records Retention and Destruction

Maintaining your business records in a logical, easy-to-find manner is important for not just legal compliance and tax reporting purposes but also to track details, help plan for the future of your business, and provide historical data. It is best to develop a records retention and destruction policy so your employees have written guidance on what to file, where to file, and how long to keep certain documents. While the Sarbanes-Oxley Act of 2002 does not apply to most small businesses, many of the requirements for publicly held companies mandated by the act simply make good business sense, including a records retention and destruction policy.

Unfortunately, no single recommendation will suffice for records retention because the federal and state governments often don't agree and both change regularly. Even legal and financial experts disagree, with some suggesting six years for the same documents that others suggest keeping for seven years. The following sections detail what is generally accepted, but just to be sure, camp professionals should seek advice from legal and accounting professionals in their states.

Documents to Keep for One Year

- Bank reconciliations
- Duplicate deposit records

Documents to Keep for Three Years

- General correspondence
- Employment applications
- I-9s: three years after hire or one year after termination—whichever is latest
- Insurance policies (expired)

Documents to Keep for Seven Years

- Accident reports and claims (settled)
- Accounts payable ledgers and schedules
- Accounts receivable ledgers and schedules
- Bank statements
- Cancelled checks (see the following exception)
- Contracts and leases (expired)
- Contracts and leases (still in effect): expiration plus seven years
- Employee personnel records: seven years after termination
- Electronic fund transfer documents
- Payroll records and pensions
- Timecards

Records to Keep Forever

- Articles of incorporation and bylaws
- Audit reports by accountants
- Cancelled checks for major purchases and important payments, such as taxes, mortgages, etc.
- Deeds, mortgages, bills of sale, titles
- Depreciation schedules
- Important correspondence
- Licenses
- Loan documents
- Minutes of board or stockholder meetings
- Property records
- Tax returns
- Trademark registrations (Massachusetts Society of Certified Public Accountants: Federal Taxation Committee, 2004)

Other Documents to Keep

- Health records of campers (separate from registration): According to *Risk and Crisis Management Planning*, "statutes of limitations vary from state to state. Even if a parent has not sued, the child, upon reaching 21, has until the statute of limitations runs out to sue on his own behalf" (Coutellier, 2008). If all health records from any year are stored together, camps may want to consider keeping health records of campers until the youngest child turns 21 plus the length of the statute of limitation in your state. Consult your attorney for more advice.
- Vehicle records: until vehicle is sold
- Warranties and instructions: keep for the life of the product

- W-4s: four years
- Workers' compensation documents: 11 years (Massachusetts Society of Certified Public Accountants: Federal Taxation Committee, 2004)

Remember that electronic documents should be retained as if they were paper documents. If a user has sufficient reason to keep an email message, the message should be printed in hard copy and kept in the appropriate file or moved to an "archive" computer file folder. Other emails and electronic documents should be purged periodically but at least every six months.

Use of Federal or State Lands

Camps using federal lands should be aware of specific regulations from the Bureau of Land Management, the U.S. Forest Service, the National Park Service, or other federal agencies—most of which will require a permit (usually an outfitter/guide permit) and/or charge camps an entrance fee or another type of fee. More and more states are requiring the same type of permits and/or fees for the use of state properties. Always check with officials from federal or state lands prior to your scheduled use and be prepared with the proper permits and fees. If you will be using such lands over a long period of time or if your camp is located on federal or state property, make a point to meet with the superintendent or manager of the land in person to review rules and regulations that will affect use by the camp.

Establishing a relationship with governmental officials is always a good business practice, responding to any questions or concerns they may have and letting them know about your program and exactly what you'll be doing. For example, if you won't be leading a trip but will employ a trip leader, take your trip leader and introduce him to the appropriate persons at the federal or state land so your on-site personnel are as familiar with the regulations and government personnel as you are. At the end of your use, it never hurts to follow up with the officials, thanking them and providing a brief report on your use of the property.

Safe Drinking Water Act and the Environmental Protection Agency

See Chapter 9 for more information about sites and facilities and related regulations.

State Sales Tax

In some states, camps must charge sales tax on all fees charged to campers. In other states, only the lodging portion of the fee is subject to sales tax. Some states exempt all camp fees from sales tax, although sales of some items in the camp store are subject to sales taxes. Camp executives should check with local authorities or their accountants to ensure that local and state laws and regulations are followed and sales taxes are remitted properly.

Current Issues

In 2013, the U.S. Congress was considering legislation related to a number of topics that could affect camps, including immigration (hiring international staff), healthcare reform (effect on camps as employers), child protection (criminal background checks), and transportation (requirement for camp van drivers to have a commercial driver's license), among others. The American Camp Association regularly updates its website when new laws that affect camp are considered, enacted, or revised. See www.acacamps.com/publicpolicy (American Camp Association, 2013f).

Other Laws Affecting Camps

The laws noted in this chapter are primarily federal laws affecting all camps in the United States, regardless of location. However, this list does not include every rule, regulation, and law that camps must follow, which vary widely from state to state. For example, in Texas, a camp could be regulated by the Railroad Commission of Texas (if it uses liquid propane gas), the Texas Commission on Environmental Quality (if it has a water system), the Brazos River Authority (if it is located on that river), and the Texas Department of State Health Services (because it's a camp). Camps will need to check with local and state authorities to determine all the regulations with which they must comply. For camp operators new to the camp business, this is another reason to get involved with your local professional camp associations–most of which are affiliated with the American Camp Association–because your local colleagues will be able to share this type of information with you.

9

Sites and Facilities

Rob Allen/iStock/Thinkstock

Site and facility management are two of the most important and perhaps least considered aspects of owning, operating, and directing your own camp business. Without question, after labor and transportation (if that's something your camp business offers), the greatest operational costs for your business will be associated with short-term, long-term, and day-to-day site and facility management costs. They are also critical to the viability of your business. After all, your camp can offer the best programming and best staff, but if your facilities or site are run down and suffering from neglect and poor management or just plain look tired, it will be hard to attract customers to your program and they will go elsewhere. The only thing that can be more costly than properly taking care of your site and facility are the costs associated with neglecting your site and facilities.

To gain a better grasp of this somewhat cumbersome topic, it may be best to break site and facility management down into the following five distinct parts:

- Day-to-day maintenance considerations
- Short-term facility planning
- Long-term facility planning
- Site management
- Other site business issues

Day-to-Day Maintenance

This may seem like something so simple that it doesn't need explanation, but what is your day-to-day plan to take care of your facility? Do you have a cleaning schedule for the bathrooms and bunks? If so, who is responsible for taking care of those jobs? Who is responsible for removing garbage? Painting the building? Mowing the grass? Bathrooms that don't smell clean, garbage on your site, buildings that look tired and worn down, and grass that needs mowing are just a few of the "minor" things that could send a potential camp family to another program. It's hard enough at times to recruit new camp families, so why give them a reason to look someplace else? This can be especially true if you are trying to recruit new campers to your business by conducting off-season tours of your facility. If all a potential customer has to base his decision on is a visual impression of a tired and worn-down facility, you'll have a hard time attracting new business.

Site and Facility Personnel

Years ago, camps had caretakers: older men—many past retirement age—who lived at the site and did minimal maintenance work. Those days are gone. It's necessary for camp executives who are responsible for a site (whether owned or leased) to have knowledgeable, skilled, and capable site personnel.

In order to address all your day-to-day maintenance issues, you first need to assess the need for a site and facility manager or at least a maintenance person (full time or part time) you can depend on to address your needs. It may be that you only need someone from the spring (to open your facility) to the early fall (when you put your facility away for winter). You may need one or more full-time site and facility employees if you are operating a facility in a year-round capacity. You may only need to contract with a company or an individual if you are seasonally leasing your site. Regardless of your staff needs and of course depending on your budget (discussed later), the point is you need someone to take care of these issues for you, as you will have more than enough to do directing and managing your camp.

While the ultimate decisions about site and facility business will be made by the camp owner or board, having someone on the site can save countless dollars and protect the investment you have in the facilities.

In *Outdoor Site and Facility Management*, Wynne Whyman has examples of site and facility job descriptions for property director, site manager, facilities manager, grounds assistant, and maintenance assistant. All include desired qualifications, essential functions, and general responsibilities (2008).

Maintenance Schedule

After you have selected how you will maintain your facility on a day-to-day basis, you need to determine what maintenance duties should be done each day. The following are items to consider:

- Collection and disposal of garbage: How often will you be collecting and how often will you have a waste hauler collect trash from your site?
- Cleaning of bathrooms, bunks, shower houses
- Landscaping
- General facility maintenance: leaky pipes, lightbulbs, unexpected repairs, etc.
- Maintenance of activity areas: pools, lakes, docks, high adventure areas
- Removal of damaged or dangerous trees
- Checking for wasps, bees, hornets, and pests in camper areas
- Procurement of maintenance supplies
- Servicing camp maintenance equipment
- Maintaining camp vehicles

> The American Camp Association website has numerous resources about site and facility maintenance at www.acacamps.org/knowledge/site-facilities, with updates and new resources provided on a regular basis.

Day-to-day maintenance and facility inspection in activity areas are usually taken care of by the camp personnel responsible for that area and maintenance personnel are called in on an as-needed basis. General janitorial duties are usually delegated to the maintenance staff and should be part of a daily schedule or rotation. Specialized duties requiring training, such as monitoring wells, pools, and other critical infrastructure, are also needs to be considered. Regulations vary by state or local statute and you need to confirm you have the right personnel with the right training to handle these matters.

Cleanliness and Campers

The importance of having a clean and neat camp simply cannot be overlooked. Some camps literally depend on child labor to keep the camp clean, assigning campers to clean bathrooms, police the grounds, and keep their cabins clean. While this works to a certain degree, such public areas as the dining hall and the bathrooms must also be cleaned—and probably not by campers. Having a clean and neat camp is a sign you care.

Your facilities don't have to be new to be clean and well maintained. Some of the most wonderful camps in the country are very old—and quite proud of some of the classic dining halls, cabins, and other buildings that were built many years ago. But these same camps take care of their facilities, doing regular maintenance and cleaning.

When camp staff members keep their clothes and personal belongings together and pick up after themselves, then campers will also be more likely to do. For some campers, camp will be the only place where they make their beds or clean the bathrooms, so opportunities for learning go along with maintaining a clean and neat facility.

Short-Term Facility Planning

Short-term facility planning can be thought of as long-term maintenance scheduling for aspects of your business that require a greater financial commitment in your budgeting. As the manager of a camp business, you need to plan on how you will take care of your facilities to get the most life out of them as possible. While some points discussed here may seem to be more related to day-to-day maintenance activities, they do require more planning because of their expense and budgetary requirements. Their importance cannot be overlooked because if you fail to properly plan and schedule these activities, the consequences can be staggering financially.

Facility maintenance activities to be considered for short-term facility planning include the following:

- Developing a schedule for painting/staining buildings and pools: every three to five years depending upon climate. You may want to set up a rotation so some painting/staining is done every year.
- Routinely scheduling maintenance for your septic/waste fields (if not on municipal sanitary): annually to every three years
- Routine maintenance of wells and water lines: every three to five years
- Maintenance for any paved roads and driveway areas of your facility: every three to five years
- Resurfacing outdoor activity areas, such as tennis or sport courts, for better safety and appearance: every five years
- Routine maintenance of HVAC systems: six months to one year annually
- Clearing brush and undergrowth

Short-term maintenance planning can be done internally with your maintenance personnel and yourself, but the actual work usually involves hiring or contracting with professional personnel outside your organization. While painting and other duties can easily be done internally, such things as servicing well systems and pavement resurfacing are usually duties best left to professionals. You cannot underestimate the importance of this activity to the viability of your camp business. Too often, camps fail to plan accordingly or, worse yet, are too frugal to spend the money necessary to paint a cabin that desperately needs it. While paint is certainly not inexpensive, it is much less expensive than replacing a building because of neglect.

Maintenance Trades

While it is preferable to have maintenance staff who have the skills, knowledge, and capabilities to make minor repairs, it's imperative to have relationships with tradespeople who can provide more involved work when necessary as well as be available for emergencies. At a minimum, it is a good practice to have an established relationship with persons from the following skilled trades, maintaining updated contact information, available on the site and at the camp office:

- Plumbing
- Electricity
- Roofing
- Water wells
- Swimming pools
- Locksmithing
- Roadwork
- Landscaping
- Framing/carpentry
- Painting
- Pest control
- Refrigeration
- Small equipment repair (food service, etc.)
- HVAC
- Fencing
- Environmental services
- Glazing (glass)

Long-Term Facility Planning

Eventually, everything needs to be replaced or at the very least needs a major renovation. Buildings, pools, tennis courts, equipment for food service, and maintenance equipment all have expected useful life spans no matter how well they have been cared for. In addition, over time, the uses for facilities change, technology changes, and previous designs and systems eventually become obsolete. When you reach the point that you're spending more time and money fixing and repairing some of your higher value assets or they no longer effectively suit your needs, it may be the time to consider replacements.

The only thing that can be harder than having to write the check for a new roof, tennis court, or well pump is not being prepared when the time comes that you have to do it—and the time will come when you will have to do it. Items to consider include the following:

- Buildings, roofs, and structures
- Major maintenance equipment, such as tractors and mowers

- Food service equipment: stoves, ovens, and dishwashers
- Computer and phone systems
- Program areas: high adventure equipment, tennis courts, sports courts
- Swimming pools and docks
- Well systems, pumps, HVAC systems
- Septic systems
- Camp vehicles

While this list is by no means inclusive, each of the items listed ranges from several thousand to several hundred thousand dollars and addressing each of them would put considerable financial pressures on the most profitable and efficient of businesses. As the director of your own camp business—whether for profit or nonprofit—you need to plan as well as you possibly can to ensure that you're protecting and managing your site and facility for the greatest possible return on investment.

When to Get Rid of Equipment

Wynne Whyman (2013) offers some sound advice about being proactive in replacing well-worn equipment that's past its anticipated useful life but still working:

- "*Think about the cost of failure:* Would you have additional costs because the repairs aren't during regular working hours? Would significant damage occur if the item failed? Is the temporary loss of the use of a building a possibility? Example: commercial hot water heater catastrophically failing.
- *Think about safety:* Does the old item pose a safety risk? Does a newer model come with additional safety features? Example: buying a newer chain saw that has additional guards and safety features that the old chain saw doesn't have.
- *Think about your organization's procedures:* Do you have pre-determined schedules? Example: Maybe you rotate computers every four years and vehicles every 10 years. Both types of equipment will still be working, but for a wide variety of reasons, it's been determined earlier when to cycle new pieces of equipment.
- *Think about the effect on guests:* Does the "older" item affect the guest (either directly or indirectly with reputation and/or aesthetics)? Example: Does the individual lodging room's heater/cooling unit provide responsive temperatures as needed? Does the unit look like it belongs in a salvage yard?
- *Think about increased utility costs:* Does the old unit draw more energy than the newer one? Example: Suppose you have an old household refrigerator for staff. Calculate how much electricity the old motor with inefficient seals is costing you."

Perhaps the most difficult aspect of long-term facility planning is that you are not always in control of making the decision when something has to be fixed or replaced. Wells, pumps, and other high-cost equipment have a funny way of always knowing the worst possible time to break down. Nothing is more frustrating than having to make a major financial decision when you have campers expected to arrive in a day or two.

In order to effectively manage your long-term facility planning, you will need to develop a schedule of all the major assets for your facility and take into account their age and their anticipated useful life. This is generally done when you're creating a depreciation schedule with your accountant (which will be discussed later). While making your assessment and developing your schedule, look at the current condition of each item, the estimated time you can expect each item to last into the future, and the cost to make the replacement in the future. You may have the expertise to do this internally with your own staff or you may want to seek input from trusted vendors or trades people in that area. Also, consider how long it will take to make the replacement in the event that it becomes an emergency necessity. For example, something like a well pump may be costly and needs to be budgeted but can wait until it actually quits working if it can be replaced in a relatively short amount of time and with minimal disruption to your business. On the other hand, something like a roof, bunk, or dining hall may need to be completed in a more preventative way so as not to interfere with your camp schedule.

After you have completed your assessment of your long-range facility planning needs and developed a timeline for the expected useful life on each item, you'll need to consider the financial demand on your budget. In a perfect world, taking care of the long-range maintenance and facility needs will fit into your normal annual budget, but it's not something that can always be depended on. To better plan and budget, it would be advisable to discuss the matter with your accountant or financial advisor. Meet with your business banker and discuss the process and timing of taking out a loan. Perhaps setting up a low-interest or no-cost business line of credit would be an option. Depending on the scope of the project, you will be able to finance the work through existing budget and a small loan—perhaps just through the existing budget if you have planned well enough. The point is that these issues need to be taken into consideration sooner rather than later. The time to consider financing a major project isn't when you finally decide the project needs to be done or when you're in emergency mode and something major needs to be replaced three days before your session is scheduled to begin. By planning well and ahead of time, you will be able to complete the long-term planning work with a minimal amount of disruption to your budget and your program.

Finally, don't be lured into complacency and decide to not do something. Always budget and plan on having to replace something. For example, if you think you are going to have to replace a roof on a structure and buy a new stove for the kitchen based on your planning schedule, by all means budget for it. If over the course of the year you find that both are still serviceable, find something else to do with the money you have budgeted to take care of another maintenance-related issue or set it aside, knowing that next year, the repairs must be done. Or move up other repairs you have been considering—resurface the sports court or make the renovations to the shower house. The most difficult thing about long-term facility planning can be that you may not have to replace anything for several years, but within a short amount of time, you may have to replace several things at one time. Be smart and plan and don't hesitate to take preventative measures. If you know you will need to do something about a cabin roof or a building in a relatively short amount of time (one to three years), do it anyway while you have the time and money to do it with the least amount of disruption to your business.

Development of a Capital Budget—Equipment and Building Replacement Schedules

Camps that have been in existence and have funded depreciation generally have cash in the bank to pay for the replacement of buildings or machines that have reached the end of their usable lives. However, because depreciation is a noncash expense, many camps (and many other businesses) choose to not fund depreciation. This can be a challenge should a need for a major capital purchase arise—either planned or unplanned.

Before developing a capital needs budget, you should know exactly what you have at the site, the anticipated use, condition, and expected life. Having a detailed schedule of fixed assets is necessary not only for site and facility planning but also for accounting purposes to properly expense depreciation. Depreciation is sometimes misunderstood, but the concept is simple. Depreciating an asset is how you expense the cost of that asset over time. (See Chapter 13 for more on depreciation.)

Your schedule of fixed assets will serve as a tool to calculate annual depreciation and then you'll be able to project replacement needs, which will be your basis for a capital budget. A typical schedule of fixed assets will include the following items:

- Name of asset, with brand and serial number if appropriate
- Date of acquisition and condition when acquired (new or used)
- Life expectancy
- Original purchase price
- Annual depreciation expense
- Accumulated depreciation
- Net depreciated value at year's end

The last three items would be repeated each year. This information is all that your accounting department will need. However, the site manager will find it helpful to add more information, such as a maintenance log, warranty information, photos, and any pertinent comments (such as "Hail damage on xx/yy/zzzz. Insurance claim paid $xxxx and actual repairs were $yyyy"). An Excel® spreadsheet can be developed to calculate the depreciation and maintain the additional information. This can be tedious because as the assets age, the spreadsheet becomes more and more cumbersome. (See Chapter 13 for a sample schedule of fixed assets.)

It is helpful to develop a capital budget, with planned expenditures to replace aging buildings, furnishings, equipment, or other assets and any expansion that requires new capital equipment or facilities. Although some fixed assets can last well beyond their projected life span, it will be important to recognize how much time, energy, and money are spent on maintenance of a fully depreciated asset. Sometimes, the repair of a fully depreciated fixed asset is just throwing away good money, continuing to pour dollars into an asset that can never be in excellent working condition or completely meet your needs. Developing a capital budget in conjunction with your maintenance manager is recommended, as he should know the time involved in maintaining fixed assets and when you need to buy and replace an asset, as opposed to repairing and holding your breath.

In developing a capital budget, it will be necessary to obtain good advice about projected costs—whether for equipment or a new building. It seems that new construction always costs more than was planned for, so when preparing a budget, allow ample room for inflation and contingencies.

A word of caution about funding depreciation: While it may be tempting to not budget for depreciation because it is a noncash expense, the best business practice is to fully fund depreciation so fixed assets can be replaced promptly. Even if you are developing a depreciation fund, remember that when it's time to replace a fixed asset, the cost of a new equivalent asset will most likely be much more than it was when originally purchased.

Site Planning/Master Plan

Whether you are developing a site that has never been utilized as a camp before or you've purchased a site that has been used for decades, you'll play a critical role in the way your site is utilized for years into the future. The decisions you make on placing buildings, paths, or program areas will quite possibly be decisions that you'll have to live with for decades. Even the removal of large trees and other unique features of your site can drastically change the character of your site. Choose wisely.

How many of you have tales of camp building designs being drawn in the dirt or sketched on a yellow legal pad? Or cabins built by the Civilian Conservation Corps or Youth Conservation Corps that have stood the test of time yet no two were exactly the same size? While some of these types of buildings give a camp "character," over the years, it may be realized that they weren't always placed in a good location and/or have suffered from the effects of weather, erosion, or, worse, neglect. Camp owners and executives are now encouraged to "listen to the land," being cognizant of cabin location in relation to water flow, prevailing winds, and topographic land features.

Like the need for a business plan, camps also need a master plan for their sites. Landscape architect Gregory A. Copeland, in his book *Camp Design: Master Planning Basics*, says: "The master planning process is a management tool for the continuous organization, improvement and development of a camp property. The process is recurring, not linear. It's a cyclical process involving four steps: study, plan, implement and reevaluate. If the process is performed properly the first time, then each cycle will be a continual update of the site plan and direction for the camp" (2011).

He goes on to state that the components of a master plan are "an existing conditions plan, a proposed facility schedule, a concept plan, a master site plan, an opinion of probable construction cost and an implementation plan. The master plan may also include a land use plan, a trail plan, a landscape plan, a schematic site utility plan and a land acquisition/deposition map. The necessary level of detail is directly related to the camp's needs and budget" (Copeland, 2011).

If you are developing a new site, it is highly advisable to seek the guidance of a site development professional. You have a vision for your business and are probably looking at the undeveloped land and already picturing campers and counselors working and playing together. Don't let these visions cloud your judgment. Instead, remove as much emotion as possible from the process. A site professional will work (free of emotion) with you to map out your property to utilize it in the most efficient way to be used for your program. They will also advise you on creating greater efficiencies for your infrastructure during the building process, which will reap benefits during the construction phase of your project as well as for long-term maintenance in the future.

If you have purchased an existing site for your business, your site planning responsibilities are even more important. You are applying your vision for your business onto the site plan that was developed by someone else who may have had an entirely different vision for his business. As with developing a new facility, it's advisable to seek professional input if at all possible. At the very least, you should consult the original site development plan to gain a clearer idea of what the original vision was in developing your site. Plan and act carefully. The grove of old oak trees that you need to remove to add an activity area or a new camper cabin can never be replaced.

Likewise, it is extremely important to make changes that fit with the character of the rest of your site and make sense from a maintenance planning standpoint. Cabins or buildings that aren't in character with the rest of the facility or pools or shower houses located great distances from water sources are all the result of poor site planning. Develop architectural standards for your camp, noting the type of materials that will be used for buildings, the color scheme, and general design standards. This will make for more cohesive and timeless facilities and will ensure that everything fits together. Camps owned by organizations that may change leadership more frequently are prone to having cabins or other facilities that can be identified as coming from "the Bob Smith era" or "the Cindy Jones era" instead of a seamless transition from one area of the camp to another.

Whether or not a camp is in a position to invest funds in construction, determining what the camp administration wants in the future and preparing a master plan are wise investments that will eventually pay off if done correctly and if re-evaluated and updated on a regular basis.

Signage

Camps can invest hundreds of thousands of dollars in facilities, but without good signage, you'll have frustrated guests and families trying to find your facility or driving around wondering where to go once inside your gate.

Start with the signs directing people to your camp. Some state or local highway departments will provide "official" highway signs for you, which is a benefit. If that is not possible, you can make your own signs or have them professionally done. That decision will depend on the impression you want to leave with families and other guests who are finding their way to your facility. Arguments can be made for both options.

Before posting signs on a highway, check with your local officials to see if any sign ordinances exist and if you can get permission to post a sign—whether permanent or temporary. You will also need permission from property owners if you need to post signs on property owned by others.

It is also important to have a clearly marked entrance to your facility—for guests and for emergencies. Consider security when deciding on your entry signage as well as whether you want your sign lighted and whether you want any type of remote control or call box at the front entry. Remember that your camp entrance is the first impression that your guests will have of your facility. The old saying that "First impressions last" is true!

Once inside your camp, guests should see clear and easy-to-understand directional and parking signs. Not only will you have families of campers and other guests, but also deliveries, trash pickup, and probably maintenance personnel. While it's easier to control the coming and going of families on drop-off and pickup days with staff carefully stationed along the way to direct traffic, consider the occasional visitor who arrives during a meal or in the evening. Clear, visible, and well-lit signs will be appreciated and will set the tone for your visitors' experiences at camp.

Site Business Issues

In addition to the day-to-day maintenance and planning for the short-term and long-term futures, some items regarding site and facility issues are just business decisions. The following sections detail choices some to consider.

Electrical Outage? Purchasing a Generator Could Be a Wise Investment

No one knows when to expect an electrical outage–whether a brownout or blackout. An outage can be caused by bad weather, an accident, or a power surge and can last a few seconds, a few minutes, or, unfortunately, hours or even days. In camp, having a generator large enough to keep your phones, refrigerators, and freezers running can save money from lost food supplies, can minimize frustration, and, most importantly, can keep your program operational until the power is restored. Remember, the best time to purchase a generator is when you don't need it. Waiting until you have an electrical outage may mean you're too late to get exactly what you need or you may pay a premium price.

Maintenance Agreements or Service Contracts

Unfortunately, no standards for maintenance agreements or service contracts exist, as every manufacturer of equipment generally develops its own. According to Portland Energy Conservation (PECI) in its publication *Operation and Maintenance Service Contracts*, usually the following four types of maintenance agreements exist:

- *Full coverage:* provides 100 percent of parts and labor
- *Full labor:* covers only labor, with the owner paying for any needed parts
- *Preventive maintenance:* covers only scheduled maintenance
- *Inspection:* offers "fly by" visits from an inspector who makes recommendations for maintenance (1997)

Varied opinions exist about the wisdom of maintenance agreements or service contracts. Your decision to purchase or not purchase a service contract for equipment or buildings depends on the skill of your maintenance staff, your proximity to qualified repair centers, and cash flow. Service contracts (sometimes known as *extended warranties*) are generally considered part of the purchase price for new equipment. After the initial term, they will most likely be treated as an annual expense. It will be important to understand exactly what is covered and what is not covered under a service contract, how quickly service calls will be answered, and the cost of service calls when a maintenance agreement is not in place. Checking references from other buyers and visiting with them about how often it was necessary to use a service contract and how reliable the service was are advisable actions before purchasing. Just like an insurance bet in Las Vegas, the purchase of a maintenance agreement can either be the smartest thing you do or a total waste of money. It is said that insurance bets have built a lot of casinos in Las Vegas. The sale of maintenance agreements has probably funded a lot of product development. Be sure to see what the regular warranty on equipment or buildings is before purchasing an additional maintenance agreement or extended warranty and what actions or inactions might void your warranty or service agreement.

Inventory/Tagging

A physical inventory of all equipment should be taken at least annually. Tagging equipment and furnishings is an excellent way to not only keep track of your equipment and furnishings but also for security. The following are some vendors for inventory control tags:

- Wasp (www.waspbarcode.com)
- ASAP Systems (www.asapsystems.com/barcloud/online_asset.php)
- Fixed Asset Tracking System (www.fatsfixedassettracking.com)
- Asset Systems (www.assetsystems.com/index.asp)

Tagging all your furnishings and equipment with bar code technology will enable you to take inventory much faster and provide you with accurate reporting of your fixed asset inventory, especially if any equipment is stolen. Because some tags can be removed, recording the serial number or another identifying number of equipment on your schedule of fixed assets is a recommended practice. Some may also choose to engrave the camp's name or another identifying mark as a secondary identifier on the equipment itself.

Publications for the Maintenance Manager

Several free publications are available in print and online that provide general information about facilities management, including some related directly to camp or recreation facilities:

- *Building Operating Management:* www.facilitiesnet.com/bom
- *Today's Facility Manager:* www.todaysfacilitymanager.com
- *Buildings:* www.buildings.com
- *Recreation Management:* www.recmanagement.com
- *Management of Outdoor Facilities:* www.callippe.com/blog

Providing resources for your maintenance manager to learn about new products and methods could save time and money for your camp business.

Business Records

Whether you own or lease property, camps should maintain certain records related to your property in a permanent and safe place. Such records should include the following:

- Property lease (if applicable)
- Property deed (if applicable) with legal description
- Any easements for utilities or other purposes that affect your property
- Any other legal agreements related to your property, including mineral leases
- Survey of the property
- Utility maps, indicating water lines, water storage tanks, irrigation system, fire protection, gas lines, location of propane or other tanks, electrical shutoff points, location of electric poles, location of meters, telephone and

other communication lines, sewer and septic tank locations, spray fields, and any other utilities

- For older sites, Google Earth can be used in conjunction with your local utility locator services to create "new" maps of water, gas, and electrical cable locations.
- Architectural and related plans for all buildings
- Maintenance equipment warranties and copies of receipts for equipment under warranty
- All licenses related to the property
- Training records related to maintenance, such as pool operators' course records, water system operators' course records, etc., including operator's licenses.
- Environmental tests, including water quality, as required by the state or locale
- Inspection reports
- Operating manuals for water wells, pools, and other major investments
- SDS (Safety Data Sheets, formerly known as Material Safety Data Sheets or MSDS) on all hazardous material (Occupational Safety and Health Administration, 2012)

Many of the above items, such as the SDS on hazardous material and operating manuals, need to be kept in an area where they're easily accessed by personnel who work with the related materials or equipment.

Asset/Facility Software and Management of Data

Several asset management software packages should be considered at some time by camp administrators who own or have responsibility for a significant number of buildings, equipment, and other assets. CPAPracticeAdvisor.com has reviewed asset management software, and while its highest ratings were given to software that might be used by an accounting firm managing multiple business' assets, it also recommends Sage 50® FAS, which can handle up to 1,000 different fixed assets and provides the opportunity to add much helpful information (CPA Practice Advisor, 2011).

However, camps may desire to turn to software geared more toward maintenance than depreciation. A few examples of facility management software that are available include the following:

- Lodgepole™ by Callippe (www.callippe.com/lodgepole)
- MaintenanceEdge by Facility Dude Software (www.facilitydude.com/industries/clubs–click on software for clubs)
- HippoFM (www.hippofm.com)
- Mpulse (www.mpulsesoftware.com/services/software-editions–four different levels for varying sizes of facilities)

The Lodgepole software has some features not typically found in general facility management software because it has been designed specifically for use by camps. This particular software is first and foremost a database that can be used to track buildings, inventory, equipment, vehicles, and everything from signs to sewer systems–and even animals. When you use it as database, you can track a great deal of information and use the software to help organize information in a way that will help you strategically plan, budget, and make decisions. Features include the capacity to develop daily maintenance logs, manage such administrative information as staff and vendors, monitor electric and water usage, and track insurance and inspections. While not all camps may need or choose to use all features, it is important to note that in this software are options that will allow all these functions to be set up as a part of your database and linked for efficiency.

It is not mandatory for all your site and facility data to be entered into a software program, but you should be intentional in your facility management decisions—whether you utilize the services of a third-party software system or create your own internal facility management system. Failing to implement some internal process in site and facility management is just a bad idea that will get worse over time. Most facilities that have been in existence for a while have their data stored in many different places, including inside the heads of the owner, director, and/or maintenance chief. As nice as that instant access is, what happens if that person is not available when you need to know where the utility cutoffs are located? What happens when you sell your property or the head of your maintenance staff retires? Will all your camp data disappear?

You may choose to organize your data in a simple spreadsheet or to develop your own database, which is fine if you can track everything you need. Over time, you may grow into the need for a more robust software program. The important thing is this: Have a system so all your data can be organized and, most importantly, accessible to more than one or two people and make sure your data is safe—with backups. With the ability to have, for example, building plans or utility maps of any size scanned and saved electronically, you won't have to worry that such important documents could be destroyed by fire or inadvertently misplaced. It is also important to note that the best use of your maintenance personnel's time is in maintenance of the site and your facilities, not in data entry for your tracking system. A knowledgeable volunteer or administrative assistant can usually update your maintenance database in a few hours per week depending on how much data you decide to track.

Advice From a Pro

"I can't say I was extremely excited about the notion of using a property management database. However, once I got started, the process didn't feel nearly as daunting. The program allowed me to layer on continuously more information as we deemed necessary and alleviated the task of remembering the most obscure facts about every structure, equipment, utilities, and contracts. Keeping an accurate inventory of our equipment, our structural maintenance, and our business contacts should help us streamline our budgeting and camp management for the future."

— Bobby Mandell, Northern Star Council,
Boys Scouts of America (MN)

Selection of how much of a maintenance software package is used is also a matter of priorities. It's probably not worth tracking every 79-cent washer that's installed on a leaky faucet. However, it is well worth your time to track the purchase of equipment, major repairs to buildings, and warranty information. Maintenance software programs are like other software programs, such as finance—a program may have the capability to track many, many things, but you don't have to use everything from the beginning. You can be as detailed as you want to be in the organizational system you choose to utilize for tracking your facility and maintenance processes. For example, one camp in a cold climate was most concerned about tracking the age and condition of roofs, as snow and winter weather were especially hard on the roofs. Nonprofit or agency-based camps may want to use facility management software to track where donations are specifically utilized or demonstrate to executive boards that they're being judicious in allocating valuable financial resources.

Regardless of your decision about what method you choose in tracking site and facility management data, remember that the most important thing is to have a plan. Set your priorities about what's most important for your program and your situation. Track what you have, where it is located at camp, where it came from, and when it needs to be replaced. Financial resources are too precious to be wasted by not taking the time to track the needs of your site and facility properly.

Climate Change and Your Carbon Footprints

Most camp executives are concerned about climate change and the effect of carbon emissions on the planet. Carbonfund.org, a nonprofit organization, has numerous resources on its website that would be helpful for camp executives who want to reduce the carbon footprint of their camps. Its recommendations include the following:

- Maintaining your vehicles on a regular basis, including keeping tire pressure at recommended levels
- Carpooling whenever possible
- Installing programmable thermostats to maintain temperatures consistently
- Insulating buildings properly
- Using energy efficient appliances
- Following its motto: Reduce what you can and offset what you can't. (Carbonfund.org, n.d.)

Additional energy saving suggestions are listed in the following sections. Check Carbonfund.org's website at www.carbonfund.org for more information about reducing your carbon footprint.

Energy Efficiency

Sometimes, doing little things can add up to big dollar savings. According to the American Public Power Association and the Association of Small Business Development Centers (now known as America's Small Business Development

Center Network) in their publication *Energy Efficiency Pays: A Guide for the Small Business Owner*, "energy-related technologies have been advancing at an amazing pace in recent years, which means upgrades can reduce energy use by up to 30 percent in some cases" (American Public Power Association and the Association of Small Business Development Centers, 2003). Some areas where minor changes can create substantial savings are the following:

- Lighting
- Office equipment
- HVAC equipment
- Refrigeration
- Hot water

Specific suggestions from www.energystar.gov related to small businesses include the following:

- Fix water leaks. Conserving water saves energy, money, and natural resources.
- Install the most efficient faucets, showerheads, toilets, and urinals to save water.
- Always check the Energy Star rating when purchasing new appliances, getting the most efficient system possible.
- On an annual basis, have a tune-up performed on all major appliances and equipment, checking coils, belts, and gaskets. On a regular basis, change air filters.
- If a dollar bill easily slips out when closed between a refrigerator door's seals, it's time to replace door gaskets.
- Use free daylight instead of turning on lights whenever possible.
- Close exterior doors when HVAC systems are on.
- Have HVAC systems serviced prior to cooling and heating seasons.
- Use fans, which can allow you to set thermostats for air conditioning three to five degrees higher, feeling just as comfortable. For each degree of higher temperature, you'll save about three percent on cooling costs.
- Plug all leaks with caulking or weather stripping.
- Install automatic sensors for lights so if no one is in a room, lights are turned off automatically.
- Consider upgrading fluorescent lamps from the older T12 tubes with magnetic ballasts to T8 tubes (1" diameter) with electronic ballasts.
- Install metal halide or high-pressure sodium vapor lamps in place of mercury vapor lamps.
- Replace incandescent lightbulbs with compact fluorescent lamps, which cost about 75 percent less to operate and last about 10 times longer than incandescent bulbs. The cost of compact fluorescent lamps has gone down substantially since their first introduction. (Energy Star, 2007)

www.energystar.gov

When constructing new buildings, opportunities will exist for even greater energy efficiency. More information about energy saving ideas can be found at www.energystar.gov. Energy savings equal cost savings and, therefore, more profit. Tax incentives may also be available when upgrading to more efficient equipment, which sometimes more than offset any increased expense. It's worth checking with governmental entities for tax incentives and utility companies for any rebate programs that apply to energy-efficiency upgrades.

Water Systems

Camps with water wells will need to understand state and local regulations and their effect on the camp. Camp water systems are usually considered public systems based on the number of people they serve or on the number of water connections.

The Environmental Protection Agency (EPA) is the federal agency charged with implementation of the Safe Drinking Water Act, which was passed by Congress in 1974, was amended in 1986 and 1996, and is the primary federal law ensuring the quality of drinking water in the United States. The EPA works with states, tribes, its own regional offices, and other partners to set standards for drinking water. States have the primary responsibility for the oversight of water systems and the implementation of water regulations as long as the state regulations meet or exceed EPA standards (Environmental Protection Agency, 2004).

The EPA says that "all public water systems must have at least 15 service connections or serve at least 25 people per day for 60 days of the year" and that the standards for drinking water are applied differently based on the type and size of the system. They continue by defining the following types of water systems:

- *Community water system:* a public water system that serves the same people year-round
- *Noncommunity water system:* a public water system that serves the public but doesn't serve the same people year-round. This is further defined as one of two types:
  - ✓ *Nontransient noncommunity water system:* serves the same people more than six months per year but not year-round (such as a school with its own water system)
  - ✓ *Transient noncommunity water system:* serves the public but not the same individuals for more than six months (Environmental Protection Agency, 2004)

www.asdwa.org

Most camps operating their own water systems would appear to be classified as transient noncommunity water systems. Laws and regulations related to water can be very complex. It is recommended that camp administrators who operate a public water system be in touch with appropriate state and local officials to ensure that the proper water system standards are in place. Camps will most likely be required to have a certified water system operator at all times. Training is typically available through state health departments on a regular basis. Additionally, camp operators should be aware that their water systems could possibly require contracted water testing by a health department–approved testing facility. Check with your local or state health departments to ensure compliance with this regulation. The Association of Safe Drinking Water Administrators (www.asdwa.org) can also be a source for additional information.

Water Rights

It has been said that he who controls the water, controls. Most camp owners or directors in the western part of the United States would agree because water rights are a huge issue there—an issue about which all camp executives in that area should be aware.

Two basic doctrines relate to water rights in the United States: the *riparian doctrine and the prior appropriation doctrine.* The riparian doctrine states that water belongs to the person whose land borders a body of water. Riparian owners can make reasonable use of water as long as it does not unreasonably interfere with use of the water in a reasonable way by others with riparian rights. This doctrine generally pertains to the eastern half of the United States (Cornell University Law School, n.d.a).

In the western part of the United States, the doctrine of prior appropriation (sometimes known as the Colorado Doctrine) came about because many people were too far away from a source of water for the riparian doctrine to make sense. The prior appropriation doctrine states that water rights are determined by priority of beneficial use—or that the first person to use water or divert water for a beneficial use or purpose can acquire individual rights to the water (Cornell University Law School, n.d.b). Under this doctrine are senior rights and junior rights based on who first used the water. Not surprisingly, it is better to have senior rights—and sometimes, these rights are available for sale.

Knowledge of water rights is especially important during times of drought, when a state may impose restrictions on the use of water wells. This topic deserves serious and ongoing attention by camp executives, who need to know what water rights are associated with their properties. Consulting with a local attorney who is well versed in the laws concerning water rights is always advised. When acquiring a new site or a camp or purchasing an existing site, always find out about the water rights in the area and exactly what type of rights the camp has. All local water rights legislation and regulatory activity should be monitored closely by camp officials on a regular basis—yet another reason to actively participate with fellow camp directors in the local unit of the American Camp Association. Without water or with limits on water, camps could face the curtailment of numerous activities or even the suspension of some camp sessions. After all, he who controls the water, controls.

Local Land Use, Building Codes, and Other Regulations

In addition to the necessity to be a good citizen in the area where your camp is located, it is also very important to stay aware of local regulations regarding use of land, building codes, and any other issues or topics that could be of importance to your camp. If your year-round office is not located at your site, one good way to maintain knowledge of local issues is to subscribe to and read the local newspaper, even if it has to be mailed or if you have to read it online.

Although it will require discipline to read this on a regular basis, you simply must be aware of what is happening in the communities closest to your camp and not be seen as someone who drops in at the beginning of the summer and drops out at the end of summer.

Building Projects

Whether you are just starting a camp, have purchased an existing camp, or run a camp that has been in operation for years, a time may come when as the camp executive you'll be responsible for a building project that will require contracting with outside individuals or entities. From a small project, such as a $5,000 fence, or a multimillion-dollar project, such as a dining hall, numerous hints will help your project coordination proceed smoothly.

- Engage the services of an architect who has camp experience, but confirm that he understands what you do at your camp—your program, traditions, history, and plans. Your architect also needs to understand from the beginning of the design process your budget, your intended use of the project, and as many details as you have about your needs, such as the size of cots or bunks you will use in cabins or the number of meals you'll serve daily in a dining hall. With the architect, establish architectural standards for building materials that will make all your facilities fit well together and stand the test of time. Architects will establish a "program," which includes all aforementioned elements but shouldn't be confused with camp professionals' normal definition of program (that is, activities offered for the campers).
- From the beginning, explain to the architect your general budget for a project or building and ask that the project be designed with that cost in mind. Have your architect explain the cost benefits of certain features, such as a metal roof versus a composition roof, giving you options to incorporate into the design that will align with not just your desires but also your budget.
- When you receive bids on a project, provide an opportunity for value engineering, which includes asking the contractor to develop alternates that will save the owner money. Some ideas you may take—others may not be acceptable.
- Ask the architect to prepare a sample board with building materials, finishes, and colors. Also, ask your architect to provide you with information about a variety of materials and compare costs, quality, and durability. Remarkable developments have occurred in building material technology and many items now reduce environmental impact, save money, and will last much longer while reducing day-to-day maintenance costs.
- Remember that this is *your* project and that recommendations from building professionals about fixtures, paint colors, and other finishes are just recommendations. These decisions are *your* decisions, not the building professional's. The more decisions you can make at the beginning of the project, the better. You do not want a project to stall while you are contemplating a laminate color, so ask that those details be decided at the beginning of the project. "Just in time" decisions will likely turn into a reason your project is delayed.

- Many builders will use a tracking software that the owner can access, which shows the schedule for various components of a project, starting with site work and noting when the slab will be poured and then through to the engagement of framers, electricians, plumbers, painters, etc. Ask if your builder uses this type of program and if you have online access so you can be aware of exactly what is happening and when and that you be notified when changes are made due to rain, other weather delays, or any other issues.
- Depending on the project, you may need a contractor who specializes in commercial building or homebuilding. For a specialized building (such as a barn or maintenance building), consider a contractor who's familiar with that type of construction, as he can work with the architect to include details with which your architect may not be familiar.
- Remember that in addition to the building itself are costs associated with utilities, roads, permits, landscaping, and furnishings/equipment as well as the architectural and design fees. Most architects will charge about six percent of the construction cost for their design and project management services.
- Discuss with your architect whether you will need geotechnical testing services on any site work. This is normally the responsibility of the owner, not the contractor, and should be included in your building project budget. While testing may feel like overkill on a camp project, you want assurance that the building site is compacted exactly as specified and that any test failures result in correcting the issues before moving on. This can save you many headaches over time. It is always better to correct an issue during the construction process, not after the project is completed. Results of testing should be reported to both you and the contractor.
- Consider how you can utilize "green technology" in your building project. Building a new project incorporating alternative energy or alternative water usage is often no more expensive than using conventional sources and it is often cost prohibitive to retrofit existing facilities. If you are considering building a LEED-certified building, learn about the requirements from the beginning of your project and work with your architect for comparisons of what will be needed for LEED certification versus green technology. Results of testing should be reported to both you and the contractor.
- Always budget for contingencies. Ten percent is typical, but that may be more or less than what's needed in your project.
- Include in your contract with the general contractor an amount for retainage. Ten percent is generally the maximum. Contractors may prefer only five percent, so include the retainage amount in your up-front communication with the contractor, as he will likely have a similar amount in his contracts with subcontractors.
- Study the plans and ask questions about anything you don't understand—and also those things you think you understand. Details are important and can cost or save you money. For example, on one recent camp construction project, the owner needed as much value engineering as possible to get the project within available funds. At the end of the project, a very nice parking sign (between two and three thousand dollars) was being installed per the plans. Had the owner been aware of that detail, a much more modest sign would have been substituted. Knowing these details is important not just for

cost management but also for intended uses of the buildings. Perhaps it's a door that opens the wrong way or the realization that there is not enough stroage in the kitchen. These things are better corrected up front than after the fact. Owners need to also be persistent, making sure that requests are either included or clearly omitted, not just left on the table because someone didn't follow up.

- Be sure you see submittals for anything that is not clearly specified on the drawings or where the contractor has included an allowance for a part of the project.
- Establish in writing the rules you expect your contractors to abide by while at your facility, such as no smoking or alcohol on the job site, where the contractors can park, the speed limit for vehicles in camp, times/days when subcontractors can be on the property, and who will be responsible for subcontractors when they are on your property. If you require criminal background checks on all subcontractors, determine what you will accept and what you will not accept, especially if the work will be done while children are in camp. If you require background checks, include that in your contract with the builder, specifying who will do the checks and who pays for them. (See the following box regarding criminal background checks for contractors.)
- Work with your architect and attorney to ensure that agreements with contractors include a provision for all the insurance you expect them to carry, including general liability, automobile liability, and workers' compensation as well as builders' risk insurance, which covers the building while it's under construction.
- Establish in writing the deadline for substantial completion of your project and if any fines will be incurred for missing the deadline or bonuses given for completing the project early.
- Learn how change orders will be communicated and agree on what type of approval will be necessary.
- Meet on a regular basis with the architect and contractor during the construction to monitor progress.
- Be sure you get all warranty information and operating manuals on all equipment that's installed.
- You will also want a complete set of "as built" plans, indicating what changes were made during construction. While printed plans are good to have, it's also preferable to have an electronic set of the "as built" plans.

Natural Resources

Many camps are fortunate to have wonderful natural environments, and as the owner of your business, it is your responsibility to properly manage the natural resources of your property. You must take an active role in the proper care and management of your site's environment if you want to maintain the character of your site and program into the future. Some steps to take include the following:

Criminal Background Checks for Contractors

One camp doing some major building projects reports that several ways exist to handle the requirement that contractors working on the camp site complete criminal background checks. The camp can have all potential contractors and their sub-contractors complete forms allowing the camp to run the background checks, but this can be a very time-consuming process and requires that a camp representative inform the contractor of those persons whose background checks did not meet the camp's standards. It also requires that contractors and sub-contractors check in daily with a camp representative, who verifies that background checks have been completed successfully.

Another way is to set up an account with a commercial firm and have an agreement with the contractor that all individuals working on the site must go to the firm and have their background checked against a list of criteria that the camp has determined would disqualify them from working on the site. The camp would still follow up to ensure that all checks have been completed, but the firm takes care of notification when individuals are disqualified. Yet another way is to write in the contract with the general contractor that all sub-contractors must have acceptable background checks, leaving the general contractor to ensure that checks are done. While this is the easiest way to handle it for the camp, there should still be some verification with the general contractor that the checks were completed.

This camp also used the following criteria found in background check reports to disqualify individuals from working at their site:

- Any sex offender records
- Any felony or misdemeanor crimes involving sex or crimes against a child (no time frame limit)
- Any misdemeanor crimes involving violence in last seven years
- Any felony records in last seven years

Each camp should consider carefully what types of incidents would result in disqualification.

- Tree removal can be necessary in the event of storm damage or disease, especially in areas where fallen trees can create a significant hazard to people or facilities. The emerald ash borer and Dutch elm disease are currently creating serious issues at camps in the eastern two-thirds of the United States.
- Invasive species are at historical levels and can create significant problems to your camp's ecosystem if not properly managed or addressed.
- Erosion in creeks or lakeshores can cause major problems for program areas, docks, boat launches, and swimming beaches as well as alter water quality used for swimming and boating.
- Invasive species in water, such as Eurasian milfoil (water weeds) and zebra mussels, can create swimming hazards and damage docks and boating equipment.

Emergency Preparedness and Response to Natural Disasters and Severe Weather

See Chapter 15 for more information on risk management related to weather issues.

Wildfire Mitigation

For larger sites, it may be advisable to consider logging portions of your property to create fire breaks to reduce the risks associated with wildfires or to induce the growth of a greater variety of species. This can also potentially be a profitable venture depending on the scope of the project and should be considered.

The Federal Emergency Management Administration (FEMA) and some state forest services offer grants to assist with wildfire mitigation on private property. Grant specifics vary, but in general, a project is designed and completed in partnership, with the camp and the governmental agency paying a portion of the cost. Some projects involve clearing undergrowth or logging, while others may include building lakes. The steps taken to mitigate for wildfire also create a healthier forest, which is more resistant to the pine beetle. Check with your state forest service or FEMA to see what programs are offered and what type of grants or financial incentives could be utilized by camps.

Mineral Leases

With advances in recent years through the process of hydraulic fracturing (also known as fracking), many areas of the United States with shale formations are now being leased for natural gas exploration, including the Barnett Shale in northern Texas, the Haynesville Shale in Louisiana, and the Marcellus Shale in West Virginia, Pennsylvania, and New York, among other shale plays. Leasing camp properties can yield a significant source of income for owners. Keep in mind that while signing bonuses may appear very attractive, the royalty paid to landowners from successful drilling operations will be more important over the years.

Some camps have also been successful in negotiating a time limit during which oil and gas companies must begin drilling and limits on how long a drilled well can be shut in, or drilled, but not producing. Also, it is important to remember that it is possible to negotiate a lease for minerals while prohibiting any drilling on your property. Camp owners need to consider not only the financial implications of a mineral lease but also the effect on camp property, security, and programs as well as any environmental concerns.

Income from mineral royalties can be substantial, but camp owners need to recognize that royalty income typically starts at its highest and then levels off after a few years. Some nonprofit camps have transferred ownership of their mineral assets to a separate foundation that exists in perpetuity to support the camp. This type of discipline is a good business practice so normal operations of the camp do not depend on mineral royalty income. Also, depending on the state, nonprofits that are tax exempt may have to pay taxes on mineral income. If you are in the fortunate situation to have active mineral leases, you will need advice from your accountant or tax professional about how royalty income is treated in your state.

Camp executives and their boards, investors, or families will have a new set of decisions to consider should they choose to lease mineral rights. Although laws vary from state to state, one thing remains the same in all states: the need for professional advice from an attorney who specializes in oil and gas law.

General Things to Consider If You Are Approached to Lease the Minerals at Your Camp

Don't sign or agree to anything until you understand the terms of the lease agreement and get professional advice.

Mineral Leases

A mineral lease is a contractual agreement between two entities: the owner of a mineral estate and another party, which is usually an oil and gas company. The lease gives the oil and gas company or an individual the right to explore for and develop the minerals that might be found underneath an area described in the lease.

When you (the lessor) sign a lease, you essentially become a partner with the company (the lessee). When a company holds a lease to your mineral property, you can't lease those mineral rights to another company until the lease term with the first company expires. When the lease terminates, all rights to the minerals revert back to the mineral owner. If you intend to only lease your minerals, make sure you're signing a lease, not a document that transfers ownership.

Check Out the Company Presenting You With a Lease to Sign

You may be contacted by a landman. A landman is the company's contact person. A landman researches the deed records to determine mineral ownership, locates the owners, and negotiates the leases with mineral owners. Ask if the company that's leasing the land is the company that will be drilling and operating the drilling site.

Inquire about the experience of the company in the area. Ask neighbors or other mineral owners and landowners about the company, which is your potential business partner. It's important to know who you're dealing with before entering into a lease. Ask for and contact references or other property owners who have dealt with or are currently dealing with the particular company.

To report any complaints related to the actions of a landman, you may contact the American Association of Professional Landmen, 4200 Fossil Creek Blvd., Fort Worth, TX 76137. The phone number is 817-847-7700.

Before You Sign a Lease

- Entering into a lease agreement doesn't necessarily mean a gas well will be drilled on your property.

General Things to Consider If You Are Approached to Lease the Minerals at Your Camp (cont.)

- By signing a lease, you're granting a right to others, which may be viewed as an encumbrance on the property.
- All the lease terms are negotiable except the owner's name and the legal description of the property.
- Until you understand the terms of the lease agreement or get professional advice, don't sign or agree to anything.
- Review the lease carefully and ask questions about anything in the lease you don't understand.
- A lease may be a long-term commitment, so be sure the forms are in a language you understand.
- Read pre-printed lease forms very carefully.
- If you're a representative of a organization—whether nonprofit or for profit (not the actual owner)—you'll probably need a resolution from the organization's board authorizing you (or someone else) to act on behalf of the organization.

Lease Provisions to Consider

The following lease provisions listed aren't a complete list nor an explanation of mineral lease terms and aren't intended to replace the advice of an attorney or another professional. Mineral owners who are unsure of their rights or who don't fully understand the terms of the lease should seek advice from an attorney or another professional who's experienced in your state's oil and gas law before signing any documents.

The following are some—but not all—of the provisions in a typical oil and gas lease:

- *A legal description* of the area and the number of acres involved.
- *An effective date* of the lease agreement and the anniversary date for the lease. Lease rental payments must be paid on or before this date in order to keep the lease in force.
- *A statement of the primary term of the lease.* The term may be any period of time, but it's commonly between one and 10 years. Standard lease provisions may allow for the renewal of the lease or hold it in force without your permission.
- *Lease rentals* are paid to maintain the lease during the primary term and vary from lease to lease.
- *A signing bonus* is a guaranteed up-front payment of money that's usually paid upon the signing of the lease.
- *A royalty clause* is the share of the oil and gas production that's reserved to the mineral rights owner. It's usually indicated as a fraction or percentage of the proceeds received from the oil or gas that's produced. Royalty may be received in kind, which means the lessor may take physical possession of the oil or gas. Usually, the oil or gas is sold to a refinery and the lessor receives payment for his share.

General Things to Consider If You Are Approached to Lease the Minerals at Your Camp (cont.)

- *Payment of royalties.* Often, it's stipulated that payment must be received within 30 days of production and each 30 days thereafter. Payment of royalties directly to the landowner by the gas purchasing company is desirable so no delay occurs while the oil or gas company does its accounting.
- *Landowner approval before a lease can be sold* to another company. This prevents the lease from being sold to an undesirable company.
- *Landowner approval in writing of well, tank, access road, and pipeline sites.* If desired, it should be stipulated that written landowner approval must be granted before any construction or drilling occurs. The maximum width of an access road, any pipeline easements, and the size of the well drilling site should also be specified. Camps may wish to specify that no drilling occur on their property, which shouldn't be an issue.
- *Payment of damages for property and crops destroyed by the operations.* Many leases contain an indemnification provision, which makes the operator liable for any and all damage and liability resulting from his oil and gas operations. (City of Fort Worth, Texas, 2013)

This list was adapted from information provided by the City of Fort Worth, Texas. This information does not constitute legal advice and is included to give landowners some basic information about oil and gas leases. It is recommended that before entering into any kind of mineral lease, an attorney specializing in oil and gas law should be consulted.

Site Security

Security systems for your camp or winter office can range from the most basic to systems that are monitored and require individual codes to enter or to systems tied in with a fire alarm panel that will automatically call your cell phone should an alarm go off. Be aware that for most security systems, permits will be required and that cities or communities may charge fees for excessive false alarms if the fire department or police respond to an alarm. If you have a security system at your camp location that includes a gate to your property, you will need to consider whether you want to install a call system and how that will be staffed or other alternatives to opening the gate should you opt to have it locked at all times.

You will also need to consider how emergency personnel can access your site if your gate (or office door) is locked. Security system or fencing company sales personnel can usually provide different options, but take time to explain how your camp operates so they can give you appropriate ideas. Items like Knox® boxes, which provide a place for a key that can only be accessed by fire departments, are inexpensive, easy to install, and will keep fire departments from breaking a door or a window. (See www.knoxbox.com for this and other options.)

Good Neighbors

Robert Frost wrote that "Good fences make good neighbors." Being a good neighbor, participating in the community, and helping your neighbors in need will build goodwill and stronger relationships within the community. Some ways that camps can work to build goodwill include the following:

- Offer tuition assistance to neighbors directly located adjacent to your site. A discount of full or half tuition will go a long way toward building good relationships with neighbors.
- Host a neighborhood cookout or back-to-school party.
- Go door-to-door and introduce yourself to your neighbors. Write up a short narrative about yourself and your intentions for your property.
- Whenever possible, hire locally. Counseling staff, kitchen staff, or contracted workers from the local community can be a tremendous asset.
- Support local community projects and initiatives. PTO and other school-based organizations are always looking for support—and not just money. Offer to let a local Boy Scout or Camp Fire youth group use your site for a campout or weekend retreat, especially during noncamp season.
- Get actively involved with local service and community organizations. Local chambers of commerce, Rotary Clubs, and other service-based organizations are great ways to get involved in your community and to also make wonderful business contacts.
- If you are served by a volunteer fire department, offer to let it use your site for training.

Remember, your business does not operate in a vacuum. You are part of the larger community, and because this industry is generally looked upon favorably, your involvement in local community events and activities holds even more meaning. Your involvement in community affairs demonstrates that you care not just about your business but also about the community. While this may not seem like much at the time, you never know when your attempts to build goodwill with your neighbors and the community will reap benefits when you need community support for a project that's important to your business.

Because so many camps are in isolated areas, it is also important for you as the camp owner and other camp management staff to know your neighbors and to have a good relationship with them for the added security of another set of eyes on your property. Additional lookouts who know when you should have people at camp and when you should not can be extremely helpful. Having a good relationship with neighbors is like having another insurance policy you hope you never have to use but are very pleased to have in place when needed. Neighbors will appreciate good fences too, delineating your property so they and your campers and staff know the physical boundaries.

Sites and facilities play a huge role in camp, as they are usually the largest assets camp owners have and the largest operational costs for your business. Paying attention to the business of sites and facilities is not optional. It is a critical and ongoing business practice.

10

Technology

Stockbyte/Thinkstock

Technology can increase productivity, aid in better organization, and, in general, make life easier. Regardless of your camp's stance on the use of technology by campers (such as a no cell phone policy or technology-free programs), your camp business must include not just technology but technology that is updated, user friendly, and designed to work in your particular situation. Whether you're considering a computer system or office copier, it is a good business practice to take time to analyze your needs, looking at future growth of your camp but taking care not to be seduced by the latest gizmo that will do things you really don't need. In general, camps should always consider the following factors when selecting technology:

- *Return on investment:* Will this purchase of technology help you attain your goals?
- *Support options:* Does the vendor offer ongoing support?
- *Cost should never be the only deciding factor:* If you buy too little, you may quickly be looking at another purchase. If you buy features you don't need or won't use, you've wasted money.

With technology evolving rapidly, to specify exactly what camp owners and directors should look for would be an exercise in futility. Every camp's circumstances are different. Therefore, the following sections address some questions and general information that may lead to a better understanding of options that camps have for technology.

Computer Hardware

Camp executives will most likely need more than a single computer and should consider a network. The following are some basic questions that should be asked when considering the purchase of a computer network:

- What are the purposes of your computer network? Is it for office tasks, camper registration, scheduling, and electronic communication? Will other potential uses occur, such as store inventory or asset management?
- Will you be using your computer for graphics?
- Will you be developing your own website and hosting it?
- Will you be using a design program for brochures or email blasts that require extra memory?
- Will you allow campers to use computers? Will you accept email to campers and staff on the camp computers?
- What operating system will you use?
- Do you prefer Mac® or PC? Can you get the software you need for your preferred system?
- Do you prefer desktop, laptop, or tablet? Do you or your staff travel a lot? Does your office configuration change seasonally? Do you have outside applications where a tablet would be desirable, such as daily attendance?
- If you are remotely located, who will you use for your Internet provider? Local cable, phone, or satellite provider? Each has its own limitations, which will determine usage and reliability.

- What comes bundled with your computer? Does it include a monitor, keyboard, mouse, and cables?
- What software comes with your computer? (Beware of "bloatware," which can take up a lot of space and reduce the speed of your processor.)
- What is your long-term technology plan? Is it different from your short-term plan?
- What is your budget for technology?
- How many people need access to your computers?
- What peripherals (printers, faxes, etc.) do you need?
- Will any of your computers be shared or public?
- Will your system be wired or wireless?
- How much Internet use do you anticipate?
- Will your software be installed on your computers or will you use "the cloud"?
- How will you back up your data?
- Do you plan to use video chat (such as Skype®)?
- Do unique factors to your camp situation exist, such as extreme temperatures, that could affect your computers?
- Do you need to access your network remotely?

Purchasing computer hardware will take time and it will take considerable research. *Consumer Reports* and *PC Magazine* are two well-known sources of current computer buying guides and product reviews for servers, desktops, and laptops. Camp executives who are tech savvy will find the entire process a rewarding challenge and approach the purchase of new computer hardware with gusto.

When purchasing or replacing computer hardware, it is helpful to maintain consistency in the brand and type of hardware as well as keep the same operating systems for all computers in your office. Note also that while the expected life span of computers may be five years or more, the usable life span appears to be two to three years at most. Depending on the use of the computer (for example, only simple word processing versus intensive data processing or accounting), older machines may perform at an acceptable level for many years. However, software companies may discontinue support for older versions, so a best practice is to upgrade the operating system and software applications on a regular basis. This may necessitate the purchase of new hardware with expanded memory.

Technology Consultants

For the camp executive who is not inclined to take on the task of learning what is currently available and the pluses and minuses of the countless options on the market, a reasonable alternative exists: engaging a knowledgeable technology consultant who knows and asks all the right questions and who can analyze your situation and make recommendations. Some consultants will just do the analysis, whereas others offer analysis, installation, and ongoing support. Most technology firms buy in bulk from major computer manufacturers, so you may get better pricing if you purchase equipment through them. Your tech consultant can also assist in advising you on a schedule for the replacement and upgrade of your computer hardware.

Look for a technology firm that can also provide installation, wiring, training, and ongoing maintenance. Many tech firms can offer you off-site, redundant backup systems to relieve you of that responsibility. They may also be able to install a program that allows them to perform maintenance on your computer system remotely, saving you time and money. Need a new user setup? Send an email to your tech consultant. Have an upgrade to download from your software vendor? Notify your tech consultant and ask him to download the upgrade at night while you're not using your computers.

To find such a consultant, check with other camp officials in the area to see who they use and recommend. If you do not have the luxury of having camp neighbors or colleagues who can share this type of information, check with other local businesses. Get references from the proposed vendor and visit in depth with the references. Find out if the tech firm delivered on its promises, if it stays current with technology, if it offers warranties for its equipment and work, if it's always responsive to requests, and how long the tech firm's prices have remained constant. Ask the proposed technology contractor for the name of a client it no longer has and then call that client to find out why.

Also ask how many people work for the firm and for how long. Although consultants who work alone can be extremely knowledgeable and cost effective, what would you do if the consultant became ill and couldn't help you? Having multiple people in a technology firm is like having redundant backup systems—always a good idea.

Confirm with your prospective consultant what hours he works. Is someone available 24/7? Will you incur additional charges if he must visit your site over the weekend or at night? Will he schedule maintenance during your off hours? If your office is in a city and your camp is in a remote location, you'll need to know if he can still service your network and individual computers.

Engaging a professional technology consultant will not absolve you of all responsibilities for technology. A recommended practice is to have at least two people on your staff who are familiar with your system and can diagnose minor problems, communicating with the tech professionals. These employees will also need to know how to provide basic instruction in all the software that you use, training others on your staff who use the technology.

www.acacamps.org/buyers-guide

Camp Software

Deciding on software is as important as deciding on your hardware—perhaps even more so. One of the best sources of camp software is the American Camp Association's *Buyer's Guide*, which lists software packages for camp registration and management, payment processing, site management, and health records. Check www.acacamps.org/buyers-guide for the most recent list.

Software packages for camp applications should address three key areas:

- General productivity suites
- Financial/accounting software
- Camp-specific applications

General Productivity Suites

The most basic software for any small business will be a productivity suite, such as Microsoft Office®, which includes word processing, spreadsheets, and presentation software.

Financial/Accounting Software

Numerous financial and accounting software packages exist, but you will want to ensure that you coordinate your purchase with your accountant, bookkeeper, bank, or payroll manager to make certain you are using compatible programs. Doing so will allow smoother reporting between all of them and in the end will save money in reduced labor expense for bookkeeping, payroll, and tax filings.

Camp-Specific Applications

You will also want to research the software that you will use to handle your registration and camp management processes. Several packaged suites are available that are specifically designed to meet the needs of camps. However, it will be necessary for you to do your research on these programs to ensure you're purchasing what you need and (like purchasing hardware with lots of bells and whistles) not paying for features that won't be utilized in your operation. Items to consider include the following:

- What specifically do you need? How adaptable is the software to be configured to your needs?
- Can the software be used for all your administrative processes—health center, transportation, food service, financial reporting?
- What are the long-term costs associated with the maintenance of the software? How much do the updates cost and how often do they need to be performed?
- Can blackout features be installed that allow for the proper dissemination of sensitive information?
- Are payments processed via your registration software? If so, what are the exchange rates you will be charged for the convenience?
- How easily is the program integrated into your other IT processes? Can it be converted to be used on PCs and tablets? Is it easy to convert to paper reports?
- How many different camp sites and programs do you run and will the software accommodate all of them?
- Will the software provide for easy online registration?
- Will the software allow for all types of registrations that you offer?
- Will the software allow for multiple discounts, such as family discounts, early registration discounts, and special session discounts?

- Can all your pricing structures be accommodated?
- What types of reports do you need and in what format do you need them?
- Can the software accommodate your store needs, including online deposits, online ordering, or other features?
- What type of reminders do you need sent by the software?
- Will the software handle all your program scheduling?
- How difficult it is to make changes when a session is closed? Can you do that without going to your software vendor?
- Do user forums exist for questions?
- Is a users group available—whether in person or virtually?
- Is the program installed on your server or will you use cloud computing? Do you need a dedicated server for the software?
- What type of training is provided for purchasers of the software? Is training included with the basic cost or will you incur an additional charge? Is online training available?
- How often are updates issued and at what expense?
- What type of maintenance program is available?
- What is the fee structure for the program? Will you need to pay a fee per registrant or can you pay an outright purchase price? If the fee is per person, is that per person per session (extremely important if you have campers who may be attending all summer and each week is a different session)?
- What additional software, if any, is needed to process online registrations and credit cards?
- If you process online registrations, how quickly is your income transferred to your bank?
- How are refunds processed?
- How long has the software developer been in business? What other software have they written and what other software do they sell?
- How many people can answer your questions? What's the usual time for consultants to return calls? How do you set up a case?
- What modules are offered?
- Does this software interface with your accounting system?

One good way to evaluate a software package is to see it in action at another camp. An alternative is for the software vendor to provide you with access to test its software with sample data. Even if you see software demonstrated at a conference, get a sample version you can evaluate at your office.

If you have chosen a technology consultant, visit with the consultant about what you need and ask for his help in analyzing which software is right for you. Involve your end users in analyzing the software packages from the beginning, as they may be spending more time using the software than you will as the owner or director. Purchasing a maintenance contract with software is generally an excellent idea, but be sure to determine if the maintenance contract includes software upgrades or you might have to pay an additional charge.

The following list includes several camp-specific programs. Be sure to check the American Camp Association's *Buyer's Guide* (www.acacamps.org/buyers-guide) for any updated information or additional software vendors.

- Rollcall®: www.bunk1rollcall.com
- CampBrain: www.campbrain.com
- CampMinder®: www.campminder.com
- CampSite: www.campmanagement.com
- Campwise®: www.campwise.com
- CircuiTree® Solutions: www.circuitreesolutions.com
- EZ-Camp2™: www.ezcamp2.com
- Active Network®: www.activecamps.com
- UltraCamp™: ultracamp.com
- Megasys®: www.megasyshms.com

You may want to consider a few other "specialty" software programs for your business including the following:

- Payment Processing
  - ✓ Payment Processing Consultants: www.ppcsales.com
  - ✓ Simply Easier Payments: www.simplyeasierpayments.com
- Purchasing Cooperative
  - ✓ Trinity/HPSI®: www.trinity-usa.net
- Camp Maintenance Software
  - ✓ Lodgepole: www.callippe.com/lodgepole
  - ✓ Megasys Hospitality Systems: www.megasyshms.com
- Health Records Software
  - ✓ MagnusHealth: www.magnushealth.com

A final thought on technology in general and software packages in particular: While you have several options for software programs (especially registration packages), the authors by no means wish to advocate or promote any particular product or program. You may choose to develop your own camp registration software. One camp has made the decision to create its own registration package utilizing its existing Microsoft Office Suite and customizing it to the point that all its processes are covered in one simple program. While it does lack some of the conveniences of the preprogrammed packages, it works for that camp's situation. Take your time, choose wisely, and don't be afraid to try things on your own. After all, it is your business.

Websites

See Chapter 11 for more information on websites.

Internet

Internet access will be a business decision and a program decision. For your business, Internet services are a must. The major question is whether your Internet access is wired or wireless. You will also need to keep in mind that most camp employees are very dependent on Internet access, so having some area of the camp for staff to get online is almost mandatory. Most directors and owners will find it necessary to develop their own policies for staff Internet access as well as social media policies.

If any of your camper programs are Internet dependent, keep that in mind when wiring or setting up your own Internet hot spots. Your technology consultants should be able to provide recommendations regarding Internet access and how you can best get what you need.

Telephone

Many options exist for telephone equipment as well as local and long-distance service. The first decision will be whether to use a traditional analog phone system or to use VoIP (Voice over Internet Protocol) if available. A VoIP system will have many of the same features as Skype or other PC-based phone systems. The main drawback to VoIP is that it depends on AC electricity for power, unlike traditional analog phones, which get their power from the telephone exchange. Because telephone communication is vital to a camp's operations, the possibility of being without telephone service due to a power interruption may outweigh the benefits of a VoIP system. If a camp decides on utilizing VoIP, it is recommended that at least a single analog telephone be available for emergencies. Some hybrids are available that can also be upgraded. In addition, because many camps are located in remote areas, not as options as one would find in a metropolitan area might be available. In addition, if using VoIP, check the bandwidth requirements.

Even if you choose a standard analog telephone system, you can use VoIP technology through your Internet provider by downloading software such as Skype for PC-to-PC videoconferencing. You will need a microphone, speakers, and a webcam. No additional charge is incurred for connecting to another PC. For camp directors, this is an excellent way to interview potential employees who aren't available for in-person interviews. Other features are available for a fee.

According to *PC Magazine:*

> Many small businesses are finding Skype suitable for their communications, especially a Skype for business account. Skype for business offers cheap calling, conference calling, IM, file sharing, and many more features. Skype for business give small business owners a unified communications (UC) platform. UC is the convergence of phone, IM, conferencing and messaging into one solution. Skype certainly isn't the only UC option for

a business. Microsoft's hosted productivity suite, Office 365™, includes Lync® Online, which provides UC at an affordable price for the small-to-mid-sized business market. (Lynn, 2012)

Camps will need to decide whether to buy or lease equipment. If yours is a seasonal operation, you may be able to have your telephone service (or at least a part of it) on vacation for the months you're not at the site, allowing you to lower your expenses. However, if that isn't possible and you choose to cancel your service, check with your telephone provider to see if you can reserve your phone number.

Your telephone system may also allow for forwarding all calls from your winter office to your summer site and vice versa. Another consideration will be the type of voice mail system you have. Some may be provided by your telephone service provider, but for larger systems, you may need to purchase separate software and a dedicated server.

Some systems will include an auto-attendant, eliminating the need for a receptionist to forward calls. The decision to use this feature becomes a philosophical one: Do you want the first impression a potential camper or parent has to be an automated attendant or a live voice?

In addition, consider your cellular phone service. Is service available at your camp? With remote locations, some areas still have spotty cellular service. Before entering into a contract with a cellular provider, confirm that service is satisfactory at your location. Most camp executives will want to have a data plan on their smartphones and then program them to receive emails.

Long-distance calling plans can be confusing, as the lowest cost per minute may not translate to the least expensive plan due to monthly fees. Read the fine print and look at the total expected monthly charge, not just the cost per minute.

Camps should look at the wisdom of purchasing a toll-free number for inbound calls. Based on the area from which you recruit campers, a toll-free number could encourage potential campers or their parents to get in touch with you instead of a competitor who has no toll-free number. If anyone at your camp makes considerable outbound calls to long-distance numbers, you may want to have inbound and outbound toll-free calls. But check the billing increments for calls. It is better to be billed in six-second increments than one-minute increments. The difference can be substantial over time.

Finally, if you are considering having camp music play while callers are on hold, be aware of potential copyright infringement issues.

Copiers

Copiers are not just a luxury item anymore. They are an integral part of the overall technology package that you choose to incorporate into your small business. Today's copiers are connected to your computer and telephone network and offer copying, faxing, printing, and scanning—just to mention a few of the options you'll have on the machine you choose for your business. Color, collating, and binding are all available on today's office machines and at speeds never before considered 15 to 20 years ago. As with any technology purchase, you need to carefully consider what you need or anticipate needing in the near future before making a purchase decision.

You should first consider what you will be using the copier for. If you are looking for something to copy a few pages of camp songs and do not anticipate making more than about 1,000 copies each month, you should probably consider outsourcing your needs altogether. However, if you are looking to make thousands of copies each month, are looking to create your marketing materials in house, or are considering large duplication projects, you should be in the market for a copier. Having your own copier with a few options, such as color and collating, will allow you to save a tremendous amount of money on outsourcing marketing and promotional projects. Of course, this will cost you money, but with the right computer software, the right copier, and the right person with the knowledge to use it, you can justify the expense.

Your second consideration should be whether to lease or to buy your own equipment. While buying your own equipment allows you some benefits, you'll also want to purchase a service contract to keep the copier maintained. This may not be a big issue in the first five years or so of ownership, but maintenance contracts do get more expensive as machines age. Not having a maintenance contract on a six-year-old machine can be very expensive in the event of a breakdown (and your copier will break down!). Also, buying your own copier locks you into the technology of that particular copier. If technology or your needs for the copier change (such as you decide to start creating your own marketing materials in house), you're locked into that machine.

Most businesses lease copiers (typically for three to five years) and many may have attractive buyouts at the end of the lease. Copiers, like computers, may last as long as five years, which is the typical lease term. One of the benefits of a lease for your copier is that you will typically receive a maintenance agreement as part of the lease, which reduces your out-of-pocket expenditures in the event of a breakdown. Also, if your copier is integrated into your computer network, periodic software updates are also included. Toner and other supplies are also usually included in your agreement, so other than the cost of your lease, your copy expenses are relatively stable. Firms that provide copiers can analyze your use and offer options for purchase or lease, size/speed of the copier, paper capacity, and such features as duplexing and maintenance. As with any major purchase or lease, when selecting a copier, it's wise to look at multiple vendors and comparison shop. (See Chapter 14 for more on procuring goods and services.) Include in your comparison the average time between calling for service and the arrival of the service technician.

In lieu of leasing one large copier, look at getting two smaller copiers—one color and one black and white—so you always have a backup and to keep your overall costs lower by using black and white whenever possible. You may also want to consider setting up account codes to track copier use and charge to different cost centers, whether it be different departments within the camp (such as food service, maintenance, or program) or different camps that are operated by the same entity. This will ensure that expenses for copies are allocated properly. Small or start-up operations may not need or want to segregate expenses, but once different departments or programs have separate budgets, it will be helpful to have the ability to charge every expense to the appropriate cost center.

BuyersLab.com/Advisor has an excellent online product search and comparison tool for copiers, multifunction products, and printers.

Copier Data Security

Be aware that digital copiers have hard drives that store data about the documents that you copy, print, scan, fax, or email. As an employer, you will need to protect that data, as it could be stolen from the hard drive. Such data can include sensitive information, including social security numbers, health records, account numbers, or credit reports. Protecting that data is important, so check with your copier supplier and technology consultant to ensure that the hard drive is sufficiently encrypted or overwritten, especially if you return a copier at the end of a lease (Federal Trade Commission, 2010).

Audiovisual Technology/LCDs

When purchasing audiovisual equipment, camp executives should consider off-season recruiting use and in-camp use. Lightweight equipment, such as LCDs, may be convenient for traveling and recruitment use, but you may find that a midweight piece of equipment is more cost effective to use during the camp season with programming than an ultralight LCD. Purchasing a case for equipment that's used by multiple people and/or is taken on trips is a necessary investment to protect the equipment.

For LCDs, you'll need to look for resolution (the sharpness of images) and lumens (brightness). To determine the resolution and lumens, you'll need to consider the size and distance of the projected image and the type of light in which you will normally be using the projector. The higher the resolution and the greater the lumens, the higher the price you will generally pay for LCD projectors. Check the aspect ratio (the ratio between the width and height), which can be 4:3 for a mostly square image or 16:9 for a wider image. Confirm that the connection between your computer and LCD is compatible. HDMI is often recommended with new equipment (Projector People, n.d.).

Technology Infrastructure

If you are fortunate enough to build a new facility for your camp, consider including the basic infrastructure for technology whether you purchase all the equipment now or later. Having conduit, cabling, switching, and a control system already installed will make the addition of equipment much simpler

Resources

Numerous resources can help you understand, purchase, and use technology at your camp. The following are a few such resources:

- www.acacamps.org/buyers-guide: The American Camp Association regularly updates this online guide to products, including camp-specific software.
- www.techsoup.org: Tech Soup focuses on nonprofits, providing "learning resources to make informed decisions about technology." They have free learning resources and offer nonprofits who join access to discounted products and services, including software and hardware.
- www.buyerslab.com/Advisor: This site is sponsored by several copier/multifunction printer manufacturers but includes a product search tab that provides information from three dozen or so different manufacturers, including model number, introduction date, price, speed per minute, maximum monthly impressions, standard paper source, and paper capacity. It gives similar information on printers. Also included is a buyer's guide, which can be downloaded and which addresses how to assess, choose, negotiate, and acquire copiers and printers.
- www.pcmag.com: *PC Magazine* features reviews from laptops to cell phones and from servers to security.
- www.consumerreports.org: *Consumer Reports* is a nonprofit that has been testing products since 1936. Its website has an extensive number of buying guides for products. Ratings and recommendations of specific products are available on a subscription basis.
- www.projectorpeople.com: This is a vendor website, but it has excellent resources, with buyer's guides, technology guides, presentation templates, and more.
- www.cio.com: The online site for *CIO* magazine, a trade publication for chief information officers, has a library of resources and white papers, primarily by vendors but covering a wide range of technology topics—from cloud computing to social media and virtualization.
- www.capterra.com: This site provides software directories in more than 300 categories.

down the road. Historically, the price for technological equipment goes down over time, so if you don't yet need a piece of equipment, think about waiting to purchase until you have a definite need.

Security for Equipment

A concern for all types of technology is security. Let common sense be your guide: Don't leave computers or expensive equipment in unsecured areas, closely monitor who has keys or access to your equipment, and never, ever leave equipment in plain view in a vehicle—whether locked or not. Insurance policies on your technology equipment are usually available and can prove to be a wise investment. Some equipment may come with the option of replacement insurance, especially items such as cell phones.

Other Business Technology

When it comes to equipment, if you can dream it, the technology is probably available to make it happen. From computerized lighting systems that will turn on and off lights in response to a smartphone command to HVAC systems that will adjust temperatures at various times of the day, technology systems are available to do many different tasks—it simply depends on how much you want to spend to computerize different systems at your camp. Be aware that with all technology comes the need to maintain it and to replace and upgrade on a regular basis.

A Final Word About Technology

In *Simplicity Rules*, Stephen Paskoff tells the story about a friend—a dynamic, nationally known leader in the area of diversity and inclusion—and how they met for dinner, catching up on family, work, and especially the pride his friend had when telling about the exploits of his four-year-old grandson, who was already using computers and other technology to learn and read. As they talked shop, his friend told him about the various delivery platforms that his firm was using, including mobile apps and various interactive learning modules. Paskoff then asked, feeling that something was missing in the technology-based learning: "Tell me; what apps are you going to use to teach your grandson to be kind, ethical, decent and honorable, just like you? Where are you going to find the app for that?" His friend paused, then looked at him and said: "*I'm* the app. That's my job. I'm the app" (Paskoff, 2011).

In camp, no matter what technology you employ and no matter how many programs or activities you add, the important thing to remember is that as camp owners or directors, you are the apps for your employees and they are the apps for your campers. Camp is one of the wonderful places where *authenticity* still matters—despite all the technology that helps people do their jobs efficiently.

11

Marketing

Daniel Hurst/iStock/Thinkstock

Marketing is the lifeblood of your business. You can have the greatest program, site, and staff, but if your customers don't know about your program, site, and staff, you will not be in business for long. Marketing is the way you define yourself to your consumers, and as a result of those efforts, they will (hopefully) register with your camp. Literally everything that you do—from advertising and your website to sponsoring a local little league team—is marketing.

Your Camp Brand

To start determining how you will be marketing your camp business to potential camper families, you first need to determine your camp brand. For the purposes of this discussion, look at your camp brand in two distinct ways:

- *The obvious representation of your business:* Your logo, mascot, colors, and anything else that's physically distinctively to your business. It's a physical representation of who you are.
- *The subliminal representation of your business:* Culturally what your business represents through your program or philosophy. This is based on principle and feeling and emotion.

Each component of your camp brand is equally important in how you'll be communicating your business to your potential customers through your marketing efforts.

Your camp logo says a great deal about your camp. If you inherited a logo, are you satisfied with it? Does it need a little freshening? Camp brands evolve over time, so if your logo is not portraying the image you want it to, look at some modifications. A change in color? Font? Even minor changes can make an old logo suddenly pop. Consider how your logo will look in print, on the web, and on clothing and other items. Decide on your logo standards: What colors are used in your logo? Is your camp name a part of your logo, and if so, do the camp name and the design have specified proportions? Then, use it on everything—printed materials, your website, bumper stickers or decals, camp shirts, camp hats, canoes, sailboats, vehicles—every time someone sees your logo, your camp is being promoted. Whether you require campers to purchase camp shirts or you give them to all your campers and staff, your campers should be promoting your camp every time they wear their camp shirt or hat and everywhere their parents drive with your camp decal on their back window.

After you have determined how you want your brand to look, you will need to consider how you want your camp brand to feel. This may be a difficult concept to embrace, but what about your program or your camp philosophy is it that you want to communicate the loudest to your potential customers? This may be done by the wording in your communications or on your website. If you represent a program that prides itself on nurturing and caring, by all means incorporate those messages into your communications. Choose the images that you present on your website or on postcards that also capture the essence of who you are as a camp. If you are a camp that philosophically positions itself as a "nature based" camp, pick out images that capture this philosophical element.

Having established your camp brand by defining who you are visually and emotionally to your customers, you need to develop a plan by which to operate as you conduct your marketing activities. Marketing is the process by which a vendor (the camp owner or director) communicates the value of his product (your camp) to the public. It is not so much about selling as it is about defining how your program meets the needs of customers. The definition of marketing has four elements: product, pricing, people, and promotion. These elements become a part of your marketing plan.

Marketing Plan

Eric Naftulin identified eight marketing strategies for camps—the first of which was to:

> create and follow a marketing plan. Your marketing program will never reach its full potential without a marketing plan to guide you. It doesn't need to be long or involved. You can write an effective marketing plan in seven sentences or less. The simpler the plan, the better. Your plan needs to be flexible enough that you can make changes on the fly, but firm enough so you know if it's working. You should know if your plan is effective after approximately six months. (Naftulin, 2011)

A good marketing plan will focus your resources and your energy. For example, if you have an urban day camp and have decided to market it as a great alternative to day care, then your marketing plan might focus on parents who need day care—either single working parents or parents who work outside the home. By focusing on those working parents who need summer child care, you have narrowed the field considerably and identified the typical camper's parent. To develop your plan, first set your marketing goals, which might look like these:

- Increase the number of camper weeks by 10 percent—from 500 to 550.
- Recruit at least four new families from the Oak Hill neighborhood in Springfield.
- Increase the number of first-time campers from 50 to 60.
- Recruit 10 new families to attend family camp week.

Once you have identified marketing goals, check them against your financial plan. Will accomplishing the marketing goals also advance your financial plan? If not, you will need to rethink one or the other.

The Four Ps of Camp Marketing

Traditionally, professionals in marketing speak about the four Ps: product, price, place, and promotion. For camp, the "place" for marketing can be predetermined, especially for day camps but also for some resident camps that serve campers from a small geographic area. However, in camp marketing, the "people" doing the marketing are extremely important, so with apologies to those in the marketing profession, for this book's purposes, "people" will be one of the four Ps in lieu of "place."

Product

Product is simply defining your program—your camp—in a way that meets the needs of your customers. What are the features of your program? Are you a specialty program or a high adventure, overnight, day, or trip and travel camp? A parent with a child who is looking for a specific type of program needs to know what your program features in order to make a registration decision.

After defining what you are, you need to define what makes you different. Dozens of programs do the exact same thing you're probably doing, so how are you any different? Does your program offer flexible scheduling, transportation, or lunch? What type of staff do you hire? What type of site do you operate from? These are all questions that your customers may have about your program and it is up to you to define yourself and your program to them. Some of the differences that your program offers can possibly be used as a competitive advantage, so be aware not only of what your program offers but also what is being offered by your competitors.

Pricing

Pricing is an element in a marketing plan that will have a significant impact on how much profit you make. All the other elements in your marketing plan will be expenses, which should, if done correctly, increase the number of campers—and, therefore, your profit. Your price should be competitive and it should reflect the image of your camp, meet your profit goals, and meet or exceed your market share. The number one piece of advice to remember about pricing is this: *You cannot own price!* Someone is always going to be less expensive or offer better discounts or offer some other pricing incentive. If all you have to offer your customers is a best or low price, you really don't have much to offer them. Set your pricing based on the needs of your business model and not on what prices your competitor is charging.

To determine your pricing structure, look at your expenses. How will your expenses change with changes in enrollment? Expenses are generally viewed on an economy of scale in that the greater the number of campers, the less per camper you will spend in expenses. You might need to make assumptions on the number of campers, which will affect the number of staff and, therefore, affect salary and benefits expense lines. What expenses will be constant? Which will be variable?

Before settling on the right price, you need to consider any price modifiers—either discounts or fees—such as the following:

- Sibling discounts
- Referral discounts
- Early registration discounts
- Credit card fees

Take these into consideration, estimating as closely as possible how any of these discounts or fees actually modify your base price, which may have to be increased to compensate for lesser income due to the price modifiers. Set up spreadsheets comparing different pricing and discount scenarios. Compare where you are currently with your pricing/discount/expense structure versus where you will be after changing your pricing or discounts. What do you estimate the effect of pricing changes will be on your expense budgets? While all this may seem like guesswork, you need to operate with a sense of purpose and a plan. Under a scenario where you have made educated estimates based on various comparisons, even if they don't work out, you still have concrete evidence to find where you had faults in your plan.

A word about "profits": *Whether for profit or nonprofit, all camps need to meet their income goals in order to stay in business.* Marketing isn't that different for for-profit and nonprofit camps—they all need to be successful financially. The goals may be different. For example, for-profit camps may have a goal to make enough money to distribute a certain amount to shareholders by the end of the season. Some nonprofit camps will have a goal of breaking even, but some will have a goal of making a profit so other services that don't make a profit can be provided. For either type of camp, financial goals will need to be met through marketing the product. For this book's purposes, the term *profit* will mean meeting the financial goals you set—whatever they may be.

People

People are key to marketing. Who will do the marketing? To whom will potential customers relate? Will you as the director or owner be responsible for all or most of the marketing? Who could help you? Do any returning staff members relate well with campers? Do you know any parents who will host you and invite other friends with children to meet you?

Generally, as the camp executive, you will play an intimate role in the marketing of your business. You are the face of the business (or should be), and in many cases, parents are "buying" you and what you represent. Think about it: How often have you ever heard of a parent sending his child to camp based solely on the reputation of a particular staff person, counselor, or program element? A parent may consider your operation because he has heard through referrals that your staff is excellent or that you offer a great depth of programming, but in the end, he will make his purchasing decision based on the trust and confidence he has in you—the camp professional. If your camp offers tours of your facility to prospective parents, you should be the person conducting the tour. If you are participating in community events, such as camp fairs, you should be the one representing your business to the parents. It is your business and nobody will be a better representative than you.

Promotion

This is the part that most camp professionals will enjoy—deciding which promotional activities are right to use in marketing your camp. In marketing is a concept called the "rule of seven," which states that to purchase a product, a prospective buyer must hear about it at least seven times. While nothing is scientific about this rule, the general meaning is that to be successful, your potential clients will have to hear or see something about your camp multiple times—whether from friends and neighbors, on a camp search website, on your own website, or from other places.

How do you "promote" your camp? Camp promotion is basically everything you do that has a point of contact with your current and potential customers. Historically, camp executives have always considered advertising in local papers, movie theaters, mass emails, and bulk mailings as normal methods of promotion and all these methods are effective to a certain point, but the following are some other forms of potential promotional contact to consider:

- In-home recruitment parties hosted by camper parents for neighborhood or school friends
- Open houses at the camp
- Personal tours of your facility for prospective families
- Family camp events
- Holiday reunions for campers and staff
- In-home visits to each camper family during the year
- Birthday or holiday cards (addressed during camp) personalized for each camper and signed by the camper's counselor
- Listings on the American Camp Association Find a Camp website (find.acacamps.org)
- Listings on other camp search websites
- Booths at festivals or camp fairs (sometimes sponsored by schools or malls)
- Free publicity from newspaper interviews or submissions to hometown papers
- Sponsorship of off-season community events
- Sponsorship of PTO family directories, especially in communities where you are trying to establish a presence

Promotion opportunities are almost limitless, but you need to act responsibly and be conscious of your budget and time constraints. One mistake that directors and owners can make is to jump at every promotion opportunity. Before accepting that invitation to speak about your camp at a civic club or paying a small fee to have a booth at the local fall festival, look at the potential return on your investment, including your investment of time. Are attendees at the fall festival looking for summer camp opportunities in October? Will the audience include the age group to whom you normally promote your camp? Time is valuable and you will have more opportunities to promote your venture than you can handle, so choose carefully where you spend your time.

Who Are Your Audiences?

To whom are you marketing? What's your target audience? If you have a single gender camp, then that narrows your market by about half, but what do you do after that?

Another way to look at people to whom you are marketing your camp is to think about the audiences with whom you are communicating:

- Potential campers who have never been to camp
- Parents who have never been to camp
- Parents who attended camp or worked at camp
- Returning campers
- Parents of returning campers

When developing messages and promotional strategies, these audiences may require different messages.

Websites

First and foremost, every camp must have a website. Your website will very likely be the first impression that many potential campers have of you and your camp, so it better be as good as you can possibly make it. Camp directors should go through a process that some marketing professionals and web designers have called "digital discovery" to determine three things:

- *Brand and strategy:* What is your brand? Are you affiliated with a national organization? Who are your competitors? Who are your customers and potential customers?
- *Functionality and technology:* What ancillary online activities will you have? Email, newsletters, search engine optimization (SEO), social media, paid search? What software will you use for content management? What are the maintenance requirements for the website? What third-party systems will plug into your website? Registration? Store? Email services, such as Constant Contact® or MailChimp®? Credit card payment systems?
- *Content:* What will the website architecture be? What content do you want included? Program descriptions? Staff biographies? Directions to the camp? History? Daily schedule? Traditions? A blog? Restricted content for registered campers and family? Session dates and prices?

From this process of digital discovery, you will be able to develop a tactical plan that could take four to six months or more to implement, including the production and testing of your new website. Take your time and be thorough. Developing your website is a critically important task and also expensive. You want to confirm that what you have developed is functional and serves you well into the future.

Along the way, you will make many decisions, such as the following:

- How many pages will you have? One hundred or more is not unusual, but you may need only a dozen or so page templates.
- How many photos and graphics will you use per page? Too many and your website will be slow to load on some computers. Too few and it could be quite boring.
- Do you have quality images? And permission to use the images? Do you want to purchase images?
- Will your site be mobile friendly, working well on smartphones?

- Will your website be integrated with social media (for example, embedding YouTube® videos)?
- Do you need to have a "dark version" to be used in case of an emergency?
- Will you provide the opportunity to not only register online but also include online health forms and opportunities to purchase from your camp store?
- Will you have a blog?
- Will you have a parent share gallery of photos to be downloaded or shared on social media?
- Will your site be easily accessible to make updates internally with your own staff so you can quickly make the changes you need at a minimal cost?

As with other technology, website design and production are dynamic and evolving rapidly. Although it may be tempting to build your website yourself with one of the many web design software packages that are available, the advantages of having a professional web developer cannot be overemphasized. To get a very fine website, camp administrators should look for a group of developers who have experience in designing and updating and who have proven skills in functionality and technology. Today's parents expect to register online and they expect the process to be flawless and simple. If you compare the return on investment of having a professional web developer with the potential for lost customers—frustrated when the website doesn't work quite as it should—the positives toward investing in a pro will become obvious.

Some additional considerations in determining the content of your website are the following:

- Most people expect websites to be simple and intuitive.
- A general rule of thumb is that nothing should be more than three clicks away.
- Websites must be compliant with ADA regulations.
- The Children's Online Privacy and Protection Act (COPPA) has strict requirements regarding the collection of information from children under age 13.
- Using text of your camp name, programs, and location, not just the logo, is important on the home page in order for your website to appear in searches.
- Blogs may move you up on Google™ searches.
- Embedded codes for Google analytics can provide you with excellent information to evaluate your web traffic.

Once you have your design and your website is functioning as you had planned, you or someone on your staff will need to update the content frequently, respond to comments or questions daily, and include in your annual budget enough to have your web developer make any design or functionality changes as needed.

If you are trying to create a website on a tight budget, several web-based tools can be used to build your own website, including the well-known WordPress®. John Brandon, writing in *Inc. Magazine*, recommends four additional tools that can be used to build your own website. Addresses for these free website building programs are:

- WordPress: www.wordpress.org
- Sidengo®: sidengo.com
- Jimdo®: www.jimdo.com
- Joomla!®: www.joomla.org
- Weebly®: www.weebly.com

As of the publication date of Brandon's article, all were free for the basic site (with ads), with nominal charges for more functionality (2012).

Advice From a Pro

"If you don't market your camp well, you are not going to be successful. The single most important source for reaching new clients is the website. You cannot skimp on the website–it has to look great, have all the information that prospective campers and parents want, and it must be updated frequently.

But if someone contacts you for more information after first seeing you on the website, how will you follow-up with them? I am a firm believer in the value of a well-done brochure, which with digital printing techniques has become less expensive than previously.

Everything we produce from our website to our brochure and letters must be high-quality–even one misspelling or grammatical error can turn off a prospective client. Remember that we are selling character growth, youth development, and outdoor education–and it is our job to educate parents about the true value of camp."

– Jane Sanborn, Sanborn Western Camps (CO)

Analytics

Google provides free analytics to track statistics on website traffic, including sales activity and performance. Other web analytics programs include:

- Open Web Analytics: www.openwebanalytics.com
- Clicky®: www.clicky.com
- JAWStats: www.jawstats.com
- GoingUp!: www.goingup.com

This is just a short list. Dozens of other web analytics programs are available–many at no cost. Your web designer will have a recommendation. The message here is to take advantage of data so you can see who is coming to your website.

Search Engine Optimization

Because most customers are searching the Internet for camps, you have to take care that your website is optimized so you show up as close to the top of search results as possible. Numerous guides exist for search engine optimization (SEO), but two in particular are Google's *Search Engine Optimization Starter Guide and Moz's The Beginners Guide to SEO*—both of which are available as free downloads and which provide excellent explanations related to SEO.

Social Media

A recent check of Wikipedia® listed more than 200 social media sites. According to the same source, 16 virtual communities had more than 100 million active users each. Camp officials will have to carefully select the ones in which to participate: Facebook and Twitter®? LinkedIn®, Tumblr®, and Instagram®? How many social media sites you participate in will be guided by how much time you (or someone you designate) can spend posting or tweeting.

Almost every camp will use social media of some type, but most will establish a Facebook page that will need to be updated frequently. Using Facebook posts, you can instantly communicate with all your Facebook fans who are checking Facebook frequently. You can post photos, remind your campers and families about registration deadlines, share the latest news, and more.

As a rule of thumb for social media site effectiveness, you should be making at least two to three posts per week in order to keep your site relevant. While this may not seem like an arduous task during the summer months, it can be more challenging during the off-season months. While social media can be an effective piece of your marketing efforts (especially with your staff), it should not be the sole focus.

If you designate someone else, consider establishing some guidelines about what types of posts are most appropriate. Your decisions about the camp's social media sites will affect also your social media policy for staff. You may also need to consider how to deal with rogue sites that could be set up by camp alumni from many years ago.

Blogs

Having a camp blog is well worth the time and energy because blogs will frequently be picked up by search engines, driving more people to your site. During camp, you may want to post to your blog several times a week. Afterward, that may drop to once a week or so. However, be faithful and post consistently! You may even want to invite guest bloggers to post—a parent, camper, or summer staff member—just to give your readers a different viewpoint. These blogs can also be linked to your Facebook posts, which will generally be shorter messages than a blog. Just remember—if you're going to blog, be consistent, be original, and be fair. Do not use copyrighted material from another person without permission and be careful what you post. Always re-read what you have written before your blog is actually posted to ensure that what you wrote is what you intended.

Printed Materials and Graphic Standards

Many camps no longer rely on printed brochures, deciding instead to use social media and websites as their primary methods for marketing. However, a lot can be said for having a good, informative brochure about your programs. With digital printing, the cost of printed materials is no longer as much of an issue as it once was and you can print in smaller quantities. You may want to have a general brochure as well as postcards or something simple that promotes only one program. This will be a decision to make when developing your marketing plans. Remember, sometimes it's grandparents who make decisions about which camp their grandchildren attend–and some grandparents (as well as some parents) are much more comfortable holding and reading a brochure than looking at a website.

In addition, it is important to have stationery for business use because an email sometimes is not the most appropriate vehicle for communication. Having a consistent look that identifies your camp is important, so work with a graphics artist or marketing professional to have graphic standards developed that include not only your website and stationery but also signage, business cards, vehicles, T-shirts, and anything else that includes your camp brand. Graphics standards will also include color treatments, fonts, and details about the placement of your logo, including the relative size of graphics and words. Your brand is a reflection of you, so protect it by making sure your camp name and logo are used consistently.

Business cards are inexpensive. Never leave home without them. Give them out whenever you have an appropriate opportunity.

Written Communications

Email is by far the most efficient method of communication, even in most business situations. However, be sure that you follow accepted email etiquette. Here are a few email etiquette rules based on recommendations by Laura Stack for Microsoft Office users:

- Be informal, not sloppy. Spelling, grammar, and punctuation rules apply.
- Keep messages brief and to the point.
- Use sentence case. USING ALL CAPITAL LETTERS LOOKS LIKE YOU'RE SHOUTING. using all lowercase letters makes you look lazy.
- Don't use a lot of color or graphics in your message because not all email programs can display them.
- Use blind courtesy copy (bcc) and courtesy copy (cc) appropriately. Overuse clutters inboxes, so copy only those people who need to be copied.
- Use the subject line for its intended purpose. Don't just say "Hi" or "Message From John."
- Email is not private, so don't put anything in an email that you would not want your mother to read, or, worse, to be used in court.
- Use group emails sparingly.
- Check the authenticity of virus warnings before you forward them.

- Remember that your tone cannot be heard in emails. The nuance of verbal communication is missing in emails, so beware of any sarcastic remarks that could be taken the wrong way.
- Use a signature that includes your email address and telephone contact information.
- Summarize long discussions and give proper attribution. (Stack, 2013)

It is the easiest and quickest, but sometimes, email is not the most appropriate. Use your business stationery for formal communications and make sure you follow general business communication etiquette there too, ensuring no misspellings or grammatical errors.

Personal notes written on camp note cards can make an impact and are a good idea for informal communication and thank-you notes.

Marketing Professionals

Selecting a professional to guide your marketing and promotion efforts should be just like finding a lawyer or accountant—look for someone who understands your business, has experience, and has a clearly stated fee structure. But with marketing professionals, you'll be able to see a body of their work, so ask to see their portfolio and inquire about the results derived from their campaigns or other work. Some firms specialize and some are generalists, working with branding, social media, advertising, and public relations.

You may wish to issue a "Request for Proposal" to various marketing agencies or individual professionals. Some firms will have specialties or a niche market. Others will have a broad range of clients. As with any consultant, look for a good fit or chemistry with the project manager. Find out what his billing practices are and how you will be updated during the project. If you are hiring a marketing professional to work with you on an ongoing basis, be certain that both of you agree on the deliverables and due dates.

Interns

If money is an issue, camp owners and directors may want to consider recruiting an intern to assist with marketing. Some colleges and universities have internship programs at no cost to the employer. Others may require a nominal fee or honorarium for the intern. Interns can assist in multiple ways, doing some of the prep work before you pitch a story about your camp or developing a system and posting on your social media sites. Actual experience with a business is valuable for interns and many times the internship sponsor will discover someone who can be hired after graduation. One word of caution though: Interns generally need direction and support, just like employees do.

Omne Trium Perfectum

When making marketing presentations, a good rule to remember is the rule of threes: *Omne trium perfectum,* which translated means: Everything that comes in threes is perfect or every set of three is complete. Simply stated, it's easy for people to remember three things. Thus, when visiting with parents or campers, be prepared with the following three things:

- Three reasons why children should attend camp
- Three top activities at your camp
- Three things that make *your* camp the one to attend

And while you're at it, be prepared with references from three families!

12

Customer Service

Dave Thoensen, Tamarak Day Camp

One needs only to look back at experiences dining out to put in perspective the importance of "service" and how it feels to get good service versus mediocre or even bad service. Think about memorable experiences when you had great food, good friends, and exceptional service. Most people have had those evenings when everything went right—and the server contributed to that with pleasant greetings, good explanations of the menus, and attentive service throughout the meal.

What you used to take for granted as service doesn't always happen anymore. Once upon a time, grocery stores paid young boys to take just purchased groceries from the store out to the customer's car, unloading all the bagged groceries into the trunk. In their general rush to get in and out, many people opt to go through the self-checkout line, avoiding any human contact at all, until you get stuck with a machine that does not cooperate when scanning a bar code.

However, camp is still one of the human-powered experiences where customer service cannot be overlooked. Perhaps the greatest casualty (for camping anyway) of the digital age is the idea that the convenience of an impersonal website is an acceptable substitute for personally interacting with your camp customers face-to-face and actively listening to their questions and concerns. While websites and online registrations are convenient (and do have their place in all businesses), camp is a "high touch, not high tech" endeavor. When you allow yourself to be viewed in the same way as any other product available on the Internet, you have lost the human element that makes the camp industry so unique.

Customer service starts from the minute a parent or potential camper sees the camp website or brochure and continues from there. It is every contact and every impression that a customer or potential customer has with the camp and it doesn't stop there. Who answers your phone at camp or are customers automatically routed to voice mail? Do you offer tours or in-home visits for prospective camp families? What about contact with parents during camp? Do you as the owner/director interact with the parents or is it one of your employees? What about your refund policy—do you offer a full refund or a partial refund?

Some excellent resources about great customer service are available. Lee Cockerell, who wrote *Creating Magic: 10 Common Sense Leadership Strategies From a Life at Disney,* shared his secrets for customer service in a book with a double entendre for the title: *The Customer Rules.* Cockerell has some common sense advice from which everyone can learn. The Disney Institute® has a publication titled *Be Our Guest: Perfecting the Art of Customer Service.* Both of these resources rely heavily on experience from years of perfecting customer service at Disney® properties—always known for consistent high quality. Finally, Leonardo Inghiller and Michal Solomon—both with many years of experience in the hospitality industry—have an excellent guide in *Exceptional Service, Exceptional Profit.* All these authors have something special to give, as their passion about customer service comes through loud and clear.

Figure 12-1. A sign seen in a restaurant

The following are about a dozen rules for customer service in the camp business—culled from sources and from camp executives' experiences.

Be, Know, Do

The U.S. Army has a leadership manual that focuses on "Be, Know, Do," with the "Be" meaning values and attributes of the individual, "Know" as the various skills and knowledge needed, and "Do" the actions, including influencing, operating, and improving (Leader to Leader Institute, 2004). Leadership skills are the same—whether it is leadership in the armed forces, a major corporation, or a camp that's focusing on customer service.

As with any organization, the key to superior customer service begins with the leadership of the owners/directors and is communicated through every single person on the staff in every action and in some cases inaction. To put it more succinctly, are you practicing what you preach when it comes to customer service? If you treat your own employees rudely, how can you ever expect them to treat your customers any differently? In addition, as the leaders of your camp organization, do you set the appropriate expectations for your staff so they know what you expect from them in the area of customer service? Are you hiring staff based on the values they possess? Each person on the camp staff needs to have the qualities necessary to serve others, which generally means they are willing to place the needs of others ahead of their own.

Too often, people mistake skills for values. Human resources has an old saying: "Hire the attitude, but teach the skill." This can apply to customer service as much as it does with swimming, arts, or sports skills. Having the skills to communicate and knowing how the camp expects counselors to interact with campers and parents are things that can be taught during pre-camp training. Doing is simply putting your customer service skills into practice. It is never enough to be and know without doing. Each person must practice what he preaches.

Everyone Is a Customer

Sometimes, it's difficult to think about your campers as customers. But in reality, camp owners and directors have several different sets of customers—all of whom are very important. First are the campers—those boys and girls who come to camp to learn or sharpen skills, to make new friends, and to have a good summer experience. Second are the parents who are paying you to take care of their children and do whatever it is you have said you would do while they are at camp. Third are your employees. You may not think about your employees as customers, but they certainly are—and they are your personal representatives with your campers and the campers' parents. Fourth is everyone else—your vendors, the mailman, your neighbors, and everyone who sees or knows you or drives by your camp entrance. Everyone who has any contact with you or your camp is a customer—or at least a potential customer! People make referrals to organizations they know and feel comfortable about and this is why everyone you come into contact with (whether actually paying or not) is a customer. This is an industry founded on referrals and reputation.

If you look at the phrase *customer service* in the context of everyone being a customer, then it is easy to see that in the camp business, you're serving everyone. Serving, of course, is the key word. You can serve others in a positive, respectful way or you can just serve.

One of the nice things about camp is that everyone is on a level playing field. At camp, it is often said that kids are just kids, not the daughter or son of someone well known or someone with or without personal financial resources. Respect should therefore flow easily in a camp setting—each counselor respecting the camper as an individual and the parents as individuals—just because they're campers or parents.

When camp administrators see their employees—the camp counselors and staff—as customers, it opens up a new viewpoint. First, you are modeling the behavior with them that you want them to model with their campers or parents. When you treat them with respect—not as a subordinate but as a fellow professional in camping—they can sense that. Who wants to be a subordinate to anybody anyhow?

Your employees are not just cabin counselors or swim instructors or cooks. Each one is a professional—a guest services manager—and an extension of the camp director.

In *The Customer Rules*, Cockerell shares his acronym A R E to describe what employees want from management: appreciation, recognition, and encouragement. He says: "A R E is like a cost-free, infinitely renewable fuel. It never runs out, no matter how much of it you use, and the more of it you give to your employees, the more they will have in reserve to give to your customers" (Cockerell, 2013).

What a terrific idea! Employees are the camp and management sets the tone for how campers and parents will be treated by the way in which camp staff are treated.

The same is true with the camp leadership and vendors, neighbors, and all others. Treating everyone with respect—whether a neighbor or stranger—is good common sense and good service for a potential customer. Think about everyone as a potential customer. You just never know who might have children or grandchildren who will end up as your campers and paying customers. Wouldn't you prefer to be known as the camp that seems to really care about not just the kids but everyone with whom you have interaction?

Mom Was Right

Expectations of customer service are fairly easy to describe if you remember the things that your moms taught you, including the following:

- Always say "please" and "thank you" and "Yes, ma'am" and "No, sir."
- Always treat others with respect, especially your elders and those in authority.
- Do unto others as you would have them do unto you.
- Be nice.
- Smile.
- Don't pout.
- Act your age.
- Look people in the eye when you talk to them.
- Have a firm handshake (but don't try to hurt anyone with it).
- If you can't say anything nice about someone, don't say anything at all.
- Look decent when you go out.
- Stand up straight.
- You're representing the whole family (or camp), not just yourself, so don't embarrass anyone.
- Remember where you came from.
- Tuck in your shirt and act like a gentleman.

Each person can likely add a few things to this list, but moms really had the right idea. It's not old fashioned to say "please" and "thank you" (although "Yes, ma'am" and "No, sir" may be somewhat regional), but courtesy is basic.

Being nice and smiling show you have a good outlook on life. As a parent, how would it feel to leave an eight-year-old who had never been away from home before with a camp counselor who didn't look like he was happy to be at camp? Or who was rude to the parents?

Camp staff may need some reminders of the Mom Rules and that's okay. You may even want to discuss these in relation to your general camp culture with each other and with the campers, getting campers to share their own Mom Rules, and don't be hesitant to let your staff know you expect them to do the same for your customers at your camp and model the behavior you expect your staff to display! What kind of example are you setting for your staff if you are smiling and polite to the faces of your customers yet speaking poorly of them behind closed doors. Setting the right example is perhaps the best way for your staff to learn your expectations for them when it comes to customer service—and the best part is, it's contagious! Moms know what they are talking about.

Practice Makes Perfect

Customer service may come quite naturally to some, but the adage that practice makes perfect is absolutely correct. Teaching customer service to your staff starts in pre-camp training. How you approach your staff, especially your newer, impressionable staff members, on the first day and week of their employment will likely shape their experiences working for you. Use this as an opportunity to make customers out of your staff. Learn their names and use them—it shows you care—and find a way for your staff to see you interacting with parents. Pre-camp training is a great place to practice meeting parents, looking them in the eye, and visiting with them. This is just one part of customer service—but an important one. Role-playing how to provide the type of service you desire will make it easier for staff to remember and who couldn't use a little extra practice?

Camp executives might also want to develop various scenarios involving angry parents or unhappy campers, reviewing the camp's philosophy on how to handle such occasions. Another good scenario might be a camp counselor on his time off in town, reminding the staff that customer service and marketing go hand in hand. Any impression left on potential customers that is not up to par is a problem for the camp.

Along with practice comes observing the staff, reinforcing good customer service and correcting service that isn't up to par. Some camps even have what is really a class for campers in customer service and doing nice things. Instead of permitting pranks, one camp encourages "random acts of kindness." Campers and their counselor decided to borrow (with permission of course—known to the counselor and director) the camp vehicle and wash it, proudly calling the director out when it was all finished to see their random act of kindness. That is a lot nicer than having to clean up after a prank!

Words Matter

In *Exceptional Service, Exceptional Profit* is a great chapter called "Language Engineering." The authors discuss how officials at the Ritz-Carlton® hotels decided on a set of ideal phrases to use with their customers, including such phrases as "My pleasure," "Right away," and "Certainly." According to the authors, this has been copied by numerous other companies, as former Ritz-Carlton employees have made their way to other hotels. They go on to recommend coming up with your own lexicon of "customer interaction guidelines" to list preferred greetings or acknowledgements and those that are discouraged (Inghiller & Solomon, 2010). This can be a wonderful exercise for the entire staff, resulting in a common understanding of how to respond in different situations. For example:

How to answer the telephone:

Acceptable: "Good afternoon. This is Chris at Camp Pine Tree. How may I help you?"

Not acceptable: "Camp Pine Tree. Who do you want?"

Worse: "Hello." Then—nothing. No identification. Nothing. And if the phone is answered by someone in the kitchen who really can't do anything but take a message that may or may not get delivered, why bother?

Greeting parents on arrival at camp:

Acceptable: "Hi, I'm Chris and I'll be Johnny's counselor. Welcome to Camp Pine Tree! Did you have a nice drive in today?"

Not acceptable: "What are you looking for? I guess nobody told you where to go."

Presentation at closing campfire with parents in attendance:

Acceptable: "This was a great week at Camp Pine Tree! I'm Chris and I'm so pleased to present these certificates to the boys who were in our cabin this week. We had a terrific time at camp and are looking forward to next year when we can all come back."

Unacceptable: "Well, I only got stuck with six kids this week, so here's your stuff."

Some of this is the result of dealing with a young workforce—many of whom have not had any jobs before—but that doesn't mean you cannot teach them the way you expect them to interact with your customers and teach them a skill they will use essentially for the rest of their lives. Be specific and leave nothing to chance. When you gather on the first day, do you shout "Shut up" at the top of your lungs or do you find a more creative way to get everyone's attention? While screaming at the top of your lungs does get attention, would you be comfortable with your staff doing the same thing with their campers? What about when you get frustrated? Do you curse and swear in front of your employees? Would you be comfortable with them doing the same with parents and campers? Decide what acceptable language is and teach it in pre-camp. Provide examples, give praise, and remind them about your expectations for them. Let them also have input into the process by role-playing and helping to establish some of the expectations. Having the staff play a part in deciding what is acceptable will create buy-in.

The same is true if your camp staff sends postcards or any notes home during the week. Give them specific examples of what to say, not just direction to write a postcard to the parents. If your staff postcard has two purposes—informing the parent about how the camper is doing at camp and reminding them of time of the closing campfire—give them an example that might read like the following:

Dear Mr. and Mrs. Jones,

Johnny is having a great time at camp this week. He's taking swim lessons and has already advanced one level! Our cabin cooked out last night and Johnny was in charge of our Dutch oven cake, which everyone loved. Later this week, we're going fishing and Johnny has told us that's one of his favorite activities, especially since he caught that big bass last spring.

We're looking forward to seeing you at the closing campfire next Friday, June 30, at 6:30 p.m. All the campers' luggage will already be in the parking lot, so you can pick it up as you come into camp. I'm sure Johnny will have lots of stories to share with you on the drive home. See you next Friday!

Sincerely, Chris

The previous letter is better than the following example:

Dear Mr. and Mrs. Jones,

We goofed and put Johnny in the wrong swim class, but after three days, we realized it and moved him up. I think he's quit crying about that now. He wasn't really happy about having to be in charge of the cake at our cookout either, but we all made it through. We're going fishing tomorrow, although no one believes Johnny's fish tale about some five-pound bass. Guess we'll see if he's really that good!

Don't forget to come get him at the end of camp—6:30 sharp. His stuff will be waiting at the parking lot.

Your friend, Chris

Words matter—a lot. While the basic information may be similar, each communication has an entirely different tone and feel. It should also be stressed that before any written communication to parents or campers is mailed, it is thoroughly proofread for the appropriate tone and content. Handing back a stack of parent or camper notes because they are poorly written or convey an inconsistent message is also a good way for staff to learn your expectations.

In *Exceptional Service, Exceptional Profit*, the authors also describe how certain visual and physical cues can negate even the best agreed-upon phrases (Inghiller & Solomon, 2010). For example, in a camp setting, you may be saying all the right things about welcoming families to camp for the closing, but do you provide them with places to sit or do they have to stand or sit on the ground? Do you have water available for them if it's very warm outside? Is someone available to greet your guests and show them where to go for the closing ceremony or do they have to wander around until they stumble upon the right place?

Whether in person, on the phone, on the website, or in other communications, words are important. You can't let your camp vocabulary get in the way of communicating or, worse yet, be insulting (*"Well, at Camp Pine Tree, we know what's best for your kid because we were trained on that"*). Young counselors can easily believe they know a great deal about kids. The parents may have a completely different take on that.

Cleanliness Is Next to Godliness, So Look the Part

Whether it's the camp truck, the front entry to camp, or inside the dining hall, cleanliness counts toward good customer service. Parents and campers alike will appreciate having a clean and neat camp. One of the most difficult things for a camp director or owner is to look at your operation in a truly objective sense. You are too close—and often too proud—of your business. Regardless of the difficulty, force yourself to walk into your camp as if it were your first time stepping foot on the property and you were looking for a camp for your own children. What's the first thing you see? Is it a clean, well-maintained check-in gate with a friendly, well-groomed counselor or is it an overgrown entrance with brush and weeds, staffed by a counselor with his feet on the table, wearing a shirt with cutoff sleeves, texting on his phone and ignoring you?

Does your maintenance staff pick up garbage regardless if it is in the cans or on the ground? Do they scrub the garbage cans frequently so they have no odor or do the garbage cans smell terrible? What about the bathrooms? Are they cleaned and disinfected daily or do they smell like poorly maintained restrooms where you would be uncomfortable with your own children using them?

You certainly get the idea, but only by looking at your facility from an objective point of view—the view of your customers—will you really be in a position to evaluate your facility. Do you like what you see? Getting customers in today's business environment is too difficult for you to be losing them over things you can truly control, such as the condition of your facility.

The same holds true for staff—all should be clean, neat, not smelly, and certainly the epitome of an all-American camp counselor. Camp administrators may laugh at the inclusion of smelly in the description, but it's true: Personal appearance—and aroma—count. Perhaps it should not, but it still does. What kind of impression is being left by a maintenance staff person who has to run into town to get a part after working hard on a plumbing problem? Although it may be hot and this one part is all that is needed to finish the project, it's worth having him either clean up before going to town on behalf of the camp or sending someone else because of the impression that could be left with others.

Equally important will be having campers and staff look their best when the parents arrive to pick up their campers at the end of the camp session. Even if the camp is not one that embraces uniforms, providing a brand-new T-shirt to every camper to wear to the closing ceremonies presents a much better picture to parents than campers who may have worn everything twice during the week or two and have picked out their least-dirty T-shirt to wear to a closing ceremony.

This leads to the topic of appropriate staff clothing. Everyone can agree that shirts advertising a counselor's antics on spring break are not appropriate for wearing at camp. But what is the condition of the rest of your staff's wardrobe? Many young people today are fond of cutting off the sleeves of their shirts and camp shirts and worse. In many cases after a creative counselor is done with the brand-new shirt you just gave him, it bears little resemblance to the original. While he may be wearing your camp shirt and camp logo, is this truly the image you are trying to convey to your customers? Many outlets at camp allow for personal expression and creativity. You don't have to include your camp uniforms as one of those outlets.

Ask Questions and Then Listen—and Keep Listening

When someone complains about anything at camp, the best thing to do is find out what happened, find out why, and then fix it. To do that, it takes listening to the complaint, digging a little deeper, and asking questions to find out more details and then listening to the customer—maybe a parent or maybe a camper—and ascertaining what went wrong. If the camp made a mistake, admit it and thank the parent for bringing this to your attention. Denial is not a good strategy (*"That would never happen here, so there must be something else going on"*). Following up with staff who were there and asking questions of them is a good strategy. If you promise to get back with a parent about a problem, do it. Remember, it isn't whether a particular situation occurred at camp. It's all in how you choose to handle the situation.

You will need to investigate every complaint, getting all sides of the story. The old saying that every story has another side is correct—and many times, witnesses offer multiple different interpretations of a single incident based on who saw what. Always remember that a complaint—whether from a camper, employee, or parent—is generally based on something credible, so it's best to ask lots of questions and find out.

Sometimes, just listening to a customer who wants to vent about something will make the situation better. Chances are, the customer (camper or parent) is not mad at you. He's probably mad at someone or something else, and if you listen, ask appropriate questions, and try to make amends, you may have found a loyal customer who returns again and again, recommending your camp to others along the way.

The Customers Are Always Right—Even When They Aren't

In *The Customer Rules*, one of the rules is to never argue with a customer. Cockerell explains that as difficult as it is to not argue, if you take the bait and snap back at a customer, you both lose. Even when the customer is wrong, it doesn't pay to tell them that nor is it acceptable to argue with them. As he says:

> Never, ever argue with a customer. Don't get defensive. Don't get rude. Don't get sarcastic. Period. Will some customers try to scam you? Sure. Will some try to take advantage of you and get something for free? No doubt. Do some people have a lousy attitude and an outsize sense of entitlement? Oh, yeah. You bet. But none of that matters, because business is business and profit is profit. (Cockerell, 2013)

One way to handle irate customers is to remember that you don't know everything they know. Maybe they have had a horrible day and you're just an innocent target. This holds true, even with campers. Perhaps they are complaining about something at camp because of a situation at home (such as a potential divorce or an illness in the family) they have no control over. The unhappy parent may have called you to complain because he couldn't complain to his boss about a terrible day at the office. One possible strategy when dealing with irate parents is to listen carefully to their concerns, letting them vent all their frustrations about their irritations. When they start winding down, tell them you want to investigate further on your end to research and gain background and that you will call them back at a specific time later in the day. Of course, you will investigate and will call them back when promised, but allowing parents the opportunity to vent and then calm down and reflect will usually result in finding a solution to the problem without emotion playing a part in the discussion. The bottom line is to not take it personally. Instead, try to fix whatever the complaint is about.

If you can't fix it the way the customer wants, consider saying *"I can't do that, but here is what I can do."* The customer then has some satisfaction that his complaint has made a difference. Coming up with a quick solution that helps the customer is much better than a prolonged wait to resolve the conflict. For example, if your policy is to send sick campers home with no refunds and you get a complaint from a parent about that, you have several options. You can give them the refund, stick to your policy, and lose the camper (and probably any friends he might influence) or come up with another solution. If the camper had enrolled for two weeks and stayed only a week before having to go home, offer to let him come back later in the summer at no charge. If it's the end of the summer, give him a week next year. Yes, that is an exception to your policy, but is that the policy you really want? Consider changing it to make it fairer to the customer, even though it's inconvenient to the camp.

Read and Network

Some customer service is simply knowing what's going on in the world and being able to respond appropriately. It is important to read, to keep up with the news, and to be aware of events taking place in your community. For example, make note of holidays (especially religious holidays) that your customers may be celebrating and make sure you refrain from calling, emailing, or sending mail to them on those days. Showing your customers that you value their beliefs and values goes a long way toward building solid customer relations. Reading the resources named earlier is important—as is reading about other ways to deal with people. Countless opportunities exist to learn program after program on how to handle situations and how to maintain good relationships. Take advantage of those and try the techniques that are suggested.

The other thing to do is to network. It is unlikely you will encounter anything in the realm of customer service that hasn't happened to someone before regardless of his occupation. Seek other business professionals in your community through civic and service organizations, such as Rotary, Optimist International, and Kiwanis® (to name just a few). Local chambers of commerce, community boards, working with the local school districts—the list is endless. Making yourself visible in your community makes a world of difference not only from a marketing standpoint but also from a customer service viewpoint. Knowing that you and your organization are actively involved with making your community a better place to live and work for everyone is perhaps the best form of customer service you can develop. Networking with other colleagues will always pay off—sometimes when you least suspect it.

Adopt the Disney Rule: Exceed Expectations

Disney has an easy-to-understand definition of quality service: "Quality Service means exceeding your guests' expectations by paying attention to every detail of the delivery of our products and services" (Disney Institute, 2011). Disney is also famous for wanting everyone to experience magic, evidenced by the minute details that go into its movies, theme parks, and other parts of the Walt Disney empire.

Camps can emulate the Disney style, creating their own magic for campers and their parents. In *Be Our Guest*, Disney executives discuss how families come to Walt Disney World not just to enjoy the rides and shows but to create a shared memory—an experience that becomes a part of the family culture. That can happen with camps if you pay attention to details, provide a few "wow" moments, and ensure you are meeting your mission. Every new Disney employee attends numerous orientation classes and one of the first things he learns is his common purpose with other Disney employees: *"We create happiness by providing the finest in entertainment for people of all ages, everywhere"* (Disney Institute, 2011).

How many of your camp counselors know your mission and philosophy? Do they also understand your camp's standards for quality? At Disney, the quality standards are safety, courtesy, show and efficiency. Each of those standards is repeated through their parks—down to the last detail.

Disney also has three service delivery systems by which it implements quality standards, the first of which is cast. Camps have a cast—the camp staff. The Disney Institute shares the following quality service cues about its cast:

- Make a memorable first impression.
- Communicate the heart and soul of the organization first.
- Speak a service language.
- Wear a service wardrobe.

- Establish a set of basic performance guidelines.
- Build a performance culture. (Disney Institute, 2011)

Think about how your camp staff "performs" as a cast. What kind of impressions do they make with the customers—primarily other campers and parents? Are you sharing with the counselors your values and philosophy and that you are more concerned about that than the paperwork that must be completed by new hires? Have you set up your camp as a service organization in the minds of your staff? Is the image of your camp the same for the counselors as it is for you? Do your staff members understand what behavior is expected of them? And do you have a "performance culture"—a set of specific behaviors and values that is communicated to the staff? Instead of telling counselors and staff what to do, constantly ask them to look at situations as a camp parent just visiting camp for the first time. What would their impressions be of a staff person lounging in the sun or talking/texting on his cell phone? Many parents would rightfully come to the conclusion that the staff is inattentive or uncaring, when in actuality, the staff person is just coming off a long night with a sick camper or dealing with a family emergency. What would the situation look like to your customers is always a great perspective from which to communicate and teach your values.

Disney's second service delivery system is the setting. What an opportunity camps have to emphasize their setting as a quality service system! Everyone at camp can and should help with maintenance of the facility, with everyone utilizing the environment in which you have established the camp. Part of Disney's environment also recognizes that employees need a special place to go and relax so the delivery of services isn't interrupted (Disney Institute, 2011). The same holds true with camps, with counselors needing a place away from program and living areas where they can relax and be off duty.

Disney's third service delivery system is processes, which for camp would include communicating between staff, campers, and parents; creating a process to take care of special situations; and fixing any flaws as soon as possible (Disney Institute, 2011).

Finally, the Disney folks speak about the integration of quality standards and processes. The standards—safety, courtesy, show and efficiency—represent behaviors that meet Disney's common purposes and the delivery systems—cast, setting, and process—are how those standards reach Disney's guests. Together, these all combine to form the magic of Disney (Disney Institute, 2011). Camps can take these Disney ideas and adapt them to create their own magic—where expectations of campers, parents, and all customers are exceeded and the customers become lifelong friends.

Find the "Yes"

In the Hollywood comedy *Yes Man*, Jim Carrey's character is challenged in a motivational seminar to find a way to say "Yes," and while at camp you do have situations where you need to draw a line with your customers, you should also always be focusing on how you can say "Yes" to a particular customer request.

Think about your own experiences from ordering food in a restaurant to asking the cable company to schedule a service appointment at a convenient time. Did you feel better about your experiences where you were told that "We can't do that" or "I'm sorry—we don't make special considerations." Or did you feel more valued as a customer when that waiter or cable company accommodated your request? How do you think your customers feel at camp when they are told the same things? While you cannot always honor a parent request, refusals should be few and far between. Do you allow a parent to call at the end of the day (in a day camp of course!) and ask that his child be sent home on a different bus? What if a parent is leaving town and asks that you pick up his child at a grandparent's home on a different bus route? Do you find a way to say "Yes"? Saying "Yes" to customer requests will require the potential for some additional work on your part (from time to time) but will pay over and over again in happy, satisfied customers.

Evaluate Your Policies

Developing a culture of excellent customer service will possibly require culture change on your part and also on the part of your organization. Do the policies of your organization lend themselves to developing customer loyalty? For example, consider your policy on refunds. If your organization has a "no refund" policy for deposits or camp fees, have you ever considered what that message is sending to your customers? While one point of your businesses is to make money and be financially stable, is keeping a $500 deposit because a camp family had a change in its situation really going to make a difference to your bottom line at the end of the year? Probably not. Many will say that if you do it for one family, you have to do it for everyone. Is that really a possibility? Probably not.

The same can be said for such policies as keeping a portion of deposits for "administrative fees," not allowing a flexible number of weeks, changes to sessions, and add-on activities, such as lunch or canteen accounts. Once in a while, you may be taken advantage of by offering flexibility to your customers, but if it's really that important to them, then so be it.

The point is, if you are trying to develop a reputation as a truly customer-driven business (and you should be!), are the policies you communicate helping you achieve your objectives? As camp professionals, you are in a unique situation where you're working with children and families and mutually share a stake in their best interests. Do antiquated business policies communicate to your customers that you share the same values they do or do they communicate a one-sided, self-serving organizational structure? The choice is yours to make.

Figure 12-2. Another sign seen in a restaurant

Peg Smith, CEO of the American Camp Association, has said that "the key difference between a good business, a great business, and an exceptional business is customer service. Customers control your brand" (Smith, personal communication, August 17, 2013). How great it would be for camps to all be in the category of exceptional businesses! By recognizing what makes customer service exceptional, paying attention to details, incorporating expectations for service and role-playing into pre-camp training, listening attentively, and intentionally adding some "wow" moments and a little magic, camps can improve their customer service—and protect their brand.

13

Financial Management

Cindy Murray/iStock/Thinkstock

Before discussing the basics of financial management in the camp business, it's important to offer a word of caution for a new start-up or before you purchase an existing camp operation: *Be careful.*

While any new business venture carries risk, remember that the Small Business Administration estimates that 50 percent of all new businesses will fail within the first five years. Statistically, the likelihood of failure is far greater than the likelihood of success. The odds are stacked against you.

While it's true that "Nothing ventured is nothing gained," your decision to purchase or start a camp is going to be a somewhat emotional decision and you can't make business decisions based purely on emotion. You may be thinking of all the great memories you had at camp as a child or you may be thinking about all the lives you'll be changing as a result of your awesome program. Whether you are borrowing a large sum from a bank or personally investing your life savings into your operation, these will also prove to be emotional events for you and be the source of countless sleepless nights.

You need to separate yourself from the emotions and be certain you're making decisions from a purely business standpoint. Items to consider if purchasing an existing operation include the following:

- Review the enrollment of the camp for at least the previous five to six years to gauge the enrollment pattern and determine if the business has been stable or has been in sharp or steady decline. If the business is in decline or has been losing campers for several years, you should negotiate your purchase price accordingly.
- Retain the services of the best legal and financial advisors your budget will allow. Good legal and financial advice is not inexpensive but it is crucial to the success of your new business.
- If you're purchasing an existing operation look closely at all the financial reports (income statements, financial statements, cash flow reports, and income tax filings) for at least the previous three years and confirm who was responsible for preparing them. Have your attorney and financial advisor or accountant do a comprehensive review of all statements.
- Make sure there is a full disclosure of assets and liabilities, including all loans and mortgages. If you have outstanding liabilities left to pay off, how will they be addressed? In many cases, you as the new business owner will inherit these liabilities and they will reduce your purchase price. If so, will the cash flow of the business be sufficient to cover the day-to-day operational costs as well as these inherited liabilities?
- Why is the previous owner leaving the business?
- What is the condition of the facility or business you're purchasing? This is especially important because if you are putting up a large investment, the last thing you want is to be saddled with huge additional expenses to repair critical infrastructure.
- Try to work out a smooth transition of ownership and if possible negotiate your purchase agreement to keep the previous owner involved in at least a small capacity for the first year. Parents don't like change for their children, and are less likely to seek another program if ownership still retains even a small level of familiarity.

If you're trying to finance a new start-up, your bank or investors may require significant proof of due diligence in terms of market research, business potential, and capacity (discussed in Chapter 4), in addition to some of the items listed (if the purchase of a property is involved).

Finally, do not leverage yourself personally more than you should. Putting yourself in a position where you risk losing your operation (and your life savings) unless you're at 100 percent capacity and every plan works perfectly is not the right way to either start or run your business. You need to give your venture (and yourself) a little breathing room. If you're so consumed about making budget that you don't have the time to devote to business-building activities and other matters that will ensure your business's long-term viability, you're setting yourself up to fail. You never want to invest your own funds so heavily that you will be personally ruined if your operation fails, so only plan on personally investing what you can afford to lose.

Plan and spend wisely and manage your business. Do your homework and be objective. Making the decision to purchase a camp is a huge step and something that will remain with you (hopefully) for decades to come.

Financial management for camps can be broken down into the following few simple questions:

- How will you finance the start-up costs, capital improvements, and ongoing expenses of operating a camp?
- What accounting system will you use?
- How will you manage cash flow?
- What systems will you put in place to deal with receipts?
- Who will be responsible for making purchasing decisions?

Financing Options

Other than your own funds, camp operators have several potential sources of financing, including the following:

- *Friends and family:* A large red flag should go up in your mind if you are considering borrowing money from friends and family, as that situation has the potential to be less than satisfactory. If for whatever reason you go this route, have legal agreements drawn up that clearly spell out the terms. If this is a loan, include all repayment arrangements. If your friends and/or family are investing in your camp, what do they expect in return? Depending on the legal structure you've chosen, they could be board members or partial owners. Either way, you'll want to have a very thorough and clear written agreement.
- *Investors:* Some individuals like to invest in new businesses, but they will expect a return on their investments. Networking with accountants or attorneys who work with small businesses may be helpful in identifying potential investors.
- *Owner financed loans:* Similar to an investor, you can utilize the previous camp owner (if applicable) to self-finance your transaction and in essence act as the bank. A payment contract agreement is created that specifically outlines payment schedules. You can also include provisions for payments should certain enrollment levels not be met. While this type of financing

usually results in a longer-term purchase arrangements and results in payments that may exceed the appraised value of the property or business, you can often negotiate this agreement with little or no money up front so you suffer very little personal financial risk.

- *Conventional bank loans:* For new businesses, banks will usually require some type of personal guaranty and collateral. Typically referred to as a mortgage, the bank utilizes the value of your property as collateral for your loan. In new start-ups or camp businesses without physical property as collateral, you may need to secure your loan with a personal investment.
- *Small business loans:* The Small Business Administration does not loan money, but it does offer guarantees on loans to small businesses from various lending institutions. Because of changing economic conditions, the amount of guaranty may vary, but it lessens the risk for the lending institution.
- *Minority business loans:* Some loans are designed specifically for businesses owned predominantly by women or minorities. Each lender may have different requirements.
- *Business lines of credit:* Business lines of credit are pre-approved loans usually given to existing bank customers. Typically ranging from $50,000 to $100,000, these loans can be used for "anything" business related—from payroll to paying bills. Interest rates are slightly higher than typical conventional bank loans, but having the funds in a pre-approved account make this an attractive option to utilize for emergency purposes, such as major unanticipated facility repairs. Be cautious about utilizing a business line of credit for day-to-day operational expenses and use it only for emergency funding. If your business needs to utilize the credit line to supplement something like payroll or day-to-day expenses, you immediately need to re-evaluate your business model.
- *Credit cards:* Using credit cards to finance start-up costs of a small business is generally considered a bad idea. However, sometimes, despite the higher interest rates charged by credit card companies, it makes sense to use credit cards—provided you can pay off the balance within a month or two. Work with your bank to secure credit cards with the lowest interest rates available. Interest rates are set according to the "risk" that the bank assumes with your account based on such factors as credit history, credit limit, and cash flow. For new businesses without credit history or cash flow history, your interest rate will most likely be higher. Pay off the balances as quickly as possible and manage the use of your credit cards judiciously to avoid carrying balances.

Obtaining money from friends, family, or investors is called *equity financing*, which means that money is lent in exchange for some type of ownership in your camp. Investors will expect to share in the profits as well as control. However, this allows the owner or director to focus on making the camp profitable instead of repaying the money. Money from loans of any type is considered *debt financing*, providing the camp owner with maximum control, but you must honor repayment agreements. If debt financed, the camp won't have all its cash flow available to do business.

Should you decide to use debt financing, it's best to comparison shop, as with any other business decision. Rates can vary substantially from lender to lender, so it's worthwhile to take the time to consider all your options. Like credit card rates, bank finance rates are based on the risk the bank is assuming by loaning you money. To secure the lowest rate possible, keep your business and personal credit rating as high as possible. As a small business (regardless of tax status), your personal credit history will have an effect on your business credit history. Pay your bills (business and personal) on time, especially any creditor or vendor who reports to the credit reporting houses, and keep the credit limits on business and personal credit cards as low as possible. By reducing your obligations, you'll make your business more attractive to lenders and receive a better finance rate.

Although it may seem that having two or three options would be enough, some financial advisors suggest looking at as many as 10 different banks, as you may strike out with just two or three that don't want to take a chance on your business. Regardless, as a borrower, you will need to get to know your banker. Most banks call their lending officers "relationship managers" for a reason: You and the bank may have a long-term relationship, so take the time to get to know your bank as it gets to know your business. Have honest discussions with your bankers about your business performance. If your registration is good or you're expanding your program to try something new and potentially profitable, tell them. You need to advocate for your business whenever possible. Look at your business plan from their viewpoint, anticipate the kinds of questions they'll ask, and be prepared to answer completely. You may also need to be flexible in how much you're requesting for a loan. A risk is involved in borrowing money, so be sure you understand your loan.

Your business plan will be a key to obtaining loans or investors. Remember the advice from new camp owner/directors—you need not just a business plan but a workable plan—carefully crafted and updated as you learn more about your new camp business.

Banking

Camp owners and directors will generally have numerous banks from which to choose. With advances in technology, the services offered by banks are changing frequently. Some of the things to consider when selecting a bank include the following:

- How is the bank's customer service? Do you already have a relationship with an existing bank? Does your bank have specialists dedicated to small businesses?
- Is your bank accessible? Are the branches convenient to your winter and summer locations? Do you use ATMs, and if so, does your bank have readily available ATMs? Some banks that don't have a large network of ATMs will refund fees their customers are charged for the use of other ATMs.
- If you will be accepting credit cards, can your bank assist you with securing a low processing rate? Credit cards are a wonderful convenience for your customers, but keep in mind that by accepting credit cards, you're paying a fee ranging from one percent to five percent (or more in some cases!) for each transaction. You need to shop for your credit card processor and review your charges and usage fees associated with your account constantly.

- Does your bank offer remote deposit capture (RDC) that allows you to scan and deposit checks from your office instead of having to deposit via mail or directly to the bank? By turning your office into a banking center with a check scanner attached to your computer, you are depositing checks into your account faster and getting access to the money faster. Also, you're notified in a day or two if a problem occurs with the check, which allows you to collect on bad checks more quickly.
- What online banking services does your bank offer? Online bill pay is a great feature, which allows you to schedule your bill payments–reducing late fees–and you can interface this feature with your in-house accounting software–reducing bookkeeping and accounting expenses.
- Some banks offer wealth management accounts, which have higher balance requirements but also pay you substantially higher interest rates for deposits (provided they are above the balance minimums). While the rate of returns may seem small, consider that in seasonal businesses like yours, large sums of money may be in your checking accounts from March to August. Any rate of return is higher than receiving nothing and even a few thousand dollars at the end of the year is better than nothing.
- What type of services do you need from a bank? What are the fees? Banks generally have product brochures and fee charts, although many will waive some fees to get your business. If your bank is willing to waive your account fees, what are the account balances necessary and will you be able to maintain them?
- Is the bank insured by the Federal Deposit Insurance Corporation? FDIC insurance covers all deposit accounts, including checking and savings accounts, money market deposit accounts, and certificates of deposit. The standard insurance amount is $250,000 per depositor per insured bank for each account ownership category. FDIC insurance doesn't cover other financial products and services that banks may offer, such as stocks, bonds, mutual fund shares, life insurance policies, or annuities or securities (Federal Deposit Insurance Corporation, 2013a). Take time to verify FDIC insurance.

In summary, shop your banking decisions carefully and choose the bank that provides you with the greatest level services with the least operating costs. Keep in mind that you don't need to keep all your bank accounts at the same bank. You may choose to keep larger sums in a bank that pays you a higher return (a wealth management account) and a daily banking account for payroll and bill paying at another because you like the services provided from that bank. It's also advisable to do annual account reviews with your business banker(s) so you can see a breakdown of all the fees you've been charged over the course of a year. This allows you to negotiate further as well as provide you with information should the need arise to seek your banking services elsewhere in the future.

Checking Accounts

After selecting your banking partner or partners, it will be necessary to establish your checking accounts. Whether you are utilizing one bank or multiple banks, it is advisable to have one account for payroll processing and another operating account for daily banking needs. Your operating account will usually be the depository account that receives money from cash, credit card, and check deposits. You will then direct the bank to "sweep" the funds into your payroll account at a pre-determined level sufficient to meet your payroll requirements. Having a separate account for operations and payroll makes reconciliation easier and provides better security for both your accounts.

When establishing your business check accounts, you need to clearly indicate who has signature authority on your accounts. While the decision is yours to make, most small businesses choose to leave the responsibility of signing checks only to the owner of the business. You need to keep track of expenditures and nobody (in most cases) is better at managing your money than you are. Print the business name on the check, but do print your name under the signature line as an extra measure of security. Guard your checkbooks closely and make sure that you limit their access–it's nobody's business what your account balances are. A locking file cabinet or a safe is best for keeping checkbooks secure and away from inquisitive employees. A good business practice is to secure unused check stock to protect yourself from losses due to forged checks. In addition, if you use online checking, you or your financial assistant can and should review your accounts on a daily basis to verify that all checks that have cleared your account were actually written on your account. Most banks will have accounts for small businesses that typically have a lower minimum balance requirement than commercial accounts. Banks will offer various packages of accounts and services geared toward different sizes of businesses. State laws vary, but many have adopted the Uniform Commercial Code, where the bank is generally held liable for any forged checks (Federal Deposit Insurance Corporation, 2013b).

Most banks also offer a positive pay service–for a fee–so when the business issues checks, a list is uploaded to the bank, which will compare any checks or Automated Clearing House (ACH) transactions (direct deposit) presented against the list you've uploaded to protect against fraud. You are notified by the bank of any mismatches, allowing you to either approve or deny payment.

Cash Management

Banks can set up your accounts so your payroll account is a zero-balance account, automatically sweeping cash from your operating account into your payroll account whenever checks are presented to the bank as another effort toward fraud prevention. Another type of account is a sweep investment account that is used to maintain higher balances that will earn interest. The funds are swept daily into investment securities, although these investment services aren't covered by the FDIC (Federal Deposit Insurance Corporation, 2013a). You may wish to check with your bank to see what types of cash management services they offer and the related fees and anticipated returns on sweep accounts. Most banks can analyze a couple months of your previous banking activity to give camps an idea of the total fees you might pay–less the anticipated returns from sweep accounts–to get a net cost of your banking business.

Fraud Prevention

Every business is vulnerable to fraud. With a scanner and laser printer, criminals can reproduce checks and easily print fraudulent checks, stealing from businesses and banks. Following are some steps that camps can take to avoid fraud:

- Monitor your bank accounts on a daily basis, reporting any unauthorized checks to your bank immediately.
- Be aware of inside jobs—whether through employee theft of cash, equipment, or inventory. The first step is to carefully screen potential employees before they are hired. When setting up your internal controls of accounting activities, segregate duties as much as possible so the person who opens the mail records all checks, another person prepares the bank deposit, and another enters the deposit into your accounting system.
- Develop a system of checks and balances to keep track of account activity. Monitor collection activities constantly, especially during times of peak activity—during registration, spring, and early summer. Monitor your receivables and deposits, comparing them periodically against your budget.
- Require that passwords are changed on a regular basis and that employees don't give out their passwords. Online banking software generally forces users to change passwords on a regular basis and may require a combination of characters (for example, uppercase, lowercase, numeral, and symbol) as an acceptable password.
- Never have your computer set to remember your password, especially for your banking or accounting information.
- Keep your computers updated with the latest versions of your operating system and antivirus system.
- Avoid using public wireless Internet connections, especially for banking online, because public hotspots could be compromised.
- Beware of any emails that are supposedly from your bank, asking that you change your password immediately or respond to the email to verify your credentials. New scams pop up every day from criminals who do a very good job of appearing to be your bank. Never respond to these emails. Instead, report these to your business banker or your bank's fraud prevention department immediately.
- If feasible, have your online banking and cash management activity on a dedicated computer with a firewall that will protect your camp business from being compromised by malware and viruses.

Electronic Payroll Distribution Systems (EPDS)

Most companies offer their employees the option of direct deposit in lieu of paper payroll checks—a much more secure way to pay employees—with the additional benefit to employees of quicker access to their money as well as saving them a trip to the bank. However, the FDIC reports that "[m]ore than one in four households (28.3 percent) are either unbanked or underbanked, conducting some or all of their financial transactions outside of the mainstream banking system" (Burhouse & Osaki, 2012). As a result, one could assume that at least some of your camp staff may not have a bank account. For those persons, an alternative method of payment, such as an Electronic Payroll Distribution System, can be very attractive. EPDS allows employers to pay their employees through the use of a payroll debit card, also known as a payment card, and/or the "convenience check," which is a paper check issued not by the employer but is self-issued by the employee (Kirsh, 2013). For employees of camps located in remote areas, this can be a major benefit.

Note that most states permit the use of direct deposit from a company to an employee's own bank account if the employee consents and some states permit employees to be paid by payment card provided that the employee consents. In addition, the Federal Reserve Board, in its Regulation E, says that employers may not require an employee to receive his wages at a particular financial institution as a condition of employment (Kirsh, 2013). Because neither direct deposit nor payment card can be mandated by an employer, paper paychecks must be an option.

Camps interested in an EPDS should ask their bank or EPDS provider the following questions:

- How does your service comply with the requirement in most states that permits employees to receive a paper paycheck if they wish?
- What type of consent do you require of employees who want to participate in the EPDS program?
- Do you use documents or nondocumentary methods to comply with the Patriot Act?
- What happens if employees fail the electronic verification or can't show proper documents?
- Is offering a direct deposit option required?
- How does your program comply with the Patriot Act and its customer identification program?

An EPDS system will be a benefit to employers, as you'll enjoy a reduction in the administration costs related to printing and distributing paper checks and reissuing checks to employees who have lost or washed them (a common circumstance among camp staff). Employees get immediate access to their money and no longer have to deal with the inconvenience of cashing or depositing a paper check.

Accounting for Your Business Finances

If you're not familiar with accounting practices or software, you will want to engage help from a professional. However, you are ultimately responsible for your finances, so it's important to learn about basic business accounting. The Small Business Administration can assist you in this, as it provides a wide variety of training opportunities that include financial management.

For persons without an accounting background, it is important to remember that the concepts of accounting are relatively simple. The first concept is that each financial transaction must have a double entry: a debit and a credit. Debit comes from a Latin word meaning "left" and is abbreviated as Dr. Credit is from a Latin word meaning "right" and is abbreviated Cr. Each transaction must have an entry on the left that equals the entry on the right, although the total entry may be spread over several different accounts. This is the basis for double-entry accounting. Note that debit and credit have nothing to do with good or bad or increase or decrease. It's just left and right entries.

Cash or Accrual?

One of the first decisions you will need to make is whether you'll operate on a cash or accrual basis. A cash basis is the easiest: If money comes in, it's income, but if money goes out, it's an expense. But that does not really tell the whole story—ever. For example, if you purchase an insurance policy for a camp vehicle, assume that the annual premium is $1,200 and is due upon receipt. If you're on a cash basis, then you have a $1,200 expense when you pay the invoice. But under an accrual system, you would pay the $1,200 expense, book it as a prepaid expense, and recognize 1/12 of the expense each month of the policy year, or $100, because $100 is the expense for the month. On an annual basis, you might not notice much difference, but most people look at their financial statements monthly, so recognizing income when it is earned and expenses when they are incurred is a much more accurate picture of where you are at any given time financially. Thus, an accrued expense is the recognition of an expense when it's incurred regardless of when you pay for it. You may have ordered—and used—food supplies for a month, but you may not have received an invoice for them by month end. Under accrual accounting, you would book the cost of the food used during that period as an accrued expense to give a fair representation of your expenses for that month.

In short, in cash accounting, you recognize income when it's received and expenses when they're paid. Accrual accounting recognizes income when it's earned and expenses when they're incurred.

Chart of Accounts

To organize all the financial transactions, you need a chart of accounts, which is organized into the following five categories:

- *Assets:* These are things you own. Assets can be cash, buildings, equipment, or receivables (because even when someone owes you money, you still account for it as an asset).
- *Liabilities:* These are things you owe. Liabilities can be accounts payable (set up when you owe for services that have already been rendered or products that are in your possession) or a mortgage or salaries payable (what you owe people who have worked for you but have not yet been paid).
- *Owner's equity:* this is what you as the owner have invested in your business. It can also include an account called retained earnings: when you make a profit but plow it back in the business. For organizations set up as nonprofit, this is called net assets (formerly known as fund balance) instead of owner's equity.

- *Income:* This is what people pay you for your programs and what you earn from other services or investments.
- *Expenses:* These are everything from salaries and benefits to supplies, rent, and utilities.

The National Center for Charitable Statistics, in cooperation with the California Association of Nonprofits, CompassPoint Nonprofit Services, and the California Society of Certified Public Accountants, has developed the Unified Chart of Accounts (UCOA) for nonprofit organizations. It is easily adaptable for for-profit organizations and includes information so nonprofits can easily translate the segments from their financial statements into the IRS prescribed categories on the IRS Form 990 as well as the federal Office of Management and Budget, for those organizations that have federal grants. The UCOA is very thorough, including many accounts that the average camp won't use. It is downloadable from the NCCS website: nccs.urban.org/projects/ucoa.cfm#Toolkit.

Two different sample charts of accounts are included in Appendix J for nonprofit and for-profit camps. In these examples, the first two digits are for the location and the next three digits are for the natural classification of expenses, such as payroll, supplies, or occupancy. The last three digits are for the functional classification, such as administration, program, marketing, or maintenance. Functional expenses can be for any program or function you as the camp executive want to track. Ideally, an employee will be responsible for each functional budget. For example, you may decide that it's important to track all your waterfront program expenses. You would assign a functional expense number for waterfront to each of the natural expenses (payroll, supplies, telephone, etc.) to assist you in determining how much your waterfront program actually costs. By careful planning of your chart of accounts and the assignment of functional expense numbers, you can group programs together or be very specific.

Assume you have five major programs for your camp: waterfront, equestrian, field sports, target sports, and arts. You want to track each major program, each department within the program, and all your programs together. Your chart of accounts for functional expenses might look like the following:

###-211	Program, Waterfront, Sailing
###-212	Program, Waterfront, Canoeing
###-213	Program, Waterfront, Swimming
###-221	Program, Equestrian
###-231	Program, Field Sports, Softball
###-232	Program, Field Sports, Soccer
###-233	Program, Field Sports, Golf
###-241	Program, Target Sports, Archery
###-242	Program, Target Sports, Riflery

###-251 Program, Arts, Music
###-252 Program, Arts, Woodworking
###-253 Program, Arts, Printmaking

Using these three-digit extensions on each of the natural classification accounts, you could then provide an audit trail (a detailed listing of all entries, including deposits, checks, or journal entries) for the following:

- All programs
- All waterfront programs
- The sailing program only
- The canoeing program only
- The swimming program only
- All equestrian programs
- All field sports programs
- The softball program only

You could also do this for cabin groups simply by carefully developing your chart of accounts. However, if you don't have a budget for each program and don't have de-centralized authority for revenue and expenditures, then you may want to limit how detailed you get with your coding and chart of accounts. The same principle would apply to separate locations or to a boys camp and a girls camp or to summer programs and winter programs. It is always a good idea to visit with other people who will be involved (your accountant or bookkeeper, department heads, other staff) and talk through how best to keep track of your finances. (See Appendix J for a sample chart of accounts.)

Effect of Debits and Credits

Increases in assets (such as cash) are booked as debits to cash and credits to income (or accounts receivable). Expenses are booked as debits to the proper expense line, with the offsetting entry a credit to cash (or accounts payable). Thus, entries as debits or credits have the effects shown in Figure 13-1 on the types of accounts.

Type of Account	Debit Entry	Credit Entry
Assets	Increases assets	Decreases assets
Liabilities	Decreases liabilities	Increases liabilities
Owners' equity	Decreases owners' equity	Increases owners' equity
Income	Decreases income	Increases income
Expenses	Increases expenses	Decreases expenses

Figure 13-1. Account debits and credits

Consider a simple transaction. Bobby Smith has registered for camp and his parents send you a check for the registration fee of $100, which you deposit into your bank account. For this transaction, you'll book $100 as a credit to Camp Fees (an income account) and a debit of $100 to cash (an asset account). The same day, your monthly telephone statement comes, indicating that you owe $25 to your phone company. You write a check immediately to pay the phone bill. That transaction is booked as a debit to telephone expense and a credit to cash. At the end of the day, you then have a net of $75 in cash, revenue of $100, and an expense of $25, leaving a gain of $75 for the day.

With accounting software, in most cases, you won't have to determine the offsetting entry. The software will do that for you. In the sample transactions, you would need to know to enter the camp registration fee of $100 into your camp registration income account and your telephone expense of $25. The software will automatically determine that the offsetting entries for both go to the cash account. With any software, you'll need to set up a chart of accounts so income, expenses, and balance sheet accounts (assets and liabilities) can be tracked consistently and efficiently. You will also be able to segregate different cost centers if you choose to do so based on the numbering system of your chart of accounts. Your software package may come with recommendations for a chart of accounts. (See Appendix J for a sample chart of accounts.)

It is important to understand the basic concepts of accounting—even if you hire an excellent bookkeeper or accountant—because it's your business. You need to review all the accounting entries and understand where your money is coming from and where it's going. It is wise to take a class in accounting—either through the Small Business Administration, a community college, another institution, or online.

Breaking Even

An additional concept of double-entry accounting you will want to understand is how to calculate a break-even point. One of the most helpful concepts to the camp owner or director, breakeven is basically how many campers paying how much will cover all your expenses for a given period of time. You'll have some expenses that will remain constant regardless of the number of campers you have, such as utilities or property insurance. You may have year-round staff costs that will also remain constant, but your summer staffing costs (likely your largest expense) will vary based on the number of campers.

Assume you are operating your camp for eight weeks and would like to charge $875 per week, with a desired capacity of 150 campers per week. You also know that over the summer, you have a special program that will involve about 40 campers and you would like to charge $50 each. Based on the ages of the campers (and to keep this simple, assuming you have a consistent number of campers of the same ages each week), you have determined that you need 15 counselors, eight activity specialists, and 10 support staff (including maintenance, kitchen, and office staff).

You calculate your fixed expenses, then add your variable expenses, including food and program supplies, awards, T-shirts, and your desired profit of eight percent. Developing a spreadsheet as follows, you make some adjustments to your fees and the number of campers until you reach a breakeven point. All these line items are based on some assumptions, including an average cost per meal ($5—but you must include all the staff meals during pre-camp as well as the camper meals) and amounts for program supplies per camper. (Note: These are all hypothetical and do not represent recommended income or expenditures.)

In Figure 13-2, starting with column A, based on the $875 per week and 150 campers, you have a deficit of (132,460). In column B, you increase the number of campers to 155, but you still have a deficit. You continue with various scenarios until you get to column 3, with a fee of $899 and projected number of campers of 171. This gets you to a slight gain—over and above your profit margin of eight percent.

However, notice that the difference of one camper—from 170 to 171—changes your bottom line from a deficit of (3,156) to a surplus of 679, without changing the fee. Because every camp is different, you can develop this type of spreadsheet to compare various fees and camper weeks. However, beware of changing your assumptions. For example, if you decide that your food costs will average only $4.80 per meal, then change all columns to include that assumption. This particular spreadsheet is built on everything keying off the fee and average number of campers. Note also that you may have additional income or expense lines and should add them.

Once you determine your breakeven point, you'll need to decide if you can realistically charge what it takes and have the number of campers that you need to break even. If not, then go back and determine what you can cut in the way of expenses and run the numbers to see what you'll need to get back to your desired fee structure and number of campers. Remember that you can eliminate a deficit in three ways: increase income, decrease expenses, or a combination of both.

Depreciation

Depreciation is another accounting concept that camp executives need to understand, as most will have either property or equipment that is capitalized. When a business makes a capital investment, it is buying something that will last for years and can be expensed over time. For example, if Camp ABC buys a small bus that costs $40,000, that expenditure is not shown as an expense for only this year. In reality, all you did was to trade one asset (cash) for another asset (the bus). You still have $40,000 in assets, but you exchanged one for another. You also expect the bus to last 10 years, as you'll take good care of it and buses have a longer life expectancy than other vehicles. Therefore, using the straight-line method of depreciation, you need to expense 1/10 of the cost every year, or $4,000. You recognize that expense by a debit of $4,000 each year to depreciation. The offset would be to an account called accumulated depreciation. After one year, your bus would be worth only $36,000—your original investment minus the $4,000 depreciation expense for one year. In year two of owning the bus, you'll expense another $4,000 and your bus will be worth $32,000.

	A	B	C	D	E	F
Income:						
Fees per week	875	875	875	890	899	899
Average number of campers per week	150	155	165	170	170	171
Number of weeks	8	8	8	8	8	8
Special program fees (extra)	50	55	65	65	65	65
Number of participants	40	40	40	40	40	40
Total Income	**1,052,000**	**1,087,200**	**1,122,400**	**1,177,400**	**1,225,240**	**1,232,432**
Fixed Expenses:						
Administrative salaries/ benefits	375,000	375,000	375,000	375,000	375,000	375,000
Year-round maintenance salaries/benefits	118,750	118,750	118,750	118,750	118,750	118,750
Telephone	4,800	4,800	4,800	4,800	4,800	4,800
Occupancy	75,000	75,000	75,000	75,000	75,000	75,000
Insurance	13,000	13,000	13,000	13,000	13,000	13,000
Equipment (noncapital)	5,000	5,000	5,000	5,000	5,000	5,000
Marketing	15,000	15,000	15,000	15,000	15,000	15,000
Conferences/training	20,000	20,000	20,000	20,000	20,000	20,000
Membership dues	1,500	1,500	1,500	1,500	1,500	1,500
Accreditation fees	3,000	3,000	3,000	3,000	3,000	3,000
Depreciation	26,500	26,500	26,500	26,500	26,500	26,500
Subtotals	**657,550**	**657,550**	**657,550**	**657,550**	**657,550**	**657,550**
Variable Expenses:						
Salaries and benefits	207,000	213,900	220,800	227,700	234,600	235,980
Food supplies	127,750	105,607	109,013	112,420	115,827	116,508
Program supplies	90,000	93,000	96,000	99,000	102,000	102,600
Awards and shirts	18,000	18,600	19,200	19,800	20,400	20,520
Profit	84,160	86,976	89,792	94,192	98,019	98,595
Subtotals	**526,910**	**518,083**	**534,805**	**553,112**	**570,846**	**574,203**
Total Expenses	**1,184,460**	**1,175,633**	**1,192,355**	**1,210,662**	**1,228,396**	**1,231,753**
Gains/Losses	**(132,460)**	**(88,433)**	**(69,955)**	**(33,262)**	**(3,156)**	**679**

Assumptions:	
Staff benefits at 25%	Program supplies average $75 per camper
Telephone averages $400/month	Awards and shirts average $15 per camper
Occupancy averages $3,750/month	Desired 8% profit
Food averages $5 per meal	

Figure 13-2. Breakeven worksheet

By expensing this amount each year, you are also building up your cash because depreciation is a noncash expense. At the end of 10 years, your cash should have increased by $40,000 and you have enough cash to purchase another bus and start the whole process over again. Anything you depreciate is called a *capital expenditure*. It will be necessary to set a capitalization policy, which will include the threshold for capitalizing any equipment or other large purchases. Depending on the nature of the business, the threshold could be as little as $1,000 or as much as $100,000 or more. For camps, it may be that you want to capitalize any expenditure of $2,500 or more—as long as the fixed asset has a life span of at least five years. With that threshold and expected life span, a $2,500 asset would be depreciated $500 a year for five years, after which it's fully depreciated and theoretically worth nothing.

The Sample schedule of fixed assets in Figure 13-3 shows all depreciation calculated on the straight-line method over the anticipated life of the asset. Note that land is never depreciated and will always be carried on your books at the price you paid for it regardless of appreciated value. In this example, the fixed assets are divided into several different categories: buildings, furnishings, other fixed assets, and equipment, in addition to land. It's also important to note which assets are fully depreciated and/or taken out of service.

Financial Statements

By using a chart of accounts and booking a debit and credit for every transaction, you'll have an audit trail of all your financial transactions that can be further organized into an income statement, owner's equity, and the balance sheet. The income statement (also known as the *profit and loss statement or the operating statement*) and balance sheet (also known as the *statement of financial position*) are important financial statements you will want to review every single month. The balance sheets list by category all your assets, all your liabilities, and the owner's equity and retained earnings. Nonprofits will have a fund balance, or net assets, instead of owner's equity. The income statements list by category all your revenues and all your expenses. Most people want to look at their income statement in comparison with their budget. After a while, instead of reviewing every transaction, you will simply look at the audit trail or general ledger at month end to see the detail of the transaction, the income statement to determine if you have more income than expenses, and your balance sheet to see your cash position. If you are borrowing money or making a financed purchase (equipment or vehicle) for your camp, the lender will want to see your income statement and balance sheet. If your camp accepts credit cards, the lender will also ask to see your income statements and balance sheets on an annual basis as a condition of its services agreement.

Item #	Item	Serial Number or Type Const	Date in Service	New or Used	Life Span	Original Cost	Accumulated Depreciation at 12/31/2012	Depreciated Value as of 12/31/2012	Depreciation Expense for 2013	Accumulated Depreciation at 12/31/2013	Depreciated Value as of 12/31/2013	Scheduled Replacement Date	Notes
	Land												
101	Land, 300 acres	n/a	1990		n/a	300,000		300,000			300,000	n/a	
	Subtotal for Land					300,000		300,000			300,000		
	Buildings												
201	Director's cabin, 800 square feet	Native stone	1990		40	80,000	44,000	36,000	2,000	46,000	34,000	2030	
202	Maintenance building, 1,500 square feet	Metal	1990		40	112,500	61,875	50,625	2,813	64,688	47,813	2030	
203	Program building, 1,800 square feet	Metal	1991		30	144,000	110,400	33,600	4,800	115,200	28,800	2021	
204	Pool equipment house	Hollow tile	1991		40	20,000	11,500	8,500	500	12,000	8,000	2031	
205	Pool restrooms and office	Frame with stone	1991		40	25,000	14,375	10,625	625	15,000	10,000	2031	
206	Cabin 1: 2,000 square feet	Frame with stone	1992		40	170,000	85,000	85,000	4,250	89,250	80,750	2032	
207	Cabin 2: 2,000 square feet	Frame with stone	1992		40	170,000	85,000	85,000	4,250	89,250	80,750	2032	
208	Cabin 3: 2,500 square feet	Frame with stone	1993		40	217,500	103,313	114,188	5,438	108,750	108,750	2033	
209	Dining Hall: 4,000 square feet	Native stone	1995		40	1,100,000	467,500	632,500	27,500	495,000	605,000	2035	
210	Director's cabin roof	Composition	2012		25	4,500	–	4,500	180	180	4,320	2037	
	Subtotal for Buildings					2,043,500	982,963	1,060,538	52,355	1,035,318	1,008,183		

Figure 13-3. Sample schedule of fixed assets

Item #	Item	Serial Number or Type Const	Date in Service	New or Used	Life Span	Original Cost	Accumulated Depreciation at 12/31/2012	Depreciated Value as of 12/31/2012	Depreciation Expense for 2013	Accumulated Depreciation at 12/31/2013	Depreciated Value as of 12/31/2013	Scheduled Replacement Date	Notes
	Furnishings and Fixtures												
301	Director's cabin furniture		1990	New	30	2,500	1,833	667	83	1,917	583	2020	
302	Program Building, 160 chairs and 20 tables		1991	New	30	5,000	3,500	1,500	167	3,667	1,333	2021	
303	36 beds (cabins A, B & C) at 80 each	Wooden	1992	New	50	2,880	1,152	1,728	58	1,210	1,670	2042	
304	36 mattresses at 75 each	4"	1992	New	10	2,700	2,700	–	–	2,700	–	2002	Still in use
305	Dining Hall: 240 chairs and 30 tables		1995	New	30	15,000	8,500	6,500	500	9,000	6,000	2025	
	Subtotal for Furnishings					28,080	17,685	10,395	808	18,493	9,587		
	Other Fixed Assets												
401	Roads through main camp	1.5 miles	1990		40	50,000	27,500	22,500	1,250	28,750	21,250	2030	
402	Water well		1990		25	50,000	44,000	6,000	2,000	46,000	4,000	2015	
403	Water lines		1990		30	13,750	13,750	3,667	458	10,542	3,208	2020	
404	Swimming pool		1991		20	20,000	20,000	–	–	20,000	–	2011	Still in use
405	Pool fence	Black chain link	1991		20	8,000	8,400	(400)	400	8,800	(800)	2011	Still in use
406	Fence at entry and sign	Stone	1991		50	12,500	5,000	7,500	250	5,250	7,250	2041	
407	Roads–extended to south camp	2.25 miles	2000		20	25,000	15,000	10,000	1,250	16,250	8,750	2020	
	Total Other Fixed Assets					179,250	129,983	49,267	5,608	135,592	43,658		

Figure 13-3. Sample schedule of fixed assets (cont.)

Item #	Item	Serial Number or Type Const	Date in Service	New or Used	Life Span	Original Cost	Accumulated Depreciation at 12/31/2012	Depreciated Value as of 12/31/2012	Depreciation Expense for 2013	Accumulated Depreciation at 12/31/2013	Depreciated Value as of 12/31/2013	Scheduled Replacement Date	Notes
	Equipment												
501	Tractor: Kubota with attachments	123W9 87X76	1990	Used	15	7,500	7,500	–	–	–	–	2005	Still in use as secondary
502	Tractor attachment mower	57893	1990	Used	15	inc	–	–	–	–	–	2005	Still in use as secondary
503	Tractor attachment box blade	802BC	1990	Used	15	inc	–	–	–	–	–	2005	Still in use as secondary
504	~~Pool equipment~~		1991		RETIR-ED		–					~~2011~~	Replaced in 2011—kept motor for emergencies
505	10 Grumman canoes at 750/each	aluminum	1992	New	25	7,500	6,000	1,500	300	6,300	1,200	2017	
506	Tractor: Kubota with attachments	789E78W 7890	2005	New	25	15,000	4,200	10,800	600	4,800	10,200	2030	
507	Tractor attachment mower	890-72	2005	New	25	3,000	840	2,160	120	960	2,040	2030	
508	Pool equipment		2011	New	20	30,000	10,500	19,500	1,500	12,000	18,000	2031	
	Total Equipment					63,000	29,040	33,960	2,520	24,060	31,440		
	Total Fixed Assets					2,613,830	1,159,671	1,454,159	61,291	1,213,462	1,392,868		
	Equipment Retired/ Removed											Date Retired	
504	Pool equipment		1991	New	20	15,000	–					2011	Fully depreciated at retirement

Figure 13-3. Sample schedule of fixed assets (cont.)

Financial Ratios

Financial ratios are a direct indication of the ability of items on the balance sheet to make money for you. They are primarily used for comparison purposes and may be quite important to bankers or investors. While numerous financial ratios can compare any financial statistics, a few are more common than others and will be more likely important for a camp business.

For example, liquidity ratios can show a business's ability to meet its short-term financial obligations or, more simply, the availability of cash to cover accounts payable and other debts and liabilities. For a camp business, the current ratio would be used (Figure 13-4).

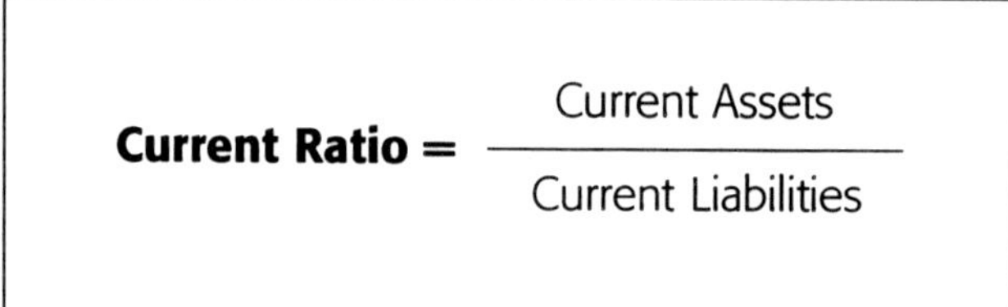

Figure 13-4. The current ratio

A high current ratio is preferred by creditors because it reduces their risk. A current ratio of 1:1 or >1 shows that you have at least one dollar of current assets for every dollar of current debt. "Current" is generally defined as within a year.

The most conservative ratio of liquidity is the cash ratio, which excludes all current assets except the most liquid, which are cash and cash equivalents (Figure 13-5).

$$\textbf{Cash Ratio} = \frac{\text{Cash + Marketable Securities}}{\text{Current Liabilities}}$$

Figure 13-5. The cash ratio

The ability to pay off current liabilities if needed is shown by the cash ratio. The long-term solvency of a business can be measured by financial leverage ratios, also defined as the extent to which a company has depended upon borrowing to finance its operations. While liquidity ratios are concerned with short-term assets and liabilities, financial leverage ratios show the use of long-term debt by the debt ratio (Figure 13-6).

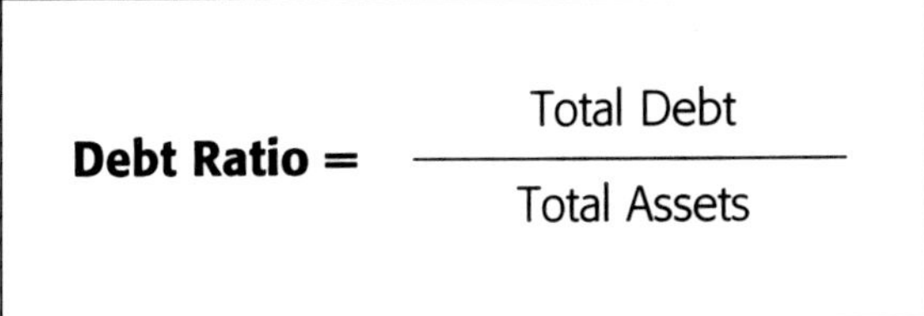

Figure 13-6. The debt ratio

A debt ratio greater than 1.0 signifies that the company is technically bankrupt and has a negative net worth. Profitability ratios indicate how well the company is using the resources of the business. One particularly useful profitability ratio is the return on assets, which measures how effective the camp is at generating a profit (Figure 13-7).

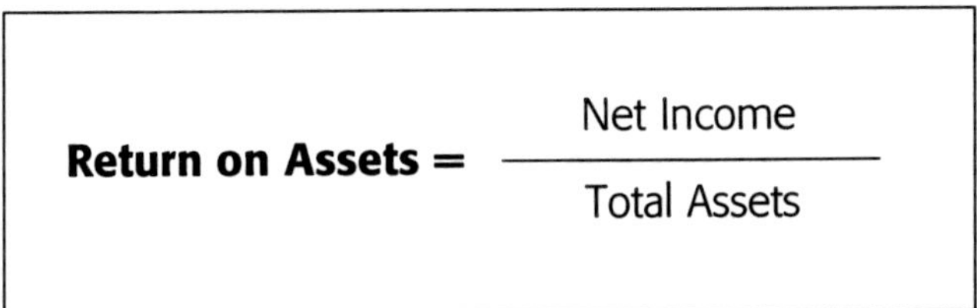

Figure 13-7. The return on assets

A low return on asset (ROA) usually indicates inefficiency, whereas a high ROA means efficient management. These numbers can be distorted by any unusual expenses and/or depreciation.

It is helpful to have historical data so the camp's ratios can be compared over time. By themselves, ratios don't mean much, but they can be viewed as indicators and taken together can be helpful. Numerous other ratios are used in accounting, but these would likely be helpful for a camp in analyzing your financial position over time.

Accounting Software

Assuming you have determined your fiscal year when you set up the camp as a business, it will be necessary to purchase an accounting software package and either learn how to use it or hire someone to maintain your financial records. Two well-known basic software packages are QuickBooks® and Sage 50® (formerly Peachtree®), although many different accounting packages are available for small businesses.

Larger operations may want to invest in midrange packages that feature more robust functionality and support more users, such as Sage 50 Quantum Accounting 2014, Netsuite® ERP, Intacct®, or QuickBooks Enterprise. Camp owners and directors will need to work with their accountant to determine if on-premises software or Software as a Service (SaaS—also known as cloud computing) is the best option for your situation. In addition, some camps may want to look at accounting systems that are also integrated with contact management software. Two good sources to check software reviews are *PC Magazine* and CPAPracticeAdvisor.com. As with most technology products, the landscape is constantly changing when it comes to accounting software, so a thorough search in consultation with your accountant is the best advice.

Accounting Policies

Through your accounting system, you are developing a method to communicate information about your business to your investors and/or managers. But your business must also establish accounting policies that conform with generally accepted accounting principles. Some of the policies you will need include capitalization–the level at which you'll capitalize purchases and expense them over time through depreciation–and revenue recognition–when you'll recognize revenue for fees.

Internal Control System

Your system of internal control will provide guidance to your employees on how you expect them to handle various situations involving money or other assets as well as help protect against fraud. Following are some sample internal controls:

- All mail will be opened by the office assistant, who will make a daily prelist of checks that arrive through the mail. This prelist will be compared to the daily deposit.
- Deposits shall not be made by the same person who is responsible for writing checks.
- The persons signing or approving checks will not enter the payables or receivables into the accounting system.
- Extra check stock shall be stored in a locked closet, with access available to only the accounting supervisor.
- Petty cash shall be kept in a locked drawer and dispensed only upon presentation of a petty cash request form with receipt attached. The maximum amount available for petty cash reimbursements is $25.00.
- Checks will be written every Thursday for distribution on Friday.
- All purchase orders shall be approved by the budget manager.
- All employees will be paid by direct deposit every other week.
- The pay period begins on Friday and continues through the second Thursday, totaling 14 calendar days. Payroll direct deposits will be made on the following Friday–six days after the pay period ends.
- All items with an original cost of at least $2,500 and a useful life of at least five years will be considered fixed assets. A schedule of fixed assets shall be maintained that includes the asset, brand, and serial number (if applicable), location, original cost, life expectancy, annual depreciation, and accumulated depreciation (recorded in the fixed asset journal and assigned a useful life). Depreciation will be calculated using the straight-line method.

The breadth and depth of internal controls for your camp will depend on your own circumstances. Because many camp businesses are small and seasonal, the likelihood of having a large administrative staff is unlikely. As a result, it will be up to you the owner/director to set the policies that make the most sense for your business, and in most instances, the processes will require your involvement. Polices and controls should include the following:

- Who has permission to use the company credit card? In working with your bank, you should have set up a company account and if necessary issued key staff personnel their own company credit card. What are the spending limits you've placed on their individual cards and what classification of items needs your approval (office supplies versus large capital expenditures)?
- While the use of petty cash should be limited, who other than yourself has access?
- Who has signature authority on your checking accounts?

In this aspect of accounting controls, many of the functions will fall upon you as the owner/director and you need to be intimately involved with this process. Of course, you trust your employees, but this is your money and you have a fiduciary responsibility to your bank or investors to make sure your financial assets are managed correctly.

Payroll

Payroll is a critical financial control system that must be managed effectively. If you ever get the feeling as a camp owner/director that much of your work goes unnoticed, fail to issue a paycheck to a counselor on payday and see how quickly you're noticed! Correctly paying your employees on time—in the correct amounts—and ensuring that all the appropriate tax information is not only the ethical thing to do, but you are also legally required to do it. Additionally, delegating payroll responsibilities to another employee in a small business can be tricky. As the administrator for your company payroll, you are being trusted with a variety of sensitive employee information and you may not feel comfortable (nor will your employees) sharing that information with anyone.

With today's tax code, issuing payroll is a complex task. Between the Federal Unemployment Tax Act (FUTA), the State Unemployment Tax Act (SUTA), FICA, social security, state social security, Medicare, and many other forms of withholding, making sure you are collecting the correct tax amount from your employees requires great attention to detail. In addition, as the employer, you're responsible for paying a variety of these payroll-based taxes (941s at the state and federal level—just to name one) that need to be paid on time or risk a steep financial penalty. Multiply all these activities by the number of employees you have working for you, plus all the other responsibilities you have during the summer, and payroll can be a time consuming activity.

While software is available to assist you with your payroll needs on your own, many camps utilize payroll service companies that rely on Windows®-based platforms to organize your payroll into a convenient spreadsheet where all that is required is for you to input the gross weekly pay or salary of the employee. You input and update personal information for each employee and you're the only one who makes updates or changes. For a small business, it allows you to be in control of the process without getting hampered by the day-to-day demands of calculating everything yourself.

Once you have communicated the weekly gross pay for each employee, the payroll company then issues paychecks or direct deposits, makes the necessary tax payments to the appropriate taxing authorities, and issues a ledger statement for your records. They take care of any quarterly payment and reporting requirements, and at the end of the year, they will also assist you with issuing W-2 statements to your employees. They are also responsible for any payment of any penalties that result from incorrectly reported or late quarterly tax payments. Payroll companies do charge a fee, generally two to three dollars per paycheck and four to five dollars per W-2, but compared to the penalties for incorrectly reporting or late payments, the fees charged are relatively nominal. With the time and attention required for reporting payroll, payroll services are certainly a financial control tool that should be considered.

Basic Accounting Principles

Generally accepted accounting principles (GAAP) are established by the Financial Accounting Standards Board (FASB) to provide for consistency across all types of businesses. Some of the GAAP principles that are important for business owners to know when presenting information statements of any kind include the following:

- *Materiality:* Is the information significant to the business?
- *Comparability:* Are you consistent, comparing the information from one year to another or from one entity to another?
- *Matching:* In accrual accounting, costs are matched to revenue so you have a cause and an effect. You don't want to overstate or understate either revenue or expenses that don't align within the same time period.
- *Fair value:* Any time you assign a value to a contribution or service, it should reflect current market value.

Audits

Another good business practice is to have an annual audit of your financial records by an independent accountant. Not only will this be helpful (and sometimes required) should you want to establish a business line of credit or seek financing, auditors will also analyze your internal controls and look at your business practices, making recommendations that will improve your business. Depending on the size of your budget, you may be required by some outside entities to have a review or a compilation—both of which are less costly to have done than an audit. Nonprofits will find that most grantors and potential funders will require an annual audit as well as a copy of the nonprofit's IRS Form 990.

Budgets

One of the most important tools for financial management of any business is a budget. Most accounting software will include a module for budgeting, but some camps may want to use spreadsheet software, such as Excel, to develop your budget. Given the seasonal nature of most camps, it will be helpful to prepare not just an annual budget but an annual budget divided by month.

A budget is a financial plan and a best practice that camp owners and directors will want to consider is the preparation of a budget that is generally based on past experiences and projected targets. It will not only track your income and expenses, but it will also help you plan for the future and economize when needed. In developing your budget, you'll have to make some assumptions about income and expenses. The first thing to know is your capacity and it must consider several factors.

How Many Campers Can You Accommodate?

For some camp owners and directors, this is simply the number of beds (less beds for staff) times the number of weeks you operate. For day camp owners, this would be the number of campers you will allow per camp group, taking into consideration allowable camper staff ratios or facility capacity. However, assume you have 10 cabins, each with 12 beds–two for staff and 10 for campers. But you pride yourself on having a lower counselor-to-camper ratio for younger campers and you don't mix ages of campers in the same cabin. You have always said that your capacity was 100 campers per week: 10 cabins times 10 campers. But it's not. Figure 13-8 presents several possibilities for determining your capacity depending on the age mix of campers.

		A		B		C		D		E	
Camper's Age	**Maximum Number of Campers per Cabin**	**Number of Campers**	**Number of Cabins**	**Number of Campers**	**Number of Cabins**	**Number of Campers**	**Number of Cabins**	**Number of Campers**	**Number of Cabins**	**Number of Campers**	**Number of Cabins**
6 to 8 years old	6	18	3	12	2	12	2	12	2	12	2
9 to 11 years old	8	32	4	32	4	40	5	40	5	32	4
12 to 15 years old	10	50	5	60	6	50	5	40	4	40	4
Total:		100	12	104	12	102	12	92	11	84	10

Figure 13-8. Determining the maximum number of campers per cabin

Looking at these scenarios, scenario A gives you your expected 100 campers, but you only have 10 cabins, so something is wrong with the mix of ages. Scenarios B and C are different mixes, but you still don't have enough cabins. Scenario D is getting closer—but still not enough cabins. Only in scenario E do you have enough cabin space, but you can only accept 84 campers, not 100, which will severely impact your total income. You have some choices: Accept fewer younger campers, start mixing ages, and build more cabins so you can accept 100 campers a week or realize that with a mix like you have, you can't take more than 84 campers.

That's when it's time to start thinking outside the box. What if you bought tents for the oldest campers? Or charged different amounts for different ages? Or limited the number of younger campers? Or accepted younger campers only certain weeks? You can solve this in numerous ways, but the bottom line is that without any changes, you can have a maximum of 84 campers per week given the mix of ages and your counselor-to-cabin ratio.

Thus, you now have the first and probably most important assumption for your budget: You have a maximum of 84 campers per week. Based on your marketing plan, you feel confident you'll come close to your maximum, but you're not quite confident enough to put 84 campers per week in your budget. You go with 80. You may have a little more miscellaneous income, but you're mainly relying on fees.

Next, look at each line item on the expense side. In many camp programs are three major expense groups: personnel, supplies, and occupancy. For personnel, you'll have to determine the following things:

- How many staff do you need? (Remember, you're assuming a maximum of 84 campers.)
- How much will you pay your staff?
- How many weeks will they work? One extra week prior to the campers' arrival for pre-camp training? Extra days to clean up camp after the campers leave?
- What will the staff benefits cost? Will you provide only the required benefits (FICA, Medicare, unemployment) or will you include anything else?
- What kind of coverage do you need when some staff members have time off?
- Will you use junior counselors or program activity specialists?
- What other staff do you need—cooks, nurse, maintenance?

If you're a day camp director, the process listed would be very similar. While you would not be addressing concerns with the number of available camper beds, you would be concerned with structuring groups that have low enough camper-to-staff ratios that allow you to accomplish your mission. If you are operating a camp that's known for low ratios and personal connections, you would want to staff accordingly. You will also need to take into consideration the required ratio for campers as determined by American Camp Association accreditation or other regulatory requirements.

A Final Note About Staffing

Consider that an extra staff person can cost you a lot less than a camper who will not return next summer. You do need to manage your staffing expenses, but don't do it at the risk, reducing the quality of your program. The money saved on an extra counselor or two will pale in comparison to the lost revenue of an unhappy camp family.

Line-Item Expenses

For supplies, you'll need to consider all the different types of supplies: food (average cost per meal times number of staff and campers), program supplies (which will depend on the programs you offer), household supplies, office supplies, and so forth.

For occupancy, you might have a different set of questions, including the following:

- Do you have historical data on utility costs for summer? Does your contract with an electric utility provider provide for a rate more or less than you paid last year? Can you take the average number of kilowatt hours and calculate this year's anticipated charges?
- What are your fixed costs for occupancy—for example, property insurance? Do you have a mortgage payment?
- Do you rent any space?
- How much do you anticipate needing for repairs?

Each line item will have specific questions you must answer and assumptions you must make. One way to handle all these lines and assumptions is to set up an Excel workbook, with different spreadsheets for each line item that automatically total and link to a budget form on another spreadsheet. Then, as you change your assumptions, your budget will automatically update.

After you make all your assumptions, drop in the number of weeks or months you have expenses, multiply everything, and then add all the expense lines together, you'll have your first estimate of total expenses you can compare to your income estimate, taking the 80 campers per week and multiplying by your proposed rate. Of course, if you give any discounts—for early registration, siblings, or staff children—then you'll need to keep those in mind too.

Remember that in your expenses, you'll need to include not just summer staff but also year-round staff. Are you expecting your summer income to cover all your year-round expenses? If your camp is part of a larger organization, how much overhead will you need to include?

If your first draft of next year's budget is typical, you will probably have more expenses than income. Thus, back to the drawing board—and time for more questions and more assumptions, including the following:

- Should you increase the rate per camper each week? How do your fees compare to other camps' fees?
- Should you adjust the personnel costs?
- Did you overestimate any expenses?

Basically, to balance your budget, you have several choices: Raise your income, cut your expenses, increase the number of campers (but what effect will that have on your expenses?), eliminate some expenses altogether, or go back to your outside-the-box thinking exercise—that temporary yurt or those large tents to accommodate more campers may be sounding really good right now.

In the budgeting process, most camp owners and directors will find that it takes a while to develop a workable budget, adjusting fees or assumptions until you find the numbers that will make your budget work for you.

A Few Ways to Save Money

Zero-Based Budgeting

The simple way of budgeting expenses is to start with last year's expenses and then add a percentage to it. However, a better practice is to start with zero and determine what you need to pay. For example, if your electric service has been $0.11 per kilowatt hour and you've been happy with the provider, that's fine. But what if you could get the same service for less than $0.10 per kilowatt hour? By starting with zero and shopping the market, you may find that you have considerable savings—all because you started over in looking for an electricity provider. However, remember that not everything changes on the first day of your fiscal year. Be sure to calculate the proper number of months at the old rate and the remaining number of months at the new rate.

Electric services are one of the easiest things to negotiate, with rates changing often and companies offering introductory packages or deals of the month almost all the time. By shopping the market, camps can realize savings that make a huge difference. If your electricity expenses average $4,000 per month, that's $48,000 a year. A 10 percent savings would go right to the bottom line—your profit. Who wouldn't take an extra $5,000 in profit for spending a few days working on your electricity contract?

Insurance Options

The same principles can be applied to numerous other purchases. For example, insurance may be one of your larger ticket items. Shopping the insurance market does not necessarily mean changing brokers or agents, although that can happen. A good agent will shop the market each year and present you with an unbiased analysis of the market for you. Granted, the camp insurance market is relatively small, but savings are available and negotiating points can be made with your current carrier as the result of your agent's market analysis. Your insurance agent can shop the market based on your experience, your claims history, and your risk management plans. Some insurance companies will give camps discounts because of American Camp Association accreditation as well as other professional certifications and affiliations.

Perhaps the greatest opportunity for insurance savings on an annual basis is with your workers' compensation policies. The workers' compensation insurance market is fairly competitive, and unless you have a poor record of claims for workers' compensation, you can usually negotiate a significant savings each year. You can also save substantially by auditing your policies to make sure you're correctly paying your policy based on job classifications.

Workers' compensation policies are based on your camp payroll by job classification. Each job class is assigned a multiplier based on your loss rating (by job class) as well as the loss rating for that job class on an overall basis. Depending on your state, employees who primarily work maintenance functions have a higher risk factor (due to claims and injuries) and multiplier than general camp counselors. In some states, all camp employees are assigned to the higher classification. Staff who are assigned primarily transportation functions also have significantly higher risk factors. You can analyze your workers' compensation policy by job type and payroll to make sure you're being correctly charged your premium.

Another way to save money on insurance is to look at your deductible. Ask your agent to quote not just $1,000 in deductibles but also $5,000 and $10,000. The more you are willing to pay in deductibles, the lower your overall premium. At the $10,000 rate, you're self-insuring for that amount but will probably save significantly over the policy with a $1,000 deductible.

Financing insurance is an option that will probably cost you money, but you may need to spend a little to preserve your cash flow. If you're paying $40,000 or $50,000 for insurance, ask your agent about any discounts for paying all at once if that is an option for you. For other big ticket items, ask about discounts for paying up front—whether for the purchase of supplies, equipment, or services—or for paying in full within a certain number of days.

Paying Just in Time

Vendors may quote their terms as "2%/10 net 30" or "1%/5 net 10," for example, where the first number represents the percent discount (in the first case, two percent) if paid before the 10th day after the invoice date. Otherwise, the entire amount is due within 30 days of the invoice date. The second example is a one percent discount if paid by five days after the date of the invoice, with the full amount due within 10 days of the invoice date. If cash flow permits, it's always good to take the discount. However, some vendors will specify "due upon receipt," which is a request for immediate payment with no option for discount.

The Power of "No"

Whether you're dealing with an employee who is submitting a budget request or a vendor, you have tremendous power in saying "No" to the first amount requested or the first price offered. Shop everything. While you typically tend to think of big purchases when it comes to shopping the best deal, you need to consider how much you could save on everything, especially items you use continually. Is your grocery supplier giving you the best price or could you save an extra $200 per week by shopping yourself at a warehouse club? Sure, the delivery from your present supplier is convenient, but is it worth an extra $1,600 for the summer for the service? Look at all your purchases. Do you have other options that can save you money over the course of a year or are you getting the best value for your money? Even if you have a longtime vendor, it's your money and you have the opportunity to get a better price. Negotiate and ask questions. If they are giving you a price increase of three to four percent while you're holding your prices steady, ask them why.

The larger the order, the more you can ask for some help in reducing the costs. You may want to ask for free shipping, which can be a tremendous savings, or a quantity discount or an early payment discount. If you're located near another camp or camps, consider forming your own purchasing group. If a wholesaler has the opportunity to sell to multiple customers with a minimum of delivery costs, it may be willing to offer you preferential pricing. As with anything else, it's your money and your business. Don't look at cost savings in the short term but rather in the long-term exponential savings that you could realize by negotiating a little harder.

Reducing Prices by Doing Some of the Work

The camp business can be a do-it-yourself business if you or your staff have the necessary skill sets or you're willing to learn to do a few things for yourself. From facility maintenance to creating your own marketing materials, you have many things you can do in house to save you significant amounts of money. For example, instead of outsourcing printed materials through conventional printing sources, utilizing a web-based provider and a little computer work (and possibly learning on your part) can yield a professional product at a fraction of the cost. In other cases, you can negotiate a price that includes materials, labor, and installation or just the cost of the goods on their own. For example, if you're ordering furniture and your vendor has quoted you a price that includes unloading all the pieces and putting the furniture together, ask if you can get a better price if you unload and put the furniture together yourself. The whole experience could be a fantastic teambuilding exercise—and you might end up with employees who have a much better appreciation for those new tables and chairs if they had a hand in putting them together—all the while saving some dollars.

Understandably, not everyone will have the skills necessary to do every task at camp, but you can always learn. For learning office and administrative functions, most public libraries offer classes on basic computer training. If you're looking for more technical skills when using more complex software programs, community colleges can be an excellent resource. Usually, the costs for taking these classed will be nominal and you will have learned a skill that can be used continually.

If you or your staff would like to save money by performing facility maintenance tasks on your own, don't overlook trusted vendors you've utilized for those tasks in the past. From equipment maintenance to winterizing your pool, most of the people you've been doing business with are usually more than happy to help you learn. If you do need to hire someone to have a repair done, watch the technician while he's making the repair and don't be afraid to ask questions. Skills learned by watching an expert can always be used in the future. Finally, use technology! YouTube and Google are amazing resources for learning how to do just about anything. Multiple descriptions are offered on just about every topic, they usually have a video that shows you how to do it, and, best of all, they're free!

Bartering

It may be old fashioned, but it can still work. Trade a week at camp for a repair or service you need. The thing to keep in mind, though, is that you get to pick the week, which obviously needs to be one that's harder to fill.

In a similar fashion, some camps have work weekends, so offer a weekend of family camping in return for a weekend of work. Some of the most successful are in the spring, when camps need some basic spring cleaning. A family camping weekend might also provide your summer staff members with an opportunity to practice some of their skills with families before trying them out on campers.

Financial Statement Reviews

A thorough and careful review of financial statements (including income statements, balance sheets, and cash flow statements) on a monthly or, at a minimum, quarterly basis is essential to help you manage your finances. One good way to review the statements includes looking at the monthly and/or year-to-date budget and income statement, along with the variance between the two. Most accountants or bookkeepers should be able to produce a monthly statement within a week to 10 days after the close of the month. Comparing your monthly income and expenditures to your budget requires diligence and discipline, but it's crucial to the success of a business.

Camp owners and directors should also consider sharing appropriate income information with key staff as direction to them and as a measurement of income and expenses compared to a budget. Employees who are responsible for various cost centers—whether it be food service, maintenance, or program—should be encouraged to take an active role in the control of not just expenditures but also the income for their department or area of responsibility. If you set up the camp chart of accounts carefully, accounting software can generally produce income statements by cost center or department, allowing camp management to drill down on income and expenses.

Cash Flow

In most new businesses, cash flow is even more important than profits. Income can be recorded not just as cash but also as receivables—and receivables can't pay for expenses. It will be important for camp executives, like any small business owner, to manage cash flow, developing a strategy for how much cash will be set aside for emergencies and how much can be used to pay for regular expenses. An income statement may be misleading when it comes to cash, so developing a cash flow projection will be important.

To develop a cash flow projection, set up a spreadsheet with "Sources of Cash" and list all incoming cash, including fees, interest, and balances in your checking accounts as well as any other sources of cash. This will be your total cash available. Next, set up "Operating Uses of Cash" for all the day-to-day expenditures you'll be paying for, most of which will be on your income statement under expenses. The third section will be "Nonoperating Uses of Cash" and will include items that normally show up on your balance sheet, such as equipment purchases, loan payments, taxes, and the owner's draw. Subtract the uses of cash from cash available and you'll have your ending cash for the month, which then becomes your opening cash for the next period.

For a business like camp that is seasonal, you may want to project your cash for an entire year at a time, noting when you'll have additional payrolls and other expenses. This will help you determine if you need to establish a line of credit or if you need to set up early payment plans to increase your off-season cash flow—or both.

Establishing a schedule for beginning registration to collect camper deposits and improve cash flow is a critical first step. Noncamp months can create a strain on camp cash flows, as you're living off the previous summer's camper fees. Instead of collecting registrations in February or March, why not September or October? Starting registration earlier will give you not only a better cash flow during the winter months but also assist you in making accurate projections for the next summer with regards to staffing and other critical financial areas of managing your camp. Also, instead of collecting a nominal deposit of $50 or $100, consider higher deposit levels. For example, if your camp tuition is $1,500 or more, asking for a deposit commitment of $250 or $500 is certainly not out of line. Of course, you do need to consider outside factors, such as what's customary in your marketplace and what competitor policies are, but you also need to do what's best for your business and has the best effect on your cash flow and your bottom line. Also, *put your refund policies in writing* and include them with your registration materials so your customers know what portion if any of the deposit and/or fee is refundable and up until what time period prior to camp.

Start-Up Cost Considerations for New Camps

Owners and directors of new camps will need to look carefully at their start-up costs, which will fall into three categories:

- *One-time expenses:* legal fees, purchase of land or construction of buildings (if applicable), equipment, licenses
- *Recurring costs:* utilities, payroll, insurance
- *Hidden costs:* costs for things you did not anticipate, so a contingency of at least 10 percent is generally recommended

If your camp is operating only in the summer as you begin, then you have additional challenges because some of your expenses (for example, payroll and utilities) will be year-round, but your income will primarily be only in the summer.

Cash Flow and Payroll

For those with year-round employees, remember that if you are paying employees every two weeks, as many employers do, two months will have three payrolls, not two. The months of three payrolls will vary from year to year, but don't be caught short because a total of 26 payrolls occur every year for biweekly employers—and every 10 or 11 years will be 27 payrolls, with three months of three payrolls.

Investments

It doesn't take large sums of money to have enough to invest. If your cash flow is such that you have extra cash at various times of the year, consider investing. A good investment advisor or financial planner can provide you with personalized advice to put your money to work. The Securities and Exchange Commission suggests that you ask the following questions when considering an investment advisor:

- Are you registered with the state securities regulator? Have you ever been disciplined by the SEC of the state?
- How long has your firm been in business?
- What training and experience do you have?
- What's your investment philosophy?
- Have you or your firm ever been involved in arbitration?
- How do you get paid? By commission? Fees? Other methods?
- How frequently do I receive statements?
- Is the return on my investment meeting my expectations and goals? (Securities and Exchange Commission, 2007)

If you need assistance in finding a financial planner, check the Certified Financial Planner Board of Standards' website at www.letsmakeaplan.org. You can search by ZIP code, investable assets, or specialty of the planner. It's never too early to look at your long-term business and personal plans.

Receivables

In addition, a good financial strategy will include how to manage receivables, although most camps require payment prior to delivery of services, which eliminates receivables. For most summer camps, income is collected in the winter (deposits for summer sessions) and spring (final payments). Some camps will increase their cash flow in the fall by offering registration discounts for families who pay for the following summer in the fall and some will advertise next year's camp at this year's rate.

Types of Income Payments

Camps will also need to determine what types of payment will be accepted. Many families now expect to register and pay online, so it will be necessary to set up a merchant account to receive credit card payments. This can be through a local bank, a bank determined by the supplier of the camp registration software, or a merchant services company. Banks typically charge different fees (known as *interchange fees*) to merchants for accepting different types of cards (primarily Visa®, MasterCard®, Discover®, and American Express®) as well as different fees for accepting a debit card versus a credit card. Credit cards are a necessary cost of business, but you need to shop your credit card provider carefully. If you've shopped well, your fees will probably range from two to three percent of the amount charged. However, some merchants may have a premium rate for "status" cards, such as gold cards or other card accounts that offer incentives. Even though you may not be aware of what cards your customer is using because it's a remote transaction, you could end up paying an even higher rate. In addition, the average ticket price may also have an effect on the fees that camps pay for accepting credit cards. Generally, greater fees are charged when a card isn't physically present, so telephone or Internet transactions may cost you as the merchant more to process.

Prior to 2013, merchants were not allowed to add a surcharge to customers for using credit cards. With the change in 2013, federal regulations now limit the amount of the surcharge, and in some states, surcharges aren't allowed at all. According to Consumer Action, retailer surcharges or "checkout fees" are not allowed in California, Colorado, Connecticut, Florida, Kansas, Maine, Massachusetts, New York, Oklahoma, and Texas (Consumer Action, 2012). Merchant interchange fees are typically between 1.5 and 3 percent. Checkout fees are not allowed for debit cards. In lieu of surcharges, some merchants give a discount to customers who pay by cash, check, or debit card. Your bank or merchant services company should make you aware of the laws and regulations that are in effect in your location. Also, review your merchant account on at least a yearly basis to monitor your charges and negotiate a better rate if possible through your merchant account provider.

Your bank or merchant services provider will also have the equipment you need to accept credit cards, including swipers, PIN pad terminals, and other types of equipment. You should have the option to purchase or rent the equipment and to purchase from another source. Some merchant services providers will also have proprietary software that can be integrated with your accounting or registration software.

Some customers still prefer to pay by check. Many banks now offer desktop deposits, known as remote deposit capture (RDC), which allows the camp to scan checks and deposit them to a bank account remotely. This is generally a much quicker and safer way to make deposits, although limits may exist as to how many checks can be deposited remotely. Your bank can make recommendations as to how long you keep the actual check and how you indicate that it has been deposited. RDC generally allows the business quicker access to deposited funds. Also available are mobile banking applications, which allow businesses to take a cell phone image of a check to deposit it.

You can also set up either one-time or recurring debits from a checking account. This could be particularly helpful for day camps, who may be charging by the week for multiple weeks.

Sales Tax

As noted in Chapter 8, state laws vary widely regarding whether camp fees are subject to sale tax. For those camps in states or locales that tax camp fees, note that the tax collected should be recorded on your books as an account payable (not income) because you're simply collecting funds that must then be transferred to the taxing authority. Check with your accountant or local officials to determine if camp fees are taxable in your locale.

Also, remember that your store sales will be taxable. Tax-exempt entities, such as nonprofit and faith-based camps, are *not* exempt from charging sales tax—only from paying it.

Records Retention

All small businesses need to retain certain records for tax or audit purposes, including all payroll records, such as timesheets, agreements, social security numbers, and tax returns themselves. More information about records retention is found in Chapter 8.

Solid financial management will be a key to your success as the executive of a camp. It's a complex subject—one that requires constant attention and monitoring of each aspect from accounts receivable to zero-based budgeting and everything in between. If you're not a "finance person" yet, you soon will be if you want to be successful in running a camp business.

14

Procurement and Purchasing Groups

Daniel Hurst/iStock/Thinkstock

Procurement is the acquisition of goods or services from an outside source. While having a specific procurement process is not required of small businesses, camps utilizing a procurement process can assure they are receiving the best pricing for the specified goods or services while also letting employees know what is expected of them when they make purchasing decisions on your behalf.

Federal and state governments have detailed guidelines regarding procurement, as do large businesses. The procurement process itself does not have to be cumbersome or long, but it should be thorough. When making major purchases, such as a car or a house, most people know what they are looking for, weigh their options carefully, and then negotiate a price. Developing a procurement process for camp is a way of formalizing what you would do for a large purchase and applying the same principles at different pricing levels.

The traditional method of procuring goods or services is to develop a request for proposals (RFP) and place an ad in your local newspaper or other sources, inviting suppliers or contractors to prepare a bid for the items or services you specify. Interested bidders would then complete a questionnaire that answers all your questions about the items you are seeking bids on, explains what their qualifications are for delivering the service or goods, and then provide you with a price. If you have been specific with your RFP, then you can compare quality, prices, and conditions from different vendors.

The benefit of having an established procurement process is that you allow more vendors to earn your business, you can reduce favoritism, you don't overlook vital information about the product or vendor that could come back and haunt you later, and, most importantly, you should save money by getting the best prices (but not necessarily the lowest prices). Your vendors will also know they are dealing with a professional organization. To develop a procurement process, start with the following questions:

- At what level is an RFP required?
- Who is authorized to require items to be purchased?
- Who is authorized to make purchases?
- How are vendors selected from whom you'll solicit bids?
- How will you select the vendor with whom you'll do business?
- What documentation will you require?
- How will you handle sole source purchases?

When to Require an RFP or Another Method of Purchasing

Not every purchase for camp will require an RFP and not every level of purchase will require multiple price comparisons. In fact, some levels of purchases may not even require approval of any sort before purchasing. Look at what you are buying to determine how you establish levels that require RFPs. Which items have historically been your largest purchases? Are you purchasing any capital equipment (items expensed over time through depreciation)? Do you have any construction projects?

You may want to pick an arbitrary number—for example, $5,000—and see what you have spent at that level or above and then look at whether it makes sense to obtain bids. Food is one category of goods where you should consider getting bids from multiple vendors if available. Printing could be another if you are printing camp brochures, stationery, cards, newsletters, and other items every year. Instead of looking at each item separately (such as the brochure and stationery), look at the category as a whole. If you promised all your business to one printer rather than shopping each time you need something printed, you might save money. If you have four or five categories of items where you spend $5,000 or more each year, consider making that your level for issuing RFPs and requiring formal bids.

Then, look at another level—perhaps at least $1,000 but less than $5,000—where you want to institute requiring written quotes but not necessarily doing a formal request for proposal.

A third level may exist—perhaps those items costing more than $100 but less than $1,000—where you simply want price comparisons—whether from catalogs, ads, or the Internet.

Finally, you may have a fourth level—anything under $100—where you decide that your designated purchasers have authority to buy without anything other than signature approval. For all the levels you set, determine if you want that level to apply to single items or to the aggregate of all items purchased from a vendor or at one time.

Your RFP should provide a clear, accurate description of the specifications of the goods or services to be procured. Specifications should not contain features that unduly restrict competition. This process is to help you get a better product, not to justify why you're buying from the vendor you have always used. You may need to use phrases such as "brand name or equal" to define what you are looking for.

Authorization of Purchase Requests, Approvals, and Purchasers

Camp owners and directors will want to identify—most likely by position—who on your staff is authorized to request that items be purchased. This may be everyone on your staff, with another level of staff authorized to approve the purchases, providing guidance on how much can be spent, whether a requested item is budgeted, and whether you have a contract with designated or approved vendors for certain products. Another group of individuals may be designated to actually make the purchase or initiate an RFP process. In a camp, the director or owner may want to approve all purchases.

Selecting Vendors

You can find potential vendors in numerous ways: through existing agreements or services, recommendations from colleagues or others, the Internet, the yellow pages, local business associations, or via membership in an association, such as the American Camp Association, which has business members and exhibitors at conferences.

Once RFPs have been issued, you should use a fair and equitable system to make your selections. For example, you may want to allocate points to each criterion in your proposal: 10 points for the supplier's location or for how fast it can deliver, 10 points for the variety of items its offers, 20 points for prices, 5 points for its experience in serving camps, 5 points for the length of time it has been in business, etc. By setting up your expectations ahead of time and letting your potential vendors know how the RFP criteria are weighted, you are ensuring fairness, which your vendors will appreciate.

Price may or may not be the most important criteria in your selection of vendors. For example, if you have a food vendor with the lowest prices but who has a limited selection of products or can only deliver to you once a week, you may decide you cannot use that vendor because you don't have adequate storage space for that much food inventory. All selection criteria must be considered, not just pricing. You may also want to select two or more vendors, but that possibility should be outlined in the RFP.

After you make your selection of vendors, you should notify the winning bidder and those who were not awarded your business as soon as possible, thanking them for providing the bid. You are looking for vendors who are responsive to your request, submitting all the materials you have asked for, as well as responsible in their abilities to deliver the product you're procuring.

Documentation

Camps will want to have written documentation not only on the specific items (including their stock number and a description) you have requested but also the vendor's financial and technical resources that will be used to be certain they can provide what you are asking for. You will want written references, the legal name of the business, its EIN (employer identification number), and its DUNS (Dun & Bradstreet number, which will allow you to get a written report on its history). You will want to know how it delivers (by mail? truck? UPS®?), how quickly it delivers, if it has a delivery charge, and if you can earn a discount for prompt payment. You will want to know its pricing on the items you have requested, any quantity discounts, how long the pricing is guaranteed, and if a discount is offered for items you have not specified but are in its catalog or on its website. Finally, you will want to know the vendor's policy on broken, damaged, and/or lost materials as well as its policy on filling back orders.

Payment, Terms, and Shipping

It is important to know how vendors expect to be paid: by check, by credit card, through a direct debit electronically, or via cash. For large purchases, some vendors may request a certain percentage payment when the order is placed—for example, 15 to 25 percent. You will also need to know how quickly a vendor expects to be paid. Many will request payment upon delivery, although net 15 or net 30 (payment within 15 or 30 days) would be preferred by most buyers. Ask the vendor for a sample invoice, too.

Ask the vendor to describe any shipping materials it uses, making sure the packaging materials are safe for children. You may also want to know if it will pick up packing materials and/or pallets from previous deliveries so you do not have to dispose of them.

Sole Source

Sometimes, you may have only one source for a particular item or one vendor who can meet all your qualifications. Be certain you provide for this in your procurement policy.

Other Services

You will want to know exactly how to place your orders—whether by phone, fax, in person, or online. Ask vendors if they have other services they can provide, such as emergency deliveries or other types of electronic ordering or inventory. For example, you may find your food supplier also handles paper goods or kitchen equipment.

Contract

The end result of having a procurement process, requesting proposals, and then selecting a vendor or multiple vendors is negotiating a contract. Your contract should include the following:

- *Services:* either a very thorough description or a list of representative goods, prices, and other terms, including discounts, delivery dates, shipping, and any other negotiated terms. Confirm that the prices will be honored through the entire term of the contract unless other arrangements have been made.
- *Term:* when the contract begins and how long it will continue
- *Payment:* when and how payment is to be made
- *Representations and warranties:* a statement that the signer is authorized to sign the contract on behalf of the vendor and usually an indemnification and hold harmless agreement from the vendor regarding all loss, liability, damage, judgment, penalty, cost, or expense, including but not limited to attorneys' fees suffered or incurred as a result of the breach of any of the representations and warranties contained in the contract
- *Assignability:* The agreement should not be assignable by the vendor.
- *Performance:* The vendor should agree to provide all services in accordance with the specifications furnished by the camp.
- *Waiver:* a statement that any waiver by either party of any of the terms and conditions of the agreement isn't a waiver for other terms
- *Termination:* a clause that allows the camp to terminate the agreement without prior written notice

If the vendor has a standard contract, you should review it carefully, making sure it conforms to what you want. In all cases, it is best to have an attorney review contracts.

Utilizing a procurement process is not always necessary and almost never the most expedient way to purchase anything. Some situations might call for purchases outside of the process, especially when speed or responsiveness is an issue. However, camps would do well to consider implementation of such a process, especially for large purchases, when quality and price are most important. Other times, the most pragmatic approach is a quick trip to the local store, but with proper planning, those instances can be limited.

Purchasing Groups

Group purchasing organizations (GPOs) leverage the collective purchasing power of their members. Organizations such as the American Camp Association have established group purchasing programs where small businesses join together, multiplying their strength, as higher purchasing power equals lower prices. Saving money when your purchase food, office supplies, equipment, and many other items means camps can spend more on their programs and missions.

Usually, GPO vendors have products needed by the group. In the case of camps, the American Camp Association purchasing program includes office supplies, facilities supplies and services, express delivery, food and food equipment, travel, postage equipment and supplies, and technology equipment and services. Many GPOs also offer employee discounts on certain products, such as car rentals and cell phones.

Historically, participants in the American Camp Association's GPO have saved in the 17 to 23 percent range on an annual basis, although savings usually depend on volume from each participating camp. Interested camps should check the American Camp Association's website at www.acacamps.org/partnerships/trinity-hpsi for the latest information, as the program features change over time.

If you have the option to participate in a GPO—whether through the American Camp Association or some other organization—it's always worth checking out, as it usually has few if any obligations. Some charge fees to the participants, others to the vendors, and still others a combination of the two. As always, read the fine print, but take time to investigate the options for participation.

15

Risk Management

Tamarak Day Camp

Ask what the words "risk management" mean to a camp owner or director and he generally jumps right to keeping his campers safe, as he should. But risk management for a business means so much more than participant safety and program rules and regulations.

Several resources that address risk management for camps in great detail are available to camp executives. The purpose is this book is not to duplicate these resources but to look at the business aspects of risk management. To a business owner or a nonprofit executive, it is critical that risks be minimized so as to protect not only the investment of the owners and/or donors but also the good name and reputation of the business, as well as the health and safety of all participants.

Definition

In *Coverage, Claims and Consequences: An Insurance Handbook for Nonprofits*, Melanie Lockwood Herman defines risk as "a measure of the possibility that the future may be surprisingly different from what we expect." Risk is neither an impossibility (which has no chance of happening) nor a certainty (which will definitely occur). Where change occurs, risk arises (Herman, 2008).

Risks for Business Owners and Directors

Business owners tend to think about managing risk as buying the right insurance. That's a good thing but certainly not all that risk management is. Mike Periu, an advisor to small businesses and contributor to the American Express Open Forum community for entrepreneurs, suggests that to put an initial risk management plan in place for your business, you should complete the following first steps:

- *Identify risks:* These can include property losses, business interruption losses, liability losses, key person losses, and injury to employees or participants
- *Determine vulnerability:* What's the likelihood a risk will materialize and how much do you stand to lose?
- *Prepare contingency plans:* This can include the development of policies and procedures, systems such as security, avoiding certain high-risk activities in your business, and training your staff on their responsibilities.
- *Acquire the right types of insurance:* Insurance remains a central part of any risk management plan.
- *Monitor and adapt as needed:* Reviewing and updating your plans, especially as your business begins to grow, will help you keep a good grasp on the risks in your camp. (Periu, 2010)

Identifying Risks at Camp

Identifying risk at camp involves so much more than just making sure the lifeguards all have the appropriate credentials. Risk management involves everything from ensuring you have the financial resources to make it through the year to ensuring the well and water system is operating in a manner that prevents people from getting sick. Camp owners and directors should identify the risks associated with their camp programs, reducing such risks by implementing thorough processes and procedures and including such things as proper safety equipment, supervision of the activities by persons knowledgeable in the safe conduct of the activity, and adherence to the accepted standards in the field, as found in the *American Camp Association Accreditation Process Guide*.

At least two excellent sources are available for developing risk management plans for camps. One that will lead camp executives in the identification of risks and the determination of how to control or reduce such risks is *Risk and Crisis Management Planning* by Connie Coutellier. This book includes worksheets for operational and program risks, with suggestions on how to address them. Another option is the online risk management planning tool *My Risk Management Plan*, which is available from the Nonprofit Risk Management Center at www.nonprofitrisk.org/tools/rm-plan/rm-plan.asp. While this tool was developed for nonprofits, it can very easily be adapted for for-profit camps.

www.nonprofitrisk.org/tools/rm-plan/rm-plan.asp

Appendix K includes a list of the topics found in of these resources. These lists point out the magnitude of the risk management process. Regardless of whether you choose to use one of these two resources or a different system, every camp needs a thorough, updated risk management plan.

Additional Strategies

In addition to the tools in Appendix K, camp owners and directors can develop other strategies to cope with risk management issues that may arise. While it is always better to be proactive, you do not always have the crystal ball that tells you when an incident will occur. Anytime an incident occurs that has resulted in or could have resulted in a negative situation, a detailed incident analysis report must be completed.

Herman, who works for the Nonprofit Risk Management Center, says that "[o]ne example of an environment where risk management can flourish is what I call the *culture of reflection*. A nonprofit that embraces a culture of reflection is committed, organization-wide, to carefully examining events that go contrary to the nonprofit's plans. When someone is hurt instead of helped while participating in a social services program, the team members of that program insist on a careful review to determine 'what went wrong'" (Herman, 2013).

Interview witnesses, talk to supervisors, take detailed notes of injuries, make note of weather conditions, take pictures—basically make a note of anything and everything you think could give you a better insight into why or how the incident may have occurred. After recording your incident analysis, meet with key leadership staff and supervisors to discuss the situation so everyone is not only informed of the situation but also trained to possibly observe and prevent a similar situation in the future.

For example, a camper turns up missing during your morning assembly. After checking attendance and confirming that the camper is indeed missing, you immediately implement your "missing camper" procedure (which of course you have practiced with your staff!). After 10 minutes of searching, the camper is located in the washroom. You call off your "missing camper" procedure and move on with your camp day—but does the situation end there? Of course not. You need to review the entire incident and determine through a thorough analysis what could have been handled differently. Better attendance or notification from staff? Who was responsible during the search to check the washrooms and why wouldn't you look there first? Did you wait too long? Ten minutes is a long time to be missing, and if the camper had indeed left camp, 10 minutes is a big head start. The purpose of the review is not to access blame but to determine what if anything you could have done better and to hopefully prevent the situation in the future.

Thus, one step after an incident should be an analysis of what went wrong. This should lead to action—whether a change in policy, a change in program, or another action or perhaps just a repair to a building or replacing worn-out equipment. Camps should develop an incident report to ensure a formal system is in place to discuss and investigate such risk management issues. It will be important for this system to be consistently implemented so all employees (and volunteers if applicable) know that issues are addressed promptly.

Other strategies can also include the following:

- Routinely meet with your insurance carrier's risk management analyst.
- Develop a maintenance routine for areas of you camp that present greater potential for risk management–related problems. Inspect tree canopies for damaged branches and limbs. Ensure that playground equipment is routinely inspected. Keep a log of all inspections.
- If camp credit card information is compromised, speak with your card provider to determine what if any measures can be done to prevent card fraud. Better card security? Was the fraud done in house?

You want to make sure you treat your risk management plan as a living document, not just something that is evaluated or discussed during your accreditation visits. Prevention is truly the best form of risk management and only by continually evaluating all aspects of your program can you truly prevent a situation from developing.

Emergency Preparedness

For one camp director from Colorado, the summer of 2013 led her to quote a well-known song: "I've seen fire and I've seen rain." Wildfires early in the summer and floods in the fall created havoc in the state and many camp professionals found that their well-thought-out risk management plans did not measure up as they had anticipated, with Mother Nature tossing some heretofore unheard-of situations their way.

The term *emergency preparedness* has many aspects. As the owner/director of a camp program, you can literally spend every working hour developing plans for the worst possible scenarios. From weather to missing campers, the critical thing to remember is to evaluate the risks and the likelihood of their occurrence. For example, if your program offers an aquatic program, you already have an emergency plan in place by providing competent and credentialed lifeguard staff. Looking more closely at your program (especially if you are accredited by the American Camp Association), you can identify many other forms of emergency preparedness you already have in place—missing camper procedures, medical preparedness, intruder procedures, etc.

However, what can be more difficult to prepare for are the freak occurrences that are usually associated with Mother Nature. As the owner or director of your business, you must assess the most likely risks that endanger your program and develop plans to address them should they occur. If you operate a camp in the Upper Midwest, you are probably not as concerned about earthquakes as you would be in other areas, but you should have a plan in the event of a serious thunderstorm or tornado. What areas will you have campers seek shelter in for protection? Who will be responsible for determining when you send campers to shelters? Who will give the all clear? Will you practice for this event? Some of this is part of the American Camp Association accreditation process, but it is still your responsibility to have an emergency plan in place.

What often gets overlooked when developing emergency plans are the events that are serious but don't result in complete property devastation and could still cause a temporary shutdown of your camp operations. A supercell thunderstorm or lightning strike that knocks out electrical power for an extended period of time can cause a camp to shut down completely and create a significant financial hardship on your program. Your customers would expect you to stop operations in the event of a tornado, but they might not have the same expectation with a thunderstorm. If you need to close camp, it can be damaging to your camp reputation and cost you lost revenues from camper refunds and possibly business in the future.

In order to prevent a possible shutdown, you should evaluate your program and facility vulnerabilities with your insurance carrier and your leadership staff. Look honestly at what are the most likely "emergency" scenarios. Not every camp or region of the country is susceptible to the same events. You may have reliable utility systems, but do they depend on roads susceptible to flooding? How will you plan on running your program in the event of a flood? What about dangerous heat situations? Do you have contingencies for program in the event that your area comes under dangerous heat advisories?

Several things that every camp needs to stay operating are (in no particular order) phones, food, bathrooms, and water. For example, you need to provide water and sanitary facilities for your campers and staff, but if you are on a well and septic system, a power outage can render your facility temporarily unusable. In addition, your phone system is useless without power and you can't expect to cook or keep food at the proper temperatures without electricity. However, if your emergency planning included an arrangement with a provider of temporary portable toilets and the delivery of large quantities of bottled water, you could meet the immediate needs for your campers and staff. A midsize portable generator could serve your needs for keeping food refrigerated properly and your phone system running to keep open the lines of communication with concerned parents. A staff person with a laptop could keep parents updated from a public place with Wi-Fi capability and you could alter your kitchen menu to serve meals that require minimal food preparation with disposable plates and utensils.

While this may not be the ideal situation for operating your camp program, it sure beats the alternative of sending unhappy campers home early and having to issue refunds to frustrated camp parents. Convince your staff and campers to buy into the new adventure and communicate every detail to your parents and you can turn a potentially disastrous situation caused by a severe thunderstorm into a model of flexibility and, most importantly, responsibility. Think outside the box and realistically about what issues specifically you can expect to have to work through in emergency situations. As camp professionals, you know all too well about the liabilities and contingencies you navigate on a daily basis in dealing with emergencies. Having a thoughtful plan can help reduce some of this stress and it is possible to create a positive situation out of a potential disaster.

Advice From a Pro

"One of the best suggestions I received when we reviewed our emergency plan was to have a list of providers to help us in case of emergency. Rather than scrambling through our contact lists during a crisis, it is much more effective to have them written down and confirmed. We have over 140 horses and we would need a lot of help if we had to move all of them. We have many neighbors that would be willing to help and I would rather talk to them before the summer. The same is true with having access to a refrigerated storage truck. It is easier to know your options before the crisis. We have a few options in case of an emergency."

— Jeff Cheley, Cheley Colorado Camps, Estes Park (CO)

www.bt.cdc.gov/disasters

Fortunately, resources exist that can provide camp executives with much food for thought when it comes to emergency preparedness. One such site is the Centers for Disease Control and Prevention's website on Emergency Preparedness & Response: Natural Disasters & Severe Weather: www.bt.cdc.gov/disasters. This site includes information on:

- Earthquakes
- Extreme heat
- Floods
- Hurricanes
- Landslides and mudslides
- Tornados
- Tsunamis
- Volcanoes
- Wildfires
- Winter weather

The CDC also has additional pages on bioterrorism, chemical emergencies, radiation emergencies, and mass casualties. The CDC pages have excellent information that include everything from what to do before a storm to how to handle the aftermath and how to cope with a disaster or traumatic event (Centers for Disease Control and Prevention, 2013). Coupled with the risk management planning tools mentioned previously, a thorough review of the CDC information can help camp executives plan for emergencies of many different types.

Insurance

From a business standpoint, most camp owners and directors do not know nearly enough about insurance. Insurance is literally what determines whether your camp stays in business as the result of a catastrophe or accident. What types of insurance does your camp need? How much coverage does your camp need and where do you obtain insurance are just a few of the many questions you may have regarding insurance. What makes understanding camp insurance even more difficult is that while countless sources offer insurance for most businesses, the camp industry has a much more limited pool of insurers. As the camp executive, your first insurance decision will be who you select as your agent, broker, or consultant. Differences exist between insurance agents and brokers, although both are licensed by state regulatory agencies. Typically, brokers represent the client, while agents represent a specific company or companies. Both have the challenge of serving both the client, who purchases insurance, and insurance markets with which they place business and generally from which they receive a commission (Herman, 2008).

Whether you work with an agent, a broker, or an insurance consultant (someone who can advise you of various options but does not actually place your insurance with an insurance market), as a camp executive, you need to establish a relationship so the insurance specialist knows your business and can provide advice based on a thorough knowledge of your operations, program, property, and risk exposure. When selecting an insurance agency or brokerage, you should interview them and ask as many questions as you might ask a potential employee, such as the following:

- For what other camps do you write insurance policies?
- What other small businesses place their insurance policies with you?
- Do you have a rate analysis annually with other companies to compare rates?
- How are the coverages on my policy assigned to my facility? Are they per incident or occurrence? Blanket coverages? Aggregate limit?
- How are claims handled? Do specific persons handle claims? Do they handle all claims or have specialties?
- How quickly does the agent or broker return phone calls? Is he responsive with renewal quotes, obtaining the necessary information from you in a timely manner?
- Can the local agency issue certificates of insurance or must they be issued by the underwriter?

- Does the agent or broker provide multiple options for coverage? Does he write insurance from only one company or does he represent multiple companies?
- Does the agent provide detailed information about the financial ratings of insurance companies?
- Has the agent or broker visited your site and made recommendations for coverage? Does he understand your business? This is an extremely important consideration due to the unique nature of each camp business and the wide variety of camp properties and camp types.

Types of Insurance

After you identify an insurance specialist with whom you want to work, he should make recommendations for the coverage you need. According to the Small Business Administration, the two fundamental types of insurance are commercial business insurance, which is not required by law, and employer insurance, which is required by law (Beesley, 2012).

Business Insurance Policies

Business insurance policies that camp owners and directors should consider include the following:

- *Commercial general liability insurance:* These policies cover three different types of liabilities: bodily injury or property damage, personal injury, and medical payments.
- *Commercial property insurance:* Whether damage is caused by fire, smoke, weather, vandalism, or a variety of other causes, this coverage is for property loss or damage. Property can include not just buildings but also equipment, computers, lost income, business interruption, and more—or less.
- *Commercial umbrella or excess liability:* A high value commercial policy typically in excess of five to 10 million dollars or more. The higher the value, the greater the cost, but it is used to cover potential damages beyond the limits of your general liability, property, or auto insurance policies—known as the underlying coverage.
- *Professional liability:* Sometimes known as errors and omissions insurance, this type of liability insurance is for individuals who provide services to the public, such as physicians, attorneys, real estate agents, and even hairdressers. Coverage for professional liability is not included in general liability policies. It can also include coverage for sexual abuse and molestation—an important coverage for camp owners and directors to consider.
- *Directors and officers liability:* For-profit and nonprofit companies often purchase liability insurance to cover their directors and officers. Many times, this type of insurance can include employment practices liability.
- *Employment practices liability:* This insurance is to cover potential losses from discrimination or other employment practices.

- *Crime:* Sometimes called a fidelity bond, crime insurance is a package of policies that includes fidelity bonds and insurance against forgery and intentional theft by employees.
- *Commercial vehicle liability:* Whether camps own, lease, or even use employee vehicles for camp business, commercial vehicle liability insurance will be important for camp owners and directors to obtain.

Nonprofits and Charitable Immunity Laws

Nonprofits should be aware of their state's laws regarding charitable immunity, which may place caps on liability. If your state has such a law, find out if it has been tested in court and discuss it with your insurance agent before eliminating your umbrella liability insurance. If you are operating in a state with such a law, you may be spending money unnecessarily if you purchase excess or umbrella liability insurance.

Crime Insurance and Computer Fraud

Crime insurance generally includes coverage for employee theft, forgery or alteration, and using counterfeit money. However, it is now possible to add computer fraud and funds transfer to this policy, which will provide some protection should your website be hacked. According to the Travelers® Insurance Company, "[f]unds transfer fraud and computer fraud are threats that every organization must plan for, particularly in light of the 2008 survey conducted by the Computer Security Institute (CSI). It found that the average annual losses that survey respondents suffered due to computer fraud was $289,000 and nearly $500,000 for financial fraud.

"'Phishing' scams make it easier than ever for criminals to access your assets. The Federal Trade Commission commented in a special alert that web-based commercial electronic funds transfers (EFTs) origination applications are being targeted by malicious software, including Trojan horse programs, keyloggers, and other spoofing techniques, designed to circumvent online authentication methods. These attacks could result in monetary losses to financial institutions and their business customers if not detected quickly" (Travelers Casualty and Surety Company of America, 2013).

Employer Insurance

Employer insurance, required by law for businesses with employees, includes:

- *Workers' compensation insurance:* Each state sets its own requirements for workers' compensation insurance, which is generally available through commercial carriers and through state workers comp programs.

- *Unemployment insurance tax:* This is also determined by your state and is different from federal unemployment taxes (FUTA). Camp owners and directors will normally not utilize the services of an insurance agent or broker because this is typically provided through a state agency. State laws vary and some camp employees who are full-time students may be exempt from the state unemployment tax. Camps may also be reimbursed, paying the tax only when someone files an unemployment claim. In addition, nonprofits may be eligible to purchase unemployment insurance through an unemployment trust, which generally provides reduced rates.
- *Disability insurance:* According to the Small Business Administration, five states—California, Hawaii, New Jersey, New York, and Rhode Island—and Puerto Rico require businesses to purchase disability insurance (Small Business Administration, n.d.b).

Workers' Compensation Insurance Class Codes

Workers' compensation insurance uses job classification as one of the primary components of pricing. The National Council on Compensation Insurance (NCCI) has developed and maintains a classification system used by most states. The exceptions are California, New Jersey, New York, Delaware, and Pennsylvania, which have developed their own classification codes, and Texas, which licenses much of the NCCI system but makes significant variations in some codes (Workers Compensation Shop, 2012). The cost of workers' compensation insurance is based on a classification code for each employee, a payroll by classification code, and an experience modification rate, derived from the ratio of claims frequency and cost of premiums paid. Camp administrators need to understand the NCCI codes and how their employees are classified. For example, employees classified in NCCI Code 9015 (camp operations) will generally have a higher exposure and therefore higher rate than those employees classified in NCCI Code 8810 (clerical). Workers' compensation carriers conduct an annual audit to confirm codes, the number of employees, and payroll during the audit period, so any misclassification could result in audit adjustments after the policy year. Having employees classified in the correct code is imperative, so be sure and visit with your insurance agent and confirm what the classifications should be.

Several insurance brokers have information on workers' compensation on their websites, including www.workerscompensationshop.com and www.cutcomp.com/guide.htm. Your insurance broker or agent can also provide information specific to your state.

Some insurance carriers offer a business owner's package, which includes all types of insurance that a business owner might need: general liability, vehicle liability, property, business interruption, and crime insurance. By bundling all the policies together, businesses can often save considerable expense as well as simplify the process should claims be filed.

The following are other types of insurance that may be applicable and should be considered:

- Equipment breakdown (sometimes known as *boiler and machinery insurance*)
- Inland marine (for movable equipment, such as tractors and mowers)
- Personal liability
- Electronic property
- Media or cyber liability
- Fiduciary liability (necessary when the business offers a pension plan)
- Terrorism
- Flood (through a government-backed program: www.floodsmart.gov)

Business Interruption Insurance

Many camps purchase business interruption (BI) insurance as a part of their commercial property insurance, given the seasonal nature of camp and the potential for huge financial losses should camps not be able to operate or have to evacuate their premises. Although the term *business interruption* sounds all inclusive, it is not. One camp in Colorado had to evacuate the camp due to smoke from fires nearby—only to find that because the fire was not on its property or within one mile of it, the business interruption insurance did not apply. In this case, the camp was under mandatory evacuation, but luckily, the fire was controlled when only two miles from their property. Upon renewal, the camp opted to pay an additional $700 annual premium to have a BI policy that will provide coverage for events within 10 miles of its property. Lesson learned—and a good question to ask your insurance agent or broker. Always find out the details and exactly what is meant by different insurance coverage, especially at what point the coverage will come into play.

Parts of the Insurance Policy

Each type of insurance policy has five parts—declarations, insuring agreements, definitions, exclusions, and conditions—and sometimes a sixth part: endorsements. The declarations, or dec page, is typically at the beginning of the insurance policy and includes the policy number, dates of coverage, the name of the insured, the type of coverage, limits of insurance, premiums, and a summary of other key information specific to the policy, including deductibles or retentions. Also included in the first section of the policy will be various schedules listing locations, any ratings classifications, and any special coverage (Herman, 2008).

The insurance agreement is what the insurance company will provide in exchange for the premiums paid, although it will typically describe what it covers and limits on or exclusions of certain coverages. If you don't gain a thorough understanding of the definitions, it is very difficult to understand exactly what the coverage is. It takes reading the entire policy, including the exclusions (which eliminate specified exposure) and conditions (which qualify the promises made), to fully comprehend the coverage and limitation of the policy (Herman, 2008).

As a policyholder, you should read and understand what you have purchased. Your agent or broker can provide help, but it is ultimately your responsibility to confirm that the coverage is what you needed and expected. As the camp owner or director, confirm that the location(s) as listed is (are) correct, that all schedules accurately portray what they should, and that your premium is what your agent or broker quoted to you. Many times, options exist to finance the premium over the life of the policy should you want to.

When You Have a Loss

Whether you have a property loss from hail, a vehicle loss from an accident, or even the potential loss due to a threatened lawsuit, it is imperative that you notify your insurance agent as soon as possible. Policies will require notification within a specified number of hours, so know this requirement and make the call in plenty of time. Better still, call immediately. If a geographic area has a hailstorm, for example, those businesses that notify their insurance agents first will probably be first on the list to have an adjuster assigned.

Many insurance companies contract with independent adjusters who will be in touch with you to set up an appointment to inspect the loss. Remember that adjusters may have never been to your property. Any help you can provide them, such as a map of the site with buildings identified as they're identified on your policy, will allow them to provide you with better service. Do not have losses repaired until after your insurance company has inspected the loss and gives you the go ahead to do so.

Payments from insurance companies for property losses will depend on the type of coverage—whether replacement cost or actual cash value, which is replacement cost less depreciation. Payments for losses are typically net of your deductible (in some cases known as the *retention*).

A final note about what to do when you incur a loss: Call your agent. Consider that when you encounter a loss, you are facing a potentially huge financial burden. While it may not seem clear cut to you if the loss is insurable or not, it doesn't hurt to ask. You may be surprised to find out what you insurance company is willing to do to assist you. Then, be prepared to spend more at your next renewal date, as claims usually lead to greater premiums at renewal.

Glossary of Risk Management and Insurance Terms

Risk management and insurance terms can be very confusing. Included as Appendix L is a "Glossary of Risk Management and Insurance Terms," originally published in *Coverage, Claims and Consequences: An Insurance Handbook for Nonprofits* (Herman, 2008) and reprinted with the permission of the Nonprofit Risk Management Center.

Employees as Risks

One of the biggest costs associated with a business—whether a camp or not—is that of the employees. Managing risks associated with employees is not just about workers' compensation insurance, although that is an important part. Camp executives need to consider additional risks and take steps to manage them, including:

- Health insurance for year-round employees to keep them healthy and at work as well as accident insurance for seasonal staff
- Human resources policies that are reviewed and updated on a regular basis and then communicated to employees
- Training to keep employees knowledgeable about their responsibilities—whether for program delivery, maintenance, or in the office

Cash Flow as a Risk

Numerous professionals who deal with small businesses on a regular basis cite cash flow as the biggest risk to be managed. In a perfect world, setting up six months of cash reserves would serve most small businesses well. With the seasonal nature of camps, even six months of cash reserves may not be enough.

Diane Tyrrell, in *Camping Magazine*, reported that new camp owners had said during a conference presentation on starting camps that:

> [s]tarting a camp is a costly proposition, and you will probably need more funding than you planned for. Don't let your dream die because you run out of money mid-stream. Make a plan for funding the long-term, and have a back-up plan for when the unexpected comes up. (Tyrrell, 2010)

This may be one of the most challenging risks to manage in a business, so be prepared. If you are starting a new business, whatever amount you have saved and you think is enough for cash flow probably isn't. It is wise to visit with your accountant and your banker to discuss specific cash flow needs and to be prepared by setting up a business line of credit.

While risk management encompasses countless program and operational situations and should be carefully addressed through one of the options listed in this chapter or another risk management tool, the insurance needed by camps as businesses is extensive. As camp executives, having a thorough understanding of all aspects of insurance is an important responsibility, as is the need to be proactive by reviewing, updating, and communicating risk management plans.

16

Health, Safety, and OSHA

Fuse/Thinkstock

As an employer, one extremely important aspect of health and safety—separate from risk management—is compliance with OSHA regulations. The Occupational Safety and Health Administration (OSHA), an agency within the U.S. Department of Labor, was started as a result of 1970 legislation passed by Congress to "assure safe and healthful working conditions for working men and women by setting and enforcing standards and by providing training, outreach, education and assistance" (Occupational Safety and Health Administration, 1989). While a few businesses do not fall under OHSA's jurisdiction (principally, those in occupations regulated by another federal agency, such as the Coast Guard), all camps are required to meet OSHA's safety and health regulations—either through the federal program or through OSHA-approved state programs, which must be at least as comprehensive as the federal OSHA program.

States With OSHA-Approved Programs

The following states and territories have approved state plans:

- Alaska
- Arizona
- California
- Connecticut*
- Hawaii
- Illinois*
- Indiana
- Iowa
- Kentucky
- Maryland
- Michigan
- Minnesota
- Nevada
- New Jersey*
- New Mexico
- New York*
- North Carolina
- Oregon
- Puerto Rico
- South Carolina
- Tennessee
- Utah
- Vermont
- Virgin Islands*
- Virginia
- Washington
- Wyoming

** The Connecticut, Illinois, New Jersey, New York, and Virgin Islands plans cover public sector (state & local government) employment only. (Occupational Safety and Health Administration,* 1989*)*

OSHA standards describe the methods that employers must use to protect their employees from hazards in three specific industries—construction, agriculture, and maritime—as well as general industry, which would be the appropriate standards for camps. OSHA standards limit the amount of hazardous chemicals that workers can be exposed to, require the use of certain safe practices and equipment, and require employers to monitor hazards and keep records of workplace injuries and illness (Occupational Safety and Health Administration, 1989). Employers must also comply with the General Duty Clause, which is usually cited when no specific OSHA standard applies to a hazard, as it requires employers to keep their workplace free of serious recognized hazards.

www.OSHA.gov

Workers have a right to file a complaint and ask for an inspection of the worksite by OSHA if they believe their employer is not following OSHA standards or that conditions in the workplace are hazardous. It is a violation of the Occupational Safety and Health Act for an employer to fire or discriminate against a worker for filing a complaint with OSHA (Occupational Safety and Health Administration, 1989).

Under OSHA standards, employers must:

- Provide their employees with a safe workplace that doesn't have serious hazards and follow all relevant OSHA safety and health standards.
- Find and correct safety and health problems.
- Try to eliminate or reduce hazards by making changes in working conditions rather than relying solely on personal protective equipment (PPE), such as masks, gloves, or earplugs.
- Inform employees about hazards through training, labels, alarms, color-coded systems, chemical information sheets, and other methods.
- Keep accurate records of work-related injuries and illnesses.
- Perform tests, such as air sampling.
- Provide medical tests or hearing exams as required.
- Post OSHA citations, injury and illness data, and the OSHA poster in the workplace where workers will see them.
- Notify OSHA within eight hours of a workplace incident in which a death occurs or when three or more workers go to a hospital.
- Not discriminate or retaliate against workers for using their rights under the law. (Occupational Safety and Health Administration, 1989)

The *Small Business Handbook*, provided on the OSHA website (www.osha.gov/Publications/smallbusiness/small-business.html), notes that nobody wants accidents in the workplace but that accidents have a cause. Investigating accidents and responding are important, but preventing accidents requires a plan. OSHA recommends the following four basic elements to all good safety and health programs (Occupational Safety and Health Administration, 1989):

- "*Management Commitment and Employee Involvement.* The manager or management team leads the way, by setting policy, assigning and supporting responsibility, setting an example and involving employees.
- *Worksite Analysis.* The worksite is continually analyzed to identify all existing and potential hazards.
- *Hazard Prevention and Control.* Methods to prevent or control existing or potential hazards are put in place and maintained.
- *Training for Employees, Supervisors and Managers.* Managers, supervisors and employees are trained to understand and deal with worksite hazards."

Regardless of the size or type of your camp, a workplace safety and health program is needed to prevent workplace accidents and possible injuries and illnesses. If you already have a workplace safety and health program, it is recommended that you review it in relation to these elements recommended by OSHA.

Additional information about establishing a safety and health plan is found on the OSHA website (www.osha.gov). Selected OSHA standards, referenced in the *Small Business Handbook*, are also included in Appendix N.

Bloodborne Pathogen Standard

In a camp setting, one of the OSHA standards where camp administrators may find the most exposure is the Bloodborne Pathogen Standard. The American Camp Association has developed a sample exposure control plan so camps can educate employees and others about issues related to exposure to body fluids. The sample plan includes job classifications that incur the risk of exposure to body fluids, job classifications that provide first-aid care as an ancillary task, and suggestions for orientation about risks as well as work practices to minimize risks. Included in Appendix M are the American Camp Association's Sample Exposure Control Plan and information on universal precautions, a part of the control plan, and a post-exposure plan for camp.

Hepatitis B

The OSHA Bloodborne Pathogens rule requires that employers provide access free of charge to the hepatitis B vaccine (HBV) to "all occupationally exposed" employees. Employees who may be exposed to blood or other potentially infectious materials should acknowledge in writing that they've either completed the HBV program or declined the vaccination. A sample vaccination statement and an exposure incident form as developed by the American Camp Association are included in Appendix M.

Standards for Health and Wellness

The American Camp Association standards address several health and wellness topics, providing the contextual education and what's necessary to demonstrate compliance. The standards go into great detail about specific requirements for these topics:

- *Healthcare provider:* availability of physician or nurse
- *First-aid and emergency care personnel:* certifications based on proximity to emergency medical system
- Healthcare away from camp
- Staff training
- Camper and staff health histories and contact information for all minors
- *Health exams:* making a determination regarding the need for campers to have a physical exam by a licensed medical provider
- Health screening for campers and staff at camp for resident and day camps
- Signed permission to provide routine healthcare, dispense medications, and seek emergency treatments

- Parent notification when campers become ill or injured
- Healthcare policies and/or procedures reviewed and signed by a licensed healthcare professional whose scope of practice allows such a review
- Treatment procedures
- Information provided to staff regarding special needs of campers
- Information provided to parents of special needs campers regarding the camp's ability to meet participants' needs
- Healthcare center minimum facilities and the ratio of beds to campers
- Availability of equipment, supplies, and emergency assistance
- Availability of automated external defibrillator
- Supervision requirements for the healthcare center
- Medication storage and administration
- Health records, recordkeeping, and record maintenance
- Healthcare planning
- Health information from rental groups (American Camp Association, 2012)

When camps are serving nonmedical religious campers, exceptions are made in scoring the standards. The health and wellness standards should be covered in an overall healthcare plan, which should also include the evaluation of risks and the plan for prevention of potential risks (American Camp Association, 2012).

Healthy Camps Study

The American Camp Association completed a significant study involving close to 300 camps, looking at camp-related injuries and illnesses over a period of five years. This study provided data that camps will be able to use to benchmark their own injuries and illnesses as well as a set of recommended practices for prevention of injuries and illnesses in camps (Garst, Marugg, & Thompson, 2013). The American Camp Association is implementing an education and monitoring program that includes numerous professional development opportunities related to maintaining the health of campers. To find out more, see www.acacamps.org/research/healthy-camp-toolbox.

www.acacamps.org/research/healthy-camp-toolbox

Other Health Resources

For camp administrators who are looking for more guidance on camp health services, *The Basics of Camp Nursing* by Linda Erceg and Myra Pravda covers the role of the camp nurse, regulations, setting up a camp health center, medication management, records systems, and much more.

Another good source of information for camp healthcare is the Association of Camp Nurses. Your camp nurse will find that:

in a practice where one nurse is often the only nurse, ACN membership [www.acn.org/membership/index.html] can be the resource which helps minimize the camp nurse's feeling of isolation and provides a way to share camp health discoveries. ACN offers access to other people who share similar interests. (Association of Camp Nurses, 2013)

State and Local Regulations

Specific laws and regulations related to camp healthcare are included in the overall state regulations for camps. Camp administrators should take note of any local or state reporting requirements for injuries or illness that could occur at camp, as some states require reports within 24 hours for various incidents. For example, the state of New York requires operators of children's camps to notify the permit-issuing official—usually the local health department—within 24 hours of any of the following situations occurring:

- "Camper and staff injuries or illnesses which result in death or which require resuscitation, admission to a hospital or the administration of epinephrine;
- Camper and staff exposures to animals potentially infected with rabies;
- Camper injuries to the eye, head, neck or spine which require referral to a hospital or other facility for medical treatment;
- Camper injuries where the victim sustains second or third degree burns to five percent or more of the body;
- Camper injuries which involve bone fractures or dislocations;
- Camper lacerations requiring sutures;
- Camper physical or sexual abuse allegations;
- All camper and staff illnesses suspected of being water-, food-, or air-borne, or spread by contact." (New York State Department of Health, 2011)

While the New York camp law requires the reporting of numerous incidents, in Indiana, the state camp regulations require that when "an injury or illness [occurs] to a camper that results in hospitalization, a [camper has a] positive x-ray or laboratory analysis, or the camper is being sent home a report shall be sent to the department within ten (10) days (24 hours if death occurs)" (Indiana State Deartment of Health, 2002).

As you can see, the reporting requirements vary considerably—from the type of injury or illness reported to the time frame in which local authorities should be notified. See Appendix F for a listing of state regulatory agencies.

17

Transportation for Campers

moodboard/Thinkstock

Transporting campers is an important program element for most camps. Transportation services can range from a day camp's daily transportation via bus to pickup services at airports for resident camps or the rental of vans for trips out of camp. Regardless of what type of transportation service your camp offers, it can be one of the most challenging and nerve-racking processes you'll encounter on a daily basis. As camp owners, you develop procedures that ensure the safety of the campers and staff in your care. However, with transportation, despite your best-made plans, you don't always have that feeling of control because of the many variables that remain out of your control. Traffic, mechanical issues, and camper and staff behavior are just a few of the many things that can present challenges—and that's all without even mentioning accidents yet. Like anything else in the camp business, it is important to have a plan for transportation and to constantly evaluate your plans, making sure you're meeting the needs of your campers while providing an efficient and, most importantly, safe experience.

Types of Camper Transportation

Camper transportation can be broken down into three distinct categories:

- Day-to-day transportation
- Airline transportation
- Out-of-camp trip transportation

www.ghsa.org/html/stateinfo/laws/childsafety_laws.html

Seatbelts

The National Highway Traffic Safety Administration recommends that children four to seven years of age be kept in a forward-facing car seat with a harness until he or she reaches the top height or weight limit allowed by the car seat's manufacturer. After that, it's time for a booster seat, which should be used by children eight to 12 until they're big enough to properly use a seatbelt. States have differing regulations regarding seatbelt requirements for children, so check the laws in your state. The Governors Highway Safety Association offers a list of state requirements at www.ghsa.org/html/stateinfo/laws/childsafety_laws.html. You may be required to provide car seats or booster seats for younger children.

Day-to-Day Transportation

For an overnight camp, day-to-day transportation in many cases takes place by bus at the beginning of a session. Campers from a particular geographical area meet at a centralized meeting place at a pre-determined time and are transported to camp. At the end of the session, the process is reversed. Campers are transported by either chartered coach or school bus or the camp may own its own bus that is driven by an employee with the appropriate commercial driver's license (CDL). In some cases where a smaller number of campers are involved, the camp may utilize large vans. Staff will of course accompany the campers, using the time on the bus to sing camp songs or engage in ice-breaking activities that allow campers to introduce themselves.

Day-to-day transportation for a day camp takes place every day, as the campers may be picked up in the morning and/or taken home in the afternoon. Some day camps provide transportation from centralized pickup locations where they meet parents at a pre-determined time. Other day camps chose to provide the convenience where they offer door-to-door transportation from the camper's home. Typically, school buses are utilized—in many cases, smaller school buses, which allow the camp to pick up campers in cul-de-sacs and dead-end roads where a larger bus would have trouble navigating. At the end of the day, the process is reversed, dropping campers off at home. In addition to the driver, counselors are assigned to the route to supervise campers.

Regardless of the method of day-to-day transportation you are offering, you need to be aware of the costs involved. For most day camps, the largest expense item each summer after staff costs is transportation. Most camps will not own their own buses, and in the case of day camps, where you may be picking up dozens or even several hundred campers each day, it is not economically feasible to own your own fleet of buses. You will need to find the services of a transportation company that will lease you the buses (on a cost per bus price) for your camp season. As with anything else in your business, you will need to interview several and determine which provides you with the best level of service for the price of the lease. Following are items you should consider:

- What are you getting for the quoted price? Is it just the bus or can you also arrange to contract for the driver, fuel, and insurance?
- Who is responsible for maintaining the buses? (Maintenance issues will happen!) Does the transportation company offer roadside assistance to an overnight camp several hundred miles away?
- What are the different capacities of buses available? Bus capacity sizes range from as few as 14 passengers up to 71 passengers, so get the bus that gives you the best capacity for your money.

Driving a vehicle carrying 16 or more passengers requires a CDL, so you will need to arrange to have a staff person on hand with a CDL. In some states, vehicles rated for 9 to 15 passengers may not require that the driver have a CDL. Check your state for specific information, as laws change. If you only need one or two drivers, you should be able to find the qualified personnel. If you need dozens of drivers (as may be the case for a day camp), this task becomes

Child Safety Switch

Many of the smaller buses commonly used by child care centers (known as *multifunction school activity buses*, or MFSABs) come equipped with a child safety switch, which requires the driver to walk to the back of the bus and deactivate the switch before leaving the bus, thus checking to see if any children are still in the bus. Leaving a child in a vehicle in the heat of the summer can be deadly, so some states are now requiring this type of safety feature in buses, especially for child care facilities. Because some camps are regulated as child care facilities, it is best to check to see what your state and local regulations are in regard to mandating any type of device that requires the driver to verify that no children are left in the vehicle.

much more difficult. An option could be to ask the bus company to quote you a contract price for the bus and a driver. In this case, the price would include insurance (which could save you money in insurance premiums) and possibly fuel too, so you want to shop and negotiate cautiously.

Airline Transportation

Camps that provide transportation from airports to the camp have not only additional costs to consider for this service but will need a clear understanding of how the airlines serving your location deal with unaccompanied minors. Just dealing with luggage can be an issue, so having adequate camp staff to assist campers and keep all the campers together will be imperative.

It is recommended that you contact your local airport security department to discuss luggage pickup and parking for camp vehicles and to determine if you can obtain escort passes to meet your campers at the gate. Parents will appreciate knowing you will meet their children at the gate and not rely on airline personnel to escort the campers to the baggage claim area. Because federal regulations regarding airport security can change, establishing a relationship ahead of time with airport security personnel will be advantageous. The American Camp Association states that airline personnel recommend the following:

- Campers should limit carry-on baggage to expedite security line procedures.
- Campers and parents should be sure that carry-on baggage does not contain items that will require separate screening and/or confiscation, such as knives, firearms, flammables, and some sports equipment.
- Campers' baggage must be with them at all times. It should be carried in the same vehicle as the camper.
- Remind campers not to joke about bombs, guns, hijacking, etc.
- Utilize skycaps wherever possible. Curbside check-in is more efficient than standing in lines in the terminal.
- Camps should be familiar with the required check-in times at the counter. (American Camp Association, 2002)

Like at any public location, your camp personnel at the airport will be representing your camp and, ultimately, you or your organization. Having everyone trained and familiar with airport regulations, parking in the designated areas, and maintaining control with campers who may be new to your camp can make a positive impression with the public and your local airport and airline officials. When in public, your staff should be easily identified as camp representatives by wearing camp logo shirts. Additional business considerations related to providing airport transportation include the following:

- Determine if you will charge a fee to pick up campers at the airport or if that service will be provided at no additional charge. Many camps do charge an additional fee for airport service. This should include not only the cost of rental buses and staff time but also associated costs, such as parking fees and meals.
- If campers' flight times and the trip to camp will last over a meal time, consider having sack lunches for the campers to eat on the bus. A hungry camper is generally not a happy camper.

- Give the campers an opportunity to use restroom facilities at the airport before boarding camp vehicles.
- If you have a large number of campers flying in, visit with a travel agent to see if any discounts can be arranged or if working through a travel agency will be beneficial to you or your camp families.
- Check with the airlines to determine their policies on camp footlockers (if you require them) and communicate this information to parents so no one will be surprised about additional fees for oversized baggage when the campers are dropped off at the airport. In addition, consider the ramifications if the camp will be taking campers back to the airport on their flight home. Who will pay for the baggage fees? Many camp families send larger pieces of luggage via UPS or FedEx®.
- Check with your insurance agent to determine if campers are covered during their trip to camp—whether by airline or driving to camp.
- Review your risk management plans to verify that you have contingencies related to late arrivals or emergencies involving public transportation, including the return trip.

Out-of-Camp Trips

The final type of transportation that day or overnight camps may offer is special out-of-camp trips that occur periodically during the course of a summer. These trips are a planned part of the camp program but typically involve a smaller number of campers for each trip. One of the greatest challenges for this type of transportation arrangement is that these trips may take place intermittently during the course of the summer and require that the trip leader also perform the driving functions. One of the major business decisions facing camp owners and directors who provide transportation of campers in any form will be the type of vehicle to use.

Much has been written about the use of 12- to 15-passenger vans due to their history of rollovers. The National Highway Traffic Safety Administration (NHTSA) issued a consumer advisory warning that "maintenance is paramount to preventing tragedies" (National Highway Transportation Safety Administration, 2010). It recommends that "vehicles have appropriately-sized tires that are properly inflated before every trip" and that "spare tires not be used as replacements for worn tires" (National Highway Transportation Safety Administration, 1999). This advisory was directed toward church groups and other nonprofit organizations that might be keeping older 15-passenger vans in service longer than usual due to budget constraints. The NHTSA went on to say that "schools should not use 15-passenger vans for transporting school children, as they do not provide the same level of safety as school buses. It's also against federal law for schools to buy new 15-passenger vans for school transportation purposes." These 15-passenger vans are considered "nonconforming buses," as they meet the federal definition of a bus but do not meet the federal occupant crash protection standards of school buses (National Highway Transportation Safety Administration, 1999).

The American Camp Association continues to monitor all legislation related to the camp industry, including transportation issues. ACA has reported that while requirements to have additional training for drivers of 15-passenger vans had previously been left up to the states, in 2012, Congress adopted a new law that may impact the camp community. The law calls for rules that would require drivers of 9- to 15-passenger (including the driver) vans used "in interstate commerce, to have a commercial driver's license passenger-carrying endorsement and be tested in accordance with a drug and alcohol testing program" (American Camp Association, 2013g). Camp directors, owners, and executives can follow ACA's educational information on transportation and other public policy issues at www.acacamps.org/publicpolicy.

Many camps still use 15-passenger vans because other vehicles simply do not meet their needs. Camp owners and directors should carefully evaluate the types of vehicles that will meet the needs of your program and become knowledgeable about the strengths and weaknesses of those vehicles before you purchase or rent. Then, create policies and practices that will make those vehicles as safe as possible. This will include excellent maintenance and driver training designed specifically for the vehicles you're using.

Other Business Considerations for Transportation

Think about the following situations to ensure you are making the best decisions for your camp:

- Before you decide on any method of transportation, consult with your insurance agent to confirm that you are covered under the terms of your auto policy. Some policies have specific driver requirements. Also, if rented vehicles are covered under your camp auto policy, decline additional coverage from the rental or leasing company to avoid additional charges. Check with your agent to see if you must notify your insurance company when you rent or lease a vehicle.
- Carefully review your contract with your transportation company so you understand all the terms of the contract. In addition, it is advisable to provide a copy of the contract, especially relating to insurance coverage, to your insurance agent to make sure the coverage is sufficient to meet the terms of your liability insurance. If the coverage is insufficient, negotiate for better coverage or consider another provider.
- If you are utilizing rental or leased vehicles, make sure you do a thorough exterior inspection when you receive and return the vehicle and make written note of any damages, no matter how minor. Have a representative of the rental company acknowledge and sign off on your written damage assessment before you accept the vehicles.
- Consider making arrangements to provide fleet fuel cards for each vehicle. You can often receive special pricing on fuel purchases made through fleet cards.

Transportation Policies

Some of the more important things to remember regarding transportation are found in the American Camp Association's standards and they include the following:

- Written communication of pickup and drop-off times to parents
- A system to communicate any changes or emergencies that would change pickup or drop-off times
- Safety rules for riding in buses or vans, explained to campers and their parents
- Established ratio of staff to campers that considers the age, mental ability, and physical condition of all riders
- Procedures that lead to an orderly loading and unloading of vehicles
- Procedures for the orderly arrival and departure of vehicles
- Proper training for all drivers
- Confirmation of driving records and verification that drivers have the appropriate licenses for the vehicles they are driving (American Camp Association, 2012)

In addition, you must have established procedures for accidents or emergencies, such as:

- How care will be provided for anyone injured
- How the uninjured will be supervised, including the provision of diversionary activities
- Who will be notified in the event of an emergency
- How witnesses will be identified (American Camp Association, 2012)

The American Camp Association offers numerous resources with regards to transportation policies on its website: www.aca.org/knowledge/transportation. Whatever you do, make sure that all your transportation policies are written down and shared with the appropriate personnel. You will also want to make certain you have your policies documented whenever possible. In the event of an accident or another catastrophic event, your best defense is proof that you have implemented safety procedures that are nationally recognized by an industry expert such as the American Camp Association.

Use of Personal Vehicles

If you use your personal vehicle or permit other staff members to use their personal vehicles for camp business, check with your insurance agent to confirm that the camp's vehicle liability insurance will cover these drivers and vehicles. In general, only liability coverage is provided, not collision. Drivers need to understand that their own insurance will usually be primary for liability purposes and that all collision insurance is the responsibility of the owners of the vehicles. Check with your agent for specifics about laws in your state.

Camp owners and directors should also consider having any employees who use their private vehicles for camp business sign an agreement acknowledging the individual's liability and responsibility for maintenance or costs associated with the private vehicles as well as the camp's responsibilities for the same. Most vehicle owners will need to provide their own comprehensive vehicle insurance for any damage that may be caused to their vehicles–unless the camp specifically arranges otherwise. Vehicle liability insurance can usually be written that includes owned, hired, or leased vehicles, but note that this is liability only. Owners of private vehicles should carry collision insurance, as damage to their vehicles will not be covered under the camp policy.

Vehicle Use as a Fringe Benefit

If camps provide vehicles to employees that can also be used for personal business, the employee will incur tax consequences on the personal use of those vehicles. A good business practice is to keep a log of all use of camp vehicles so bona fide business use is substantiated. Otherwise, the IRS will assume that the vehicle was used entirely for personal use. The value of the personal use of vehicles should be included as income. Conversely, any use of a personal vehicle for business purposes may be considered a deductible business expense (Internal Revenue Service, 2013e).

Maintenance of Vehicles

Maintaining all your vehicles at camp is vitally important for the safety of your campers and staff as well as ensuring that your valuable assets are protected and last as long as they possibly can. As with any physical asset, it will last a lot longer and more reliably if you take care of it. Key maintenance issues include the following:

- *Tires:* Tires must be inflated properly and not show excessive wear. All tires should be checked on a regular basis and replaced promptly when worn. It is always better to replace tires too soon than too late. Check the owner's manual to see what the proper inflation should be and then verify that each vehicle has a tire gauge in it that the driver can use.
- *Transmission and brakes:* Follow your vehicle manufacturer's recommended maintenance schedule for such items as transmissions and brakes. Drivers should check the brakes before departing on any camp trip.
- *Routine maintenance:* Establish a routine maintenance schedule for such tasks as changing the oil and filters and for performing other minor maintenance tasks.
- *Gas:* It's better to refuel when you are not carrying campers. Always turn the vehicle off completely and put the vehicle in park when refueling.
- *Lights, hazard lights, and emergency warning lights:* Check to confirm these are working properly.
- *Windshield and wipers:* Drivers should check that windshields–front and back–are clean and that wipers are not worn.
- *Horn:* The horn should be checked before leaving on a trip.
- *Fluids:* At least weekly, the oil, windshield washer fluid, and transmission fluid should be checked by camp maintenance employees who are knowledgeable and can change or top off fluids as necessary.

When is it necessary to replace tires?

According to the National Highway Transportation Safety Administration's website, safercar.gov.:

> "... the structural integrity of a tire can degrade over an extended period of time. When that occurs, tires are more prone to catastrophic failure, which could, at best, cause an inconvenience, or, at worst, lead to a crash. The degradation of a tire occurs over time, mostly the result of a chemical reaction within the rubber components. That aging process can be accelerated by heat and sunlight." (National Highway Transportation Safety Administration, n.d.)

The NHTSA goes on to recommend the following steps:

- Check tires for wear after five years of use, then annually.
- If you are unsure of the age of tires, check the tire identification number on the sidewall of the tire. The identification number will begin with the letters "DOT" and the last four digits will represent the week and year of manufacture.
- Be sure that tires are maintained regularly, inflated properly and that vehicles are not overloaded. Poor vehicle and tire maintenance can lead to tire failure and may contribute to vehicle crashes. (National Highway Transportation Safety Administration, n.d.)

Driver Training

Driver safety begins with the application process, when the applicant's motor vehicle report is checked. Camp staff with a history of vehicle accidents should never be put in a position to drive campers or to drive any vehicle on behalf of the camp. All drivers should be at least 21 and have experience driving the type of vehicle they will drive for camp. One camp in its driver training says that "[d]riving children in a camp vehicle is the most serious responsibility you can be entrusted with, and your driving at all times should be defensive and extremely careful. Remember that you accept a professional responsibility when you drive a camp vehicle. This is very different from what you might do in your own car" (Sanborn Western Camps, 2013). Training for drivers should include at least the following:

- *General maintenance of vehicles:* Each driver should have a checklist to complete before departing on any camp trips.
- *Medication/weariness:* If drivers are tired or are taking medication that might hamper their effectiveness as a driver, they should be instructed to tell the director and be replaced as a driver. All concerned will be appreciative.
- *Route and campers:* Drivers should know exactly where they are going, have a map on how to get there, and take a cell phone (with car charger) and travel money for gas and/or emergencies.

- *Emergency equipment:* Drivers should be aware of the location in the vehicle of the first-aid kit, a flashlight, reflectors, and a fire extinguisher and know how to use each item. Before leaving on any trip, drivers should also confirm that the jack, lug wrench, and spare tire are in their proper locations. Drivers must know how to change a tire.
- *Stopping for emergencies:* Drivers should make certain that the vehicle is well off the road and the emergency flashers are turned on. If the vehicle is disabled, it should be removed from the roadway and the campers should get out of the vehicle and go to a safe location with a staff member to wait. The driver should stay with the vehicle and call for help if it is not possible to fix the problem.
- *Phone numbers:* Camp and insurance company phone numbers should be programmed into the cell phone as well as included in the first-aid kit and the glove compartment.
- *Accident protocols:* Drivers should know accident protocols, which should include providing first aid; calling local authorities (or asking a passerby to do so); notifying the camp ASAP; having uninjured staff provide diversion activities to uninjured campers and moving them away from the accident; getting names, addresses, and phone numbers from any other drivers involved in the accident and witnesses; and then waiting for police or sheriff to arrive, providing them with all requested information.
- *Accident report form:* Many states will have an accident report form online that can be printed and copies provided in the glove compartment of each vehicle.
- *Vehicle registration information:* All vehicle registration information and insurance cards should be kept in the glove compartment. If available, an accident report form from the state should also be kept there.

Driving in Less Than Perfect Conditions

Driver training should include a review of the types of driving conditions that could be encountered, such as rain, snow, downhill/uphill, gravel roads, and any other types of conditions that could be less than ideal, and how best to handle such conditions. Camps located in rural areas or mountains may have additional hazards that should be covered in driver training, such as wildlife on roads, gravel, washboard conditions, soft shoulders or no shoulders, clay that becomes slick when wet, dust, horses, bikes, other campers, large delivery trucks or buses, farm equipment, blind curves, deep ruts after a rain, large rocks, cattle guards, or road construction.

Other Driving Considerations

Drivers should always know exactly how many campers and how many staff are in their vehicles. Each time a stop occurs and it's necessary to reload, the driver should take roll and account for everyone. Drivers should also check that the following recommended rules are observed:

- The vehicle should never be overloaded.
- Each person in a vehicle must wear a seatbelt. The driver should confirm that all passengers are wearing seatbelts before moving the vehicle. All passengers should remain seated and belted while the vehicle is moving.
- Everyone should stow loose objects, such as water bottles, in their day packs.
- Each vehicle should have at least one staff member in addition to the driver.
- Counting the driver, the staff to camper ratio should be no more than 1-to-7.
- Campers aged 12 or younger should not sit in the front seat.
- Fill the seats from front to back.
- Health forms/permission to treat forms should be in the vehicle with the campers and staff (unless the camp is closer than another medical treatment facility).

Most van accidents occur while backing up. Drivers should walk around the vehicle before getting in to see if trees, rocks, backpacks on the ground, other vehicles, or other hazards might present issues. If necessary, the second staff person can stay outside the vehicle while the driver maneuvers a vehicle in a tricky place.

Vans should never be driven more than 55 mph even if the speed limit is higher. Camps should determine the safe maximum speed on camp roads. The driver's responsibility is not to entertain or monitor the campers. Other staff members should keep the noise level reasonable, and if the driver asks for quiet, the staff should make that happen.

Distracted Driving

The use of cell phones, although addressed in a camp's human resources policies, should also be considered when developing transportation protocols at camps. The National Safety Council (NSC) reports that one of the biggest reasons for crashes is the danger associated with driver distraction. "Drivers using cell phones are four times as likely to crash, and there is no difference in crash risk between handheld and hands-free phone use." (National Safety Council, 2013). Beyond the safety for your campers and employees, motor vehicle crashes are costly to employers and can result in lawsuits and ongoing time spent dealing with insurance and liability claims. The NSC also reports that distracted drivers talking on cell phones:

- Are more likely to commit driver errors and traffic violations
- Have slower reaction times than drivers impaired at a .08 blood-alcohol level
- Look but fail to see much of the driving environment
- Have cognitive impairment, as more than one-third of the brain's processing resources are drawn away from driving tasks (National Safety Council, 2012)

Cell Phone Use and Texting Laws

According to the National Highway Traffic Safety Administration, forty-one states and the District of Columbia ban text messaging for all drivers and 12 states and D.C. prohibit all drivers from using handheld cell phones while driving. They also report that "11% of all drivers under the age of 20 involved in fatal crashes were reported as distracted at the time of the crash. This age group has the largest proportion of drivers who were distracted." (U.S. Department of Transportation, NHTSA, n.d.)

To see all state laws regarding cell phone use and texting, visit www.distraction.gov/content/get-the-facts/state-laws.html

Camp owners and directors should consider the development of a specific policy that includes typical scenarios relevant to your camp, including enforcement and discipline related to violations of the policy. The NSC recommends that a distracted driving policy contain the following points:

- Employees should not be permitted to use any type of cell phone, PDA, or a similar device while operating any motor vehicle on behalf of the camp.
- Employees should not be permitted to read or respond to email, text messages, or any other visual message while operating any motor vehicle on behalf of the camp.
- Calls should not be answered by an employee while he is driving. Instead, he should allow the call to go to voice mail.
- If a driver needs to make a phone call while driving, the employee should stop at a safe location to make the call. (National Safety Council, 2012)

As with any human resources policy, your legal counsel should review these points and assist in the development of an appropriate policy for your circumstances, including the ramifications of not abiding by the policy. In addition, your insurance broker can provide assistance in reviewing your vehicle and liability coverage, making sure you have adequate coverage for the transportation activities at your camp. Many insurance companies will provide online or other training related to transportation safety, so take advantage of services such as these.

Vehicle Cleanliness and Driving Courtesy

Most camps identify their vans, buses, trucks, or other vehicles with a camp logo, which is an excellent marketing tool and a reminder to all in the communities where the vehicles are driven that that camp exists. However, it is important for camp owners, directors, and executives to remember that every time a vehicle leaves camp, that vehicle has become a rolling billboard, advertising your camp program. The impression created by a vehicle—whether it is being driven too fast or too slow, whether it's clean and shiny or covered with dirt and mud, and whether it is being driven courteously—is a direct impression on you and your camp.

Did one of the maintenance staff have a minor fender bender backing into a tree at camp that crushed the side of the camp van? It's best to get it repaired as quickly as possible. Otherwise, you could leave the impression that camp is unsafe or that you don't take care of property–or, even worse, that you don't take care of people. Camp executives can never go wrong by making certain that vehicles are clean–inside and out–and that drivers understand the importance of safe, courteous driving as a representative of your camp.

Camps providing any type of transportation–whether a single maintenance vehicle or a fleet of vans or buses–need to be aware of all regulations, have proper insurance, provide a driver training program, and include comprehensive guidance for their staff on all transportation-related issues. Common sense, preparedness, courtesy, and responsibility for children–these are all components of the business of camp transportation.

Thanks to Sanborn Western Camps for its assistance in the section on driver training and transportation safety.

18

Food Service

waldru/iStock/Thinkstock

Whether the camp provides food service or campers bring their own lunches, the camp has a responsibility to see that food is stored at safe temperatures, that meals are served at the proper temperatures, and that proper handwashing facilities are available. From a business perspective, food service presents multiple challenges, including the following:

- Good memories of food may not equal a returning camper, but a bad food experience can keep a camper from coming back to camp.
- Controlling costs of food while providing adequate amounts that are nutritious and enjoyed by the campers and staff alike
- Providing special meals for children with food allergies
- Keeping food safe at all times when serving a large number of campers and staff
- Providing training for all food service personnel

American Camp Association Standards

For purchasing, preparing, or serving food, American Camp Association standards and local regulations will govern the food service. American Camp Association standards include the following:

- Keeping food preparation and storage areas free from accumulated dirt and grease and protected from rodents and insects
- Proper storage of potentially hazardous foods in refrigeration units and maintaining temperatures at 40° or below
- Verifying the training and experience of a food service manager
- Minimizing the time that potentially hazardous foods remain in the food temperature danger zone of 40°F to 140°F
- Using only clean and sanitized utensils and equipment
- Washing and rinsing dishes at the prescribed temperatures
- Air-drying all dishes and food service utensils and protecting them from dust and contamination between use
- Advising rental groups of appropriate procedures in food service (American Camp Association, 2012)

The American Camp Association also recommends food service professional practices which, while not standards, are important reminders to camp owners, directors, and executives, including the following:

- Permanent, enclosed dining facilities to provide protection from problem insects
- Menus planned and/or approved by a nutritionist, dietician, or another person qualified to evaluate the level of nutrition and balance of the meals served
- Food service staff wearing appropriate head covers as required by state/local regulations and wearing clean, neat, practical clothing
- Cans in dining/kitchen areas covered when not in use (American Camp Association, 2012)

State and Local Regulations

Food service to the public is generally regulated by a state or local governmental agency, most of which adopt the Food and Drug Administration's Food Code (Food and Drug Administration, 2013). Appendix O lists the state agencies that regulate food service in public locations, which may include camps depending on circumstances. Camp operators need to be aware of food service regulations in addition to any state or local camp regulations. Separate licenses may be required at several different jurisdictional levels. It is also important for the camp director to understand exactly what the food service license requirements are for his location. In some cases, simply storing lunches brought from home—as is common in most day camps—subjects the camp to the food service requirements of local health departments.

Food Costs

Food supplies, personnel expenses, equipment costs, and utilities will most likely be a major part of resident camp expenses and at day camps if meals are served. Camp executives will want to know a cost per person per meal so food costs can be factored in the decisions related to pricing. Raw food costs can be determined by the formula in Figure 18-1.

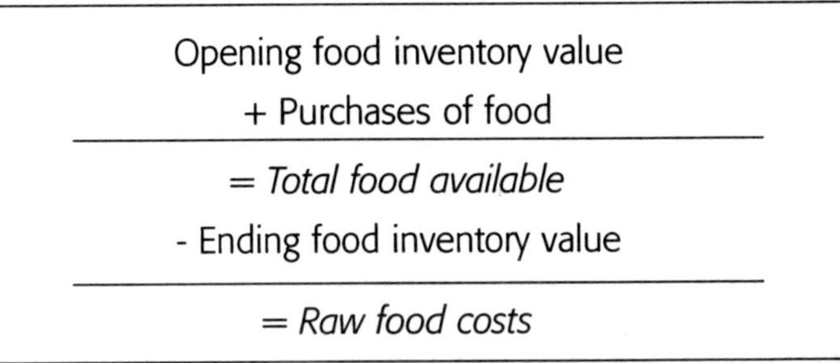

Opening food inventory value
+ Purchases of food

= *Total food available*
- Ending food inventory value

= *Raw food costs*

Figure 18-1. Determining costs for raw food

This calculation takes into consideration not only food served but any wasted food. The camp director should then calculate the remaining costs to determine the total cost of food service. The additional costs are labor, expendable supplies (paper goods, cleaning supplies, etc.), and utilities, plus other building expenses, such as garbage and trash removal. When dividing the total expenses by total meals served, be mindful of not just the campers but all staff who are eating to determine a cost per person. However, you may want to also calculate a cost per camper, knowing that the camper fees must also pay for the cost of meals served to staff.

Note that capital equipment is not included in the calculation. You may choose to add that by including the annual depreciation expense of your food service equipment with the other items listed. Additional expenses may be incurred, such as training, travel, or allocated overhead, which should be added depending on your situation.

Monitoring the costs of raw food on a regular basis will be necessary to maintain control over food costs, which can quickly skyrocket. Food service personnel should be required to use portion control, consistently serving the amounts specified per item per meal. To help control portion size, it will be necessary to provide food service personnel with not only standardized recipes but also the utensils to properly portion food. Guesswork with portions will quickly lead to waste.

Waste is one of the most controllable costs. To minimize waste, have your cooks keep a waste log, noting how much food is wasted before it is served, how much comes back from tables (if family service), how much is overcooked/undercooked, and how much is spoiled and must be thrown away. Together, analyze the amount of waste and how to prevent it. You may need to change menus, change the way in which the food is prepared, change presentation, or change how much food is ordered.

Another critical area of waste is related to following established recipes. Experienced kitchen staff may rely on memory when it comes to recipes, which is generally not a good idea. Try posting recipes so they will be easy to follow. This will not only cut down on waste but will also ensure consistency.

Vendor Assistance

Many food suppliers will include recipes, buying guidelines, newsletters, and pricing trends on their websites. Checking these on a regular basis will assist your food service manager in forecasting costs. Some suppliers also offer menu planning assistance, providing menu rotations of various lengths.

Program Considerations—Cafeteria or Family Style?

Camp owners and directors will want to coordinate their food service operations with programming needs and the camp's philosophy. For example, if the camp considers the small group experience as a major part of the program experience, then serving food family style and having campers eat as a cabin group will most likely be important. Other owners or directors may want to emphasize individual choice by campers, serving cafeteria style and allowing campers to choose where they sit for each meal. In general, cafeteria style will be more efficient and control portions better, while you might have more waste and less portion control with a family-style food service. The choice of serving type should depend on the camp's philosophy.

In *Basic Camp Management: An Introduction to Camp Administration*, Armand and Beverly Ball chart the advantages and disadvantages of cafeteria style versus family style (Figure 18-2).

Cafeteria Style	
Advantages	*Disadvantages*
• Portions are more easily controlled. • Quantities served are more easily controlled, as are costs. • Table setting is not required prior to the meal. • If dining area is too small for the entire community, this style enables persons at the back of the line to fill tables vacated by persons in the front of the line.	• Some people will be completing the meal while others are being served (unless the camp is very small). • It is difficult to have any all-camp activity (announcements, singing) at this type of meal setting.
Family Style	
Advantages	*Disadvantages*
• The counselor can better observe how much and what each camper eats. • Family atmosphere and group spirit are better. • Everyone starts and finishes at the same time. This factor is helpful if singing and/or any announcements follow the meal, and dishes can be cleared before campers leave the table. • It provides opportunities for camper groups to share in tasks around the meal service.	• More food is wasted unless service is controlled by the kitchen and counselors. • Tables must be set in advance. • More time is generally required for the meal.
Ball, A., & Ball, B. (2012). *Basic camp management*. Third edition. Monterey, CA: Healthy Learning. Used with permission.	

Figure 18-2. Determining which meal style to use in your camp

Comparing Vendors

In most areas, food vendors offer significant competition and you can use this to your advantage. However, you have to weigh the time it takes to compare prices among competing vendors, doing this at least once a year—and more often if at all possible.

If you choose to have competitive bids through the procurement process, you will have a better idea of the specific differences in pricing and quality of each product. However, you may want to forgo a formal procurement process and simply get food pricing for a given period of time. Your vendors may guarantee prices for a short period of time—even the entire summer—but you will need to carefully compare each invoice with the guaranteed prices that were quoted. Be sure to get those guarantees in writing, as what your salesman says is of no value if it is not in writing. When comparing food items available from different vendors, take into consideration the following factors:

- Is the quality for each item the same?
- Is the price you were quoted for a particular product or applied to similar products from other manufacturers? Not all products are the same and camper tastes can be finicky.
- Can the vendor supply you with ingredient lists from each food label? This is critically important if you are serving campers with special dietary needs.
- Is the quantity on each item the same? Packaging varies from company to company, so if you have a 64-ounce package of frozen corn, be sure you are not comparing the price to a 72-ounce package of frozen corn.
- Is the service you receive from each vendor the same? If you need something on a day other than your scheduled delivery date, can the vendor make a special delivery? Will he charge you for it?
- What is the delivery schedule? Is this the best day—and time—for you to receive food supplies? Are the deliveries consistent? If the delivery is due by 10 a.m. and what you're planning for lunch is on the truck, will you get it by 10 a.m.?
- Do the vendors provide the same services with regards to unloading the food?
- Is ordering from each vendor a simple process? Do they have online ordering or do you have salespeople who meet with you?
- If vendors could also sell to other camps in the area, would they be willing to negotiate a group rate for you?
- What are the terms and discounts your vendor is offering? Most vendors today are adding fuel or delivery expenses, which substantially affect the price you pay. If you pay "on time" or upon delivery, what is your vendor willing to do for you?

Keep in mind that food might have cost spikes—based on weather and other factors—so be prepared to alter your menu should some items exceed your budget and not be available at a reasonable price. Always have alternatives in mind when planning menus, especially with any items that are subject to sudden price spikes.

Grades of Fruits and Vegetables

It is important to know the grades of fruits and vegetables and the differences between grades. Most fruits and vegetables are graded U.S. Grade A, B, or C, with those in Grade A being the most uniform in shape and size (U.S. Department of Agriculture, 2012). Some vendors may refer to their highest quality as "fancy," followed by "extra standard," and "standard" (grading hasn't been uniform across the industry). It is important to remember that all grades are nutritious. The difference in grades is generally related to consistency, not nutrition. You may save money if you purchase a lower grade of fruit or vegetable—whether fresh, frozen, or canned—with no loss of nutritious value or taste. At a minimum, you should ask your food service director to discuss the price differences of the different grades of all foods with your vendors.

Receipt of Food

Even if your food deliveries come at one of your busiest times, it is important to check all deliveries against the packing slips or delivery receipts. Count not only the case lots, but also check for individual items that may also have been ordered. Verify that all items are as specified on the order and that no substitutes have been made. If you were shorted, note that on the driver's paperwork before you sign off for all the food received. If anything was ordered by weight, check it and verify that you received what was ordered. Also, carefully inspect any damaged boxes to see that the contents are still usable. You should not have to pay for damaged or unusable food or food supplies.

Produce deserves special attention when it is received, as you are more likely to have quality issues with produce than with anything else. Be certain that your produce is fresh and exactly what you ordered. It can—and should—be refused if it doesn't meet your quality standards.

Fresh Foods and In-Season Foods

Serving fresh meat and fruits and vegetables that are in season will almost always be less expensive and provide a higher quality than using processed frozen products. However, you need to realize that time is involved in using fresh products—whether it be shucking corn or peeling tomatoes. Sometimes, the downside of additional preparation time outweighs the benefits of fresh food, especially if you are short on kitchen staff.

You may want to develop a relationship with local farmers and take advantage of fresh vegetables and fruits that are grown locally. One challenge to remember is that you may need to be very flexible with menus because pinpointing exactly when crops are ready to be picked can be difficult as well as knowing how much the farmer can provide you.

Some camps will have a garden as a program area. If you choose to do this, keep in mind that you might have to tend the garden more often than the campers can do themselves and that gardening will require attention before and after the summer camp season. However, having fresh onions, tomatoes, peppers, and other items that can be used in salads (perhaps supplemented by purchased fresh vegetables) can add a special touch to your camp, combining program and food service.

Using Leftover Foods

Some camps serve "must-goes" toward the end of the week, which can be a popular meal, especially if you normally serve family style and utilize all leftover but never served food on a cafeteria line for a change. This can save money and eliminate waste, but it is extremely important to ensure that all standard food safety procedures are followed. In most cases, once food has left the kitchen, it can't be served again.

Also remember that by planning your menus carefully, you can prepare extras of some food items to intentionally be used later in the week, such as vegetables or meats that can be added to soup, thus saving some preparation time later in the week.

Allergies and Special Diets

It is simply not sufficient anymore for camps to eliminate peanut butter from the menu or create a peanut-free table for campers and declare that they have addressed the issue of allergies at camp. According to a 2011 study published in *Pediatrics*, the journal of the American Academy of Pediatrics, as many as 15 million people have food allergies and nearly six million or eight percent of children have food allergies, with young children affected most (Gupta et al., 2011). Take the time to consider that approximately one in 13 campers in your camp program could potentially have some form of food allergy, so you are dealing with an important percentage of your camp business. In addition, parents of campers with food allergies are exceptional advocates for their children and will seek camp opportunities for their families based on your policies toward food safety for their children.

Establishing a "food safe" kitchen will take a coordinated effort on the part of your food service staff, your healthcare staff, your food vendors, your cabin and group counselors, and yourself. Essentially, it will take the efforts of all your staff to make the decision to offer a variety of menus and choices available to ensure the safety of all your campers. It is now a best practice to use no nut oils or hidden nut products, so check all food items to be certain they do not contain nuts or nut oils. Ask your food suppliers about "nut safe" food items in their warehouses. You must confirm all these in writing and have your healthcare specialist review all the items to confirm their safety. What makes this especially difficult is the fact that such allergens as soy, peanuts, and nut oils are so prevalent in food processes today. In addition, many manufacturers are not claiming on packaging if the food was made in a facility that also produces other foods that contain nuts. While it may be difficult to establish a food safe kitchen, it is manageable.

You will need to have a clear policy on how you handle special diets. Do the parents need to provide some of the special foods needed by campers on these diets? Will you charge extra and provide everything needed? Will you simply absorb the cost? Will you need additional kitchen staff to meet the needs of providing vegetarian, gluten-free, and lactose-free meals and other options at every meal? Have cooks been trained in the importance of avoiding cross-contamination? Not only are these considerations for campers, but also for staff.

www.foodallergy.org/resources/camps

Food Allergy Research & Education (FARE)

Food Allergy Research & Education (FARE) reports that every three minutes, a food allergy reaction sends someone to hospital emergency departments, resulting in more than 200,000 emergency room visits per year. A reaction to food can range from a mild response (such as an itchy mouth) to anaphylaxis, a severe and potentially deadly reaction. According to FARE, the following eight foods account for 90 percent of all food-allergic reactions:

- milk
- eggs
- peanuts
- tree nuts (e.g. walnuts, cashews, pecans, etc.)
- wheat
- soy
- fish
- shellfish

It also reports that food allergy is the leading cause of anaphylaxis outside the hospital setting and that teenagers and young adults with food allergies are at the highest risk of fatal food-induced anaphylaxis. Even small amounts of a food allergen can cause a reaction. In addition, FARE reports that symptoms of anaphylaxis may recur after initially subsiding and that experts recommend an observation period of about four hours to monitor that the reaction has been resolved (Food Allergy Research & Education, 2013).

For guidelines on managing food allergies at camp, as developed with the Association of Camp Nurses, see www.foodallergy.org/resources/camps.

Special Food, Special Days

If your camp uses themes for sessions or special days, try to incorporate the food service with the program. For example, if you have a Hawaii theme, work with the food service staff to have a luau. If you have a Western event, plan on having barbeque. Other opportunities may exist for special things just in the area of food service. Whether it's a fiesta meal with tacos, enchiladas, and piñata decorations or a sleep-in Sunday with waffles or omelets to order, having a little variety is always nice.

Also remember that you will have campers and staff who celebrate their birthdays while at camp. Decide ahead of time what you will do for each birthday: A cake for the cabin? A tray of cookies for the cabin? A goofy hat that's worn by the birthday kid? It is important that birthdays are recognized, but that all birthdays are treated equally. Having something special for the entire cabin group is preferable than singling out just the birthday camper so all can celebrate.

The food service staff needs to be aware of special occasions and birthdays ahead of time so it can be prepared and can be part of the planning.

Customer Service and Food Service Staff as a Part of Camp

An important consideration in the selection and training of food service staff is an emphasis on service. Although cooking for several hundred hungry staff, teenagers, and children is certainly not the easiest job in camp, it is important that the food service staff be friendly and pleasant with the staff and campers. When served with a growl, even the best food will not be as good as it should be. Kitchen employees need training in how to deal with their customers—the youngest camper through the most senior of the staff.

Like any other employees, the kitchen staff needs to be a part of the overall camp experience and should be expected to attend staff meetings, participate in camp activities, and get to know campers and other staff. This may be a challenge, especially if your kitchen staff does not live on-site. However, with careful planning, you can incorporate them into general camp activities. For example, you may have a cooking class—and not just outdoor cooking over a fire or coals. One camp had a small kitchen built so campers could learn to bake cookies from scratch, which seemed like a lost art because so many of their campers had never done that before. Following are other ways in which your food service staff can be involved in camp programs:

- Incorporate your food service staff into parts of your staff orientation and training week.
- Your food service director should be included in any leadership team meetings. If you are expecting your food service employees to be involved in camp, they need to be in the "know" like any other program employees at camp.
- Allow them to nurture their culture and share it with the campers and program staff. Songs, cheers, skits, or special talents that are unique to your food service program or staff would be welcomed entertainment at meal time and a great way to increase their involvement in camp.

The occasional use of food service staff in program areas can be a benefit for campers and the employees working in food service.

Cleanliness in Food Service Areas

Cleanliness in food service areas is paramount in camps. Whether feeding 30 or 300 at a time, food service areas must be clean and meet all local and state regulations. In addition, food service personnel must wear hair covers and be clean and neat. If cooks have splattered tomato sauce on their shirts or aprons, have them change and wear a clean apron or chef's jacket before serving food. Think of them just like medical personnel—when the clothes get messy, they need to be changed.

It is also important that in addition to being clean, the kitchen and food service preparation areas should be neat. When deliveries come in, they should be put away as soon as possible and the empty boxes taken to your recycling bins. Just because you run camps doesn't mean that your food service should be any less than a top-quality restaurant. It is important to have clean and neat equipment, clean and neat preparation and service areas, and clean and neat people preparing and serving food. Any one of these falling below standard will negate the high quality of the others.

In short, food service personnel need to look the part! You want a high-quality food service, so make sure your employees look sharp. It will be well worth the investment to provide your food service staff with extra staff shirts or chef's jackets to ensure that they always look clean when serving food.

Business Considerations for Food Service

Numerous factors should be considered when planning for food service and almost all will affect your expenses. Following are a few to keep in mind:

- Inefficiency and waste, which can be controlled
- Available equipment, which will allow personnel to cook more efficiently and provide opportunities for a greater variety of food
- Health considerations for campers—those without special dietary needs and those with special dietary needs
- Types of activities and programs provided by the camp that affect the type of food provided and the amount that campers eat
- Ages and gender of campers
- Typical weather patterns during your primary camp season (Do you really want to serve hot soup for lunch in Texas in July when your dining hall isn't air-conditioned?)
- The availability of food storage space, including dry, refrigerated, and frozen, and the frequency of food deliveries
- The training and experience of food service personnel
- Planned use of leftover foods for the following day's meals
- Policies in place that discourage the theft of food (e.g., no food to be taken home by any food service personnel under any circumstances)
- Regular inventory of food
- Regular maintenance of food service equipment
- Security of kitchen and food service storage, keeping locked during off hours
- Prohibition of "kitchen raids" by staff and campers
- Careful review of food orders prior to ordering
- Confirmation that deliveries include every item on the packing slip and/ or invoice

- Comparison of invoices with packing slips/delivery confirmation
- Emergency contingencies for your refrigeration and freezer units. A well-placed generator dedicated to your kitchen operation can pay for itself with one power outage. Plan on where you can move perishables in the event of an emergency–neighboring camp, restaurant in town, church with a large kitchen, neighborhood school, etc.

Food Service Program as a Marketing Tool

With the changes in camper and camp family dietary habits, the traditional institutional kitchen has changed considerably. It is no longer possible to simply purchase processed frozen foods, reheat them in camp ovens, and call this either dinner or cooking. While it is almost always cheaper (and more delicious) to prepare fresh food, it is also possible to use your food service operation as a point of difference between you and your competitors and garner camper and camper parent interest in your camp program. You can accomplish this in a variety of ways, including the following:

- Organic or natural offerings. While purchasing organic can be more expensive, many families today are interested in consuming a food supply that is free of chemicals.
- Make sure you have an actual cook.
- Offering specialized menus designed around specific dietary needs. Most camp directors would not hesitate to offer vegetarian options in their dinner service. However, they may hesitate at a special request from a camper with celiac disease or anaphylactic peanut allergies. With planning, it is possible to design your program to meet the needs of all your campers.

Parents of campers with severe food allergies or who are extra conscious about health are extremely well educated about food safety. Offering them real choices and having specific food service processes in place to meet the needs of their campers can potentially give you the edge when registration opens.

Training for Food Service Staff

Everyone in every staff position needs ongoing training. For your food service staff, that may mean sending them to formal training events, such as ServSafe®, doing your own training prior to your season with the help of some of your vendors, or something as simple as sending your food service staff to a vendor's product show. In addition, one or more of your food service staff should belong to a professional organization so they can take advantage of not only the organization's training but also receive the periodical published by the organization. Some food service magazines, such as the Association of Nutrition & Foodservice Professionals' journal, are available online, with most articles available at no charge.

States and counties or cities within states vary in their requirements for food service personnel. ServSafe, a well-known program of the National Restaurant Association, provides in-person and online courses. Information is available at its website (www.servsafe.com) for all states and locales, indicating which training is required, any options that are available, and other information, including links to state laws (National Restaurant Association, 2013).

Other Professional Resources

Even encouraging some of your food service staff to use some paid time to read professional journals online can pay off in keeping your menus fresh and costs down. It is also helpful to build up a good food service library with not only cookbooks and recipes, but resources such as the following:

- *Food for Fifty* by Mary K. Molt
- *Principles of Food, Beverage, and Labor Cost Controls* by Paul R. Dittmer
- *Food Service Manual: Lessons in Group Food Service* by Viki Kappel Spain
- *101 Camp Cooking Tips* by Viki Kappel Spain
- Association of Nutrition and Foodservice Professionals: www.anfponline.org
- National Restaurant Association's ServSafe: www.servsafe.com
- USDA: www.nutrition.gov
- RestaurantOwner: www.restaurantowner.com
- National Restaurant Association: www.restaurant.org

Employment Agreements

As the camp administrator, you may want to have human resources policies specific to food service employees, including your policy for taking home any leftover food, what food is available for consumption by the food service staff, where staff eats, and dress code requirements. Some of these items may be regulated by local or state entities, but it is important to acknowledge any expected situations before issues arise.

Contracted Food Service Companies

Food services companies can also provide everything related to food service for camps—often charging on a cost-plus basis—so you still have control of what is served, paying for the cost of labor and food supplies, plus the management fee and profit. This transfers all responsibility to a different entity but will most likely be more expensive. If you're considering using a contracted food service, it will be important to analyze the costs versus the benefits.

Tax Considerations for Meal Services to Employees

Meals provided for employees are generally not considered as taxable income because they're provided for the convenience of the employer and are furnished on your site. However, if you allow employees to receive additional pay instead of eating meals at your camp, then the exclusion won't apply to anyone.

Food service for camps comes with a myriad of challenges—from controlling waste to providing for campers with severe food allergies. However, one overriding factor to keep in mind about food service is that good food service may be taken for granted, but poor food service will do serious harm to a camp's reputation. Bon appétit!

19

Store and Camper Recognition Items

Matthew Ragen/iStock/Thinkstock

The camp store can be a source of additional income as well as a program opportunity. As with other areas, what you sell in the camp store and for how much will depend on your goals and philosophy. Most camps with a store stock the following items for sale to campers:

- T-shirts with the camp name
- Hats or caps with the camp name
- Shorts and other clothing items
- Stationery and stamps
- Water bottles
- Sweatshirts and jackets (for camps in cooler climates)

Other items for sale sometimes include the following:

- Games
- Books
- Pencils and pens
- Stuffed animals
- Blankets
- Specialty items related to camp activities (sports, nature, music, horses, etc.)
- Craft kits or supplies
- Personal care supplies (toothpaste, soap, combs, etc.)

How much or how little you stock in a camp store depends on the emphasis you want to place on the store. Some camps have a scheduled time for campers to go to the store every day, whereas others open the store after meals for drop-in business and still others open the store only when parents are in camp. Online stores are also popular, especially with camps that require uniforms.

How to collect money for the store can take many different forms. Campers can bring cash and keep it with them, they can have cash deposited into a camp store account, or they can have a credit account established for them that parents will pay at the end of camp. Most directors don't want campers to keep cash with them out of concern for potential loss.

Basic Selling Principles

For years, retailers used keystone pricing, establishing the selling price of an item by simply doubling the cost. This method is not commonly used now, with major stores calculating the selling price based on the costs of goods sold, plus operating costs, plus desired profit—much as you would set your pricing for camp sessions. Before setting your prices for items in the camp store, ask the following questions:

- Do you require your campers to purchase camp shirts, etc., as uniforms?
- Do you want the camp store to be a profit center?
- If so, what is the profit margin you need?

- What historical data is available regarding past sales?
- Do you need to allocate expenses to your camp store, such as utilities, salaries, etc., or will you operate strictly off the wholesale cost of the items you sell?

Online Sales

Some camps set up their stores with an online component so campers can purchase required items. Signing up with an online store that serves multiple camps is also a possibility. Some camp management software includes a store module, so you have a variety of choices if you want to sell online.

Purchasing Branded Items

T-shirts are probably the universal item carried at camp stores. You'll need to remember the following things when purchasing shirts and comparing the prices of shirts from different vendors:

- Check the minimum number of shirts that must be ordered. Some shirt companies will require at least 144, while others may require as few as 24.
- Will you incur a screen or setup charge? If so, add this to the cost per shirt to compare.
- Will you have to pay additional fees for multiple colors?
- What does delivery cost? Are you responsible for paying the shipping costs?
- Confirm that the quality of shirts is the same. Ask to see sample shirts in the color and brand so you can compare shirts side by side. You may even want to wash the sample shirts to see how they hold up.
- What are the vendor's policies on reordering?
- Is a deposit required upon ordering? How quickly must the invoice be paid?
- What is the delivery time?
- After adding the additional fees, compare to get a cost per shirt.

As you can see in Figure 19-1, while vendor A had the lowest base cost per shirt by a considerable amount, the fees for vendors A and B increased the final cost per shirt to more than the base cost per shirt for vendor C. It is important to validate that all fees and any hidden costs are included when comparing vendors.

Costs	**Vendors**		
	A	B	C
Base cost per shirt	$3.00	$4.00	$5.00
Base cost times the number of shirts ordered (100)	$300.00	$400.00	$500.00
Setup charge	$150.00	$50.00	$0.00
Screen charge	$35.00	$50.00	$0.00
Estimated shipping	$78.00	$25.00	$0.00
Total cost	$563.00	$525.00	$500.00
Final cost per shirt	$5.63	$5.25	$5.00

Figure 19-1. Comparing costs for shirts

Also, you may be able to offer a variety of shirts and keep costs down (if you must pay a screen charge) by using the same design on different shirts. You may also want to discuss with vendors the possibility of multiple shirt orders during the summer so you can spread out your payments, ordering just enough shirts for each week or two. Once you find a vendor and develop a relationship with him, he will probably be eager to work with you.

Shirt vendors may also offer other items that can be imprinted with your logo. Remember, any item with your camp logo that is purchased by a camper is free advertising for you, so consider the types of merchandise that will be seen by others—clothing, hats, bumper stickers, perhaps water bottles—and make your camp name and/or logo very identifiable.

Advice From a Pro

"The camp store is not only a wonderful profit center but it is a huge opportunity for marketing. The revenue from the camp store helps us further reach our mission and promote our program. I realize that the items included in our store represent our brand. Therefore, I only put our name on quality items. I want the sweatshirt purchased at camp to become their favorite sweatshirt that lasts many years. I want the t-shirt to be one of the shirts they grab when they go on vacation. It is not about finding the best deal on clothing or taking the lowest bid, it is partnering with a quality company that can provide cutting-edge artwork, quality items, and can deliver on time."

— Jeff Cheley, Cheley Colorado Camps, Estes Park (CO)

Pricing Points

It is advisable to have merchandise for sale in several different pricing points—some items under $5, some under $10, some between $10 and $20, and a few at $20 or more. After you have established your store, you may want to add more higher-priced items, especially if parents or camp alumni have the opportunity to visit your store. Blankets, jackets, or other higher-priced items can also be sold to your own staff.

Sales Tax and Unrelated Business Income Tax

Store sales will be taxable, even for nonprofits that are tax exempt and don't normally pay sales tax. A difference exists between purchasing items for your use and purchasing items for resale. You will need a resale certificate from your state and will need to charge tax on everything that is taxable in your state. For example, some states may not tax food items, but others do, so it's important to know what's taxable and the rate for your location. Note that the tax rate at your camp may be different from the tax rate at your office due to locally imposed sales taxes. Check with the state taxing authority for clarification on how this should be handled. Also, when you are purchasing items for resale, you may not have to pay sales tax to your vendors on those items because you will be selling them and charging tax. Again, the laws vary from state to state, so be sure to understand how your state and location treat sales tax.

For tax-exempt camps, store income will most likely be treated as unrelated business income and will therefore be subject to taxes. If you normally file an IRS Form 990—the information return to report your income and expenses—you will most likely also need to file an IRS Form 990-T and be subject to Unrelated Business Income Tax, commonly known as UBIT. However, it is not uncommon for stores to show a loss once occupancy and salaries have been allocated. Therefore, it may be that no UBIT is due. Regardless, nonprofits will still need to file a Form 990-T. Your accountant can provide additional information and guidance on how to segregate your store income and expenses for the purposes of UBIT.

Store Location and Layout

Where you locate your store can make a huge difference in sales. Some camps carve out a part of their dining hall for the camp store, opening it after lunch or dinner. Others have a separate building. Either way, it is important to establish a secure area where merchandise can be locked to prevent possible theft. The location should be convenient for campers and preferably available to parents on check-in, closing, or visiting days.

Camps may be able to obtain fixtures from stores going out of business or upgrading their fixtures. Other opportunities to showcase items are shelves, pegboards, slatwalls (which can be configured in a variety of ways), clothing racks, or glass/plexiglass display cases.

Arranging items for sale is almost an art form, but in general, less expensive items should be placed near the cash register. If you are developing a display with multiple items, place the largest items in the display first, filling in with smaller items in an asymmetrical design. Don't crowd items. You can also use camp props—whether a saddle, canoe paddles, or some other camp-related props—to add a little variety and pizzazz to your displays.

Camper Recognition Items

Most camps provide some type of recognition item for campers—whether it's a patch, shirt, charm, or some other type of branded item. If your camp has been established for a while, it may already have a tradition you want to continue or change. New camps establish a new tradition for camper recognition. Working with your vendors, you can find some type of appropriate recognition item or you can consider using a natural product from your camp. If you decide to use a natural product, keep in mind the time it will take your staff to prepare the items.

Snacks

Some camps also sell snacks at their stores, opening the store during times when snacks are permitted. Selling or not selling snacks will depend on your personal preference, but you do need to consider trash as a result of snack sales and place waste receptacles near the store for wrappers, cans, or empty bottles. Snack service may also come under food service regulations, so check with your state and local officials.

Camp stores can be a major or minor part of the camp experience and should either break even or make a profit. How much emphasis is placed on the camp store is up to the camp administrator, but any branded items sold in the store are opportunities for free exposure and marketing of the camp throughout the year.

20

Year-Round Use

Daniel Hurst/iStock/Thinkstock

Year-round use of a camp can be a huge opportunity or a substantial challenge—or both. Having a site with buildings, program areas, perhaps a food service facility, and probably in a quiet, picturesque area is a wonderful thing. But when the facility is designed for summer camp (and the assumption is that most persons reading this are operating camp programs in the summer), you will have limitations and issues related to using the property for other purposes.

This is where as the camp owner or executive you need to put on your "business hat" and weigh the options in operating your facility in some revenue-generating capacity during the non–summer camp season. What are the benefits and what are the detriments to using your facility more than just the eight to 10 weeks each summer that you are currently using your facility? First of all, consider the obvious fact that you are paying for your facility 365 days per year. Mortgages, taxes, bank loans, and fixed expenses are all drains on your camp business cash flow, not to mention your bottom line, and having the ability to have a secondary business that can help generate income and pay a few bills between seasons can be a good thing. As attractive as an infusion of cash into your business during the non–summer camp season may be, you also need to consider how adaptable your facility is to uses other than summer camp. Things you need to consider include how usable your facilities are in the winter, the cost of operation in the off-season, and the opportunities or potential opportunities you feel are available to make an "off camp season" operation feasible.

Some possible uses for camp properties during the off-season include the following:

- School groups, in particular outdoor education
- Corporate and other retreats
- Church and youth group campouts
- Family camping
- Early childhood education programs
- Seasonal sports opportunities (snowmobiling, skiing, etc.)

Outdoor Education

Outdoor education is probably the most closely related program to a summer camp, and as a result, it is usually the most considered option for camps seeking off-season opportunities. Many camps have developed very successful outdoor education (or environmental education, depending on the area) programs using an existing resident camp. Some considerations for outdoor education programs include the following:

- Will the program be for day use only or will it include overnight experiences?
- What will the exact program be? Most schools who want to purchase outdoor education programs for their students need the lessons to be aligned with state educational objectives. How will the program be developed? Do you have the staff to develop curriculum or will you need to outsource?

- Will you offer a full menu of program services similar to your camp program or will you treat potential off-season businesses as a user group where you offer facilities and limited services only?
- Who will deliver the program? Will you hire staff, and if so, where will they live? Will they work all nine months of the school year or just when outdoor education classes are held?
- How will the outdoor education program be marketed?
- What will you charge?
- Will you provide food service, linen service, and other value-added services similar to your offerings for the summer? Perhaps this could be an additional option (for a larger fee).
- Will you provide any additional services or programs—for example, swimming, horseback riding, or other traditional camp programs?
- Will you need to make any modifications to accommodate boys and girls or perhaps adult chaperones (teachers and parents)?
- Will the school transport the students themselves or will you offer this as an additional service? If you have the ability, transportation services can be extremely lucrative if positioned correctly.

Program Content for Outdoor Education

Most camp directors may think that outdoor education is simply a slight change to their existing camp program. This would be a gross misjudgment. Those camp executives who already have an outdoor education program in place would note that the culture and dynamics of school groups are entirely different. Most are much more structured due to the formality of the educational system.

Program content for school groups can be divided into two areas: educational activities and recreational/adventure activities. For recreational/adventure activities, camps can usually take their existing programs, such as archery and challenge courses, and adapt them easily for school groups use. For educational activities, unless the camp has already developed more formal curriculum guidelines, it will probably be necessary to write programs for outdoor education.

To develop educational activities, look at the opportunities presented by your site. Do you have a lake? Can you do water studies? Do many birds live at your site? Other animals? Do you have a variety of trees and wildflowers that would lead to educational units? Do you have a terrific place to watch the stars? Can you set up a weather station? Does your site have interesting rock formations or fossils? All these natural features can be the springboard to outdoor education activities that can be developed into units with educational objectives.

Camp administrators should investigate what types of outdoor education opportunities exist in the area, visiting as many as possible, to see what schools are currently doing. Then, visiting with school administrators and surveying what they want—and what they will pay—will provide even more information that will help you develop your program. Countless resources exist for outdoor education, but keep in mind that programs will need to be adapted to your own site and surroundings.

Staffing

Just like in your summer program, staffing will be crucial. Your program will not grow and develop overnight, so you may have to be creative with staffing, utilizing summer staff when available (although many caveats come with that–the first being that during the school year, most are not available), contracting with former staff who may not have jobs, or hiring other individuals on an as-needed basis. Granted, this is one of the most challenging parts of any off-season use–having staff when you need them but not paying for staff you do not need.

Staffing for off-season programs will depend on what you are specifically going to be offering, but as with your summer program, staffing is crucial to the success and potential growth of your new ventures. Regardless, make sure you hire the very best people you possibly can. Hiring poorly will not only reduce the chances of your new programs being successful but will also reflect poorly on your existing camp program. You don't want to hurt one business while trying to build another. A potential benefit, however, may be that you develop a reliable base of year-round staff working your summer program and your "new" business venture.

Marketing Outdoor Education Programs

Marketing an outdoor education program is different from marketing summer camp–whether resident or day camp. It takes developing personal relationships with school officials and, to a certain extent, parents. But in most cases, the individual school principal is the person who will make decisions about where the students will be going for off-campus activities. You may first want to survey what programs are currently available to see how much competition you have and if you can make it as another vendor to schools. It is also a good idea to do your research and find out how many students are in the geographic area you serve. One camp looked at all the schools districts within a one-hour drive of its location to determine the number of students in public and private schools, finding more than half a million students. This research can help not only with your outdoor education program but is also a great by-product to use with your regular camp program marketing.

www.nces.ed.gov/globallocator

One source of data that may be helpful in determining the total school-age population by city is the National Center for Education Statistics (www.nces.ed.gov/globallocator). For example, searching ZIP code 76049 (Granbury, Texas, the location of a camp not far from Fort Worth) and asking for all public and private schools within 50 miles yielded 994 schools. A search of ZIP code 60069–a Chicago suburb–for all public and private schools but within only 30 miles yielded 2,068 different schools. Using this type of data, you can more easily determine on which schools you want to concentrate. Much more data is available on this particular site than just location, including school population by grade level. For example, looking again at ZIP code 76049, a search asking for just the third through sixth grades in public schools within 50 miles returned 27,287 students. Tools such as this are invaluable, adding hard data to your options for decisions. Once you have a defined program to sell, marketing your program can be accomplished but will generally take a different path from marketing your summer programs.

Determining What to Charge and Other Decisions

This exercise is not a simple one, as your ability to make a profit will depend on quantity and scale. If you have only a few outdoor education programs, you simply cannot make a profit if you allocate staff time and occupancy—among other things—for the nine-month school year to only two or three outdoor education groups. If you decide to get in this business—or perhaps any other off-season business—realize that until you can take this business to scale, you will be losing money. However, that must be offset by the fact that in some cases, you would have these expenses anyway and would have been absorbing them into your summer budget.

Of course, the differences are that with outdoor education, you may now have more staff and may be keeping your site open for 12 months instead of four or five. Until you build your business, setting your fee for outdoor education will be less based on exact costs and more on what the market will bear. This is not a particularly good thing to do with a fledgling business!

Realize, of course, that school districts seem to always be notoriously short on money. Most will ask parents to pay at least a portion of outdoor education camp fees, but the school also has to come up with money for transportation. Some will also hold fund-raisers, so having this information in your back pocket when visiting with schools is always a good idea.

Advice From a Pro

"The benefit of camp-school partnerships forms relationships that will last for many years. The partnership will help camps grow not only during the summer months but more during the off season.

It's important to learn how to talk the talk and understand the vocabulary used by the educational community. Be patient and find your niche, such as team building or environmental studies; recognize what makes your camp special or unique.

Schools and educational learning programs need to be educated on the overall benefit of the camp experience. Follow through with off -season contacts.

Having the right staff made of mature well-educated leaders will make the camp-school partnership stronger."

— Tony Oyenarte, Director, Lochearn Camp for Girls (VT)

You will need to look at whether you will have just day groups, just overnight groups, or both. If you have overnight groups, then you must have food service and you may need to make changes in your sleeping accommodations. Keep in mind that most adults don't care for sleeping in bunk beds, so if you have a cabin for adult teachers, you may lose half your capacity in those cabins.

Outdoor education is a good year-round program to complement your camp business, but it is a different business than summer camp. You have to be prepared to look at all the things that are different, modify your site and program as necessary, develop curriculum that will meet the needs of your intended audience, and decide if this is a business in which you want to invest your time, energy, and money.

Camps Located Near Urban Areas

In evaluating the viability of additional off-season programming, day camp operators have the distinct advantage because they are generally located closer to population centers that can create a greater demand and larger potential market for additional ventures. A few resident camps will fall into this category based on their location, but to some degree, all camps may consider some of these options. The possibilities are unlimited depending on your facility and your willingness to make the venture work. Many camps located close to metropolitan areas offer the following services during the school year:

- *Corporate retreats/events:* If you are located in an urban area and provided your facility is of sufficient size, you could offer programming based on teambuilding and adventure/challenge activities. Large and small companies see the value in teambuilding exercises for their employees, especially adventure challenge–based programs.
- *Corporate picnics for local companies:* The beauty of these events is that you can also offer them on weekends during the camp season. In addition, if you have the food service facilities and staff to do it, you can possibly cater the event yourself and make additional revenue from another unused asset (kitchen equipment).
- *Facility rental for sports organizations:* With the large offering of community and private sports organizations, athletic field space is at a premium. You may have the opportunity to contract with a local park district for your athletic fields or open spaces if you have the acreage available.
- *Churches and youth organizations:* This market possesses a huge opportunity for camp facilities on single-day and short-term bases. While the potential for per day/event revenue is not as high as what a corporate retreat may offer, it's worth investigating. Renting your facility for an evening of tent camping to a group of younger children and their parents always has potential with a minimum of staff expense. Youth organizations also offer a potential camper a first exposure to your camp facility and program and is also a wonderful marketing opportunity.
- *Early childhood programming:* Early childhood (pre-school) programs are in huge demand, especially high-quality programs. These programs do have more licensing requirements due to state and local regulations and you need to hire the appropriate staff and create curriculum, but the return on investment can be significant. As with churches and youth organizations, early childhood programming can have a positive effect on your marketing and enrollment for your camp program by exposing children and parents

to the wonderful things your facility offers. It also broadens your marketing efforts because they are specifically targeted toward young children and families. Not all parents realize the benefit of summer camp programs and youth development, but they universally accept the fact that pre-school is mandatory. Also, because early childhood programs typically follow the traditional September to June school calendar, they make an excellent companion activity for day camps. If this is an avenue you choose to pursue, be prepared because a variety of mandatory licensing requirements exist that vary from state to state that are different from those required to operate a camp program.

You have really no limit to the number of additional uses for your camp facility, provided that you are willing to put in the additional effort to make them successful and that is really the caveat you need to keep in mind. If you are going to seek additional ventures, do them to the best of your ability and do them well. The way the public views your new business will also reflect on your camp business. Doing something new poorly will have a negative effect on all your efforts to make your camp business successful and in the long run won't be worth the additional time and effort.

It is also important for you to evaluate what the value will be of the new business venture from a revenue standpoint. The opportunity to rent your facility for a corporate party for several thousand dollars has obvious appeal. Renting your indoor space for yoga instruction at $200 per month may not seem worth the time or the effort. Those decisions are strictly yours to make, but you need to evaluate the value for the amount of extra effort (on your part) and also the wear on your facility.

For example, consider that you decide you are going to rent your facility to groups each weekend for the summer. You decide based on your market research that you can charge $1,000 per day for the exclusive use of your property. Each summer has roughly 20 weekend days, and if you were to rent each Saturday and Sunday, you would receive an additional $20,000 in revenue for the year—from private picnics alone. The purpose of considering noncamp programming is to generate additional revenue, so it may be worth your time to explore everything. Be creative and think outside the box. While you don't want to venture into businesses that would potentially harm your existing camp business, you can find a variety of uses that generate revenue and stay congruent with your existing mission.

Directors From Nonprofit Agencies

Directors who work for nonprofit agencies may have a different set of responsibilities during the school year or camp-related responsibilities. In addition to the items listed previously, nonprofit youth organizations also have the option to use their camps for weekend activities for their year-round members.

Other Off-Season Activities

Other camps have included the following activities in their off-seasons:

- Christmas wreaths made from camp evergreens and shipped all over the country
- Wedding rentals and other special events
- Horseback riding lessons and stabling services
- Growing and selling pecans

Opportunities will vary—be creative, think outside the box, and think about how your site could be utilized year-round.

Capacity and Site Utilization

Another important formula when looking at your year-round use of your site involves comparing your capacity to the utilization of your property. This is addressed in Chapter 9 in more detail but is noted in this chapter because of the effect on facility use decisions.

Camps can determine their utilization by developing a chart that includes each month or week of the year and the capacity for that time of year. For example, you may be able to accommodate 200 campers each week in the summer but only 100 during the winter months due to your facilities. Or if you're renting a facility, you may only have access to six weeks, so your maximum utilization would be calculated over the six-week period. Figure 20-1 is one example of a camp's capacity and utilization.

Month	**Capacity per Week**		**Number of Available Weeks**	**Total Capacity for the Month**	**Current Utilization per Month**	**Percent Utilization**
	Campers	*Staff*				
January	100	15	3	345	0	0%
February	100	15	4	460	50	10.8%
March	100	15	4	460	75	16.3%
April	200	30	4	920	200	21.8%
May	200	30	5	1,150	300	27.3%
June	200	30	4	920	850	92.3%
July	200	30	4	920	900	97.8%
August	200	30	4	920	750	81.5%
September	200	30	4	920	300	32.6%
October	200	30	4	920	400	43.5%
November	100	15	3	345	60	17.3%
December	100	15	2	230	30	13.0%
Total				8,510	3,915	46.0%

Figure 20-1. How a camp can utilize its space

Looking at this figure, it appears that the summer months are almost at 100 percent capacity but that opportunities for growth exist in the fall and winter. Using this type of data, the camp owner or director will be better able to make sound financial decisions and see that the data tells the story. In this case, the story is the underutilization of an asset for all but the summer months.

The corollary, however, is the staffing and occupancy costs for year-round use. At what point do you look at the data and determine that it's costing you more to be open year-round than you can afford? What is it worth to have groups in over the year? You might find it sensible to operate a less-than-profitable outdoor education program or to open up your facility to families or corporate or church groups on weekends. If you see these as important to marketing your summer camp operation—and you track data to prove it—then year-round use by other programs may be one of your best marketing events.

No one can tell you it is always best to use your site year-round or that it's never a good idea. You will have to take into consideration everything unique to your site: the expense of operating year-round versus the expense of having to shut down your site and then open it up again; the cost of having a year-round staff on site and the security that brings versus having staff there only when you need it; and the identity of your camp as many different things to different people versus the single identity of being a summer camp—among other options.

Regardless, following are the important things for camp administrators to remember about using their sites on a year-round basis:

- If it's a different business, treat it that way. Develop a business plan, a budget, a marketing plan, and all the other business pieces necessary to develop a separate business.
- Visit with other camp owners and directors to learn from them about the challenges of operating a second business.
- Evaluate whether you can be in charge of both businesses or if you need to hire someone else.
- Re-evaluate your situation every two or three years, as the climate for different businesses may have changed.

The challenges with non–summer camp uses of your site include staffing, maintenance, marketing to different audiences, and operating a completely separate type of business than your summer camp program. "Because we've always done it this way" is never a good answer to why you would or would not operate additional programs during the year. But basing your decision to use or not use your site year-round on your mission, on your goals, and, in particular, on data will serve you well.

21

Succession

mandygodbehear/iStock/Thinkstock

An important part of building a successful business—particularly a camp business—is developing a succession plan in the eventuality that you as the individual owner or executive of an organization are no longer in charge of the day-to-day operating responsibilities of your camp program. This may be the result of retirement after many years of successfully managing your business, a change in management structure, or an unexpected life event. Regardless of the reason for a succession plan to be necessary, the point is that in order for your organization to remain relevant into the future, it will rely in large part on the plans you make many years in advance.

In an article titled "Succession Planning: Raising Up the Next Generation of Leaders," Kurt Podeszwa (2010) writes:

> What will this industry look like in twenty years? That depends on us. That's right; don't look over your shoulder to see who else is going to step up. As leaders of youth, we know that we shape the future. But how much thought have you put into how you will shape the future of your organization and our industry? Empowering the next generation of leaders will make our organizations stronger as we train others to handle our responsibilities when we are not there. As role models, we can help shape our developing industry, and by offering professional development, we will keep our own skills fresh. This is not something that just happens. Raising up the next generation of leaders needs to be as intentional as the goals and outcomes we set for our campers. In order to offer intentional experiences to help staff develop, we have to overcome barriers in our way of thinking and in our organizational processes.

Succession planning is not just a sound and necessary business function. It is also your responsibility as one of the stewards of this amazing industry. Without your continual efforts to "pay it forward" to the next generation of camp professionals and foster their development, you will be doing the youth in your communities a disservice and jeopardize the future of camping. However, as with anything, the development of succession plans is somewhat complex and needs to be viewed by your classification as one of the following:

- Agency (nonprofit) or faith-based based programs
- Privately owned (for profit or nonprofit) programs

Succession Planning for Agency or Faith-Based Programs

While slightly less complicated than succession planning in privately owned entities (because no transfer of ownership occurs), succession plans in agency or faith-based programs are equally important to ensure a seamless delivery of high-quality youth programs. Efforts for this business segment should focus on the development—either internally or externally—of high-quality staff—some of whom may (or at least should be) in the grooming process for the eventuality that the current executive will no longer be in his current position. To this end, it is critical that as the camp executive you actively recruit and develop individuals who will have the skills necessary to possibly assume camp leadership one day in the future.

Your current kitchen manager or assistant program director may be a wonderful person and very good at what he does in his current position, but does he really possess the skills that are required to do all that an executive director needs to do in order to suitably do the job? Take a hard look at the individuals who are working for you. Do you see them presenting an annual budget to your board? Do they have the social and business skills required to solicit funding from potential donors? If any of these questions give you pause, your program may not be prepared for a successful transition in leadership to someone currently employed on your staff.

This is not to say your staff needs to be replaced or that you need to look elsewhere for a possible succession candidate, but you need to look objectively at your staff and determine who is really capable of doing your job effectively. This is a very difficult process for any manager to go through. As "camp people," you're pre-disposed to appreciate all your staff members for the wonderful individuals they are. However, in this situation, you can't look at all your staff as being capable of doing your job. Some are going to be better than others, and no matter how unpopular your decision may be, it is your responsibility to identify those individuals who truly have the potential to succeed you. It won't be easy, but remember that the future of your organization depends on your decision.

When going through this process, you may also come to the realization that your staff just isn't ready for the responsibilities of executive leadership. This is where you as a manager need to put on your staff development hat and start mentoring your staff members in the skills they need to develop. Perhaps you could involve them in workshops or seminars offered by your local American Camp Association section. If specific skills need to be addressed, maybe you need to look at offering continuing education for your potential succession candidates at local community colleges or other professional development programs. The point is that you need to develop, coach, and mentor suitable candidates who possess the skills and aptitude to possibly take over your job one day.

Succession Planning for Privately Owned Camps

As an individual entity, entirely different sets of succession planning concerns and difficulties for privately owned camps exist. A family member or several family members might be interested in taking over the camp business. Other family members might feel entitled to your position, which further complicates matters, as one can imagine. Also worthy of consideration is the fact that as the owner and director of your camp business, you have large financial and sentimental attachments to your camp. You may also decide to look outside your family for a possible successor. The issue of succession in an individual or family-owned camp business is complicated and requires thoughtful planning to ensure that the legacy and financial stability of the camp business continue long into the future.

Family Business

While on the surface family businesses seem to be simple, idealistic small entities, in reality, they are quite complicated. Not only are they susceptible to the same economic pressures of their larger counterparts, but the family dynamic can play a significant role in the development and functioning of the family itself. Simply put, family businesses aren't for everyone. You work closely with those that are closest to you, and unlike other professions where you work for a small family-owned camp business, the business itself becomes an extended member of your family whether you want it to or not. When the phone rings at 3 a.m. with a call from the alarm company saying you have a trouble signal coming from the dining hall, what choice do you have but to get up and investigate?

At the same time, family-owned businesses (camp businesses included) are the cornerstone of the U.S. economy. According to the Small Business Administration, family-owned businesses account for 90 percent of all businesses—large and small—in the United States (Small Business Administration, 2011). Family businesses are a powerful force in the economy, and certainly within the family, powerful forces are at work related to the business. But when it comes to succession, the following are questions that must be faced:

- What are your family goals for the future?
- What are the plans for the next generation? Who is interested in staying in business and leading the way? Does more than one person stand out as a potential leader? Who is best equipped to lead? What role will the other members play?
- What if no one from your family is interested in succeeding you in operating your business? (Small Business Administration, 2011)

The time to ask these questions—and many others—is well before succession is necessary. Part of the difficulty with developing a succession plan is having the difficult discussions with your family members about who you feel should be the person to lead the organization into the future. Telling someone you are not choosing him to be part of the next generation of leadership is hard, but telling a close family member you're not going to sell him your life's work can be impossible. A clear chain of command should exist, especially in situations where succession occurs earlier than planned, so the next generation is well prepared as well as knows who should be in charge.

The Next Generation

McKinsey & Company®, a global management consulting company, noted on its website that:

> [a]s family businesses expand from their entrepreneurial beginnings, they face unique performance and governance challenges. The generations that follow the founder, for example, may insist on running the company even though they are not suited for the job. And as the number of family shareholders increases exponentially generation by generation, with few actually working in the business, the commitment to carry on as owners can't be taken for granted. Indeed, less than 30 percent of family businesses survive into the third generation of family ownership. (Caspar, Dias, & Elstrodt, 2010)

Some decisions to be made about family-owned camps include the following:

- Who will be in charge? Are there next-generation family members who are not only qualified but are also committed to running the business? If not, to whom do you turn? Will you sell a part of your business to an outsider or someone who has worked at the camp?
- Whether a family member or not, the next leader of your camp should be mentored. An owner will do a disservice to the family business by neglecting such mentorship. Provide opportunities for the designated successor to be a part of important decisions. Provide for training—through the American Camp Association or other entities—for the designated successor.
- Determine your timetable and let it be known to all involved.
- Decide on your role in the future. Consult experienced camp owners who have made the change from being the active director to that of director emeritus or consulting director.

Advice From a Pro

"Camp owners have two important assets: their family and their camp. Planning for prompt leadership succession is insurance for keeping the camp business viable and the camp experience intact for our nation's children. Timeline? Make succession plans NOW!"

— Jean McMullan, Alford Lake Camp, Hope (ME)

Valuing the Family Business

Selling the family business to another family member can be a tricky experience. Baylor University's Bill Worthington, assistant professor at the Hankamer School of Business, was quoted in an article by the National Federation of Independent Businesses: "There's a whole different dynamic to consider and deal with when your successor is a family member. Both parties know the other's weaknesses, for example, and that can cause hesitation on the part of the incumbent or aggression on the part of the successor" (National Federation of Independent Business, 2013).

Getting an outside appraisal and assistance from your accountant and your attorney will be advantageous for the seller and the buyer because capital gains may take a considerable bite out of the seller's proceeds and the buyer—even if a family member—will be reassured that the value of his investment is accurate.

Additional Succession Considerations

Another difficulty when developing succession plans for privately owned camp businesses has to do with how the assets of the camp business are treated during the succession itself. The value of even a small camp business can be substantial when considering the values of the land, business, and facilities. Careful legal and financial plans need to be developed to ensure that in the eventuality of succession, the next generation owner/director isn't saddled with staggering tax liabilities or legal requirements that divert attention away from building and maintaining the success of the camp business. To this end, it is imperative that you receive professional legal and financial advice from your lawyer and accountant and perhaps also retain the services of a reputable estate planning professional.

Succession Without Family Involvement

In the event you find yourself without a family member to take control of the camp business, it is possible to still sell the business and continue the legacy you've created. While it is always possible to find an outside buyer, you need to make sure you're finding the *right* buyer. You have years of your own hard work at stake and, more importantly, you have a large financial interest. For many private camp owners, the single largest investment they own is their camp business, and as with any financial instrument, it must be protected to maximize its value. Following are different ways in which you can sell your camp business:

- Conventional sale
- Business purchase with a land lease
- Owner-financed sale

Conventional Sale

In a conventional sale arrangement, the buyer and the seller agree on the terms of a purchase for the business and the property and the seller arranges to make the purchase using funds gathered from personal funds, investors, or conventional business loans. While this is a great arrangement for the seller, as he receives the money at closing, it is becoming unusual to have this kind of financing arrangement. Simply put, as land prices have increased over time, it is increasingly difficult for camp businesses to support the value of the property. In many cases, especially in more urban locales, the values of the land alone far outweigh the values of the businesses that operate on them. When you arrange for financing, a bank or group of investors may question why you would operate a camp business when you could probably be better off financially in developing the property for another use.

Business Purchase/Land Lease

In a business purchase/land lease arrangement, the seller agrees to pay a sum up front for the value of the camp business and agrees to rent the property from the seller for a finite period of years. For example, after purchasing the business, you may choose to lease the facility from the seller for an extended period of 10 to 20 years. At the end of the lease period, the seller would then be free to either sell the property to you the buyer, take the land for his own use, or find another use for the property altogether. While this is an attractive and potentially less expensive way for you to own your own camping business, it does pose more risk due to the fact that at the end of the property lease agreement, you would potentially own a camp business without a place to operate. The seller could choose not to re-lease or sell the property to you in the future. If the camp you're looking to purchase is closely tied to the environment of the facility, this makes the purchase potentially risky. Also, if you need to borrow money from an outside source, you may incur the risk of having very little collateral with which to guarantee your note, meaning you will pay a significantly higher interest rate on the note or not receive financing at all.

Owner-Financed Sale

In an owner-financed sale, the seller agrees in essence to operate as the mortgage lender and receive payment from the buyer for the value of the property as well as the value of the business. Depending on the value of the transaction and the duration of the agreement, payments will be made by the buyer to the seller for a duration of several years on a monthly or quarterly basis. The buyer may agree to make a down payment to "secure" the transaction and these transactions are usually of a much longer duration of 15 to 20 years. They do pose an equal element of risk to both parties. The risk to the seller is that the buyer may decide to back out of the business after several years and the risk to the buyer is that the business may not be all that was represented by the seller during the negotiation process. What is most attractive, however, is that for a well-established camp business, this type of agreement minimizes the issue of the value of the land being too valuable to be supported by the business.

The biggest caveat for the owner-financed sale is that the parties involved really need to be comfortable with each other, as they are entering into a potentially decades-long business agreement. If you are not comfortable working closely with others for long periods of time, this may not be the financing arrangement for you.

Changing the Structure of Your Camp

Some for-profit camps have made the decision to change their structure from a family- or individually owned for-profit entity to that of a nonprofit. This sometimes happens when a family (especially a second- or third-generation one) no longer wants or is unable to continue private ownership or if a concern arises about the camp property being sold to a developer. Many times, camp alumni have formed a nonprofit foundation to purchase the camp and have established it as a tax-exempt entity, thus keeping the property as a camp and keeping alive the vision and mission of the original camp leaders. The purpose of the foundation must align with those in the IRS code for tax-exempt organizations, generally as an educational entity. This can be a complicated situation and takes expert guidance from an attorney who specializes in nonprofit organizations.

The Aloha Camps made the transition to nonprofit successfully over time. Posie Taylor, director emeritus of the Aloha Foundation, offered the following suggestions in an article in *Camping Magazine*:

- "Make a very careful self-examination. Think really hard about how such a dramatic change will affect your future, your dreams for yourself, and your family. Picture this new and different relationship with camp: Does it feel right and good from most perspectives? A little angst is fine. After all, you are sending your "baby" out into the nonprofit world. But are you at least 85 percent sure it will be the right move? Hold multiple conversations with any family members who'll be touched by your decision. Do they understand and support you? Are they waving multiple red flags? Are they asking good questions, and is the conversation generally positive? Proceeding in the face of family disagreement is possible, of course, but time spent talking through the issue and developing consensus early generally tends to create a happier outcome!
- Speak with a trusted lawyer. At this point, a good attorney can give you the questions to ask and the information to gather before making any sudden moves.
- Speak with your accountant or auditor. Talk about assets and what might be included in the nonprofit. Ask about financial risks and essential records. Consider with this knowledgeable person the financial ramification on your family and your needs going forward. Make a financial plan.
- Share ideas with select valued alumni, staff, parents, and friends. Listen carefully and objectively to their feedback. Ask them to share positive and negative reactions. Have another person with you as you listen to their thoughts, as hearing clearly may be harder than you think. Compare notes and write down all relevant points, positive or negative.
- Revisit all the feedback received so far. You will have a first reaction to all you have learned and heard. Write it down. Write down your elevator speech. Keep a file of legal opinions you have gathered and any other relevant feedback." (Taylor, 2012)

It should be noted that making the change from for profit to nonprofit isn't a solution when a camp is losing money nor is it a way to shore up a faltering organization. However, a change in structure might make sense and should be considered, especially when dealing with succession planning.

Communication With Camp Families

Changes in camp ownership or leadership can be difficult on camp families, many of whom may have attended the camp for generations. After one camp owner made a difficult decision to close the camp for family reasons, he suggested in a note to camper parents that campers and parents might feel

Advice From a Pro

> *"If you're contemplating working with others to establish a foundation that would purchase a for-profit camp and establish it as a nonprofit, follow the advice of Posie Taylor, director emeritus of the Aloha Foundation, which was successfully formed to purchase the Aloha camps in Vermont in the late 1960s. She suggests that you "[s]et up a meeting with a camp or two who have taken this path recently: ACA may well be able to help you locate several that are similar in many aspects to your own. Invite the directors to lunch or dinner. Relax with them and hear their stories. What worked easily? And what was unexpectedly hard? Talk finances and talk family. Hear the challenges they faced and what they would have done differently, knowing what they know today. Ask how their board works and whether being educational and philanthropic feels natural or like a tight shoe every day." (Taylor, 2012)*

heartbroken, with campers not having "their" camp to return to the next summer and never being able to realize their dreams of someday being a counselor. Camper families can get very attached to a camp due to the influence that the camp experience has on so many people. This particular camp owner made a very thoughtful decision in contacting the families so they heard about the camp closing directly from him, not via the rumor mill.

You also have to keep in mind that ownership changes at camp create a level of uncertainty for your camp families. You know that any changes you make (as the incoming camp owner) are only going to enhance the experience for your campers and their families, but you need to reassure them of this. Change is difficult, especially when it involves an institution such as a camp. One of the many endearing qualities about camps is that they hold traditions and culture in such high regard. Your customers do too, which is why so many of them return to you year after year and generation after generation.

If you are taking over an existing program, you might have a long list of things you would like to change once you assume ownership. Be cautious and change only those things you feel are essential to the enhancement of a camper's experience. Make improvements to the facility, but be careful about how much change you ask your camp population to accept at one time. Hopefully, you will own your camp business for a long time and you'll have plenty of opportunities to change your program in the future. Too much change at one time will only push customers away at a time when you need them the most.

Some key points regarding communicating with camp families during a time of transition include the following:

- As soon as you begin implementing your camp succession plan, communicate it to your camp families. You want them to hear it from you, not from someone else.
- Make sure the current owner/director is the person making the introductions of the new owners/directors. Detail their credentials, experience, and what their roles will be during the transition.
- Make sure the current owner/director specifically outlines his role during the transition period. Such titles as director emeritus or consulting director are great ways to differentiate.
- If possible, design your transition plan so leadership is passed over the period of at least one camp season and make sure the former owner/director has a visible presence at camp.
- All marketing communications (letters, emails, website pages, and brochures) should include the former owner/director as well as the incoming owner/director.
- In most cases, you want to give the impression that little is changing at the camp as a result of the transition, so be careful how you word your communications. Too much talk about all the things that will be changed as the result of the new management structure may have a negative effect on your customer base.
- Gradually, as you pass through your first year, slowly phase out any mention of the previous owner so your customers begin to rely on you and your decision making in all aspects of your camp operations.
- Communication to camp families concerning the transfer of leadership, however, can be a very upbeat message, especially if the new owner or director has been a member of the camp staff for a while and is known to the current group of campers.
- Camp owners or directors may want to engage professional assistance from a trusted marketing advisor in making announcements about leadership or ownership changes, knowing whether to communicate by email or via social media.

The McKinsey & Company article concluded that:

> [a]lmost all companies start out as family businesses, but only those that master the challenges intrinsic to this form of ownership endure and prosper over the generations. The work involved is complex, extensive, and never-ending, but the evidence suggests that it is worth the effort for the family, the business, and society at large. (Caspar, Dias, & Elstrodt, 2010)

22

Advisors, Relationships, and You

nimis69/iStock/Thinkstock

Said the reader who thought he wanted to start a camp and then got this far before screaming: *"Help! The more I read, the more complicated this becomes!"*

Owning and operating a camp is not as complicated as it seems, but no ever one said that starting or purchasing a camp would be easy. It's a business with many different parts and will take concentrated effort to plan and get off the ground. The good news is that you don't have to figure out everything on your own. Although camp professionals can do many, many things, avoiding the engagement of professional assistance in some areas of your business can be a costly if not fatal mistake. The expense in hiring quality advisors and consultants is minor when compared with the cost of trying to fix errors in legal documents or realizing too late that your insurance did not provide the coverage you thought it did. Some of the professionals that you need include the following:

- An attorney familiar with small business organizations
- An accountant also familiar with small businesses
- A banker
- An insurance broker
- A public relations/marketing professional
- A technology/information systems consultant

For all these advisors, referrals from friends and colleagues are often the best way to find someone who can be of assistance to you. As mentioned previously, getting actively involved in networking within your community is a great way to build business relationships inside and outside the camping world. Networking in your community will put you in contact with other professionals from other fields and is an excellent resource in finding professionals you feel comfortable working with.

While you can "in house" some tasks, you should never underestimate the value gained by looking outside your organization for professional assistance. One of the biggest dangers you'll face as a camp professional is becoming complacent in the operation of your day-to-day businesses. Face it, you don't come into contact with many other camp professionals as you go about the day-to-day operation of your business. Getting outside input keeps you current with developments in your industry and in the world of business in general.

Attorneys

If you need assistance in locating a good attorney, check the Martindale-Hubbell website at www.martindale.com. Before you engage an attorney, determine if his area of specialty corresponds to your needs or if he has other attorneys in the firm for those services.

You will most likely need an attorney who knows employment law, small business administration, and who is familiar with laws relating to children. You will also want to determine his level of expertise in the field of building and zoning as well as general land use. As rural and unincorporated urban communities continue to expand, many camps are seeing an increased need to conform with various government regulations in topics ranging from zoning uses to septic and well requirements. While you can try to sort out the maze of government requirements yourself, it is advisable to seek competent legal advice.

Financial Advisors

Your state board of accountancy or local chapter of CPAs can be of assistance in locating an accountant who has small business experience, knowledge of personnel and benefits, and tax issues. Local chambers of commerce and the Better Business Bureau are also great places to start seeking accountants and financial advisors. It will also be extremely helpful if the accountant you select has experience in using the accounting software you use.

You will also need to seek input from a qualified financial advisor with regards to estate planning, tax regulations, and succession planning. While this may also be a task handled by an attorney, at some point in owning your own camp business, you will need sound financial advice in planning for your estate and how your business will be managed into the future.

Banking

You may have even more choices when looking for a banker. With the consolidation of many community banks into larger banks, many can offer a greater range of services. You will want your banker to have lending authority, which is sometimes easier to find with relationship managers at community-based banks. At a minimum, you will want your bank to provide not only checking and savings accounts for the camp, but also payroll services for direct deposit, a line of credit, small business loans, and perhaps wire transfers and merchant services for credit cards. Shop your choices carefully and be thorough in researching and asking questions from potential bankers. Be sure to ask for the fees for various transactions—from credit card charges to overdraft fees—then comparison shop. You have the opportunity to bundle your services with one bank, but make sure it's giving you the combination of service and fees you are comfortable with. Your bank may also provide a bank-at-work program, offering discounted checking accounts for your employees. The banking industry has changed drastically in recent years, and as a result, banks are as competitive as ever in working to get your business.

Insurance

Your insurance agent should be able to offer all types of insurance coverage you require and get competing bids from different carriers. This process should be conducted every year and your agent should also take the time to show you not only competing bids but also how adjusting your deductibles will affect your premiums. The business of camp is different from other businesses, so having an agent who understands what you do at camp can save you considerable dollars by shopping your business for you.

Information Technology

Your technology professional will need to have a complete knowledge of your hardware and software and should be able to assist you with installation, wiring, training, and ongoing maintenance.

Marketing Consultants

For marketing pros, ask to see what they have produced for other youth-related clients. Camp executives probably want to have a full-service firm that can handle websites, social media, press releases, promotional material, and other forms of marketing services.

Interviews

Regardless of the consultants you are seeking, take time to interview them. Some business owners/camp directors may spend more time researching the purchase of a new canoe than they do looking for their professional advisors. These are crucial decisions to make for the long-term success of your business. The following are some questions you may want to ask potential advisors:

- What experience do you have working with small businesses (and with start-ups if that applies)? If the camp is organized as a nonprofit, ask about experience in working with other nonprofits. If yours will be a family-owned camp, ask about experience working with family businesses.
- What experience do you have with camp? Did you ever attend camp, work at a camp, or have children who attended camp? Do you have other clients who operate camps? Any advisor who will be working with your organization needs to understand the unique nature of what camp executives do.
- Would I be working directly with you or with one of your subordinates? Who else will be on the team that works for me?
- What are your fees and the fees with others in your firm or company who would work with me?
- What additional services can you offer that might add value to our relationship?

While you can certainly make changes in any of these professionals at any time, look for long-term relationships. Consider not just your current needs but also your potential needs in the next couple years. The best relationships with outside advisors are those that are developed over time because those individuals truly understand your history and what makes your business unique.

It's a good idea to think of all your advisors as potential camp parents or marketers for your programs, inviting them to come to your site, see the program in action, and become engaged in what you are doing. The more they know about you and your camp, the better service they can provide you.

Camp Relationships

www.ACAcamps.org/membership/join-aca-today

As has been noted previously, if you do not already belong, join the American Camp Association and attend local and national meetings and workshops, making a point to meet people and get to know what they do. Always have your business cards with you and exchange cards with everyone you meet. Camp professionals are known for sharing ideas even when competing for the same customers. Through your involvement with the American Camp Association, you will find many opportunities for continuous learning—whether through attendance at conferences, reading their numerous publications on an array of relevant topics, or involvement in governance or leadership positions within the association. A camaraderie is shared among camp professionals, many of whom develop relationships with colleagues from all segments of the profession and all parts of the country. Within these relationships, you may find a mentor with whom you can share your challenges and successes and who will provide valuable guidance about your camp business.

Characteristics of a Good Leader

Much has been written by very bright and successful people about the characteristics needed to be a good leader or executive. But a recent post by Georgina Stamp (2013), an executive with a firm specializing in placing interim managers, offered the following 10 characteristics that seemed to hit the mark for camp executives who want to be successful:

- *Good communication skills:* For a camp executive, you have multiple groups with which you must communicate and communicate well: campers, their parents, your staff, your investors or donors, and the public. As Stamp said in her blog: "You must be able to stand confidently in front of everyone and speak coherently whenever you are addressing important issues. Always maintain eye contact to make sure everyone is listening when you are talking to them. Most importantly, you should always listen to your juniors or customers when they have something to say and act accordingly" (Stamp, 2013).
- *Commitment and passion:* Camp executives do not get into this line of work without both of these. Enough said.
- *High self-esteem:* You can't please everyone all the time and you will have some failures. As the leader, you have to learn from your mistakes, and even when you fail, still be yourself and keep your principles firmly intact.
- *Quick thinking:* Identifying and solving issues are things camp executives do every day at camp. Whatever the situation, be prepared to analyze quickly and make a decision about what to do.
- *Ability to multitask:* You will face this every day, as you will have many decisions and actions you have to take as a camp director—from the mundane to life changing.
- *Flexibility:* This is no surprise to camp professionals! Being flexible is something you may have to do every single day at camp, ready with activities and alternate programs due to weather or changing work assignments when employees are ill.

- *Humility:* This may seem like the opposite of high self-esteem, but these two characteristics go hand in hand. If you are approachable—by your staff, by your campers, by the parents—communication will be better and you will open up the possibility for some potentially wonderful suggestions to make your camp even better.
- *Motivator:* Show your appreciation to your staff and the campers and lead them toward their (and your) goals.
- *Risk-taker:* If you have come this far, then you are obviously ready to take some risks. The key is to control the risks when you can—just as you tell your campers.
- *Good sense of humor:* Even camp can sometimes become stressful and hectic, so never lose your sense of humor. Enjoy yourself at camp—it's a great life!

Some of the Best Advice Ever

- Be firm, be fair, and be consistent.
- You can never go wrong being kind.
- You can't spend more than you make—even if you're running a nonprofit.
- Shop everything!
- The key difference between a good business, a great business, and an exceptional business is customer service. Customers control your brand.
- Find the "Yes." You are in a customer service business, and even if it goes against "policy," the customer is always right.
- You cannot own price. Identify what makes your program unique and market yourself on the merits of the program, not on how much you charge.
- Listen more and talk less.
- Hire the attitude but teach the skill.
- Treat every staff employee the same as you would your own child. Remember they are someone's son or daughter.
- What we tolerate, we teach.
- Don't just say it—behave it.
- If you manage the business, the bucks will take care of themselves.

Conclusion

Many owners, directors, and executives become camp professionals because they either had a positive experience at camp as a child or because they grew up through the ranks, advancing from counselor to leadership positions in a camp. The transition from camper to program staff to that of being the owner or director of a business can bring challenges, realizing that the buck now stops with you. But you cannot get so caught up in the emotion of all the amazing "feel good" moments that you enjoy every day working with children and families that you forget that at their core, all camps are businesses. You manage millions of dollars in business and facilities every day—all in an environment of liability and risk that keeps your insurance agents awake each night!

This book began by sharing the need for a balance in decision making—always considering the mission of the camp as well as good business practices. It can be a delicate balance. You may remember a TV commercial from long ago that had a little angel whispering in one ear of the protagonist and a little devil whispering in the other ear. Sometimes, it's hard to decide what is best—and luckily, not every decision in managing a camp business will have diametrically opposed options representing a good business decision or a good program decision.

Some decisions will be easy. If a law or regulation applies, then of course you follow it. The tough ones are those that involve considering your head and your heart together. This is where the decision-making process can become difficult. Nelson Mandela wrote, "A good head and a good heart are a formidable combination." Everyone should be proud of the work he does, but you cannot become so focused on the "soft" aspects of your profession that you ignore the "hard" realities of your businesses. As the chief executive of your business, it is up to you to make those hard decisions that may often determine the success or failure of your operations. To do otherwise would be fiscally irresponsible and make your individual mission as a champion of youth development unattainable.

Camp owners, directors, and executives will find that with guidance from knowledgeable consultants, support from camp colleagues, resources from your professional association, assistance from neighbors, and an immense amount of personal hard work, your camp will accomplish its mission and fulfill your dreams, evolving and growing into a valued part of the community, a well-run business, and an oasis for the children and families you serve. It is crucial that you run your camp as a business, but you still need the heart and soul of camp to shine through because camp isn't just any business—it's *camp*. And your camp isn't just any camp—it's *your* camp.

Appendices

Stockbyte/Thinkstock

Appendix A

State Listing of Resources for Small Businesses

State	Office/Agency	Website
Alabama	Office of Small Business Advocacy–Alabama Department of Commerce	www.commerce.alabama.gov
Alaska	State of Alaska–Business	www.alaska.gov/businessHome.html
Arizona	Arizona Commerce Authority	www.azcommerce.com/programs-and-services/small-business-services
Arkansas	State of Arkansas–Business	www.arkansas.gov/business
California	Governor's Office of Business and Economic Development	www.business.ca.gov/StartaBusiness.aspx
Colorado	Business Express	https://www.colorado.gov/apps/jboss/cbe//start-business.xhtml
Connecticut	Business Response Center	www.ct-clic.com/default.asp
Delaware	Economic Development Office	www.dedo.delaware.gov
District of Columbia	Small Business Development Center	www.dcsbdc.org
Florida	MyFlorida	www.myflorida.com/taxonomy/business
Georgia	Business Resources–Small Business	www.georgia.org/business-resources/small-business-resources/small-business-georgia/Pages/default.aspx
Hawaii	Business Development and Support	www.invest.hawaii.gov
Idaho	Business Idaho	www.business.idaho.gov
Illinois	Department of Commerce and Economic Opportunity	www.ildceo.net/dceo/Bureaus/Business_Development
Indiana	Secretary of State	www.in.gov/sos/business/3783.htm
Iowa	For Business	www.iowa.gov/For_Businesses
Kansas	Business Center	www.kansas.gov/businesscenter/starting
Kentucky	One Stop Business Portal	www.onestop.ky.gov/start

State	Office/Agency	Website
Louisiana	Grow a Business	www.louisiana.gov/Business/Grow_a_Business
Maine	Business	www.maine.gov/portal/business/starting.html
Maryland	Department of Business and Economic Development	www.choosemaryland.org/startbusiness
Massachusetts	Business	www.mass.gov/portal/business/start-business
Michigan	Business One Stop	www.michigan.gov/business
Minnesota	Employment and Economic Development	www.positivelyminnesota.com/Business
Mississippi	Small Business Development Center	www.mssbdc.org
Missouri	Business Portal	www.business.mo.gov
Montana	Department of Commerce	www.mtfinanceonline.com/startbusiness.mcpx
Nebraska	Secretary of State	www.sos.ne.gov/business/corp_serv/businessstartups.html
Nevada	Secretary of State	www.nvsos.gov/index.aspx?page=415
New Hampshire	Division of Economic Development	www.nheconomy.com/business-services/starting-a-business-in-nh.aspx
New Jersey	Business Portal	www.state.nj.us/njbusiness/starting
New Mexico	Small Business Development Center	www.nmsbdc.org/suguide.html
North Carolina	Thrive North Carolina	www.thrivenc.com/locationtools/overview
North Dakota	Business	www.nd.gov/category.htm?id=160
Ohio	Business Gateway	www.business.ohio.gov/starting
Oklahoma	Department of Commerce	www.okcommerce.gov/new-and-existing-business/starting-a-new-business
Oregon	Business Oregon	www.oregon4biz.com/Grow-Your-Business/Starting-a-business-in-Oregon
Pennsylvania	Business Online	www.pabizonline.com/Pages/default.aspx
Rhode Island	For Business	www.ri.gov/business
South Carolina	Business	www.sc.gov/Business/Pages/startingABusiness.aspx
South Dakota	Governor's Office of Economic Development	www.sdreadytowork.com
Tennessee	Department of Economic and Community Development	www.tn.gov/ecd
Texas	Wide Open For Business	www.texaswideopenforbusiness.com/small-business/index.php
Utah	Governor's Office of Economic Development	www.business.utah.gov
Vermont	Agency of Commerce and Community Development	www.accd.vermont.gov/business
Virginia	Business	www.virginia.gov/business
Washington	Department of Commerce	www.commerce.wa.gov/Pages/default.aspx
West Virginia	Business and Workforce	www.wvcommerce.org/business/default.aspx
Wisconsin	Economic Development Association	www.weda.org
Wyoming	Business Council	www.wyomingbusiness.org

Appendix B

Sample Human Resource Policies

Please note: These policies are provided as samples only and do not represent recommended policies. You should develop your own policies with your legal counsel.

1.0 Employment

1.1 Equal Employment Opportunity Policies

Camp XYZ (hereafter "the camp") is an equal opportunity employer. The camp will not discriminate against any individual because of race, color, religion, creed, sex, age, national origin, disability, or any other reason prohibited by the fair employment laws. Reasonable accommodation will be provided in an effort to advance employment opportunities for individuals with disabilities.

1.2 Terms and Conditions of Employment

Employment at Camp XYZ is on an at-will basis. The employee and the camp are each free to terminate the relationship at any time without cause.

1.3 Criminal Background Investigations and Other Verifications

Criminal history background investigations may be made of any employee. It is the policy of the camp not to employ anyone who has been convicted of any felony criminal offense that may involve but is not limited to: (1) dishonesty or breach of trust; (2) child abuse or neglect; or (3) attempted or actual bodily injury or property damage.

Camp XYZ will check the status of every potential employee with the National Sex Offender website.

Camp XYZ will obtain at least three nonfamily references on all potential employees.

Camp XYZ may 1) disqualify and prohibit employment of staff and/or 2) terminate or reassign current employees who the camp or its representative in its sole discretion determines, learns, or has knowledge that the employee has committed or is alleged to have committed any conduct that is inconsistent with the purposes and goals of Camp XYZ whatsoever.

1.4 Classification of Employees

Resident camp employees are exempt from the minimum wage and overtime pay provisions of the Fair Labor Standards Act. Other employees will be classified as exempt or nonexempt as described by the U.S. Department of Labor's Wage and Hour Division and determined by the camp CEO.

1.5 Pay Dates and Methods

Exempt and nonexempt employees are paid biweekly on Fridays. Pay periods begin on Friday and continue through the second Thursday following that Friday. Timesheets for nonexempt employees are due the following Friday morning by 10 a.m. to the camp office. Pay to employees will be one week later (six days after the pay period ends) and will be made through direct deposit to the employee's bank account.

1.6 Hours of Work

Camp XYZ is a resident camp. Therefore, most employees may be on call 24/7, although planned times will occur when employees are free from responsibilities.

1.7 Personal Conduct, Including the Use of Tobacco, Alcohol, and Controlled Substances

Camp XYZ is committed to conducting its business affairs with honesty and integrity. This commitment applies to relationships with competitors, campers, volunteers, vendors, employees, and the public. Under the standards, an employee should not knowingly conduct any business that is not in the full spirit of honest and ethical behavior nor shall any employee cause another employee or nonemployee to act otherwise—either through inducement, suggestions, or coercion.

Camp XYZ employees are required to adjust their personal habits and actions to the customs, policies, and ideals of Camp XYZ and to conduct themselves at all times—at camp and away from camp—in such a manner that will be a credit to themselves and to the camp and to keep hours and habits that will enable them to meet the customs, policies, and ideals of Camp XYZ.

No tobacco or alcohol use is permitted at Camp XYZ. Any employee who engages in the use of tobacco or alcohol at camp or during time off away from camp may be dismissed from employment.

The use of controlled substances is not permitted at Camp XYZ.

1.8 Physical Examinations, Drug Screens, and Medications

The camp may require any employee to submit to and pass a drug screen by a physician or entity selected by the camp as a condition of continued employment. Drug screens may be conducted at any time. A positive drug screen is grounds for dismissal.

All medications—whether prescription or nonprescription—must be stored with the camp nurse or designee and dispensed only as directed by medical personnel.

1.9 Sexual and Other Forms of Harassment

The camp strongly disapproves of and does not tolerate sexual, racial, or other harassment of any kind. All employees must avoid offensive or inappropriate behavior at work and are responsible for assuring that the workplace is free from sexual or other harassment at all times.

Camp policy prohibits unwelcome sexual advances as well as requests for sexual acts or favors, with or without accompanying promises, threats, or reciprocal favors or actions, or other verbal or physical conduct of a sexual nature that has the purpose or effect of adversely affecting an employee's performance or which creates an intimidating, hostile, or offensive working environment. Examples of prohibited conduct include but are not limited to sexual propositions, unwelcome touching, lewd or sexually suggestive comments, jokes of a sexual nature, slurs and other verbal, graphic, or physical conduct relating to an individual's sex, or any display of sexually explicit materials.

Camp policy prohibits racial slurs and other forms of harassment based on race, color, religion, creed, sex, age, national origin, or disability.

Complaints of harassment will be promptly and carefully investigated and all employees are assured that they will be free from any and all reprisal or retaliation from filing such complaints. Any employee who has a complaint of harassment at work by anyone, including supervisors, coworkers, visitors, clients, or volunteers, should immediately bring the problem to the attention of management. Employees may bring the complaint to the attention of their supervisor or, if the complaint involves supervisory personnel in the employee's line of command, to another supervisor or the camp director.

Employees are assured that the camp will not tolerate any acts of retaliation against any complainant who utilizes this procedure. The camp will make every effort to strike a balance between the parties' desires for privacy and the need to conduct a fair and effective investigation.

If the investigation reveals that the complaint appears to be valid, immediate and appropriate disciplinary action—up to and including discharge—will be taken to stop the harassment and prevent its recurrence.

1.10 Privacy Policy

Camp XYZ has access to certain private information about employees. We will at all times honor the privacy of our employees and will not disclose private information including, but not limited to, dates of birth, home addresses, social security numbers, income, dependent status, credit card information, telephone numbers, and similar information.

We will not sell, rent, or in any manner share personal or credit card information that we obtain from employees. Camp XYZ will not intentionally disclose any personal information to any third party unless we have permission of the individual.

Camp XYZ is also entrusted with the care of minors. At times, employees will have access to private information about both our participants and their parents, as well as our volunteers, the board, donors and other employees. Protecting the privacy of an individual's personal information is very important to Camp XYZ. All employees are required to treat personal information with the utmost respect, including all information to which our employees may have access.

2.0 Benefits

2.1 Statutory Benefits (social security, Medicare, unemployment, workers' compensation)

Camp XYZ contributes funds to the Social Security Administration on behalf of each employee in an amount equal to the FICA and Medicare taxes withheld from each employee's paychecks. The camp also pays federal unemployment taxes (FUTA).

The camp provides benefits under the workers' compensation law. This law ensures compensation for loss of wages due to illness or injury that occurs in or as a result of employment. Salary benefits paid by the workers' compensation insurance carrier are paid directly to the employee and such payments are usually based on a percentage of the employee's regular pay. Salary normally paid by the camp is not paid in addition to this benefit and if paid must be returned to the camp. It is the employee's responsibility to report injuries immediately to the camp director.

Employees who are injured on the job and lose work time may be compensated by the insurance carrier after a specified waiting period. Full-time injured employees who return to work for less than full-time duty will be paid a proportionate amount of their regular pay for the hours worked and should schedule treatment or physician's appointments during nonwork time. Part-time injured employees who return to work will be paid for actual hours worked only and should schedule treatment or physician's appointments during nonwork time. The workers' compensation insurance rules and regulations will supersede these policies should any discrepancy occur between these policies and the workers' compensation insurance rules and regulations.

2.2 Housing, Meals, and Laundry (if provided)

Housing and meals for resident camp employees are provided at no charge to the employee and are for the convenience of Camp XYZ. No food should be kept in cabins. Designated areas for staff and camper snacks are provided.

Laundry facilities for personal laundry of resident camp staff are furnished by the camp and include a washing machine, dryer, and laundry detergent.

2.3 Dress Requirements and Uniforms

Camp XYZ employees will be required to provide mid-length navy blue shorts to wear on session opening and closing days. Employees will be provided with two camp staff shirts to be worn on session opening and closing days. Additional staff shirts may be purchased. Whenever camp employees are representing Camp XYZ in public, they are expected to wear this uniform.

On all other days, employees should wear mid-length shorts or long trousers and modest shirts. Closed-toe shoes and socks should be worn at all times (the exception being at the pool or river) for safety. Camp XYZ employees should dress conservatively and in good taste at all times, refraining from wearing tight-fitting or see-through clothing or clothing with advertised products, sayings, or graphics that would not be in keeping with the mission or spirit of Camp XYZ.

2.4 Training Provided by the Camp—Pre-Camp and in Service

Camp XYZ will provide all resident camp employees with a minimum of seven days training prior to the summer season. In addition, during the summer season, additional in-service training options will be available. Camp XYZ may request that employees take training from outside vendors, such as lifeguard or archery instructor training, and will cover the cost of such training, providing a written training agreement exists with the employee before the training occurs.

2.5 Time Off and Leaves of Absence

Each resident camp staff member will have approximately two hours off per day, although the staff member may not leave the camp during that time. In addition, resident camp staff members will have 20 to 40 hours off each weekend. All time off will be scheduled by the administrative staff so sufficient staff will always be in camp. In addition, a staff retreat is provided for staff use only during time off in camp.

Leave without pay may be granted in the event of personal illness or death in the family, urgent business, or individual circumstances at the discretion of the camp director.

2.6 Health and Accident Insurance

Camp XYZ provides a health and accident insurance policy for all summer staff.

3.0 Operations

3.1 Safety at Camp

Camp XYZ has established safety rules for all activities and provides these rules in the camp staff manual. All employees are expected to uphold and promote these safety rules.

3.2 Use of Camp-Owned Equipment and Vehicles

Camp XYZ provides sports and activity equipment for use in programs. When such equipment is not in use by campers, employees may use it, provided they have been cleared by the activity program director and have passed the safety test on an annual basis.

Camp XYZ owns several vehicles. Employees must be at least 21 years old, have the appropriate driver's license, have passed a motor vehicle screening, and have successfully completed and passed the Camp XYZ class for each type of vehicle in order to drive any of the camp-owned vehicles. No vehicle should be driven without permission of the appropriate supervisor. See also 3.11.

Camp XYZ assumes no responsibility for an employee's personal equipment, including but not limited to cell phones, musical instruments, computers, cameras, vehicles, and any other electronic or other equipment. Camp XYZ provides a locker in the staff retreat for each employee to secure small equipment or personal items.

3.3 Authority to Purchase and Represent the Camp

Some employees will be authorized to purchase on behalf of Camp XYZ or to represent the camp at public events. No employee should commit to purchasing anything on behalf of the camp without proper authorization, which can come only from the camp director or the assistant director. Those persons with purchasing authorization will be provided guidelines for purchasing and budget information.

3.4 Pets and Weapons

No pets or weapons are permitted at Camp XYZ.

3.5 Tips, Gratuities, and Gifts

Tips, gratuities, and gifts from campers or parents are prohibited.

3.6 Accident Reporting

All work-related accidents and/or injuries must be reported to the supervisor immediately and to the assistant director within 24 hours. Reports to the assistant director must be written and include a statement of what happened, names and statements from any witnesses, when and where the accident or injury occurred, and a description of the accident/injury. The supervisor will investigate and add any comments as necessary. Camp XYZ may require an immediate drug screen of the employee involved in such an accident or injury. Failure to report a work-related accident or injury may result in disciplinary action—up to or including termination. Camp XYZ strictly prohibits false or fraudulent claims. All claims will be reviewed and investigated by the appropriate insurance carrier.

3.7 Reporting of Suspected Child Abuse

Every employee who works with children has a responsibility to report suspected child abuse to Child Protective Services at xxx-xxx-xxxx.

3.8 Supervision Ratios Used in Camp, Including Exceptions to the Ratios

Camp XYZ will maintain the following ratios of counselor to campers:

Campers 6 to 8	One counselor for every 6 campers
Campers 9 to 11	One counselor for every 8 campers
Campers 12 to 15	One counselor for every 10 campers
Campers 16 to 18	One counselor for every 12 campers

During rest hour and during the evening when the campers are in bed, one counselor may supervise two cabins.

3.9 Use of Computers, the Internet, the Telephone, and Other Electronic Equipment

A. Privacy: The camp respects the privacy of its employees. A Camp XYZ employee may not expect such privacy rights to extend to the use of Camp XYZ–owned systems, property, equipment, or supplies or to work-related conduct. This policy is intended to notify all Camp XYZ employees that no reasonable expectation of privacy exists in connection with your use of Camp XYZ's systems, property, equipment, or supplies. Camp XYZ employees are prohibited from withholding information maintained within company-supplied containers, including but not limited to computer files, computer databases, desks, lockers, and cabinets, and they acknowledge and agree that any such items may be viewed or searched by Camp XYZ at any time with or without notice.

B. Prohibited Content: Camp XYZ employees are prohibited from using Camp XYZ's telephone, electronic, or computer network systems at any time in any manner that may be offensive or disruptive to others. This includes but is not limited to the transmission of racial or ethnic slurs, gender-specific comments, sexually explicit images or messages, any remarks that would offend others on the basis of their age, political or religious beliefs, disability, national origin, or sexual orientation, or any messages that may be interpreted to disparage or harass others. No telephone, electronic, or computer network communications may be sent that represent the sender as from another company or as someone else or which try to hide the sender's identity.

C. Computers: The computer hardware provided to employees is owned by the camp and is provided for organization business. Camp XYZ purchases and licenses the use of various computer software for business purposes and does not own the copyright to this software or its related documentation. Unless authorized by the software developer, Camp XYZ does not have the right to reproduce such software for use on more than one computer. Employees may only use software stored on their Camp XYZ computers or the local area network according to the manufacturer's software licensing agreement. Camp XYZ prohibits the illegal duplication of software and its related documentation. Failure to observe manufacturer's copyright or license agreements may result in disciplinary action from the organization and/or legal action by the copyright owner.

The camp provides standardized software, which is to be used by all employees. This includes the operating system, office automation, graphics, databases, email, Internet browsers, and virus protection software. No other software may be installed on any Camp XYZ–owned computer without express permission from the network administrator and the camp director. This includes screen savers, graphics programs, and any software that is downloadable from the Internet, especially video-sound programs.

D. Internet: Camp XYZ provides employees with Internet access to facilitate the operations of the organization and for employee use with their personal computers. Copyrighted materials belonging to entities other than the camp may not be transmitted by employees on the Internet. Employees may not download or upload unauthorized software over the Internet. Failure to observe copyright or license agreements may result in disciplinary action from Camp XYZ or legal action from the copyright owner.

   Camp XYZ reserves the right to review Internet activity and analyze usage patterns to assure that Internet resources are devoted to maintaining the highest levels of productivity. Camp XYZ further reserves the right to inspect any and all files stored in any directory on the network or workstation if needed in order to assure compliance with Camp XYZ policies and procedures.

E. Telephone: Camp XYZ provides employees at most locations with telephone and voice mail access to facilitate the operations of the organization. In general, employees should use the telephone for business purposes only. The telephone should not be used while at Camp XYZ in a manner that is unethical, discriminatory, disruptive, threatening, or offensive to others or in ways that may be harmful to workplace morale. This includes but is not limited to unlawful or offensive conversations or voice mail messages that contain sexual implications, racial slurs, gender-specific comments, or other messages that offensively address someone's age, sexual orientation, religious or political beliefs, national origin, or disability.

F. Responsibilities of Employees/Misuse of Equipment or Software: Employees of Camp XYZ are responsible for abiding by the policies of the organization and all laws related to the use of electronic equipment and computer software. Employees learning of any misuse of software or related documentation within Camp XYZ shall notify their supervisor. According to applicable copyright law, persons involved in the illegal reproduction of software can be subject to civil damages and criminal penalties, including fines and imprisonment. Camp XYZ does not condone the illegal duplication of software or the illegal use of any electronic equipment. Camp XYZ employees who make, acquire, or use unauthorized copies of computer software or whose use of electronic equipment is illegal or is deemed inappropriate based on prevailing standards of conduct shall be disciplined as appropriate under the circumstances and such discipline may include termination.

3.10 Social Networking

Philosophy: Camp XYZ recognizes the potential value of social networking, blogging, and similar online activities and that such activities are accepted methods of communication and tools for business development. These policies are designed to provide guidance to employees of the camp and to protect and uphold the camp's reputation and that of all employees. The camp recognizes that technology and the utilization of social media change rapidly. Therefore, our policies will be reviewed and updated often to be as comprehensive as possible so camp employees have appropriate and clear guidance in the use of technology and social media.

Scope: These policies apply to all online activities—whether they involve access to the Internet via use of the camp network, a home computer, Internet-capable devices such as smartphones, or any other means. These policies cover social media, business and social networking, blogging, microblogging, and other online activities, including commenting on blogs and participating in chats or Q&A sessions. Social media and applications include but are not limited to the following: blogs, forums, message boards, wikis, podcasts, LinkedIn, Twitter, Facebook, MySpace, personal websites, Digg, Flickr, YouTube, and Socializr. For purposes of this policy, any social media or social networking site or application will be considered "social media" or "social networking."

Blogging, Posting, and Commenting Online: Camp staff should be mindful that any blog, post, or comment online is permanent, easily searchable, and easily found by anyone. Such activity is the same as being interviewed or having an opinion published in the newspaper under your name. Even when posting or commenting as an individual, you may be perceived to be representing Camp XYZ.

Always use good judgment and common sense when online—whether for personal or business purposes. A general rule of thumb is, if you wouldn't want your mother, your children, or your boss to read something, don't post it. If using personal pages, such as Facebook or LinkedIn, be aware of how open and available your personal information is. The camp recommends that employees' personal pages be set as private and available only to friends.

Only employees approved by the camp director may serve as official spokespersons for the camp. Employees who want to participate in any type of online activity through social media on behalf of the camp must have permission to do so before participating. Any personal posts, blogs, or comments that do not reflect the high standards of the camp may result in disciplinary action—up to and including termination.

Productivity Impact: Social networking activities are not to interfere with an employee's primary job responsibilities. Although business-related networking can be appropriate, each employee is expected to limit personal use of social networking during regular work hours. Use of personal computers for social networking or any other purpose should be limited to time off.

Website and Social Media Sites: The camp maintains a website and several presences on social networking sites. Information disseminated through these sites is the responsibility of the camp director or his designate. All resident camp staff will be asked to join a private Facebook page. No nonsanctioned pages or sites are permitted.

Photos: Photos posted on any camp website or social networking site must be approved for such use by the assistant camp director, and if the photos include images of youth participants, a photo release must be obtained. Generally, youth should not be identified in photos. Employees should be aware of the provisions of the Children's Online Privacy Protection Act of 1998 (COPPA), which generally requires a release to post a child's photograph online. Employees may not post any photos of children on their personal Facebook page or other social media sites.

The camp does not provide email for resident camp employee use nor does the camp provide for remote use of the camp network by resident camp staff.

All employees should recognize the potential harm in establishing online and/or other social networking relationships with campers or their parents. Although campers or their parents may ask to become friends on Facebook with a Camp XYZ employee, the camp strongly recommends against becoming online "friends." As an alternative to becoming an online "friend," employees should recommend that clients become "fans" of any of the camp's social networking pages.

Employees are expected to maintain a professional, not personal, relationship with camp families and should not participate with camp families in any social setting except those organized by the camp. Camp XYZ provides several opportunities during the year for campers, their families, and camp staff to socialize at officially sanctioned events.

Resident camp staff are requested to maintain these policies even after their seasonal employment ends, recognizing that as former staff, their behavior and relationships with campers are still perceived as related to Camp XYZ programs and activities. Failure to maintain these policies after seasonal employment could result in disqualification as employees in a subsequent season.

3.11 Cell Phone Use While Driving and at Camp

The safety and well-being of all employees and any passengers are of utmost importance to Camp XYZ. Distracted driving has been found to lead to a substantial increase in injury accidents. Therefore, when driving any vehicle on behalf of Camp XYZ—whether owned by the camp or not—employees are not permitted to use any type of cell phone, PDA, or similar device. Employees must not read or respond to email, text messages, or any other visual or aural message while operating any vehicle on behalf of the camp. Calls should not be answered by the employee while driving. Any call should go to voice mail. If it is necessary to make a phone call while driving, employees must stop at a safe location—away from traffic—before making the call. Any employees found to not comply with this policy will be subject to disciplinary action—up to and including termination of employment.

Employees may be asked to keep their cell phones with them during work hours for emergency communication. All other use of cell phones by camp employees while supervising campers is prohibited. Employees should use cell phones for personal use only on time off, when campers are not with them.

4.0 Evaluation, Discipline, and Separation

4.1 Evaluation and Discipline Processes

All resident camp employees will receive at least two formal evaluations during the summer. Such evaluations will be conducted by the supervisor in conjunction with the assistant camp director.

Supervisors may have conversations about employee performance or conduct that do not rise to the level of formal disciplinary action. Performance or conduct necessitating such a conversation may occur at any time during the year and, if so, should be addressed promptly, not delayed until the formal review. In all cases, the supervisor should keep documentation of performance issues or inappropriate conduct.

Certain conduct or actions of an employee may result in immediate termination of employment. Except in cases that Camp XYZ deems to necessitate immediate termination of employment or if circumstances require an immediate written warning and/or probation period, the following general procedures are to be used in handling unacceptable performance or behavior.

All disciplinary actions must be documented, including verbal warnings. The documentation defines the problem, refers to previous discussions, outlines the corrective action to be taken, and establishes a specific time period for its solution. The disciplinary process has three steps:

A. Verbal Warning: The supervisor must discuss unacceptable performance or behavior with the employee. This discussion should indicate the nature of the problem and the action necessary to correct it. The supervisor should write a memo for the personnel file, indicating that a verbal warning has been given and describing the discussion with the employee. Copies of this documentation should be kept by the supervisor, reviewed by the appropriate supervisor, and also filed with the camp director.

B. Written Warning: When a problem continues despite verbal warning, the supervisor should consult with the camp director. After approval from the camp director, the supervisor should discuss the written warning with the employee and forward it for inclusion in the employee's personnel file. If circumstances warrant, a written warning may be issued without prior verbal warnings.

C. Release: If the disciplinary procedure fails to solve the problem, the supervisor should document the recommendation for release. The camp director must approve all terminations. The employee is then notified of the termination by the supervisor.

4.2 Problem Resolution Procedure

The camp will attempt to review and resolve employee problems in a prompt and equitable manner. An employee problem exists when an employee feels a job-related problem has not been satisfactorily resolved. Employees are encouraged to present all such problems in writing to their immediate supervisor. If the problem is of such a nature that the employee cannot raise it with the immediate supervisor, then it may be raised directly with the assistant camp director. If an agreement is not reached, the staff member may request through the supervisor to have the problem reviewed by the camp director. The decision of the president/CEO is final.

4.3 Administrative Leave

At the discretion of the president/CEO, the camp may place an employee on administrative leave–with or without pay–for the investigation of any situation that may require that the employee be removed from contact with children or from other situations deemed appropriate.

4.4 Separation

Separation may be initiated by either the camp or the employee at any time–with or without notice. The date of separation is the date on which an employee ceases active work with the camp. The employer and the employee have a responsibility to time separation in such a way as will be least upsetting to the camp and the individual concerned.

An employee will be removed from active employment of the camp and lose all employment benefits should any of the following occur:

A. The employee quits or is discharged–with or without cause.

B. The employee has not actively worked during any three consecutive days–unless on an approved and documented leave of absence.

C. The employee fails to return to work after the expiration of an approved leave of absence–regardless of reason.

4.5 Voluntary Termination

A resignation should be given in writing. Because of the seasonal nature of working at a resident camp, employees who resign must give at least one week's notice. The camp may permit the employee to continue employment during the notice period or accept the resignation immediately and pay the employee in lieu of notice. Persons terminating without proper notice are generally not eligible for rehire.

4.6 Involuntary Termination

In the event the camp terminates the service of an employee, it may or may not provide prior notice due to the nature of temporary employees' jobs. The camp is not required to give advance notice, pay in lieu of notice, or severance pay when terminating an employee.

4.7 Reasons for Involuntary Termination

Involuntary termination may be immediate or at a date following the occurrence of the act causing the discharge. The following are some–but not all–examples of conduct that may result in termination of employment:

- Failure to maintain a satisfactory level of any job performance aspect, including negligence of duty
- Poor judgment related to camp resources, programs, participants, or property

- Engaging in practices that are not in the best interests of the campers' health, safety, or happiness
- Failure to maintain a reasonable standard of dress, grooming, cleanliness, personal conduct, or speech
- Reduction of staff
- Using cell phones while driving on behalf of the camp
- Discrimination against anyone associated with the camp because of race, color, age, creed, sex, disability, national origin, or family status
- Unauthorized possession of or being under the influence of drugs, narcotics, or intoxicants while on or off the job
- Theft, pilfering, fraud, or other forms of dishonesty or breach of trust
- Absence without cause or without authorization
- Commission of an immoral or criminal act whether on or off the job
- Child abuse or neglect
- Any conduct that is inconsistent with the purposes and goals of the camp whatsoever
- Any other item or conduct as determined by the camp and/or the camp director

4.8 Exit Report/Interview

On separation, an exit or end-of-program report should be completed and an interview held with the supervisor, assistant camp director, and/or the camp director if practicable.

4.9 Employment References on Former Employees

A terminating or former employee may request that the camp provide an employment reference.

Appendix C

State Payday Requirements

State	Weekly	Biweekly	Semi-monthly	Monthly
Alabama[1]				
Alaska			X	X
Arizona			X[3]	
Arkansas			X	
California	X[9]	X[9]	X	
Colorado				X
Connecticut	X[4]			
Delaware				X
District of Columbia			X	
Georgia			X	
Hawaii			X	X[5]
Idaho				X
Illinois			X	X[2]
Indiana		X		
Iowa	X	X[6]	X	X
Kansas				X
Kentucky			X	
Louisiana		X	X[7]	
Maine			X[8]	
Maryland		X		
Massachusetts	X	X		
Michigan[9]	X	X		X

State	Weekly	Biweekly	Semi-monthly	Monthly
Minnesota				X[10]
Mississippi		X[11]	X[11]	
Missouri			X	
Montana[12]				
Nebraska[13]				
Nevada			X	X[2]
New Hampshire	X			
New Jersey			X	
New Mexico			X	X[2]
New York	X[14]		X[14]	
North Carolina[15]				
North Dakota				X
Ohio			X	
Oklahoma			X	
Oregon				X
Pennsylvania[13]				
Rhode Island	X[16]			
South Carolina[1]				
South Dakota				X
Tennessee			X	
Texas			X	X[17]
Utah			X[18]	
Vermont	X	X[19]	X[19]	
Virginia		X[20]	X[20]	X[20]
Washington				X
West Virginia		X		
Wisconsin				X
Wyoming			X	

1. Alabama and South Carolina. No regulations or not specified.
2. Illinois, Nevada, New Mexico and Virginia. Monthly payday requirements for Executive, Administrative, and Professional personnel.
3. Arizona. Payday two or more days in a month, not more than 16 days apart.
4. Connecticut. Longer interval (up to monthly) permitted if approved by labor commissioner.
5. Hawaii. Employees may choose to be paid on a monthly basis under special election procedure. Director of labor and industrial relations also may grant exceptions to the general semi-monthly payday requirement. Payday requirement applies only to private sector employment.

6. Iowa. Any predictable and reliable pay schedule is permitted as long as employees get paid at least monthly and no later than 12 days (excluding Sundays and legal holidays) from the end of the period when the wages were earned. This can be waived by written agreement; employees on commission have different requirements.
7. Louisiana. Applicable to entities engaged in manufacturing, mining, or boring for oil, employing 10 or more employees, and to every public service corporation. Payment is required once every two weeks or twice during each calendar month.
8. Maine. Payment due at regular intervals not to exceed 16 days.
9. California and Michigan. Frequency of payday depends on the occupation.
10. Minnesota. Employees engaged in transitory employment, i.e. migrant workers, which require an employee to change the employee's place of abode, because the employment is terminated either by the completion of the work or by the discharge or quitting of the employee must be paid within 24 hours.
11. Mississippi. Applicable to every entity engaged in manufacturing of any kind in the State employing 50 or more employees and employing public labor, and to every public service corporation doing business in the State. Payment is required once every two weeks or twice during each calendar month.
12. Montana. Wages must be paid within 10 business days after the wages are due and payable.
13. Nebraska and Pennsylvania. Payday designated by employer.
14. New York. Weekly payday for manual workers. Semi-monthly payday upon approval for manual workers and for clerical and other workers.
15. North Carolina. None specified, pay periods may be daily, weekly, bi-weekly, semi-monthly or monthly.
16. Rhode Island. Childcare providers shall have the option to be paid every two weeks.
17. Texas. Monthly payday for employees exempt from overtime provisions of the Fair Labor Standards Act.
18. Utah. Payments are to be paid at regular intervals, but in periods no longer than semi-monthly.
19. Vermont. Employers may implement bi-weekly and semi-monthly payday with written notice.
20. Virginia. Employees whose weekly wages total more than 150 percent of the average weekly wage of the Commonwealth may be paid monthly, upon agreement of each affected employee.

Note: South Carolina. Employers with 5 or more employees are required to give written notice at the time of hiring to all employees advising them of their wages agreed upon, and the time and place of payment along with their expected hours of work. The employer must pay on the normal time and at the place of payment established by the employer.

Reprinted from the Department of Labor's Wage and Hour Division: www.dol.gov/whd/state/payday.htm.

Appendix D

State Minimum Wages
(as of January 1, 2014)

Federal minimum wage	**7.25**		Nebraska	7.25
			Nevada	8.25
Alabama	n/a		New Hampshire	7.25
Alaska	7.75		New Jersey	8.25
Arizona	7.90		New Mexico	7.50
Arkansas	6.25		New York	8.00
California	8.00		North Carolina	7.25
Colorado	8.00		North Dakota	7.25
Connecticut	8.70		Ohio	7.95
Delaware	7.25		Oklahoma	7.25
Florida	7.93		Oregon	9.10
Georgia	5.15		Pennsylvania	7.25
Hawaii	7.25		Rhode Island	8.00
Idaho	7.25		South Carolina	n/a
Illinois	8.25		South Dakota	7.25
Indiana	7.25		Tennessee	n/a
Iowa	7.25		Texas	7.25
Kansas	7.25		Utah	7.25
Kentucky	7.25		Vermont	8.73
Louisiana	n/a		Virginia	7.25
Maine	7.50		Washington	9.32
Maryland	7.25		West Virginia	7.25
Massachusetts	8.00		Wisconsin	7.25
Michigan	7.40		Wyoming	5.15
Minnesota	6.15		District of Columbia	8.25
Mississippi	n/a		Guam	7.25
Missouri	7.50		Puerto Rico	7.25
Montana	7.90		U. S. Virgin Islands	7.25

- The state minimum wage rate requirements, or lack thereof, are controlled by legislative activities within the individual states.
- Federal minimum wage law supersedes state minimum wage laws where the federal minimum wage is greater than the state minimum wage. In those states where the state minimum wage is greater than the federal minimum wage, the state minimum wage prevails.
- There are four states that have a minimum wage set lower than the federal minimum wage. There are 21 states (plus DC) with minimum wage rates set higher than the federal minimum wage. There are 20 states that have a minimum wage requirement that is the same as the federal minimum wage requirement. The remaining five states do not have an established minimum wage requirement.
- The State of Washington has the highest minimum wage at $9.32/hour. The states of Georgia and Wyoming have the lowest minimum wage ($5.15) of the 45 states that have a minimum wage requirement.
- Note: There are 10 states (AZ, CO, FL, MO, MT, NV, OH, OR, VT, and WA) that have minimum wages that are linked to a consumer price index. As a result of this linkage, the minimum wages in these states are normally increased each year, generally around January 1st. The exception is Nevada which adjusts in the month of July each year. Effective January 1, 2014, nine of the 10 states increased their respective minimum wages. The exception was Nevada.

From the U.S. Department of Labor's Wage and Hour Division's Office of Communications. For current rates, see www.dol.gov/whd/minwage/america.htm or visit your state's employment commission website.

Appendix E

Sample Voluntary Disclosure Statement

Name: ____ Birth date: ____________________
Last First Middle

Home address: ____
Street Address City State Zip

Social security number: __________________________ Email address: ____________________

Other names by which you are known (e.g., maiden name): ________________________________

Home phone: ___________________________ Cell phone (optional): ____________________

School or college: ____

Address: ____
Street Address City State Zip

Driver's license number: ___________________ State: _____ Expiration date: _______________

1. Previous residence(s) for last five years (including college and home residences):

City: ____ State: _____ Years: _______________

City: ____ State: _____ Years: _______________

City: ____ State: _____ Years: _______________

(Continue on a separate sheet if necessary.)

2. Have you ever been convicted of any crime related in any manner to children and/or your conduct with them? ❑ Yes ❑ No

If yes, please explain: (Use a separate sheet if necessary.)

___

___

___

3. Have you ever been convicted of any crime, including but not limited to, indecent assault and battery; rape of any kind; assault with intent to commit rape; kidnapping; distribution and trafficking of narcotics or other controlled substances; intent to commit any of the aforementioned crimes; or any crime similar in any manner to the aformentioned crimes? ❑ Yes ❑ No

If yes, please explain: (Use a separate sheet if necessary.)

___

___

___

4. Have you ever been adjudged liable for civil penalties or damages involving sexual or physical abuse of children? ❑ Yes ❑ No

If yes, please explain: (Use a separate sheet if necessary.)

___

___

___

5. Are you now or have you ever been subject to any court order involving sexual or physical abuse of a minor, including but not limited to a domestic order or protection? ❑ Yes ❑ No

If yes, please explain: (Use a separate sheet if necessary.)

___

___

6. Have your parental rights ever been terminated for reasons involving sexual or physical abuse of children? ❑ Yes ❑ No

If yes, please explain: (Use a separate sheet if necessary.)

___

___

I understand that:

a. The camp may deny employment to any person who answers "Yes" to any one of questions 2 through 6. If hired and the employer later discovers circumstances that would indicate a "Yes" answer to any of the these questions, employment may be terminated immediately.

b. The information provided on this form is subject to verification, which may include a criminal history check and a request from any central registry of child abusers.

c. The camp may terminate employment or volunteer service of any person if that person is found—regardless of when discovered—to:

1. have a history of complaints of abuse of a minor;
2. have resigned, been terminated, or been asked to resign from a position—whether paid or unpaid—due to complaint(s) of sexual abuse of a minor; and/or
3. have falsified or omitted information in this disclosure statement.

d. This disclosure statement must be updated yearly.

Signature: ______________________________

Date: ______________________________

Signature of Minor's Parent or Guardian: ______________________________

Date: ______________________________

Appendix F

State Camp Licensing and Governing Bodies

State	License Required	Governing Body
Alabama	Yes	Alabama State Board of Health, Bureau of Environmental Services, Division of Food, Milk and Lodging
Alaska	Yes	Alaska Department of Commerce, Community, and Economic Development
Arizona	Yes	Arizona Department of Health Services, Office of Environmental Health
Arkansas	Yes	Arkansas Department of Health, Division of Child Care and Early Childhood Education
California	Yes	California Department of Public Health
Colorado	Yes	Colorado Department of Human Services, Division of Child Care
Connecticut	Yes	Connecticut Department of Public Health, Youth Camp Licensing Program
Delaware	Yes	Delaware Department of Health and Social Services, Division of Public Health, Recreational Camp Program
District of Columbia	Yes	D.C. Department of Consumer and Regulatory Affairs
Florida	No	Florida Department of Children and Families; Florida Local County Health Departments
Georgia	Yes	Georgia Department of Human Services
Hawaii	Yes	Hawaii Department of Health; Hawaii Department of Human Services
Idaho	No	Idaho Department of Health and Welfare; Idaho Division of Building Safety
Illinois	Yes	Illinois Department of Public Health, Division of Environmental Health, Recreation–Campgrounds and Youth Camps

State	License Required	Governing Body
Indiana	Yes	Indiana State Department of Health
Iowa	Yes	Iowa Department of Human Services; Iowa Department of Public Health—Camps With Food Service
Kansas	Yes	Kansas Department of Health and Environment
Kentucky	Yes	Kentucky Department for Public Health
Louisiana	Yes	Louisiana Department of Health and Hospitals
Maine	Yes	Maine Department of Health and Human Services, Division of Environmental Health
Maryland	Yes	Maryland Department of Health and Mental Hygiene, Youth Camp Certification
Massachusetts	Yes	Massachusetts Office of Health and Human Services, Camps—Recreational
Michigan	Yes	State of Michigan, Department of Human Services
Minnesota	Yes	Minnesota Department of Health, Environmental Health Division
Mississippi	Yes	Mississippi Department of Health, Child Care and Youth Camp Licensure
Missouri	No	Missouri Department of Health and Senior Services
Montana	Yes	Montana Department of Public Health and Human Services
Nebraska	Yes	Nebraska Department of Health and Human Services
Nevada	Yes	Nevada Department of Health and Human Services, State Health Division
New Hampshire	Yes	New Hampshire Department of Environmental Services Drinking Water and Groundwater Bureau
New Jersey	Yes	New Jersey Department of Health and Senior Services, Consumer, Environmental, and Occupational Health Service
New Mexico	Yes	New Mexico Environment Department
New York	Yes	New York State Department of Health, Children's Camps; New York City Department of Health and Mental Hygiene
North Carolina	Yes	North Carolina Department of Environment and Natural Resources
North Dakota	Yes	North Dakota Department of Health, Local Health Units
Ohio	Yes	Ohio Department of Health, Local Health Departments, Ohio Department of Jobs and Family Services
Oklahoma	Yes	Oklahoma Department of Human Services, Division of Child Care
Oregon	Yes	Oregon Health Authority; Community Liaison for Local Health Departments
Pennsylvania	Yes	Pennsylvania Department of Health, Pennsylvania Department of Agriculture, Bureau of Food Safety and Laboratory Services
Puerto Rico	Yes	Government of Puerto Rico, Departamento de la Familia
Rhode Island	Yes	State of Rhode Island, Department of Health
South Carolina	Yes	South Carolina Department of Health and Environmental Control, Department of Social Services
South Dakota	No	South Dakota Department of Health

State	License Required	Governing Body
Tennessee	Yes	Tennessee Department of Health
Texas	Yes	Texas Department of State Health Services
Utah	Yes	Utah Department of Health, Division of Disease Control and Prevention; Utah Department of Environmental Quality; Utah Department of Human Services, Outdoor Youth Programs
Vermont	Yes	Vermont Department of Health; Vermont Department for Children and Families, Agency of Human Services
Virginia	Yes	Virginia Department of Health, Office of Environmental Health Services; Virginia Department of Social Services, Child Care and Development Division
Washington	No	Washington State Department of Health
West Virginia	Yes	West Virginia Department of Health and Human Resources, Office of Environmental Health Services; West Virginia Department of Health and Human Resources, Bureau for Children and Families
Wisconsin	Yes	Wisconsin Department of Health Services, Bureau of Environmental and Occupational Health, Food Safety and Recreational Licensing
Wyoming	Yes	Wyoming Department of Family Services, Division of Early Childhood

Courtesy of the American Camp Association

Appendix G

State Equine Liability Laws
(Updated August 2013)

Note that California, Maryland, Nevada and New York do not have equine liability laws.

Statute Name	Citation	Summary
AK - Equine - Equine Activity Liability Statute	AK ST § 09.65.145; AK ST § 09.65.290	Two Alaska statutes are provided here that relate to the limitation of liability for equine activities. The first is the equine activity liability statute, which states that livestock are unpredictable and inherently dangerous and all persons who knowingly place themselves in proximity to livestock for any reason involving an activity that includes livestock are considered a participant in livestock activity and assume the risk. Exclusions include gross negligence of the equine sponsor, knowledge of faulty tack or equipment, and failure to properly ascertain the level of competence by the participant. The second statute reiterates that a person who participates in a sports or recreational activity assumes the inherent risks in that sports or recreational activity, including horseback riding.
AL - Equine - Immunity of those involved in equine activities.	AL ST § 6-5-337	This Alabama statute embodies the legislature's recognition that persons who participate in equine activities may incur injuries as a result of the risks involved in those activities. This statute provides that for the immediate preservation of the public peace, health, and safety, and to encourage equine activities, civil liability of those involved in equine activities is limited by law. Liability is not limited when the equine sponsor intentionally injures a participant or engages in willful or wanton behavior that causes injury or death.

Statute Name	Citation	Summary
AR - Equine - Equine Activity Liability	AR ST § 16-120-201 to 202	This Arkansas statute provides that an equine activity sponsor or an employee of an equine activity sponsor shall not be liable for an injury to or the death of a participant resulting from the inherent risks of equine activities. Liability is not limited when the equine agent knew the equipment or tack was faulty, failed to make reasonable and prudent efforts to determine the ability of the participant, was aware of dangerous latent condition on the land that the equine agent owed or possessed, committed an act or omission that constituted willful or wanton disregard for the safety of the participant, or when the owner or agent intentionally injured the participant. Warning signs alerting participants to the assumption of risk in equine activities are also required by law.
AZ - Equine Activity Liability Statute	AZ ST § 12-553	This Arizona statute provides that an equine agent or owner is not liable for injury if the participant took control of the equine prior to injury, if a parent or guardian signed a release on behalf of a minor, if the owner or agent has properly installed suitable tack or the participant has personally tacked the equine, or the owner or agent assigns a suitable equine based on a reasonable interpretation of the person's representation of his or her skills, health and experience with and knowledge of equines. Liability is not limited, however, when an equine owner or agent is grossly negligent or commits willful, wanton or intentional acts or omissions.
AZ - Equine Transport - Transporting equine in a cruel manner; violation; classification; definitions. § 28-912. Vehicles transporting equine; violation; classification; definitions	AZ ST § 3-1312; § 28-912	These Arizona laws provide the requirements for transporting equines to slaughter. A vehicle used to transport equine for slaughter may have no more than one level or tier in the compartment containing the equine. Violation of the laws constitutes a misdemeanor.
CO - Equine Activity Liability Statute - Article 21. Damages.	CO ST § 13-21-119	This Colorado statute embodies the intent of the general assembly to encourage equine activities and llama activities by limiting the civil liability of those involved in such activities. This section also contains specific provisions related to llama activities. Liability is not limited by this statute where the equine or llama sponsor provided faulty equipment or tack, failed to make reasonable and prudent efforts to determine the ability of the participant to engage safely in the activity, owned or otherwise possessed the land upon which an injury occurred where there was a known latent condition, or if he or she commits an act or omission that constitutes willful or wanton disregard for the safety of the participant or intentionally injures the participant.

Statute Name	Citation	Summary
CT - Equine Activity Liability Statute - Chapter 925. Statutory Rights of Action and Defenses	CT ST § 52-557p	This unusually short Connecticut statute limits the liability of equine sponsors by providing that each person engaged in recreational equestrian activities assumes the risk for any injury arising out of the hazards inherent in equestrian sports. However, if the the injury was proximately caused by the negligence of the person providing the horse or by the failure to guard or warn against a dangerous condition, use, structure or activity, liability if not limited by law.
DE - Equine Activity Liability - § 8140. CHAPTER 81. PERSONAL ACTIONS.	DE ST TI 10 § 8140	This Delaware statute provides that an equine activity sponsor, an equine professional or any other person shall not be liable for an injury to or the death of a participant resulting from the inherent risks of equine activities. Liability is not limited, however, when the equine professional knowingly used faulty tack, failed to make reasonable and prudent efforts to determine the ability of the participant to engage in the activity, owns or otherwise is in lawful possession of the land upon which the participant sustained injuries because of a dangerous latent condition which was known, commits an act or omission that constitutes willful or wanton disregard for the safety of the participant, or intentionally injures the participant. Equine professionals and sponsors are also required to post warning signs alerting the participants to the limitation of liability by law.
FL - Equine Activity Liability Statute- Chapter 773. Equine Activities.	FL ST § 773.01 - 773.06	This Florida statute provides that an equine activity sponsor, an equine professional, or any other person shall not be liable for an injury to or the death of a participant resulting from the inherent risks of equine activities. Liability will not be limited by statute, however, where the equine professional or sponsor knew the tack or equipment was faulty, failed to make reasonable and prudent efforts to determine the ability of the participant to engage safely in the equine activity, owns or is otherwise in lawful possession of the land or facilities where the injury is attributable to a known dangerous latent condition, commits an act or omission that constitutes willful or wanton disregard for the safety of the participant, or intentionally injures the participant. Posting of warning signs alerting participants to the limitation of liability by law is also required.
GA - Equine Liability Act - Chapter 12. Injuries from Equine or Llama Activities.	GA ST §§ 4-12-1 to 5	This act stipulates that an equine sponsor or professional, or a llama sponsor or professional, or any other person, including corporations, are immune from liability for the death or injury of a participant, which resulted from the inherent risks of equine or llama activities. However, there are exceptions to this rule: A person will be held liable for injuries if they display a willful and wanton or intentional disregard for the safety of the participant and if they fail to make reasonable and prudent efforts in ensuring the safety of the participant.

Statute Name	Citation	Summary
HI - Equine Activity Liability Statute	HI ST § 663B-1, B-2	Hawaii is unique in how it treats liability for injuries incurred during equine activities. The relevant section provides that, in any civil action for injury, loss, damage, or death of an equine participant, there shall be a rebuttable presumption that the injury, loss, damage, or death was not caused by the negligence of an equine activity sponsor, equine professional, or their employees or agents, if the injury, loss, damage, or death was caused solely by the inherent risk and unpredictable nature of the equine. Liability is not limited by this statute where the equine professional knowingly provided faulty tack or equipment, failed to make reasonable and prudent efforts to determine the ability of the participant to engage safely in the equine or activity, owns or otherwise is in lawful possession of the land or facilities upon which the participant sustained injuries because of a known, dangerous latent condition, or if he or she commits an act or omission that constitutes willful or wanton disregard for the safety of the participant or intentionally injures the participant.
IA - Equine Activity Liability Statute - Chapter 673. Domesticated Animal Activities.	IA ST § 673.1 - 673.5	This Iowa statute provides that a domesticated animal professional, sponsor, or exhibitor is not liable for the damages, injury, or death suffered by a participant or spectator resulting from the inherent risks of a domesticated animal activity. However, this section shall not apply to the extent that the claim for damages, injury, or death is caused by an act committed intentionally, recklessly, or while under the influence of an alcoholic beverage or other drug, the knowing use of faulty equipment or tack, the failure to notify a participant of a known dangerous latent condition on real property in which the defendant holds an interest, a domesticated animal activity which occurs in a place designated as a place for persons who are not participants to be present, or a domesticated animal activity which causes damages, injury, or death to a spectator who is in a place where a reasonable person would not expect a domesticated animal activity to occur. Not only does the statute require the displaying of warning signs alerting participants to the limitation of liability of the equine operators, but in cases where a written contract is executed, special provisions must be present on the contract.
ID - Equine Activity Liability - CHAPTER 18. EQUINE ACTIVITIES IMMUNITY ACT.	ID ST § 6-1801 - 1802	This Idaho statute provides that an equine activity sponsor or an equine professional shall not be liable for any injury to or the death of a participant or equine engaged in an equine activity and no participant may maintain an action against an equine activity sponsor or professional. Statutory definitions are provided, including "participant," "equine," and who is considered an "equine sponsor" or "equine professional." Liability is not limited by this statute where the equine professional knowingly provided faulty tack or equipment, failed to make reasonable and prudent efforts to determine the ability of the participant to engage safely in the equine activity, owns or otherwise is in lawful possession of the land or facilities upon which the participant sustained injuries because of a known, dangerous latent condition, or if he or she commits an act or omission that constitutes willful or wanton disregard for the safety of the participant or intentionally injures the participant.

Statute Name	Citation	Summary
IL - Equine Liability Act - Equine Activity Liability Act	IL ST CH 745 § 47/1 - 47/999	This act stipulates that an equine sponsor or professional, or any other person, is immune from liability for the death or injury of a participant, which resulted from the inherent risks of equine activities. However, there are exceptions to this rule: a person will be held liable for injuries of an equine activity participant if he or she displays a willful and wanton or intentional disregard for the safety of the participant and if he or she fails to make reasonable and prudent efforts in ensuring the safety of the participant. In addition, a person will also be held liable for the injury of an equine activity participant if he or she is injured on the land or at a facility due to a dangerous latent condition of which was known to the equine sponsor, professional or other person.
IN - Equine Activity Statute - Chapter 5. Equine Activities	IN ST 34-31-5-1 to 5	This Indiana statute states that an equine activity sponsor or equine professional is not liable for an injury to a participant or the death of a participant resulting from an inherent risk of equine activities. Liability is not limited by this statute where the equine professional knowingly provided faulty tack or equipment, failed to make reasonable and prudent efforts to determine the ability of the participant to engage safely in the equine activity, owns or otherwise is in lawful possession of the land or facilities upon which the participant sustained injuries because of a known, dangerous latent condition, or if he or she commits an act or omission that constitutes reckless disregard for the safety of the participant or intentionally injures the participant. The statute also requires the visible displaying of warning signs or warnings provided in contracts that alert participants to the limitation of liability by law.
KS - Equine Activity Liability - Article 40. Assumption of Risk of Domestic Animal Activity.	KS ST § 60-4001 - 4004	This Kansas statute provides that any participant in domestic animal activities assumes the inherent risks of when such participant engages in a domestic animal activity. This limitation of liability operates legally as an affirmative defense of assumption of risk pleaded by the domestic animal activity sponsor or domestic animal professional. The statute also requires the visible displaying of warning signs that alert participants to the limitation of liability by law and any written contract must provide explicit language outlined in the statute.
KY - Equine Activity Liability Statute - Chapter 247. Promotion of Agriculture and Horticulture. Farm Animal Activities.	KY ST § 247.401 - 4029	This Kentucky statute embodies the legislative intent to encourage farm animal activities by limiting the civil liability of those involved in such activities. Statutory definitions are provided, including "inherent risks of farm animal activities" and "engages in farm animal activity." The statute also requires the visible displaying of warning signs that alert participants to the limitation of liability by law. Failure to comply with the requirements concerning warning signs and notices provided in this section shall prevent a farm animal activity sponsor or farm animal professional from invoking the provisions of KRS 247.401 to 247.4029.
LA - Equine Activity Liability - § 2795.1. Limitation of liability of farm animal activity sponsor or professional; exceptions; required warning	LA R.S. 9:2795.1 - 9:2795.3	The Louisiana law regarding equine activity liability is divided into two sections; one related to "farm animal activity" and one specific to "equine activity sponsors." Both statutes have identical terms, save for the animal to which the statute pertains. Under both, engaging in the farm animal or equine activity does not include being a spectator at a farm animal activity, except in cases where the spectator places himself in an unauthorized area and in immediate proximity to the farm animal or equine activity. The statute also requires the visible displaying of warning signs that alert participants to the limitation of liability by law and any written contracts must include the statutory language provided. Failure to comply with the requirements concerning warning notices provided prevents a farm animal activity sponsor or equine sponsor from invoking the privilege of immunity provided by this section.

Statute Name	**Citation**	**Summary**
MA - Equine Activity Liability Statute - Chapter 128. Agriculture.	MA ST 128 § 2D	This Massachusetts law provides that an equine activity sponsor, an equine professional, or any other person shall not be liable for an injury to or the death of a participant resulting from the inherent risks of equine activities. The statute sets out several definitions related to equine activities, but specifically notes that the term "engage in an equine activity" shall not include being a spectator at an equine activity, except in cases where the spectator places himself in an unauthorized area or in immediate proximity to the equine activity. Liability is not limited by this statute where the equine professional knowingly provided faulty tack or equipment, failed to make reasonable and prudent efforts to determine the ability of the participant to engage safely in the equine activity, owns or otherwise is in lawful possession of the land or facilities upon which the participant sustained injuries because of a known, dangerous latent condition, or if he or she commits an act or omission that constitutes willful or wanton disregard for the safety of the participant or intentionally injures the participant.
ME - Equine Liability - Chapter 743. Equine Activities	ME ST T. 7 § 4101 - 4103-A	This act stipulates that an equine sponsor, equine professional, or any other person engaged in an equine activity, is immune from liability for the death or injury of a participant, as well as property damage, which resulted from the inherent risks of equine activities. However, there are exceptions to this rule: A person will be held liable for injuries of an equine activity participant if he or she displays a willful and wanton or intentional disregard for the safety of the participant and if he or she fails to make reasonable and prudent efforts in ensuring the safety of the participant. In addition, a person will also be held liable for the injury of an equine activity participant if he or she is injured on the land or at a facility due to a dangerous latent condition of which was known to the equine sponsor, professional or other person.
MI - Equine Liability - Chapter 691. Judiciary. Equine Activity Liability Act	MCLA 691.1661 - 1667	This statute sets out the liabilities for those that own and use horses: both commercial horse operations and horse shows. It limits liability of owners in certain circumstances.
MI - Equine Liability Act - Chapter 691. Judiciary. Equine Activity Liability Act	MI ST 691.1661 - 1667	This act stipulates that an equine sponsor or professional, or any other person, is immune from liability for the death or injury of a participant, which resulted from the inherent risks of equine activities. However, there are exceptions to this rule: a person will be held liable for injuries if he or she commits a negligent act or omission that results in the proximate cause of injury or death, and if he or she fails to make reasonable and prudent efforts in ensuring the safety of the participant. In addition, a person will also be held liable for the injury of an equine activity participant if he or she is injured on the land or at a facility due to a dangerous latent condition of which was known to the equine sponsor, professional or other person.

Statute Name	Citation	Summary
MN - Equine Activity Liability - 604A.12. Livestock activities; immunity from liability.	MN ST § 604A.12	This Minnesota statute comprises the state's equine activity liability statute. The act is not limited to equines, but rather extends protection from liability to participants engaged in "livestock activities." It is important to note that this provision and exemption from liability applies only to non-profit entities. Liability is not limited where the livestock professional knowingly used faulty tack, the person failed to reasonable care to protect the participant from a known, human-made dangerous condition, the person is a livestock activity sponsor and fails to comply with the notice requirement, or the act or omission of the person was willful or negligent.
MO - Equine Activity Liability - Chapter 537. Torts and Actions for Damages.	MO ST 537.325	This Missouri statute provides that an equine activity sponsor, an equine professional or any other person shall not be liable for an injury to or the death of a participant resulting from the inherent risks of equine activities and no participant shall make maintain an action against an equine operator. Statutory definitions are provided, including "participant," "inherent risk," and who is considered an "equine sponsor" or "equine professional." The term "engages in an equine activity" does not include being a spectator at an equine activity, except in cases where the spectator places him or herself in an unauthorized area. The statute also requires the visible displaying of warning signs that alert participants to the limitation of liability by law.
MS - Equine Activity Liability - Chapter 11. Liability Exemption for Livestock Shows and Equine Activities	MS ST § 95-11-1 to 95-11- 7	This Mississippi statute embodies the intent of the Legislature to encourage equine and livestock activities by limiting the civil liability of those involved in such activities. Liability is not limited by this statute where the equine professional knowingly provided faulty tack or equipment, failed to make reasonable and prudent efforts to determine the ability of the participant to engage safely in the equine or livestock activity, owns or otherwise is in lawful possession of the land or facilities upon which the participant sustained injuries because of a known, dangerous latent condition, or if he or she commits an act or omission that constitutes willful or wanton disregard for the safety of the participant or intentionally injures the participant. The statute also requires the visible displaying of warning signs that alert participants to the limitation of liability by law.
MT - Equine Activity Liability - Chapter 1. Availability of Remedies--Liability.	MT ST 27-1-725 to 27-1-728	The Montana equine activity liability act provides that it is the policy of the state of Montana that a person is not liable for damages sustained by another solely as a result of risks inherent in equine activities if those risks are or should be reasonably obvious, expected, or necessary to persons engaged in equine activities. Liability is not limited by this statute where the equine professional knowingly provided faulty tack or equipment, failed to make reasonable and prudent efforts to determine the ability of the participant to engage safely in the equine activity, owns or otherwise is in lawful possession of the land or facilities upon which the participant sustained injuries because of a known, dangerous latent condition, or if he or she commits an act or omission that constitutes willful or wanton disregard for the safety of the participant or intentionally injures the participant.
NC - Equine Activity Liability - Article 1. Equine Activity Liability	NC ST S 99E-1-99E-3	This act stipulates that an equine sponsor or equine professional, or any other person, including corporations and partnerships, are immune from liability for the death or injury of a participant, which resulted from the inherent risks of equine activities. However, there are exceptions to this rule: a person, corporation, or partnership will be held liable for injuries of an equine activity participant if he or she displays a willful and wanton or intentional disregard for the safety of the participant and if he or she fails to make reasonable and prudent efforts in ensuring the safety of the participant.

Statute Name	Citation	Summary
NC - Equine Activity Liability - Article 1. Equine Activity Liability	NC ST S 99E-1-99E-3	This act stipulates that an equine sponsor or equine professional, or any other person, including corporations and partnerships, are immune from liability for the death or injury of a participant, which resulted from the inherent risks of equine activities. However, there are exceptions to this rule: a person, corporation, or partnership will be held liable for injuries of an equine activity participant if he or she displays a willful and wanton or intentional disregard for the safety of the participant and if he or she fails to make reasonable and prudent efforts in ensuring the safety of the participant.
ND - Equine Activity - Chapter 53-10. Equine Activity Sponsor or Professional.	ND ST 53-10-01; ND ST 53-10-02	This North Dakota statute provides that an equine activity sponsor or an equine professional is not liable for an injury to or the death of a participant engaged in an equine activity and no participant may maintain an action against an equine activity sponsor or professional. Statutory definitions are provided, including "participant," "equine activity," and who is considered an "equine sponsor" or "equine professional." Liability is not limited by this statute where the equine professional knowingly provided faulty tack or equipment, failed to make reasonable and prudent efforts to determine the ability of the participant to engage safely in the equine activity, owns or otherwise is in lawful possession of the land or facilities upon which the participant sustained injuries because of a known, dangerous latent condition, or if he or she commits an act or omission that constitutes willful or wanton disregard for the safety of the participant or intentionally injures the participant.
NE - Equine Activity Liability - Article 21. Actions and Proceedings in Particular Cases. (EE) Equine Activities	NE ST § 25-21,249 - 253	This Nebraska statute provides that an equine activity sponsor, an equine professional, or any other person shall not be liable for an injury to or the death of a participant resulting from the inherent risks of equine activities and no participant shall make any claim against, maintain an action against, or recover from an equine activity sponsor. Statutory definitions are provided, including "participant," "inherent risk," and who is considered an "equine sponsor" or "equine professional." Engages in an equine activity does not include being a spectator at an equine activity except in cases when the spectator places himself or herself in an unauthorized area. The statute also requires the visible displaying of warning signs that alert participants to the limitation of liability by law.
NH - Equine Activity Liability - Chapter 508. Limitation of Actions.	NH ST § 508:19	This New Hampshire statute provides that an equine activity sponsor, an equine professional, or any other person engaged in an equine activity, shall not be liable for an injury or the death of a participant resulting from the inherent risks of equine activities. However, liability is not limited by this statute where the equine professional knowingly provided faulty tack or equipment, failed to make reasonable and prudent efforts to determine the ability of the participant to engage safely in the equine activity, owns or otherwise is in lawful possession of the land or facilities upon which the participant sustained injuries because of a known, dangerous latent condition, or if he or she commits an act or omission that constitutes willful or wanton disregard for the safety of the participant or intentionally injures the participant. The statute also sets out several definitions and specifically states that the term "engages in an equine activity" does not include being a spectator at an equine activity, except in cases where the spectator is in an unauthorized area and in immediate proximity to the equine activity.

Statute Name	Citation	Summary
NM - Equine Activity Liability - Article 13. Equine Liability	NM ST § 42-13-1 to 42-13-5	This act stipulates that any person, corporation or partnership is immune from liability for the death or injury of a rider, which resulted while the rider was engaged in an equine activity. However, there are exceptions to this rule: a person, corporation, or partnership will be held liable for injuries if he or she displays a conscious, reckless, or intentional disregard for the safety of the rider, and if the person, corporation, or partnership fails to make reasonable and prudent efforts in ensuring the safety of the rider.
OH - Equine Liability Act - Chapter 2305. Jurisdiction; Limitation of Actions. Miscellaneous Provisions.	OH ST § 2305.321	This act stipulates that an equine sponsor, equine activity participant, equine professional, veterinarian, farrier, or any other person is not liable in damages in a tort or other civil action for harm that an equine activity participant allegedly sustains during an equine activity, which resulted from the inherent risks of equine activities. However, there are exceptions to this rule: an equine sponsor, equine activity participant, equine professional, veterinarian, farrier, or any other person will be held liable for injuries of an equine activity participant if he or she displays a willful and wanton or intentional disregard for the safety of the participant and if he or she fails to make reasonable and prudent efforts in ensuring the safety of the participant. In addition, an equine sponsor, equine activity participant, equine professional, veterinarian, farrier, or any other person will also be held liable for the injury of an equine activity participant if he or she is injured on the land or at a facility due to a dangerous latent condition of which was known to the equine sponsor, professional or other person.
OK - Equine Activity Liability - Title 76. Torts. Livestock Activities Liability Limitation Act.	OK ST T. 76 § 50.1 - 50.4	The Oklahoma Livestock Activities Liability Limitation Act provides that it is the intent of the Oklahoma Legislature to encourage livestock activities by limiting the civil liability of livestock activities sponsors, participants and livestock professionals involved in such activities. A livestock activity sponsor, a participant or a livestock professional acting in good faith and pursuant to the standards of the livestock industry shall not be liable for injuries to any person engaged in livestock activities when such injuries result from the inherent risks of livestock activities. Oklahoma also has a unique provision that explicitly states that two or more persons may agree, in writing, to extend the waiver of liability pursuant to the provisions of the Oklahoma Livestock Activities Liability Limitation Act.
OR - Equine Liability Act - Chapter 30. Actions and Suits in Particular Cases. Actions Arising Out of Equine Activities.	OR ST § 30.687 - 697	This act stipulates that an equine sponsor or an equine professional is immune from liability for the death or injury of a participant, arising out of riding, training, driving, grooming or riding as a passenger upon an equine. However, there are exceptions to this rule: an equine sponsor or professional will be held liable for injuries of an equine activity participant if he or she displays a willful and wanton or intentional disregard for the safety of the participant.
PA - Equine - Chapter 13. Equine Activity.	PA ST 4 P.S. § 601 - 606	These statutes comprise Pennsylvania's Equine Activity Act, which sent into effect on February 21, 2006. Under the law, liability for negligence shall only be barred where knowing voluntary assumption of risk is proven in a particular case. However, the Act provides immunity only where a sign that states, "You assume the risk of equine activities pursuant to Pennsylvania law," is conspicuously posted on the premises in two or more locations.

Statute Name	Citation	Summary
RI - Equine Activity Liability - Chapter 21. Exemption from Liability Arising from Equine Activities	RI ST § 4-21-1 - 4	This Rhode Island section provides that an equine professional, or any other person, shall not be liable for an injury to or the death of a participant resulting from the inherent risks of equine activities unless the equine activity sponsor, professional or other person are demonstrated to have failed to exercise due care under the circumstances towards the participant. Liability is not limited by this statute where the equine professional knowingly provided faulty tack or equipment, failed to make reasonable and prudent efforts to determine the ability of the participant to engage safely in the equine activity, owns or otherwise is in lawful possession of the land or facilities upon which the participant sustained injuries because of a known, dangerous latent condition, or if he or she commits an act or omission that constitutes willful or wanton disregard for the safety of the participant or intentionally injures the participant.
SC - Equine Activity Liability - Article 7. Equine Liability Immunity.	SC ST § 47-9-710 - 730	This South Carolina section provides that an equine activity sponsor or an equine professional is not liable for an injury to or the death of a participant resulting from an inherent risk of equine activity. The statute also requires the visible displaying of warning signs that alert participants to the limitation of liability by law. Failure to comply with the requirements concerning warning signs and notices provided in this section prevents an equine activity sponsor or equine professional from invoking the privileges of immunity provided by this article.
SD - Equine Activity Liability - Chapter 42-11. Equine Activities.	SD ST § 42-11-1 - 5	This act stipulates that an equine sponsor, equine professional, doctor of veterinary medicine or any other person, is immune from liability for the death or injury of a participant, which resulted from the inherent risks of equine activities. However, there are exceptions to this rule: a person will be held liable for injuries of an equine activity participant if he or she displays a willful and wanton or intentional disregard for the safety of the participant and if he or she fails to make reasonable and prudent efforts in ensuring the safety of the participant. In addition, a person will also be held liable for the injury of an equine activity participant if he or she is injured on the land or at a facility due to a dangerous latent condition of which was known to the equine sponsor, professional or other person.
TN - Equine Activity Liability - Chapter 20. Equine Activities--Liability	TN ST § 44-20-101 - 105	This act stipulates that an equine sponsor or equine professional, or any other person, including corporations and partnerships, are immune from liability for the death or injury of a participant, which resulted from the inherent risks of equine activities. However, there are exceptions to this rule: a person, corporation, or partnership will be held liable for injuries of an equine activity participant if he or she displays a willful and wanton or intentional disregard for the safety of the participant and if he or she fails to make reasonable and prudent efforts in ensuring the safety of the participant. In addition, a person will be held liable for the injury of an equine activity participant if he or she is injured on the land or at a facility due to a dangerous latent condition of which was known to the equine sponsor, professional or other person.

Statute Name	Citation	Summary
TX - Equine Activity Liability - Chapter 87. Liability Arising from Equine Activities or Livestock Shows.	TX CIV PRAC & REM § 87.001 - 005	This Texas section provides that any person, including an equine activity sponsor, equine professional, livestock show participant, or livestock show sponsor, is not liable for property damage or damages arising from the personal injury or death of a participant in an equine activity or livestock show if the property damage, injury, or death results from the dangers or conditions that are an inherent risk of an equine activity or the showing of an animal on a competitive basis in a livestock show. The statute also requires the visible displaying of "clearly readable" warning signs that alert participants to the limitation of liability by law.
UT - Equine Activity Liability - Part 2. Limitations on Liability for Equine and Livestock Activities	UT ST § 78B-4-201 - 203	This Utah section states that it is presumed that participants in equine or livestock activities are aware of and understand that there are inherent risks associated with these activities. Thus, an equine activity sponsor, equine professional, livestock activity sponsor, or livestock professional is not liable for an injury to or the death of a participant due to the inherent risks associated with these activities. The section also requires an equine professional to give notice to participants of the limitation of liability, either by the posting of a sign or by the execution of a written release.
VA - Equine - Chapter 62. Equine Activity Liability/Chapter 63. Ox Activity Liability	VA ST § 3.2-6200 - 6302	This Virginia section provides that an equine activity sponsor, an equine professional, or any other person shall not be liable for an injury to or death of a participant resulting from the intrinsic dangers of equine activities. Liability is not limited where the equine professional intentionally injures the participant, commits an act or omission that constitutes negligence for the safety of the participant, or knowingly provides faulty equipment or tack that causes injury. The statute seems to imply that a waiver should be executed when a participant engages in equine activities to adequately insulate the equine professional.
VT - Equine - § 1039. Equine activities; acceptance of inherent risks	VT ST T. 12 § 1039	This statute represents Vermont's equine activity liability law. Under the Act, no person shall be liable for an injury to, or the death of, a participant resulting from the inherent risks of equine activities, insofar as those risks are necessary to the equine activity and obvious to the person injured. An equine activity sponsor may (it does not say "shall") post and maintain signs which contain the warning notice specified in this subsection.
WA - Equine Activity Liability - Chapter 4.24. Special Rights of Action and Special Immunities.	WA ST 4.24.530 - 540	This Washington section provides that an equine activity sponsor or an equine professional shall not be liable for an injury to or the death of a participant engaged in an equine activity, nor may he or she maintain an action against or recover from an equine activity sponsor or an equine professional for an injury to or the death while engaged in an equine activity. Liability is not limited by this statute where the equine professional knowingly provided faulty tack or equipment, failed to make reasonable and prudent efforts to determine the ability of the participant to engage safely in the equine activity, owns or otherwise is in lawful possession of the land or facilities upon which the participant sustained injuries because of a known, dangerous latent condition, or if he or she commits an act or omission that constitutes willful or wanton disregard for the safety of the participant or intentionally injures the participant.

Statute Name	Citation	Summary
WI - Equine Activity Liability - 895.481. Civil liability exemption; equine activities	WI ST 895.481	Under this Wisconsin statute, a person is immune from civil liability for acts or omissions related to his or her participation in equine activities if a person participating in the equine activity is injured or killed as the result of an inherent risk of equine activities. Notably, the statute provides that a person whose only involvement in an equine activity is as a spectator shall not be considered to be participating in the equine activity. The statute also requires the visible displaying of warning signs or bold print in a written waiver that alerts participants to the limitation of liability by law.
WV - Equine Activity Liability - Article 4. Equestrian Activities Responsibility Act.	WV ST § 20-4-1 - 7	This West Virginia section expressly recognizes the value of equestrian activities to the state. Thus, in order to limit liability to those who provide equine services, the duties of both the horsemen who provide such services and the participants who engage in such activities are stated. Each participant in an equestrian activity expressly assumes the risk of and legal responsibility for any injury, loss or damage to person or property which results from participation in an equestrian activity. Horsemen are required to ensure the safety of the participants and the equipment provided.
WY - Equine Activity Liability - Chapter 1. General Provisions as to Civil Actions	WY ST § 1-1-122 to 123	The Wyoming equine liability provisions immunize equine professionals by declaring that those who engage in equine activities or any recreational activities assume the inherent risks in the sport or recreational opportunity. However, actions based upon negligence of the provider wherein the damage, injury or death is not the result of an inherent risk of the sport or recreational opportunity shall be preserved pursuant to W.S. 1-1-109.

Courtesy of Michigan State University, College of Law, Animal Legal and Historical Center, Professor David Favre, Editor-in-Chief. Equine activity liability laws are updated by the Animal Legal and Historical Center on an annual basis. See http://animallaw.info/articles/armpequineliability.htm for the most recent updates.

Appendix H

Mandatory Reporting of Child Abuse by State

Camp personnel and those likely to be employed at camp, plus child care personnel and youth recreation program personnel

✓ = named in state law
= implied by law*

State	Any person who knows or in good faith suspects child abuse or neglect:	Medical personnel:	Child care personnel:	Camp personnel:	Youth recreation program personnel:	Other persons who might be similar to camp personnel:
Alabama		✓	✓			
Alaska		✓	✓			
Arizona		✓	#	#	#	Any person who has responsibility for the care or treatment of minors
Arkansas		✓	✓			
California		✓	#	✓	#	Individuals providing services to minor children
Colorado		✓				
Connecticut		✓	✓			
Delaware	✓	✓				
District of Columbia		✓	✓		✓	
Florida	✓	✓	✓			

State	Any person who knows or in good faith suspects child abuse or neglect:	Medical personnel:	Child care personnel:	Camp personnel:	Youth recreation program personnel:	Other persons who might be similar to camp personnel:
Georgia		✓	✓			
Hawaii		✓	✓	#	✓	
Idaho	✓	✓	✓			
Illinois		✓	✓	#	✓	
Indiana	✓	✓				
Iowa		✓	✓			
Kansas		✓	✓			
Kentucky	✓	✓	✓			
Louisiana		✓	✓	✓	✓	
Maine		✓	✓	✓		
Maryland	✓	✓				
Massachusetts		✓	✓	#	#	Persons paid to work in program that provides child care or residential services to children
Michigan		✓	✓			
Minnesota		✓	✓			
Mississippi	✓	✓	✓			
Missouri		✓	✓	#	#	Other persons with responsibility for children
Montana		✓	✓			
Nebraska	✓	✓				
Nevada		✓	✓	✓	#	Adult persons who are employed by entities that provide organized activities for children
New Hampshire	✓	✓	✓			
New Jersey	✓					
New Mexico	✓	✓				
New York		✓	✓	✓		
North Carolina	✓					
North Dakota		✓	✓			
Ohio		✓	✓	✓		
Oklahoma	✓					
Oregon		✓	✓	✓		

State	Any person who knows or in good faith suspects child abuse or neglect:	Medical personnel:	Child care personnel:	Camp personnel:	Youth recreation program personnel:	Other persons who might be similar to camp personnel:
Pennsylvania		✓	✓			
Puerto Rico	✓	✓	✓			
Rhode Island	✓	✓				
South Carolina		✓	✓			
South Dakota		✓	#			Child welfare service providers
Tennessee	✓	✓	✓			
Texas		✓	✓	#		An employee of a facility licensed by the state who has direct contact with children (camps must be licensed)
Utah	✓	✓				
Vermont		✓	✓	✓		
Virginia		✓	✓	✓	✓	
Washington		✓	✓	#	#	Persons who supervise employees who have regular unsupervised access to children
West Virginia		✓	✓	✓	#	Employees of entities that provide organized activities for children
Wisconsin		✓	✓			
Wyoming	✓					

*Note: This is the interpretation of the authors. See state law for more information.

Information derived from *Mandatory Reporters of Child Abuse and Neglect*, Child Welfare Information Gateway, Children's Bureau, Administration for Children and Families, U.S. Department of Health and Human Services. Available online at http://www.childwelfare.gov/systemwide/laws_policies/statutes/manda.cfm.

Appendix I

Websites and Phone Numbers for Reporting Child Abuse by State

State	Reporting Agency	Phone Number
Alabama	http://dhr.alabama.gov/services/Child_Protective_Services/Abuse_Neglect_Reporting.aspx	Local: 334-242-9500
Alaska	http://www.hss.state.ak.us/ocs/default.htm	Toll free: (800) 478-4444
Arizona	https://www.azdes.gov/dcyf/cps/reporting.asp	Toll free: (888-767-2445) (888) SOS-CHILD
Arkansas	http://www.arkansas.gov/reportARchildabuse	Toll free: 800-482-5964
California	http://www.dss.cahwnet.gov/cdssweb/PG20.htm	*
Colorado	http://www.colorado.gov/cs/Satellite/CDHS-Main/CBON/1251633944381	Local: (303) 866-5932
Connecticut	http://www.state.ct.us/dcf/HOTLINE.htm	TDD: (800) 624-5518 Toll free: (800) 842-2288
Delaware	http://kids.delaware.gov/services/crisis.shtml	Toll free: (800) 292-9582
District of Columbia	http://cfsa.dc.gov/service/report-child-abuse-and-neglect	Local: (202)-671-SAFE (202-671-7233)
Florida	http://www.dcf.state.fl.us/abuse	Toll free: (800) 96ABUSE (800-962-2873)
Georgia	http://dfcs.dhs.georgia.gov/child-abuse-neglect	*
Hawaii	http://www.hawaii.gov/dhs/protection/social_services/child_welfare	Local: (808) 832-5300
Idaho	http://healthandwelfare.idaho.gov/Children/AbuseNeglect	Toll free: (800-926-2588)
Illinois	http://www.state.il.us/dcfs/child/index.shtml	Toll free: (800) 252-2873 Local: (217) 524-2606
Indiana	http://www.in.gov/dcs/protection/dfcchi.html	Toll free: (800) 800-5556
Iowa	http://www.dhs.state.ia.us/dhs2005/dhs_homepage	Toll free: (800) 362-2178
Kansas	http://www.srskansas.org/services/child_protective_services	Toll free: (800) 922-5330

State	Reporting Agency	Phone Number
Kentucky	http://chfs.ky.gov/dcbs/dpp/childsafety.htm	Toll free: (877) 597-2331
Louisiana	http://dss.louisiana.gov	Toll free: (855) 452-5437
Maine	http://www.maine.gov/dhhs/ocfs/hotlines.htm	TTY: (800) 963-9490 Toll free: (800) 452-1999
Maryland	http://www.dhr.state.md.us	*
Massachusetts	http://www.mass.gov/eohhs/gov/departments/dcf/child-abuse-neglect	Toll free: (800) 792-5200
Michigan	http://www.michigan.gov/dhs	Fax: (616) 977-1154 Local: (616) 977-1158 Toll free: (855) 444-3911
Minnesota	http://www.dhs.state.mn.us/main	*
Mississippi	http://www.mdhs.state.ms.us/fcs_prot.html	Toll free: (800) 222-8000 Local: (601) 359-4991
Missouri	http://www.dss.mo.gov/cd/rptcan.htm	Toll free: (800) 392-3738
Montana	http://www.dphhs.mt.gov/cfsd/index.shtml	Toll free: (866) 820-5437
Nebraska	http://www.hhs.state.ne.us/cha/chaindex.htm	Toll free: (800) 652-1999
Nevada	http://dcfs.state.nv.us/DCFS_ReportSuspectedChildAbuse.htm	Toll free: (800) 992-5757
New Hampshire	http://www.dhhs.state.nh.us/dcyf/cps/contact.htm	Toll free: (800) 894-5533 Local: (603) 271-6556
New Jersey	http://www.nj.gov/dcf/reporting/how/index.html	TDD: (800) 835-5510 TTY: (800) 835-5510 Toll free: (877) 652-2873
New Mexico	http://www.cyfd.org/content/reporting-abuse-or-neglect	Toll free: (855) 333-7233
New York	http://www.ocfs.state.ny.us/main/cps	TDD: (800) 369-2437 Toll free: (800) 342-3720 Local: (518) 474-8740
North Carolina	http://www.dhhs.state.nc.us/dss/cps/index.htm	*
North Dakota	http://www.nd.gov/dhs/services/childfamily/cps/#reporting	*
Ohio	http://jfs.ohio.gov/ocf/reportchildabuseandneglect.stm	Toll free: (855) 642-4453
Oklahoma	http://www.okdhs.org/programsandservices/cps/default.htm	Toll free: (800) 522-3511
Oregon	http://www.oregon.gov/DHS/children/abuse/cps/report.shtml	*
Pennsylvania	http://www.dpw.state.pa.us/forchildren/childwelfareservices/calltoreportchildabuse!/index.htm	Toll free: (800) 932-0313
Puerto Rico	Spanish: http://www2.pr.gov/agencias/adfan/Pages/AdministracionAuxiliardeProteccionSocial.aspx	Toll free: (800) 981-8333 Local: (787) 749-1333
Rhode Island	http://www.dcyf.ri.gov/child_welfare/index.php	Toll free: (800) RI-CHILD (800) 742-4453
South Carolina	http://dss.sc.gov/content/customers/protection/cps/index.aspx	Local: (803) 898-7318
South Dakota	http://dss.sd.gov/cps/protective/reporting.asp	*
Tennessee	https://reportabuse.state.tn.us/	Toll free: (877) 237-0004

State	Reporting Agency	Phone Number
Texas	https://www.dfps.state.tx.us/Contact_Us/report_abuse.asp Spanish: http://www.dfps.state.tx.us/Espanol/default.asp	Toll free: (800) 252-5400
Utah	http://www.hsdcfs.utah.gov	Toll free: (855) 323-3237
Vermont	http://www.dcf.state.vt.us/fsd/reporting_child_abuse	Toll free: (800) 649-5285 (after hours)
Virginia	http://www.dss.virginia.gov/family/cps/index.html	Toll free: (800) 552-7096 Local: (804) 786-8536
Washington	http://www1.dshs.wa.gov/ca/safety/abuseReport.asp?2	TTY: (800) 624-6186 Toll free: (800) 562-5624 Or : (866) END-HARM (866-363-4276)
West Virginia	http://www.wvdhhr.org/bcf/children_adult/cps/report.asp	Toll free: (800) 352-6513
Wisconsin	http://dcf.wisconsin.gov/children/CPS/cpswimap.HTM	*
Wyoming	http://dfsweb.state.wy.us/protective-services/cps/index.html	*

*Go to website for information on reporting or call Childhelp® at 800-422-4453 for assistance.

These numbers were current as of August 11, 2013. If you have any difficulties in reporting, call Childhelp at 800-422-4453 for assistance.
Source: Child Welfare Information Gateway
www.childwelfare.gov

Appendix J

Chart of Accounts

Sample Chart of Accounts—Nonprofit							
In the form xx-yyy-zzz, where: *xx = location* *yyy = natural classification (listed below)* *zzz = department*							
Assets			**Miscellaneous Income**			**Local Transportation**	
Cash			611	Store		781	Mileage Reimbursements
101	Operating Account		612	Snacks		782	Maintenance & Gas
102	Savings Account		613	Photos		783	Vehicle Insurance
103	Equipment Account		619	Miscellaneous Other		784	Vehicle Rental
Accounts Receivable			**Expenses**			785	Tolls and Parking
131	Accounts Receivable Fees		*Salaries*			789	Other Transportation
132	Accounts Receivable Other		701	Salaries Exempt		*Conferences & Travel*	
Prepaid Expenses			702	Salaries Nonexempt		801	Airfare
151	Prepaid Insurance		703	Salaries Temporary		802	Registration
159	Prepaid Other		709	Salaries Other		803	Lodging
Inventory			*Benefits*			804	Meals
161	Inventory Store		711	Health Insurance		805	Ground Transportation
162	Inventory Food		712	Pension		809	Other Conferences
169	Inventory Other		*Payroll Taxes*			*Subscriptions & References*	
Liabilities			721	FICA/Medicare		811	General Subscriptions

Sample Chart of Accounts—Nonprofit (cont.)					
Accounts Payable		722	Workers' Compensation	812	General References
201	Accounts Payable General	723	Unemployment	813	Advertising
202	Accounts Payable Sales Tax	*Professional Fees & Contract Labor*		814	Website
Deferred Revenue		731	Professional Fees	815	Software
301	Deferred Revenue Fees	732	Contract Labor	819	Other Subscriptions & References
309	Deferred Revenue Other	739	Other	*Assistance to Individuals*	
Net Assets		*Supplies*		821	Assistance–Camp Fees
401	Net Assets	741	Medical	829	Assistance–Other
Income		742	Program	*Dues & Fees*	
Contributions		743	Food	831	Membership Dues
501	Contributions Individuals	744	Household	832	Fees & Licenses
502	Contributions Foundations	745	Office	839	Other Fees
503	Contributions Corporations	746	Horse	*Equipment*	
509	Contributions Other	749	Other Supplies	841	Medical
Special Events		*Telephone*		842	Program
531	Special Events Live Auction	751	Landlines	843	Food
532	Special Events Ticket Sales	752	Cellular	844	Household
533	Special Events Table Sales	753	Internet	845	Office
539	Special Events Other	*Postage*		846	Rental
United Way Income		761	Postage, Meter	849	Other
551	United Way Smith County	762	Postage, Stamps	*Insurance*	
552	United Way Jones County	763	Bulk Mail	851	Participant Accident
553	United Way Brown County	764	Mail House	852	Liability
554	United Way Johnson County	765	Permits	853	Directors & Officers
Fee Income		*Occupancy*		854	Fidelity
591	Fees Summer Camp	771	Rent	855	Equipment
592	Fees Outdoor Education	772	Utilities, Electric	859	Other Insurance
593	Fees Weekend Programs	773	Utilities, Gas	*Miscellaneous*	
594	Fees Transportation	774	Utilities, Water	861	Awards & Gifts
599	Fees Other	775	Care of Buildings	862	Credit Card Fees
Interest and Dividends		776	Care of Grounds	863	Other Miscellaneous
601	Interest	777	Property Insurance	*Transfer to Other Funds*	
602	Dividends	779	Other Occupancy	901	Transfers

Sample Chart of Accounts—For Profit

In the form xx-yyy-zzz, where:
xx = location
yyy = natural classification (listed below)
zzz = department

ASSETS		**EXPENSES**		*Local Transportation*	
Cash		*Salaries*		781	Mileage Reimbursements
101	Operating Account	701	Salaries Exempt	782	Maintenance & Gas
102	Savings Account	702	Salaries Nonexempt	783	Vehicle Insurance
103	Equipment Account	703	Salaries Temporary	784	Vehicle Rental
Accounts Receivable		709	Salaries Other	785	Tolls and Parking
131	Accounts Receivable Fees	*Benefits*		789	Other Transportation
132	Accounts Receivable Other	711	Health Insurance	*Conferences & Travel*	
Prepaid Expenses		712	Pension	801	Airfare
151	Prepaid Insurance	*Payroll Taxes*		802	Registration
159	Prepaid Other	721	FICA/Medicare	803	Lodging
Inventory		722	Workers Compensation	804	Meals
161	Inventory Store	723	State Unemployment	805	Ground Transportation
162	Inventory Food	724	Federal Unemployment	809	Other Conferences
169	Inventory Other	*Professional Fees & Contract Labor*		*Subscriptions & References*	
LIABILITIES		731	Legal Fees	811	General Subscription
Accounts Payable		732	Accounting Fees	812	General References
201	A/P General	733	General Contract Labor	813	Advertising
202	A/P Sales Tax	739	Other Contract Labor	814	Website
Deferred Revenue		*Supplies*		815	Software
301	Deferred Revenue Fees	741	Medical	819	Other Subscriptions & References
309	Deferred Revenue Other	742	Program	*Assistance to Individuals*	
OWNERS EQUITY		743	Food	821	Assistance—Camp Fees
401	Owners Equity	744	Household	829	Assistance—Other
402	Retained Earnings	745	Office	*Dues & Fees*	
INCOME		746	Horse	831	Membership Dues
Fee Income		749	Other Supplies	832	Fees & Licenses
591	Fees Summer Camp	*Telephone*		839	Other Fees
592	Fees Outdoor Education	751	Landlines	*Equipment*	
593	Fees Weekend Programs	752	Cellular	841	Medical
594	Fees Transportation	753	Internet	842	Program
599	Fees Other	*Postage*		843	Food
Interest and Dividends		761	Postage, Meter	844	Household
601	Interest	762	Postage, Stamps	845	Office

Sample Chart of Accounts—For Profit (cont.)							
602	Dividends		764	Mail House		846	Rental
Miscellaneous Income			765	Permits		849	Other
611	Store		769	Other Postage		*Insurance*	
612	Snacks		*Occupancy*			851	Participant Accident
613	Photos		771	Rent		852	Liability
619	Miscellaneous Other		772	Utilities, Electric		853	Directors & Officers
			773	Utilities, Gas		854	Fidelity
			774	Utilities, Water		855	Equipment
			775	Care of Buildings		859	Other Insurance
			776	Care of Grounds		*Miscellaneous*	
			777	Property Insurance		861	Awards & Gifts
			779	Other Occupancy		862	Credit Card Fees
						863	Other Miscellaneous

Appendix K

Risk Management

Risk management topics, as found in *Risk and Crisis Management Planning* by Connie Coutellier:

Operational

1. Who is in charge where?
2. Emergency phone numbers
3. Agency emergency contacts
4. Emergency procedures for hazards and/or disasters—office
5. Emergency procedures for office evacuation and fires
6. Utilities—office
7. First aid/CPR and exposure to bloodborne pathogens—office
8. Death of a participant, volunteer, staff member, or family member
9. Emergency media plan
10. Report of alleged child abuse
11. Legal liabilities of trustees/directors
12. Legal counsel
13. Office/site hazards
14. Office operations, maintenance, and fire prevention and safety
15. Storage and handling of hazardous, flammable, or poisonous materials
16. Food handling and foodborne illness
17. Serving persons with disabilities
18. Insurance coverage
19. Reevaluating insurance
20. Insurance safety audit for organization-owned sites
21. Record retention and destruction
22. Operational financial risks
23. Business use of vehicles and drive authorization and responsibility
24. Fundraising and special events
25. Security
26. Technological usage and record security
27. Contracts for services

28. Screening of staff and volunteers
29. Employment practices
30. Harassment—sexual and other
31. Complaints
32. Supervision of staff
33. Product tampering
34. Intellectual property, copyrights, and royalties
35. Incident report
36. Risk reduction analyses

Program

1. Who is in charge where?
2. Emergency phone numbers
3. Agency emergency contacts
4. Emergency procedures for hazards and/or disasters
5. Utilities
6. Firefighting and other emergency equipment and procedures
7. Emergency communication and warning systems
8. Security
9. Parent contact
10. Missing persons
11. Diversion activities
12. Site evacuation
13. Participant and staff whereabouts
14. Emergency on-site transportation
15. Transportation emergencies
16. First aid
17. Exposure to bloodborne pathogens
18. Insect and rodent-transmitted diseases
19. Youth suicide and self-mutilation
20. Death of a participant, volunteer, staff member, or family member
21. Site hazards—natural and man-made
22. Site operations and maintenance
23. Property use and liability
24. Safe water supply
25. Notification of operation
26. Fire prevention and safety
27. Serving persons with disabilities
28. Foodborne illness
29. Storage and handling of flammable/poison materials
30. Transporting participants and staff
31. Health services and supervision
32. Health screening and records
33. Personal medications
34. Insurance safety audit for organization-owned sites
35. Federal, state, and local laws
36. Interstate and international laws
37. Waivers, permissions, and agreements for participation
38. Program record retention and destruction
39. Intellectual property infringements, copyrights, and royalties
40. Contracts for services
41. Operational financial risks
42. Participant risk-reduction analyses
43. Incident report
44. Emergency drills
45. Registration—check-in and check-out
46. Drop-in programs
47. Guests on-site
48. Parent notification of changes
49. Weapons and firearms
50. Business use of vehicles/driver authorization
51. Complaints
52. Participant supervision plan
53. Conduct of participants and staff

53. Conduct of participants and staff
54. Screening of staff and volunteers
55. Staff selection and training for emergencies
56. Employment practices
57. Staff training
58. Supervision of staff
59. Harassment–sexual and other
60. Preventing child abuse
61. Activities requiring staff with specialized training or certification
62. Weather and/or environmental health effects on the program
63. Participants in off-site field trips or excursions

List courtesy of Healthy Learning and Connie Coutellier

Sections in *My Risk Management Plan,* an online tool from the Nonprofit Risk Management Center: www.nonprofitrisk.org. Each section includes numerous questions and sample language that can be used, with options to insert custom answers.

- Introduction
- Risk management program
- Governance
- Human resources
- Programs and services
- Client safety
- Financial management
- Fundraising and public relations
- Facility/site safety and security
- Technology and information management
- Transportation
- Crisis management
- Volunteer management
- Insurance program

Used with permission © Nonprofit Risk Management Center

Appendix L

Glossary of Risk Management and Insurance Terms

This glossary was originally published in *Coverage, Claims and Consequences: An Insurance Handbook for Nonprofits*, 2nd Edition. For more information on this resource, see the Nonprofit Risk Management Center's website at www.nonprofitrisk.org.

Accident: Unexpected or chance event. This term is frequently defined in older commercial general liability (CGL) policies.

Accident medical reimbursement insurance: Covers medical expenses for injuries arising out of accidents, regardless of liability. Traditionally also provides a schedule of payments for death or severe injury, such as loss of limb or sight. Can be written to provide coverage for volunteers in the course of their work for the insured, participants in the insured's activities, or clients while under the insured's supervision.

Actual cash value (ACV): Replacement cost of damaged or lost property less depreciation.

Actual damages (also known as compensatory damages): Sum of money a plaintiff (injured party) is entitled to, to compensate him for actual economic loss sustained.

Additional insured endorsement: An additional insured endorsement is the contract by which an additional insured (a person or entity, other than the named insured) is protected by a particular insurance policy.

Admitted carrier: An insurance company licensed by a particular state, monitored by the state for financial stability, covered by the state's guaranty fund, and subject to the state's regulations for licensed insurance companies.

Agent: An insurance professional/intermediary who markets and explains insurance products to insureds and prospective insureds. Agents, like brokers, are licensed by state regulatory agencies. However, they are restricted in the marketing and placement of coverage to those carriers with whom they have a contractual relationship. Some agents have relationships with a number of companies, while others represent a single insurer. An agent, therefore, represents the company or companies with whom she or he has a relationship.

Aggregate limit: Maximum amount that the insurer will pay under a liability policy during one annual policy period, regardless of the number of occurrences, usually in addition to legal defense costs. For general liability, policies are sometimes written with the aggregate limit applying separately to each scheduled location.

Alternative market: Nontraditional risk financing, including risk retention groups, risk pools, self-insurance and captive insurance companies.

A.M. Best Company, Inc.: An independent company that rates insurance companies on their financial stability and future claims-paying ability (see www.ambest.com).

Appraising risks: Identifying the portfolio of risks and assigning values or weights to the risks. Risk appraisal is a hybrid of list making and brainstorming. This is the second step in the risk management process.

Auto insurance:

Business auto policy (BAP): A standard business automobile policy that is designed to cover the liability and physical damage of motor vehicles. Liability coverage can be provided for the organization, regardless of whether a nonprofit, a staff member, volunteer or other party owns the vehicle.

Broker: An insurance professional/intermediary who markets and explains insurance products to insureds and prospective insureds. Brokers are typically licensed by a state to place insurance on behalf of clients (individuals and organizations) with any number of companies, while others represent a single insurer. A broker technically represents the client.

Business auto policy: A hybrid policy that provides both property and liability coverage; main coverages are auto liability and physical damage coverage.

Business interruption insurance (loss of income coverage): Insurance coverage designed to protect the insured against loss of earnings resulting from the interruption of business caused by an insured peril, subject to the policy provisions.

Captive insurance company: Subsidiary of one or more parent or member organizations formed for the purpose of insuring the exposures of the parent or member organization(s).

Certificate of insurance: A form that indicates the types of insurance policies written, policy dates, and coverage limits.

Charitable immunity: Legal defense by which charitable organizations were protected from litigation by virtue of their charitable status. The common law doctrine of charitable immunity exists—to some degree—in nine states: Alabama, Arkansas, Georgia, Maine, Maryland, New Jersey, Virginia, Utah and Wyoming. The states with the least restrictive forms of charitable immunity are Arkansas, New Jersey, and Virginia.

Charitable risk pool: A nonprofit property/casualty insurance company that insures nonprofit organizations and qualifies as a charitable risk pool pursuant to federal tax laws and is exempt from federal income tax. A qualified charitable risk pool may only be comprised of nonprofit organizations that qualify under section 501 I(3) of the Internal Revenue Code.

Claims-made basis: A liability coverage form that requires that claims be reported to the insurance company while the policy is still in force in order for coverage to apply. In other words, a claim must be made while the policy is in force. The claims-made form is one of two types of liability policy forms. The other more common form is called occurrence form. Under an occurrence form policy, a claim occurring during the policy term may be reported to the insurance company at any time, even years after the policy expires.

Claims management: Involves proper and timely notification and recordkeeping of specific claims and overall loss history for the organization.

Commercial general liability (CGL) insurance: Covers liability exposures that are common to all organizations; a combination of three separate coverages, each with its own insuring agreement and exclusions: Coverage A = general liability; Coverage B = personal injury and advertising injury liability; and Coverage C = medical payments.

Commercial property insurance: Covers risk of loss to an organization's buildings or personal property. Usually includes buildings, personal property of the insured, personal property of others on site and in insured's possession. Coverage can be on an all risk or specific perils basis.

Conceptual competition: A method of choosing an insurance provider. Establish a comfortable relationship with a new insurance provider (agent, broker, or consultant) prior to obtaining firm coverage proposals.

Conditions: Part of every insurance policy; qualify the various promises made by the insurance company.

Consequential damage insurance: Optional coverage for equipment insurance that insures against spoilage of specified property (food or plants) from lack of power, light, heat, steam, or refrigeration.

Context: The environment and circumstances facing your nonprofit that affect risks and risk management efforts. For example, a nonprofit that serves vulnerable clients is exposed to a different array of risks than an organization that doesn't. A nonprofit that has never faced an incident or lawsuit may be somewhat less enthusiastic about risk management activities. Exploring the context for risk management in a nonprofit is the first step in the risk management process.

Crime coverage: A package of policies that protects an organization against intentional theft by insiders as well as theft of assets by third parties. Crime coverage generally includes a fidelity bond plus a basic menu of other coverages.

Declarations: Usually the first page of an insurance policy; summarizes key information specific to the policy; sometimes called a dec page.

Deductible: Amount deducted from a loss. The deductible is an amount assumed in advance by an insured as required by the insurance company or as a means of obtaining a lower premium for the coverage. Also, the amount of the loss that the insured must pay.

Defendant: Individual or organization against whom a lawsuit has been brought.

Defense coverage: Source of funding for the defense of a legal challenge filed against the nonprofit.

Definitions: Part of every insurance policy. Explain the special meaning of the designated words (identified in bold print or set off by quotation marks) within the context of insurance.

Dimensions of risk: The three dimensions of risk are 1) directional (positive/negative), 2) probability (more/less often) and 3) magnitude (major/minor) dimension of risk.

Directors' & officers' liability insurance (D&O insurance): Insurance that provides coverage against wrongful acts which might include actual or alleged errors, omissions, misleading statements, and neglect or breach of duty on the part of the board of directors and other insured persons and entities. Many D&O policies include employment practices liability coverage.

Disability insurance: Provides an employee security by providing an income should he or she become sick or injured and unable to work.

Doctrine of contra proferentem: Latin term referring to practice of reviewing courts to construe ambiguous insurance policy terms in favor of the insured policyholder.

Earthquake coverage: Purchased as separate policy as most property policies do not protect against damage by earthquake.

Electronic property coverage: An inland marine floater designed specifically for computers and other electronic equipment. Provides coverage for perils not normally included in a standard property policy, such as electrical surge and loss of data.

Employee benefits liability (EBL): Covers errors and omissions in the administration of the insured's employee benefits, such as health insurance or pension benefits.

Employment practices liability insurance (EPLI or EPL): Insurance that provides coverage for claims arising out of employment practices. EPLI policies generally cover the organization, its directors, officers, and employees.

Employer's liability insurance: Coverage protecting an employer against claims, which are not covered under workers' compensation statutes, alleging employer negligence stemming from work-related injuries, illness or death. Claims may be filed by injured workers or their spouse or family members for economic losses. This policy is generally bundled with workers' compensation coverage.

Endorsement: Part of most insurance policies; policy forms that modify the main coverage form; changes to the policy language.

Equipment breakdown insurance: Supplements property insurance (which specifically excludes physical damage and the financial damage stemming from equipment breakdown) to cover the unique causes that can damage equipment. Was known as boiler and machinery coverage.

Excess and surplus lines carrier: Insurer that is not admitted (not licensed) to do business in a particular state, but is permitted because coverage is not available through licensed insurers.

Excess liability insurance: Provides coverage over and above primary insurance. The coverage is triggered when the amount of a loss exceeds (exhausts) an existing primary policy. Excess liability coverage mirrors the terms and conditions of the underlying policy.

Exclusions: Part of every insurance policy; policy provisions that eliminate coverage for specified exposures.

Extra expense insurance: Covers the extra cost of continuing to deliver services following the destruction or damage to a nonprofit's facility or equipment due to a covered peril. Extra expense coverage is generally sold in tandem with business interruption coverage.

Fidelity bond: A bond that reimburses an employer, up to the stated amount, in the event that an employee commits a dishonest act covered by the bond. Also known as employee dishonesty coverage. A nonprofit can purchase a fidelity bond as a standalone or part of a crime coverage package.

Fiduciary liability: Protects the fiduciaries of health and welfare, or pension plans from claims by employees alleging financial loss due to mismanagement of funds.

Group insurance programs: Special programs generally developed to serve homogeneous or geographically similar groups of organizations; may offer better rates, specialized coverages or features, fewer restrictions and better acceptance of the risks inherent in the group programs.

Hammer clause: A policy provision that acts as a financial incentive for an insured to agree to a settlement proposed by the insurer.

Hard market: A phase of the insurance market cycle during which time coverage may be more costly, terms may be more restrictive, and policy conditions and requirements more stringent.

Health insurance: Covers medical expenses for accidents or sickness, on a first-party basis, and regardless of fault.

Hired and non-owned auto liability: Coverage that protects a nonprofit for claims that result from the use of a vehicle not owned by the nonprofit but used on the nonprofit's behalf (for example, an employee's or volunteer's personal vehicle). Hired and nonowned coverage is excess over the insurance on the auto involved in the accident. The policy protects the named insured, not the driver of the vehicle. This coverage can be purchased as an add-on to the CGL policy, as an adjunct to the business auto policy, as part of a business owners policy, or as a separate policy.

Hold harmless agreement: Contract by which legal liability for damages of one party is assumed by the other party. One party agrees to hold the other party harmless (and usually indemnify) from the liabilities associated with the hazards of a particular activity or venture. Contracts may contain a hold harmless clause.

Hybrid policies: Have both liability and property coverages. Examples are business auto policy, international coverage, volunteer accident medical reimbursement and personal liability policies.

Immunity: A provision in the law which shields a person or organization from legal obligations.

Improper sexual conduct coverage: Coverage that protects an organization against claims alleging improper sexual conduct.

Indemnification agreement: When one party (the indemnitor) assumes the liability of another (the indemnitee) in the event of a claim or loss. An example is a hold harmless agreement.

Indemnify: To compensate for actual losses sustained.

Individual causing harm: The person whose actions led to the injury or loss.

Inland marine coverage: Also known as a floater endorsement. Insures special items, such as computers, light and sound equipment, and camera equipment at an agreed amount.

Insurance: Traditional risk-financing tool used to transfer the financial hazard of risk. An insurance policy spells out what is or is not covered caused by all or specific perils (causes of damage or injury). Insurance is also a contract whereby an organization agrees to indemnify another and/or to pay a specified amount for covered losses in exchange for a premium. For many nonprofits, insurance provides the funds to pay for the nonprofit's unexpected losses of people, property and income, while ultimately keeping the organization in operation.

Insurance policy: A legally binding contract that defines the obligations of both the insured and the insurer.

Insurance professional: An agent, broker or consultant.

Insurance program review: A review of the nonprofit's existing insurance coverages for the purpose of identifying coverage gaps, overlaps and commenting on the adequacy of specific policy terms, limits and deductibles.

Insurance Services Office (ISO): An insurance industry-supported agency that creates standard policy forms and collects premium and claims statistics.

Insured versus insured exclusion: Negates coverage for claims brought by one insured against another insured.

Insuring agreement: Part of every insurance policy; specifies what the insurance company has agreed to pay for or to provide in exchange for the premium.

Intentional acts: Deliberately fraudulent acts or omissions, wanton, willful, reckless or intentional disregard of any law or laws.

Joint liability: A form of liability in which liability is shared by more than one person or organization.

Latent injury: Injury that manifests itself years after the event occurred such as those from asbestos, medical malpractice, and sexual abuse or molestation.

Liability: Any enforceable legal obligation. For example, the failure to meet the duty of care of a reasonable person under similar circumstances.

Liability insurance: Insurance covering the financial risk of civil lawsuits.

Liquor liability: Liability arising out of the manufacture, distribution or sale of liquor. Under the standard CGL, coverage is excluded if the insured is in the business of serving alcohol.

Long-tail exposure: Exposures for which a claim might be filed long after the insurance policy or policies expire. Loss may not be recognized for many years, involving such latent injuries as asbestos, medical malpractice, and sexual abuse or molestation.

Loss control: Analyzing hazards and determining a course of action to reduce the risk of loss while carrying out the nonprofit's mission.

Loss experience report: Compiled by the insurance company, it provides detailed history of an insured's claims information. Also known as loss runs or hard copy loss runs. Every insured is entitled to receive an account history from its insurance company.

Market assignment: Method of choosing an insurance provider. Choose several insurance agents or brokers as bidders for your account and assign one or more insurance companies (markets) to each.

Media liability: Policy protects the insured from extensive personal and advertising injury, as well as publishers' liability for all forms of media.

Moody's: An insurance rating service that provides credit ratings on an estimated 700 insurance companies worldwide (see www.moodys.com).

Named insured: An individual, business or organization that is identified on the policy declarations page as the insured(s) under a policy. Most policies, especially liability policies, will have insureds or additional insureds other than the named insured (such as employees, volunteers, board members, landlords), but only the named insured is responsible for premium payments, receipt of notices, and adjustment of losses.

Negligence: Failure to use the standard of care that a reasonably prudent person would exercise in a similar circumstance.

Obedience, duty of: Standard of care that obligates a director or officer (of a board) to act in a manner that demonstrates faithfulness to the organization's mission and obeys all applicable laws, statutes and regulations.

Occupational accident: Accident to an employee that occurs within and arises out of the course of employment.

Occurrence basis: A liability coverage form that covers claims that occur during the policy period, and for which claims can be reported to the insurance company at any time during or after the policy period.

Open bidding: Method of choosing an insurance provider. Send a request for proposal to a list of firms asking them to bid for your business.

Personal injury liability: Injury to a person or organization caused by slander, invasion of privacy, false arrest or detention, malicious prosecution, or wrongful entry or eviction.

Personal liability policy (volunteers): Provides protection if the volunteer is liable for bodily injury or property damage arising out of the performance of his or her duties; generally written on an excess basis. Purchase separately or bundled with accident medical reimbursement and/or excess automobile liability insurance for volunteers.

Personally liable: Liability that an individual assumes when he/she is directly involved in the occurrence and cannot defer the liability to another person or entity.

Plaintiff: Individual or organization that initiates a lawsuit to obtain a remedy for an injury. An injury.

Premium: The payment for an insurance policy or bond.

Prior acts coverage: Coverage for all acts that occurred before the policy was issued. Prior acts coverage is one of the means of covering the gap in coverage when switching from a claims-made policy to another claims-made policy or to an occurrence policy. The prior acts coverage is provided by the new policy, as opposed to tail coverage that is added by endorsement to an expired claims-made policy.

Professional liability insurance: Also known as malpractice coverage or errors and omissions (E&O) coverage; covers liability for damages arising from the rendering of or failure to render professional services.

Property: Category of nonprofit assets at risk that includes real property (buildings, improvements and betterments), personal property (furniture, fixtures, valuable papers and records, equipment, and supplies) and intangible property (copyrights, business goodwill and trademarks).

Property insurance: Insurance that covers direct damage to the nonprofit's property and equipment including consequential losses (business income, loss of rents, extra expense) caused by an insured peril.

Punitive damages: Damages awarded by the court in excess of those required to compensate the plaintiff for the loss sustained. These damages are a type of punishment for the offender for failing to take proper care.

Reinsurer: A company that insures upper layers of coverage for commercial carriers, risk retention groups, captive insurance companies and other insurance providers.

Replacement cost basis: The cost of replacing the appraised or inventoried property.

Respondeat superior: Legal principle by which employers are held responsible for the actions of those they supervise. Literally, the master shall answer for the acts of his servant. In the context of volunteer organizations, the nonprofit is the master and paid and volunteer staff are the servants working on the organization's behalf.

Risk: A measure of the possibility that the future may be surprisingly different from what we expect. Downside risk of loss and upside risk of gain.

Risk assessment: A thorough examination of the exposures of the nonprofit, both insurable and uninsurable.

Risk-financing plan: The monetary tools that you will use to protect the nonprofit's resources so the lion's share may be devoted to its community-serving mission. Primarily used to protect an organization from catastrophic financial loss.

Risk-financing pools: A nonprofit association that benefits it members by pooling their contributed premiums in order to finance losses.

Risk management: A discipline for dealing with the possibility that the future may be surprisingly different from what we expect (see Strategic risk management).

Risk management committee: A representative group of staff, volunteers and advisors who identify exposures, develop a risk control program, and establish a risk-financing strategy for the nonprofit. May act in place of a staff designee in small nonprofits. In midsize and large organizations, they may work in partnership with the staff designee (such as finance director or professional risk manager).

Risk management program: Educated projections about the future and sound management practices.

Risk retention: A method of funding loss using internal money.

Risk transfer or sharing: A method of funding loss using external funds (such as insurance) or risk sharing with another organization. Examples of risk sharing include mutual aid agreements with other nonprofits, and sharing responsibility for a risk with another through a contractual agreement.

Self-insurance: When an organization's own resources (internal) are used to fund losses. A nonprofit may self-insure risks through a formally structured risk-financing program, such as a captive insurer, or by setting aside funds to pay for losses. A nonprofit can also be self-insured on an informal basis when it has made no arrangements to finance losses and must use operating funds when losses occur.

Self-insured retention: Similar to a deductible except that until the SIR is exhausted the insured will generally be responsible for performing the loss adjustment functions that would otherwise be undertaken by an insurance company. For umbrella liability, the SIR is the amount the insured is obligated to pay for claims when there is no underlying insurance.

Soft insurance market: Insurance companies are eager to write new business.

Special endorsement: Written language appended to an insurance policy that changes the coverage in regards to special circumstances.

Special events insurance: General liability insurance for events that are outside the day-to-day operations of the insured, such as fund-raising events.

Speculative risk: An insurance term that includes the possibility of gain or loss.

Sponsored insurance program: Members, chapters or affiliates of a national, regional or statewide organization create a group insurance program by partnering with a commercial insurance provider or endorsing the services of an agent or broker.

Standard & Poor's: A nationally recognized organization that rates insurance companies on their financial strength (see www.standardandpoors.com).

Standardized form: A document prepared in a prescribed arrangement of words and layout.

Strategic risk management: A discipline that counters downside risks by reducing the likelihood, magnitude, and unpredictability of losses and financing recovery from these losses; and seizes upside risks by searching for opportunities to more fully, more certainly, and more efficiently achieve an organization's nonprofit goals, and developing plans to act on these opportunities when the future presents them.

Strategic risk management process: Five steps to empower an organization to be all it can be in a less-than-fully-predictable world.

1. Establish the risk management context.
2. Appraise risks.
3. Decide what to do.
4. Take action on your decision.
5. Follow up and adjust.

Umbrella liability insurance: Provides excess coverage over several primary policies, such as CGL, auto liability and employers liability. Increases the amount of liability insurance beyond that of the basic policies carried by the nonprofit and reaches out to cover areas of unknown exposures lacking in the basic insurance policy.

Underwriting: The process of determining whether coverage will be offered, what policy provision will be included and at what price.

Volunteer excess automobile liability insurance: Auto liability insurance that covers claims arising from a volunteer's use of his or her own vehicle. This policy pays in excess of the volunteer's personal auto policy. No coverage is provided to the nonprofit.

Waiver: The giving up of a right or privilege. Nonprofits frequently require participants in recreational or other programs to waive the right to sue in the event of injury. Courts often invalidate waivers on the grounds that the individual did not fully appreciate the rights being waived or that the waiver did not specifically indicate that it covered liability for negligence.

Workers' compensation and employers' liability insurance: The first part covers expenses an employer is mandated to pay by state statute to cover specific benefits for employee injuries. The second part protects employers from employee-related suits that are separate from WC claims.

Sources

Head, George L., Ph.D., editor, *Essentials of risk control*, Volume I, Second Edition, Insurance Institute of America, Malvern, Pa., 1989.

Head, George L., Ph.D., Elliott, Michael W., and Blinn, James D., *Essentials of risk financing, volume 2, Third Edition,* Insurance Institute of America, Malvern, Pa., 1996.

Head, George L., Ph.D., and Herman, Melanie L., *Enlightened Risk Taking: A Guide to Strategic Risk Management for Nonprofits, Nonprofit Risk Management Center*, Washington, DC, 2002.

Elliott, Michael W., *Risk Financing,* First Edition, Insurance Institute of America, Malvern, Pa., 2000.

Glossary of Insurance and Risk Management Terms, Fifth Edition, International Risk Management Institute, Inc., Dallas, Texas, 1991.

Smith, Barry D., and Wiening, Eric A., *How insurance works*, Second Edition, Insurance Institute of America, Malvern, Pa., 1994.

Nonprofit Risk Management Center
15 N. King St., Suite 203
Leesburg, VA 20176
www.nonprofitrisk.org

Appendix M

OSHA Requirements

Sample Exposure Control Plan, Hepatitis B Vaccination Statement, Exposure Incident Report, Post-Exposure Plan for Camp, Information on Universal Precautions

All courtesy of American Camp Association

Sample Exposure Control Plan

This information is provided to camp employees in partial compliance with OSHA's Bloodborne Pathogen Standard. It is the intent of the camp to educate people about issues related to exposure to body fluids, to use management techniques and equipment to minimize exposure risks for employees, and to monitor individuals' use of these techniques. The camp program recognizes universal precautions as an effective control measure. This handout describes the application and monitoring of potential sources of risk in the camp program, the steps taken by camp to protect employees, and the actions taken by camp if blood or body fluid exposure occurs.

JOB CLASSIFICATIONS WHICH, BY VIRTUE OF JOB DESCRIPTION, INCUR THE RISK OF EXPOSURE TO BLOOD AND OTHER BODY FLUIDS: nurse, nursing assistant

JOB CLASSIFICATIONS WHICH, BY VIRTUE OF JOB DESCRIPTION, PROVIDE FIRST-AID CARE AS AN ANCILLARY TASK RATHER THAN A PRIMARY TASK: Designated wilderness first aider in camp tripping programs, lifeguarding staff when on duty at the waterfront.

(ALL OTHER JOB CLASSIFICATIONS ARE NOT EXPECTED TO PROVIDE FIRST AID BUT RATHER REFER PEOPLE IN NEED OF HEALTHCARE TO THE NURSE/ NURSING ASSISTANT.)

Camp nurses and nursing assistants (Nas) can reasonably expect to come in contact with blood and other body fluids. The potential for exposure to transmitted diseases is greatest for these staff members. Consequently, the recommended exposure control plan involves the following practices:

Members of the camp healthcare team are oriented to the potential for exposure by camp's healthcare administrator. A record of who received the education and its content is kept for three years by the administrator. The orientation includes:

- Identification of risk areas: contact with bloodborne pathogens (e.g., hepatitis, HIV), contact with airborne pathogens (e.g., common cold, TB), contact with surface-borne pathogens (e.g., staph infections).
- Education about the nature of the risk: method of transmission, virulence of pathogens, resistance factors related to potential host, symptoms, and information sources which provide clues to potential risk areas.
- Work practices designed to minimize exposure:
  - ✓ Availability of personal protective equipment (PPE)–gloves, CPR mask, antimicrobial soap, (eye, nose, and mouth) shield, body fluid spill clean up kits.
  - ✓ Double bagging via red bag and disposal procedure for hazardous waste.
  - ✓ Screening individuals who come to the program.
  - ✓ Requiring participants to provide health information.
  - ✓ Use of universal precautions by staff.
  - ✓ Education for people working in risk areas: healthcare team members, lifeguards, housekeeping, kitchen staff.
  - ✓ Hepatitis B vaccination for nurses: camp pays for vaccinations done by the local provider during the nurse's contracted time. Camp encourages nonvaccinated nurses to get vaccinated.
  - ✓ DVD/video which teaches effective use of the CPR mask.
  - ✓ Sharps container provided which has biohazard label affixed.
  - ✓ Resource personnel to answer questions: camp healthcare administrator, camp supervising physician, and State Dept. of Health epidemiologist.
- Behavior expected from employees to minimize risk:
  - ✓ Use of PPE:
    - ⇨ Gloves are used when in contact with body fluids or providing skin treatment (e.g., applying medication to poison ivy, washing a rash).
    - ⇨ CPR mask is used to provide CPR/artificial respiration.
  - ✓ Minimum 15-second hand washing with antimicrobial soap after: removing gloves, contact with potential risk, unprotected contact with any body fluid.
  - ✓ Minimum 60-second hand washing with antimicrobial soap after blood splash.
  - ✓ Use of body fluid spill clean up kit.
  - ✓ Vaccination to protect from hepatitis B.

- ✓ Sharps disposed of properly: no recapping of needles, all sharps (lancets, needles) placed in sharps container immediately after use, full sharps container given to Administrator for disposal through local hospital.
- ✓ Participation in education about disease control.
- ✓ Immediate reporting suspected exposure (e.g., needle stick) to supervisor and Administrator.
- ✓ Performing job tasks in a manner which minimizes/eliminates exposure potential.

Evaluation of compliance with the camp exposure control plan as part of the camp personnel-management system.

Camp Counseling Staff

While the potential for exposure to bloodborne pathogens is minimal for general counseling staff, it does exist. The camp healthcare plan vests authority in general staff to respond to emergencies at the level of their training while initiating the camp emergency response system. Since camp emergency response occurs within minutes, the potential for exposure is limited and most likely confined to initiating CPR/artificial respiration and slowing severe bleeding.

In keeping with accepted practices, the camp healthcare administrator educates camp staff during orientation about appropriate response practices:

- Staff are instructed to use a CPR mask for CPR and artificial respiration; masks are kept at the waterfront and health center.
- Staff are instructed to use gloves when potential for contact with blood or blood tinged fluids exist. Gloves are in all first-aid kits. Staff members who want to carry a pair on their person may obtain them from the health center.
- Staff are instructed to respond in emergency situations to the level of their training per State Good Samaritan regulations.
- Staff are instructed to initiate the camp emergency response system immediately.
- Staff participate in a discussion of "emergency" to establish defining attributes of their response.
- Staff are educated to approach care of minor injuries from a coaching perspective and specifically directed to refer injured people to the camp healthcare team if self care is inappropriate or impossible.

american CAMP association®
enriching lives, building tomorrows

HEPATITIS B VACCINATION STATEMENT

(In response to the OSHA Bloodborne Pathogens rule [1992], which requires that employers provide access to the Hepatitis B vaccine to "all occupationally exposed" employees, this form has been used by some ACA camps. This form may be a piece of the camp's OSHA-required Exposure Control Plan your local OSHA regulating agency.)

I understand that due to my occupational exposure to blood or other potentially infectious materials, I may be at risk of acquiring the Hepatitis B virus (HBV) infection. I have been given information on the Hepatitis B vaccine, including information on its efficacy, safety, method of administration, the benefits of being vaccinated, and that the vaccine and vaccination will be offered free of charge.

- OPTION 1

________________________ has completed the following inoculations using:
(name of employee)

- Recombivax-HB or Enerix-B vaccine [circle one]

Inoculation 1: Date ______________ Given at ____________________
Inoculation 2: Date ______________ Given at ____________________
Inoculation 3: Date ______________ Given at ____________________

OR See attached medical form for additional information

- OPTION 2

I have been given the opportunity to be vaccinated with the Hepatitis B vaccine at no charge to myself. I decline the vaccination at this time. I understand that by declining this vaccine, I continue to be at risk of acquiring Hepatitis B, a serious disease. If, in the future, I continue to have occupational exposure to blood or other potentially infectious materials and I want to be vaccinated with the Hepatitis B vaccine, I can receive the vaccination series at no charge to me.

Please check either Option 1 or Option 2 above, then sign and date below:

Employee Name (please print) ________________________________

Employee Signature ___________________________________

Date ____________________

Exposure Incident Should any staff member have a blood exposure incident, an Exposure Incident Report Form (see next handout) must be completed as soon as possible.

american CAMP association®
enriching lives, building tomorrows

CONFIDENTIAL EXPOSURE INCIDENT REPORT

Employee name ____

SS# ______________________ Date of Birth ________________

Home phone (____) __________ Business phone (____) __________

Job title ____

Date of exposure ______________ Date completed ______________

Time of exposure _____AM _____PM Vaccination Status ____________

Location of incident (be specific):

Describe what happened:

What task was the employee performing when the exposure occurred?

Was the employee wearing PPE? _____No _____Yes Type:

Did the PPE fail? _____No _____Yes If yes, in this way:

To what body fluid(s) was the employee exposed?

On what part of the employee's body did this fluid fall?

Estimate the size of the area covered by the fluid (consider taking a photo)

For how long was the fluid in contact with the employee's body?

Did a foreign body (needle, nail, dental wire, machine part, etc.) penetrate the employee's body? _____ No _____Yes If yes, what was the object and where did it penetrate?

Was any fluid injected into the employee's body? _____No _____Yes If yes, what fluid and how much?

Did the employee receive medical attention? _____No _____Yes If yes, where? When? By whom?

Name, address and phone of the source individual(s)

Other pertinent information

Signature of person completing this report ______________________

Print name of person completing this report ______________________

Post-Exposure Plan for Camp

Camp employees who have a blood exposure incident are eligible for follow up treatment. Follow up is initiated by the employee who must immediately (within fifteen minutes) notify the camp nurse when a blood exposure incident occurs. The following plan is initiated. Records of the incident are maintained for the duration of employment plus thirty (30) years by the Camp Director and according to OSHA requirements (i.e., separate from personnel records). Camp administration debriefs each incident in an effort to identify ways to improve the camp's exposure risk.

Timeline	Employee's Actions	Camp Nurse's Actions	Camp Director's Actions
Within 24 hours	Exposure incident occurs. Report the incident to the camp nurse within 15 minutes of it happening. Begin a prophylactic treatment. Complete the workers' compensation form and file an incident report with the camp director.	Notify the camp director. Begin a 15-second scrub of the area with bacteriostatic soap, followed by the application of a disinfectant. Contact the supervising doctor and refer the client for assessment. Begin the psychosocial support process.	Determine the source of contamination. Initiate a request to the have source screened for infectious diseases. Notify the insurance company. Create an incident report file, including supporting documentation. Contact the mental health professional for the employee. Complete the workers' compensation form and help file an incident report with the employee.
Within next 48 hours	Continue medical follow up per doctor's orders. Begin counseling support.	Monitor the client's adjustment to the situation and answer questions as needed. Provide needed cares.	Follow the testing of the source individual as warranted. Consult with a mental health professional to arrange post-camp therapy if needed.
Beyond first three days	Continue post-exposure prophylaxis, as directed by the doctor. Participate in a review of the incident.	Participate in a review of the incident.	Maintain contact with the employee to follow up on the incident. Lead a review of the incident. Review the incident and adapt camp practices as needed to manage risk and to minimize a chance of repeating the situation. Maintain records for the employee's duration of employment, plus 30 years.

Information on Universal Precautions

As part of an overall exposure control plan, mandated by the OSHA Bloodborne Pathogens Standard, "universal precautions" are part of infection-control practices. They are specific guidelines which must be followed to provide every person protection from diseases which are carried in the blood. Since blood can carry all types of infectious diseases, even when a person does not look or feel ill, knowledge of universal precautions is essential for anyone who might come into contact with blood or other body fluids.

The following are sample guidelines, recommended by the Centers for Disease Control, to prevent cross- contamination from bloodborne pathogens:

1. All healthcare providers should use appropriate barrier precautions to prevent skin and mucous-membrane exposure when contact with blood or body fluid of any person is anticipated. Personal protective equipment such as latex or vinyl disposable gloves should be readily available in healthcare, housekeeping and maintenance areas, in all first-aid kits, and in vehicles.
2. Any person giving first aid should always wear latex or vinyl disposable gloves if blood is visible on the skin, inside the mouth, or if there is an open cut on the victim. Gloves should be changed after contact with each person.
3. Gloves should always be worn when handling items or surfaces soiled with blood or bloody fluids. Such areas (floor, counter, etc.) should be flooded with bleach solution (1 part bleach to 10 parts water), alcohol, or a dry sanitary absorbent agent. However, routine cleaning practices are all that are needed if blood is not visible or likely to be present. With regard to the requirement to wear gloves, these items should always be worn when cleaning up blood from a counter after a cut finger, but gloves do not usually need to be worn to handle urine-soaked bedding, unless blood is obvious. Disposable towels and tissues or other contaminated materials should be disposed of in a trash container lined with plastic. Biohazard bags ("red bags") are to be used for dressings or other materials used to soak up blood or other infectious waste.
4. Remove gloves properly – pulling inside out. Place gloves in bag with waste. Hands and other skin surfaces should be washed with soap and water immediately and thoroughly if contaminated with blood or other body fluids.
5. Masks, protective eye wear, gowns or aprons should be worn during procedures that are likely to generate droplets or splashes of blood or other body fluids.
6. Needles should NOT be recapped, purposely bent or broken by hand, removed from disposable syringes, or otherwise manipulated by hand. After use, disposable syringes and needles, scalpel blades and other sharp items should be placed in puncture-resistant "sharps" containers for disposal.
7. Mouthpieces, resuscitation bags, or other ventilation devices should be available for use in areas in which the need for resuscitation is predictable.
8. Healthcare workers who have draining lesions or weeping dermatitis should refrain from all direct care and from handling equipment until the condition resolves.

All procedures should be specific to the staff and clientele served. All persons who might come into contact with blood or other body fluids must be trained to follow appropriate procedures.

american CAMP association
enriching lives, building tomorrows

Appendix N

OSHA Self-Inspection Checklists—Selected Items

The following are some of the OSHA self-inspection checklists that might apply to camps. The entire list is included in OSHA's Small Business Handbook. OHSA suggests referring to OSHA standards for specific guidance that could apply to your situation. These items are typical for general industry. This list is not exhaustive, as many more standards apply to camps. These are listed for example only and should not be considered comprehensive or definitive.

Employer Posting

- Is the required OSHA Job Safety and Health Protection Poster displayed in a prominent location where all employees are likely to see it?
- Are emergency telephone numbers posted where they can be readily found in case of emergency?
- Where employees may be exposed to toxic substances or harmful physical agents, has appropriate information concerning employee access to medical and exposure records and Material Safety Data Sheets (MSDSs) been posted or otherwise made readily available to affected employees?

Recordkeeping

- Are occupational injuries or illnesses, except minor injuries requiring only first aid, recorded as required on the OSHA 300 log?
- Are employee training records kept and accessible for review by employees, as required by OSHA standards?
- Are operating permits and records up-to-date for items such as air pressure tanks, liquefied petroleum gas tanks, etc.?

Safety and Health Program

- Do you have an active safety and health program in operation that includes general safety and health program elements as well as the management of hazards specific to your work-site?
- Is one person clearly responsible for the safety and health program?

Medical Services and First Aid

- Is there a hospital, clinic, or infirmary for medical care near your workplace or is at least one employee on each shift currently qualified to render first aid?
- Have all employees who are expected to respond to medical emergencies as part of their job responsibilities received first aid training; had hepatitis B vaccination made available to them; had appropriate training on procedures to protect them from bloodborne pathogens, including universal precautions; and have available and understand how to use appropriate PPE to protect against exposure to bloodborne diseases?
- If employees have had an exposure incident involving bloodborne pathogens, was an immediate post-exposure medical evaluation and follow-up provided?
- Are emergency phone numbers posted?
- Are fully supplied first aid kits easily accessible to each work area, periodically inspected and replenished as needed?

Fire Protection

- Is your local fire department familiar with your facility, its location and specific hazards?
- If you have a fire alarm system, is it certified as required and tested annually?
- If you have outside private fire hydrants, are they flushed at least once a year and on a routine preventive maintenance schedule?
- Are portable fire extinguishers provided in adequate number and type and mounted in readily accessible locations?
- Are fire extinguishers recharged regularly with this noted on the inspection tag?
- Are employees periodically instructed in the use of fire extinguishers and fire protection procedures?

Personal Protective Equipment and Clothing

- Has the employer determined whether hazards that require the use of PPE (e.g., head, eye, face, hand, or foot protection) are present or are likely to be present?
- Are protective goggles or face shields provided and worn where there is any danger of flying particles or corrosive materials?
- Are hard hats required, provided and worn where danger of falling objects exists?
- Are approved respirators provided when needed?

General Work Environment

- Are all worksites clean, sanitary and orderly?
- Are all work areas adequately illuminated?

Stairs and Stairways

- Do standard stair rails or handrails on all stairways have at least four risers?
- Are all stairways at least 22 inches (55.88 centimeters) wide?
- Are steps slip-resistant?
- Are stairway handrails located between 30 inches (76.20 centimeters) and 34 inches (86.36 centimeters) above the leading edge of stair treads?
- Do stairway handrails have at least 3 inches (7.62 centimeters) of clearance between the handrails and the wall or surface they are mounted on?

Exiting or Egress—Evacuation

- Are all exits marked with an exit sign and illuminated by a reliable light source?
- Are the directions to exits, when not immediately apparent, marked with visible signs?
- Is the number of exits from each floor of a building and the number of exits from the building itself appropriate for the building occupancy load?

Portable Ladders

- Are all ladders maintained in good condition, joints between steps and side rails tight, all hardware and fittings securely attached, and moveable parts operating freely without binding or undue play?
- Are non-slip safety feet provided on each metal or rung ladder, and are ladder rungs and steps free of grease and oil?
- Are employees prohibited from placing a ladder in front of doors opening toward the ladder unless the door is blocked open, locked, or guarded?
- Are employees prohibited from placing ladders on boxes, barrels, or other unstable bases to obtain additional height?

Fueling

- Are employees prohibited from fueling an internal combustion engine with a flammable liquid while the engine is running?
- Are fueling operations performed to minimize spillage?
- Are fuel tank caps replaced and secured before starting the engine?

Hand Tools and Equipment

- Are all tools and equipment (both company and employee-owned) used at the workplace in good condition?
- Are employees aware of hazards caused by faulty or improperly used hand tools?
- Are appropriate safety glasses, face shields, etc., used while using hand tools or equipment that might produce flying materials or be subject to breakage? Is eye and face protection used when driving hardened or tempered studs or nails?

Portable (Power Operated) Tools and Equipment

- Are power tools used with proper shields, guards, or attachments, as recommended by the manufacturer?
- Are portable circular saws equipped with guards above and below the base shoe?
- Are all cord-connected, electrically operated tools and equipment effectively grounded or of the approved double insulated type?

Welding, Cutting and Brazing

- Are only authorized and trained personnel permitted to use welding, cutting, or brazing equipment?
- Does each operator have a copy of and follow the appropriate operating instructions?

Environmental Controls

- Are all work areas properly illuminated?
- Are employees instructed in proper first aid and other emergency procedures?
- Are hazardous substances, blood and other potentially infectious materials, which may cause harm by inhalation, ingestion, or skin absorption or contact, identified?
- Are spray painting operations performed in spray rooms or booths equipped with an appropriate exhaust system?
- Are restrooms and washrooms kept clean and sanitary?
- Is all water provided for drinking, washing and cooking potable?
- Are all outlets for water that is not suitable for drinking clearly identified?

Lockout/Tagout Procedures

- Is all machinery or equipment capable of movement required to be de-energized or disengaged and blocked or locked out during cleaning, servicing, adjusting, or setting up operations?

- Does the lockout procedure require that stored energy (mechanical, hydraulic, air, etc.) be released or blocked before equipment is locked out for repairs?
- Is the locking out of control circuits instead of locking out main power disconnects prohibited?

Compressors and Compressed Air

- Are compressors equipped with pressure relief valves and pressure gauges?
- Are air filters installed on the compressor intake?
- Are employees strictly prohibited from directing compressed air towards a person?
- Are employees prohibited from using highly compressed air for cleaning purposes?

Flammable and Combustible Materials

- Are approved containers and tanks used to store and handle flammable and combustible liquids?
- Are fire extinguishers selected and provided for the types of materials in the areas where they are to be used?
  - ✓ Class A–Ordinary combustible material fires.
  - ✓ Class B–Flammable liquid, gas or grease fires.
  - ✓ Class C–Energized-electrical equipment fires.
- Are all extinguishers serviced, maintained and tagged at intervals not to exceed one year?
- Are all extinguishers fully charged and in their designated places?

Electrical

- Are all employees required to report any obvious hazard to life or property in connection with electrical equipment or lines as soon as possible?
- When electrical equipment or lines are to be serviced, maintained, or adjusted, are necessary switches opened, locked out or tagged, whenever possible?
- Are exposed wiring and cords with frayed or deteriorated insulation repaired or replaced promptly?

From: www.osha.gov/Publications/smallbusiness/small-business.html

Appendix O

State Food Service Regulatory Agencies

State	Regulatory Agency
Alabama	Department of Public Health, Division of Food, Milk and Lodging
Alaska	Department of Environmental Conservation, Food Safety and Sanitation Program
Arizona	Department of Health Services, Food Safety and Environmental Services
Arkansas	Department of Health, Food Protection Program
California	California Department of Public Health, Food Safety Program
Colorado	Colorado Department of Public Health and Environment, Retail Food Program
Connecticut	Department of Consumer Protection, Food and Standards Division; Department of Public Health, Food Protection Program
Delaware	Department of Health and Social Services, Office of Food Protection
Florida	Department of Health, Food Hygiene Program
Georgia	Department of Agriculture, Food Safety Section; Department of Community Health, Food Service Program
Hawaii	Department of Health Sanitation Branch
Idaho	Department of Health and Welfare, Food Protection Program
Illinois	Department of Public Health, Foods, Drugs and Dairies
Indiana	Department of Health, Food Protection Program
Iowa	Department of Inspections and Appeals, Food and Consumer Safety Bureau
Kansas	Department of Agriculture, Food Safety and Lodging
Kentucky	Cabinet for Health and Family Services, Food Safety Branch
Louisiana	Department of Health and Hospitals, Retail Food Program
Maine	Department of Health and Human Services, Health Inspection Program; Department of Agriculture, Consumer Food Inspection Unit
Maryland	Department of Health and Mental Hygiene, Division of Food Control
Massachusetts	Department of Public Health, Food Protection Program

State	Regulatory Agency
Michigan	Department of Agriculture, Food Safety and Recalls
Minnesota	Department of Health, Food Safety; Department of Agriculture, Dairy and Food Inspection Division
Mississippi	Department of Agriculture and Commerce, Consumer Protection; Department of Health, Food Safety Division
Missouri	Department of Health and Senior Services, Food Safety
Montana	Department of Public Health and Human Services, Food and Consumer Safety Section
Nebraska	Department of Agriculture, Food Division
Nevada	Department of Health and Human Services, Environmental Health Services
New Hampshire	Department of Health and Human Services, Food Protection
New Jersey	Department of Health and Senior Services, Food and Drug Safety Program
New Mexico	Environment Department, Food Program
New York	Department of Agriculture and Markets, Division of Food Safety and Inspections; Department of Health, Food Handling, Preparation and Storage
North Carolina	Department of Health and Natural Resources, Environmental Health Services; Department of Agriculture and Consumer Services, Food Program
North Dakota	Department of Health, Division of Food and Lodging
Ohio	Department of Health, Food Safety Program; Ohio Department of Agriculture, Food Safety Division
Oklahoma	Department of Health, Consumer Protection Division
Oregon	Department of Human Services, Foodborne Illnesses Prevention Program; Department of Agriculture, Food Safety Division
Pennsylvania	Department of Agriculture, Bureau of Food Safety and Laboratory Services
Rhode Island	Department of Health, Office of Food Protection
South Carolina	Department of Health and Environmental Control, Division of Food Protection
South Dakota	Department of Health, Office of Health Protection
Tennessee	Department of Health, Division of General Environmental Health; Department of Agriculture, Regulatory Services Division
Texas	Department of State Health Services, Food Establishments Group
Utah	Department of Agriculture, Division of Regulatory Services
Vermont	Department of Health, Food and Lodging Program
Virginia	Department of Agriculture and Consumer Services, Food Safety and Security Office
Washington	Department of Health, Food Safety Program
West Virginia	Department of Health and Human Resources, Public Health Sanitation Division; Department of Agriculture
Wisconsin	Department of Agriculture, Trade and Consumer Protection Division of Food Safety; Department of Health Services, Food Safety and Recreational Licensing
Wyoming	Department of Agriculture, Consumer Health Services Section

Courtesy of the U.S. Food and Drug Administration

References and Recommended Resources

American Camp Association. (2002). Airport arrivals. *Campline*. Retrieved August 2013 from www.acacamps.org/campline/s-2002/airport-arrivals.

American Camp Association. (2003). Camps and vans: The latest update. *Campline*. Retrieved from www.acacamps.org/campline/03o-vans.

American Camp Association. (2011). Criminal background checks: Background information and guidance for camps. Retrieved August 2013 from www.acacamps.org/sites/default/files/images/accreditation/standards/05-HR/CBC_Education_7_2011.pdf.

American Camp Association. (2012). *Accreditation process guide*. Martinsville, IN: Healthy Learning.

American Camp Association. (2013a). Staff hiring policies guide sample. Retrieved from www.acacamps.org/standardstool/nutsbolts/resources-by-section/human-resources.

American Camp Association. (2013b). Child Protection Improvements Act. Retrieved from www.acacamps.org/publicpolicy/cbc.

American Camp Association. (2013c). State by state information for camps – regulations and other info. Retrieved from www.acacamps.org/print/29754.

American Camp Association. (2013d). Showing movies at camp? Know the licensing laws. Retrieved from www.acacamps.org/membership/mplc.

American Camp Association. (2013e). Music licensing at camp – know the law. Retrieved from www.acacamps.org/membership/ascap.

American Camp Association. (2013f). Public policy and government relations. Retrieved from www.acacamps.org/publicpolicy.

American Camp Association. (2013g). Federal motorcoach laws – new updates. Retrieved from www.acacamps.org/publicpolicy/motorcoach-laws.

American Camp Association. (2013). ACA buyer's guide. Retrieved from www.acacamps.org/buyers-guide.

American Camp Association. (2013). Human Resources standards. Retrieved from www.acacamps.org/standardstool/nutsbolts/resources-by-section/human-resources.

American Camp Association. (2013). Public policy and government relations. Retrieved from www.acacamps.org/publicpolicy.

American Public Power Association and the Association of Small Business Development Centers. (2003). *Energy efficiency pays: A guide for the small business owner.* Retrieved from www.asbdc-us.org/Resources/Energy_Efficiency_Pays.pdf.

Animal Legal & Historical Center. (2013). Equine liability laws. Retrieved from www.animallaw.info/statutes/topicstatutes/sttoeql.htm.

Armstrong, S., & Mitchell, B. (2008). *The essential HR handbook: A quick and handy resource for any manager or HR professional*. Pompton Plains, NJ: Career Press.

Association for Challenge Course Technology. (2012). ACCT standards information. Retrieved from www.acctinfo.org/displaycommon.cfm?an=1&subarticlenbr=89.

Association of Camp Nurses. (2013). About ACN. Retrieved from www.acn.org/aboutacn/index.html.

Ball, A., & Ball, B. (2012). *Basic camp management*. Martinsville, IN: American Camp Association and Healthy Learning.

Bangs, D. H. Jr. (2002). *The business planning guide: Creating a winning plan for success* (9th ed.). Chicago, IL: Kaplan Publishing.

Beesley, C. (2012). Small business insurance, part 1: What type of insurance do I need? Retrieved from www.sba.gov/community/blogs/community-blogs/small-business-matters/small-business-insurance-part-1-what-type-ins#nav.

Bicycle Helmet Safety Institute. (2013). Helmet laws for bicycle riders. Retrieved from www.helmets.org/mandator.htm.

Brandon, J. (2012). 4 easy-to-use tools for building websites. *Inc. Magazine*. Retrieved from www.inc.com/magazine/201210/john-brandon/4-easytouse-tools-for-building-websites.html.

Burhouse, S., & Osaki, Y. (2012). 2011 FDIC national survey of unbanked and underbanked households. Retrieved from www.fdic.gov/householdsurvey.

Carbonfund.org. (n.d.). How to reduce your carbon footprint. Retrieved from www.carbonfund.org/reduce.

Caspar, C., Dias, A. K., & Elstrodt, H-P. (2010). The five attributes of enduring family businesses. Retrieved from www.mckinsey.com/insights/organization/the_five_attributes_of_enduring_family_businesses.

Centers for Disease Control and Prevention. (2013). *Emergency preparedness and response*. Retrieved from www.bt.cdc.gov/disasters.

Child Welfare Information Gateway. (2012). Mandatory reporters of child abuse and neglect. Retrieved from www.childwelfare.gov/systemwide/laws_policies/statutes/manda.pdf.

Child Welfare Information Gateway. (2013). What is child abuse and neglect? Recognizing the signs and symptoms. Retrieved from www.childwelfare.gov/pubs/factsheets/whatiscan.pdf.

City of Fort Worth, Texas. (2013). What should I do if a gas well company wants me to sign a lease? Retrieved from http://fortworthtexas.gov/uploadedFiles/Gas_Wells/should%20I%20sign_Copy.pdf.

Cockerell, L. (2013). *The customer rules*. New York: Crown Business.

Consumer Action. (2012). Checkout fees: Consumer rights and retailer responsibilities. Retrieved from www.consumer-action.org/downloads/english/checkout_fees.pdf.

Copeland, G. A. (2011). *Camp design: Master planning basics*. Akron, OH: Domokur Architects.

Cornell University Law School. (n.d.a). Riparian doctrine. Retrieved from www.law.cornell.edu/wex/riparian_doctrine.

Cornell University Law School. (n.d.b). Prior appropriation doctrine. Retrieved from www.law.cornell.edu/wex/prior_appropriation_doctrine.

Coutellier, Connie. (2004). *Day camp from day one: A hands-on guide for day camp administration*. Martinsville, IN: American Camping Association.

Coutellier, C. (2008). *Risk and crisis management planning* (3rd ed.). Martinsville, IN: Healthy Learning.

CPA Practice Advisor. (2011). Effective asset management is more than depreciation. Retrieved from www.cpapracticeadvisor.com.

Disney Institute. (2011). *Be our guest: Perfecting the art of customer service*. New York: Disney Editions.

Energy Star. (2007). *Putting energy into profits: A guide for small business*. Retrieved from www.energystar.gov/buildings/sites/default/uploads/tools/smallbizguide.pdf?c000-91dd.

Environmental Protection Agency. (2004). *Understanding the Safe Drinking Water Act*. Retrieved from www.epa.gov/safewater/sdwa/pdfs/fs_30ann_sdwa_web.pdf .

Federal Deposit Insurance Corporation. (2013a). Deposit insurance summary. Retrieved from www.fdic.gov/deposit/deposits/dis.

Federal Deposit Insurance Corporation. (2013b). Money smart for small business. Retrieved from www.fdic.gov/moneysmart.

Federal Trade Commission. (2010). *Copier data security: A guide for businesses*. Retrieved from www.business.ftc.gov/sites/default/files/pdf/bus43-copier-data-security.pdf.

Federal Trade Commission. (2012). Using consumer reports: What employers need to know. Retrieved from http://business.ftc.gov/documents/bus08-using-consumer-reports-what-employers-need-know.

Federal Trade Commission. (2013). Children's online privacy protection rule: A six-step compliance plan for your business. Retrieved from www.business.ftc.gov/documents/bus84-childrens-online-privacy-protection-rule-six-step-compliance-plan-your-business.

Federal Trade Commission. (2013). Fair Credit Reporting Act. Retrieved from www.ftc.gov/enforcement/rules/rulemaking-regulatory-reform-proceedings/fair-credit-reporting-act.

Food Allergy Research & Education (2013). Food allergy facts and statistics for the U.S. Retrieved from www.foodallergy.org/document.doc?id=194.

Food and Drug Administration. (2013). *FDA food code*. Retrieved from www.fda.gov/Food/GuidanceRegulation/RetailFoodProtection/FoodCode/default.htm.

Garst, B., Marugg, M., & Thompson S. (2013). Building a "healthy camp": Strategies that worked! *Camping Magazine*. Retrieved from www.acacamps.org/campmag/1303/building-healthy-camp.

Google. (2010). *Search engine optimization starter guide*. Retrieved from https://static.googleusercontent.com/external_content/untrusted_dlcp/www.google.com/en/us/webmasters/docs/search-engine-optimization-starter-guide.pdf.

Gregg, C. R., & Hansen-Stamp, C. (2009). Caution! Participant agreements containing a release of liability. Retrieved from www.outdoored.com/Professional/subscriptions/recreation-law-center-case/recreation-law-center/2009/01/09/caution!-participant-agreements-containing-a-release-of-liability.

Gupta, R. S., Springston, E. E., Warrier, M. R., Smith, B., Kumar, R., Pongracic, J., & Holl, J. L. (2011). The prevalence, severity, and distribution of childhood food allergy in the United States. *Pediatrics*. Retrieved from pediatrics.aappublications.org/content/128/1/e9.full.

Hansen-Stamp, C., & Gregg, C. R. (2013). HIPPA and camps – compliance required? *Campline*. Retrieved from www.acacamps.org/campline/spring-2013/hipaa-camps-compliance.

Hanson, K. (2013). *What is business ethics?* Retrieved from www.scu.edu/ethics/practicing/focusareas/business/introduction.html.

Herman, M. L. (2008). *Coverage, claims and consequences: An insurance handbook for nonprofits* (2nd ed.). Leesburg, VA: Nonprofit Risk Management Center.

Herman, M. L. (2013). Back to basics: Effective risk management may require culture change. Retrieved from www.myriskmanagementplan.org/article.asp?id=64.

Herman, M. L. (2009). Risk management culture and your volunteers. Retrieved from www.nonprofitrisk.org/library/enews/2009/enews090209.htm.

Herman, M. L. (2011). *Ready or not: A risk management guide for nonprofit executives* (2nd ed.). Leesburg, VA: Nonprofit Risk Management Center.

Hodges, C. (2010). Quick summary of Equine Activity Liability Acts (EALA). Retrieved from www.animallaw.info/topics/tabbed%20topic%20page/spusequineliability.htm.

Howard, J. (2011, July 11). What you do in seven words [Web log post]. Retrieved from www.ceffect.com/blog/communicating/what-you-do-in-seven-words.

Inc.com. (n.d.). Financial ratios. Retrieved from www.inc.com/encyclopedia/financial-ratios.html.

Indiana State Deartment of Health. (2002). *Applications, bulletins, forms, laws and regulations: Youth camps*. Retrieved from www.in.gov/isdh/21962.htm#General_health.

Inghiller, L., & Solomon, M. (2010). *Exceptional service, exceptional profit: The secrets of building a five-star customer service organization*. New York: AMACOM.

Internal Revenue Service. (2012). *Publication 503: Child and dependent care expenses*. Retrieved from www.irs.gov/pub/irs-pdf/p503.pdf.

Internal Revenue Service. (2013a). *Publication 557: Tax-exempt status for your organization*. Retrieved from www.irs.gov/pub/irs-pdf/p557.pdf.

Internal Revenue Service. (2013b). *Publication 15 (Circular E): Employer's tax guide: For use in 2014*. Retrieved from www.irs.gov/pub/irs-pdf/p15.pdf.

Internal Revenue Service. (2013c). *Publication 15-A: Employer's supplemental tax guide*. Retrieved from www.irs.gov/pub/irs-pdf/p15a.pdf.

Internal Revenue Service. (2013d). Affordable Care Act tax provisions for employers. Retrieved from www.irs.gov/uac/Affordable-Care-Act-Tax-Provisions-for-Employers.

Internal Revenue Service. (2013e). *Publication 15-B: Employer's tax guide to fringe benefits*. Retrieved from www.irs.gov/pub/irs-pdf/p15b.pdf.

J. J. Keller & Associates. (2013). *OSHA compliance manual*. Neenah, WI: J. J. Keller & Associates.

Karageorge, K., & Kendall, R. (2008). The role of professional child care providers in preventing and responding to child abuse and neglect. Retrieved from www.childwelfare.gov/pubs/usermanuals/childcare.

Kirsh, R. (2013). *Eliminating paper paychecks: Best practices for implementing a successful, compliant electronic payroll distribution program*. Retrieved from www.firstdata.com/downloads/thought-leadership/4376_Paycard_Best_Practices_WP.PDF.

Leader to Leader Institute. (2004). *Be, know, do: Leadership the Army way*. San Francisco: Jossey-Bass.

Leiken, J., & Riggio, J. (2002). Creating your ideal camp culture. *Camping Magazine*. Retrieved from www.acacamps.org/members/knowledge/mission/cm/027creating.

Lynn, S. (2012). Small business technology: A step-by-step guide to getting started. *PC Magazine*. Retrieved from www.pcmag.com/article2/0,2817,2386537,00.asp.

Markkula Center for Applied Ethics. (n.d.). Resources for analyzing real-world ethical issues and tools to address them. Retrieved from www.scu.edu/ethics-center.

Massachusetts Mutual Insurance. (2010). *The MassMutual FamilyPreneurship Study: What every entrepreneur wants to know about being in business with a family member*. Retrieved from www.massmutual.com/mmfg/pdf/FamilyPreneurship_Study.pdf.

Massachusetts Society of Certified Public Accountants: Federal Taxation Committee. (2004). *The record retention guide*. Retrieved from www.cpa.net/resources/retengde.pdf.

Moz. (2013a). Our TAGFEE code. Retrieved from moz.com/about/tagfee.

Moz. (2013). *The beginners guide to SEO*. Retrieved from http://moz.com/beginners-guide-to-seo.

Naftulin, E. (2011). Top eight marketing strategies for 2011. *Camping Magazine*. Retrieved from www.acacamps.org/campmag/1103/top-eight-marketing-strategies-2011.

National Federation of Independent Business. (2013). How to sell your company to a family member without losing your shirt. Retrieved from www.nfib.com/business-resources/business-resources/item?cmsid=63265.

National Highway Transportation Safety Administration. (2010). Consumer advisory: NHTSA reissues 15-passenger van safety caution. Retrieved from www.nhtsa.gov/CA/10-14-2010.

National Highway Transportation Safety Administration. (1999). Highway special investigation report – pupil transportation in vehicles not meeting federal school bus standard. Retrieved from www.ntsb.gov/news/events/1999/sir-99-02/index.html.

National Highway Transportation Safety Administration.(n.d.). Tire aging. Retrieved from www.safercar.gov/Vehicle+Shoppers/Tires/Tires+Rating/Tire+Aging.

National Restaurant Association. (2013). *ServSafe regulatory information*. Retrieved from www.servsafe.com/regulatory.

National Safety Council. (2013). *Why focus on cell phone use while driving? What about other distractions?*. Retrieved from www.nsc.org/safety_road/Distracted_Driving/Documents/2013 DDAM Public Fact Sheet.pdf.

National Safety Council. (2012). *Cell phone policy kit*. Retrieved from www.nsc.org/safety_road/Distracted_Driving/Pages/CellPhonePolicyKit.aspx.

National Swimming Pool Foundation. (2013). Resources. Retrieved from www.nspf.org/en/Resources.

New York State Department of Health. (2011). *Health & safety in the home, workplace and outdoors: Children's camps*. Retrieved from www.health.ny.gov/regulations/nycrr/title_10/part_7/subpart_7-2.htm.

Occupational Safety and Health Administration. (1989). *OSHA small business handbook*. Retrieved from www.osha.gov/Publications/smallbusiness/small-business.html.

Occupational Safety and Health Administration. (2012). Hazard communication standard: Safety data sheets. Retrieved from www.osha.gov/Publications/OSHA3514.html.

Office of Child Support Enforcement. (1996). The Personal Responsibility and Work Opportunity Reconciliation Act of 1996. Retrieved from www.acf.hhs.gov/programs/css/resource/the-personal-responsibility-and-work-opportunity-reconcilliation-act.

Paskoff, S. (2011). *Simplicity rules: 12 thoughts for the 2012 workplace*. Retrieved from www.eliinc.com/Portals/139296/downloads/ebook_simplicity_rules.pdf.

Paskoff, S. M. (2002). *How we do things here*. Retrieved from www.eliinc.com/Portals/139296/downloads/how-we-do-things-here.pdf.

Periu, M. (2010). Risk management 101 for small business owners. Retrieved from www.openforum.com/articles/risk-management-101-for-small-business-owners-1.

Podeszwa, K. (2010). Succession planning: Raising up the next generation of leaders. *Camping Magazine*. Retrieved from www.acacamps.org/campmag/1011/succession-planning-raising-next-generation-leaders.

Portland Energy Conservation. (1997). Operation and maintenance service contracts. Retrived from www.energystar.gov/buildings/tools-and-resources/operation-and-maintenance-service-contracts.

Projector People. (n.d.). Projector resources. Retrieved from www.projectorpeople.com/resources.

Sadler, J. M. Jr. (2013). Are waiver/releases worth the paper they are written on? Retrieved from www.sadlersports.com/riskmanagement/sports-insurance-waiverrelease.php.

Sanborn Western Camps. (2013). Driver training. In *Staff Manual*. Florissant, CO: Author.

Securities and Exchange Commission. (2007). Questions you should ask about your investments ... and what to do if you run into problems. Retrieved from www.sec.gov/investor/pubs/askquestions.htm.

Small Business Administration. (n.d.a). What is SBA's definition of a small business concern? Retrieved from www.sba.gov/content/what-sbas-definition-small-business-concern.

Small Business Administration. (n.d.b). Determine your state tax obligations. Retrieved from www.sba.gov/content/learn-about-your-state-and-local-tax-obligations.

Small Business Administration. (2013). Build your business plan. Retrieved from www.sba.gov/business-plan/1.

Small Business Administration. (2011). Small business matters: 5 tips for managing successful family business. Retrieved from www.sba.gov/community/blogs/community-blogs/small-business-matters/5-tips-managing-successful-family-business.

Stack, L. (2013). 12 tips for better e-mail etiquette. Retrieved from http://office.microsoft.com/en-us/outlook-help/12-tips-for-better-e-mail-etiquette-HA001205410.aspx.

Stamp, G. (2013). What personal characteristics do you need to become an executive? Retrieved from leadchangegroup.com/what-personal-characteristics-do-you-need-to-become-an-executive.

Starr, K. (2012). The eight-word mission statement. *Stanford Social Innovation Review*. Retrieved from www.ssireview.org/blog/entry/the_eight_word_mission_statement.

Steen, M. (2013). Building and nurturing an ethical culture. Retrieved from www.scu.edu/ethics/practicing/focusareas/business/BuildingEthicalCulture.html.

Taylor, P. (2012). 20/20 toolbox: From family to foundation – a path to perpetuity. Camping Magazine. Retrieved from www.acacamps.org/campmag/1211/family-foundation.

The Trustees of Reservation. (2013). Our mission. Retrieved from www.thetrustees.org/about-us/our-mission.

Travelers Casualty and Surety Company of America. (2013). Travelers wrap: Funds transfer fraud and computer fraud. Retrieved from www.travelers.com/business-insurance/management-professional-liability/documents/59545.pdf.

Tyrrell, D. (2010). 20/20 toolbox: Tomorrow's camps, today's realities. *Camping Magazine*. Retrieved from www.acacamps.org/campmag/1009/todays-camps-tomorrows-realities.

U.S. Citizenship and Immigration Services. (2013). *Handbook for employers: Guidance for completing Form I-9*. Retrieved from www.uscis.gov/files/form/m-274.pdf.

U.S. Coast Guard Boating Safety Resource Center. (2013). Regulations. Retrieved from www.uscgboating.org/regulations/default.aspx.

U.S. Consumer Product Safety Commission. (2012). Pool & Spa Safety Act. Retrieved from www.poolsafely.gov/pool-spa-safety-act.

U.S. Copyright Office. (2011). *Copyright laws of the United States and related laws contained in Title 17 of the United States Code*. Retrieved from www.copyright.gov/title17/circ92.pdf.

U.S. Department of Agriculture. (2012). *Agricultural marketing service*. Retrieved from www.ams.usda.gov.

U.S. Department of Health and Human Services. (2013). Understanding health information privacy. Retrieved from www.hhs.gov/ocr/privacy/hipaa/understanding.

U.S. Department of Justice. (2011a). Information and technical assistance on the Americans with Disabilities Act. Retrieved from www.ada.gov/2010_regs.htm.

U.S. Department of Justice. (2011b). ADA update: A primer for small business. Retrieved from www.ada.gov/regs2010/smallbusiness/smallbusprimer2010.htm.

U.S. Department of Labor. (n.d.a). The Uniformed Services Employment and Reemployment Rights Act (USERRA). Retrieved from www.dol.gov/compliance/laws/comp-userra.htm.

U.S. Department of Labor. (n.d.b). Posters. Retrieved from www.dol.gov/compliance/topics/posters.htm.

U.S. Department of Labor. (2008a). Fact sheet #17A: Exemption for executive, administrative, professional, computer & outside sales employees under the Fair Labor Standards Act (FLSA). Retrieved from www.dol.gov/whd/regs/compliance/fairpay/fs17a_overview.pdf.

U.S. Department of Labor. (2008b). Fact sheet #18: Section 13(a)(3) exemption for seasonal amusement or recreational establishments under the Fair Labor Standards Act (FLSA). Retrieved from www.dol.gov/whd/regs/compliance/whdfs18.pdf.

U.S. Department of Labor. (2008c). Fact sheet #36: Employee Polygraph Protection Act of 1988. Retrieved from www.dol.gov/whd/regs/compliance/whdfs36.pdf.

U.S. Department of Labor. (2012a). State payday requirements. Retrieved from www.dol.gov/whd/state/payday.htm.

U.S. Department of Labor. (2012b). Fact sheet #28: The Family and Medical Leave Act. Retrieved from www.dol.gov/whd/regs/compliance/whdfs28.pdf.

U.S. Department of Labor. (2013a). Child labor provisions for nonagricultural occupations under the Fair Labor Standards Act. Retrieved from www.dol.gov/whd/regs/compliance/childlabor101_text.htm.

U.S. Department of Labor. (2013). *Employment law guide on occupational health and safety.* Retrieved from www.dol.gov/compliance/guide/osha.htm.

U.S. Department of Transportation, NHTSA. (n.d.). Distraction.gov. Retreived from www.distraction.gov.

United States Power Squadrons. (2010). Boating laws & license requirements by state. Retrieved from www.americasboatingcourse.com/lawsbystate.cfm.

Whyman, W. (2008). *Outdoor site and facility management: Tools for creating memorable places.* Champaign, IL: Human Kinetics.

Whyman, W. (2013). *Management of outdoor facilities.* Retrieved from callippe.com/blog/?s=when+to+replace&x=0&y=0

Workers Compensation Shop. (2012). *Workers compensation insurance.* Retrieved from www.workerscompensationshop.com.

About the Authors

Ann Sheets is senior vice president for administration and finance at Camp Fire First Texas in Fort Worth, Texas, and is a past national president of the American Camp Association.

Dave Thoensen is the owner and director of Tamarak Day Camp and Country School in Lincolnshire, Illinois, and is active in various local and national American Camp Association programs.